Careers
in
Multimedia

Careers in Multimedia

 by **vivid** studios

ZIFF-DAVIS

ZD

PRESS

Ziff-Davis Press
Emeryville, California

Development Editor	Cheryl Holzaepfel
Copy Editor	Margo Hill
Proofreaders	Margo Hill and Nicole Clausing
Project Coordinator	Barbara Dahl
Book Design	**vivid** studios
Page Layout	M.D. Barrera
Indexer	**vivid** studios

Ziff-Davis Press books are produced on a Macintosh computer system with the following applications: FrameMaker®, Microsoft® Word, QuarkXPress®, Adobe Illustrator®, Adobe Photoshop®, Adobe Streamline™, MacLink®*Plus*, Aldus® FreeHand™, Collage Plus™.

If you have comments or questions or would like to receive a free catalog, call or write:
Ziff-Davis Press
5903 Christie Avenue
Emeryville, CA 94608
1-800-688-0448

ISBN 1-56276-311-3
Manufactured in the United States of America
♲ This book is printed on paper that conatins 50% total recycled fiber of which 20% is de-inked postconsumer waste.
10 9 8 7 6 5 4 3 2 1

vivid studios

Senior Writer and Editor	Ken Fromm
Managing Editors	Kathleen Egge, Henri Poole
Creative Director	Nathan Shedroff
Associate Editor	Drue Miller
Researchers and Writers	Bondy Bondurant, Peter Christy, Sam McMillan, Drue Miller, Zeb Rice, Nathan Shedroff, Misty West
Illustrators	Steve de Brun, Kathleen Egge, Nathan Shedroff, Maurice Tani
Photographer	David Wasserman
Book Designer	Drue Miller
Layout Artists	Nigel French, Candice Kollar
Production Assistants	Francesca Milone, Marsha Plat
Gaffer	Paul Guth
Best Boy	Steve de Brun
Catering	Chavo's

vivid studios
510 Third Street, Suite 420, Box 7
San Francisco, CA 94107-1814 USA

TEL	(415) 512 7200
FAX	(415) 512 7202
NET	info@vivid.com
LINK	vivid
WEB	http://www.vivid.com

Acknowledgments

In the course of putting this book together, we talked to a wide variety of people in all fields of multimedia development, from all over the world. vivid studios thanks the following individuals for their contributions to this book as well as the many others not listed here who provided ideas, comments, and encouragement.

Abbe Don, Interactive Multimedia Artist

Adrian Miles, Educator, Royal Melbourne Institute of Technology

Allan Rinkus, Agent, International Computer Group

Alma Derricks, Producer/Technology Consultant, United Media

Anthony Perkins, Publisher, *The Red Herring*

Aric Wilmunder, Manager of Software Tools and Technologies, LucasArts

Barbara Bell, Director of Outside Production, Starwave

Bill Rollinson, VP Marketing, Internet Software

Bjorn Omer, Technical Communicator

Brad Brewster, Producer/Publisher, Bent Media

Brenda Laurel, Member of Research Staff, Interval Research

Bret Dahlgren, Interface Engineer and Brenda Laurel fan, Interbold

Brian Coburn, Sound Artist, Sega

Carl Loeffler, Artist and Researcher, Carnegie Mellon University

Catherine Kirkman, Attorney, Wilson, Sonsini, Goodrich & Rosati

Cesar A. Zevallos Heudebert, Developer and Educator, ASIX S.A., Pontificia Universidad Catolica del Peru

Cheryl Weiner, Director of Product Development, McGraw Hill Home Media

Chris Okon, Writer and Instructor

Chris Shen, Game Designer, Sega

Christina Cheney, Electronic Entertainment

Clifford Lau, Animator, Sega

Cynthia Hudson, President, Ziff-Davis Press

Dana Atchley, Multimedia Performer

David 'Zero' Humphreys, Producer/Designer

David Steuer, Producer/Publisher

David Tee, Business Development Manager, Acorn Computers

David Wasserman, Photographer

David Wicks, Executive Producer, Grolier Multimedia Encyclopedia

Deborah Todd, Interactive Scriptwriter

Dezsö Molnár, Sound Producer

Donna Campbell, Executive Producer, Hearst New Media

Eric Hunting, Literary Computing Researcher and Developer

Frank Boosman, General Manager, Virtus Corporation

Frank Scales, Video Producer

Gitta Solomon, Interface Designer

Gray Holland, Modeler/Animator, Alchemy

Howard Rheingold, Author, *The Virtual Community*

J. Sterling Hutto, General Manager, Electric Classified

JA Nelson, Programmer

Janine Firpo, Marketing Consultant

Jeffrey C. Kimmel, General Manager, WAOA/WTAI Radio

Jim Donovan, Video Producer

Jim Wiseman, DigitalMedia

John Nyenhuis, Producer/Publisher, Purdue University

Jonathan Steuer, Founder, The Cyborganic Cafe

Jose-Carlos Mariategui, President, Phantasia Multimedia

Karen Burch, Producer, Synapse Technologies

Kim Daus, General Manager, AGORA Digital

Larry Doyle, Programmer

Larry Kay, Interactive Scriptwriter

Larry Miller, Editor, Go Digital magazine

Liisa Lind, Producer/Editor-in-Chief, National Board of Education

Lim Cheng Chye, Information Technology Engineer

Linda Jacobson, Writer

Linda Stone, Director of Advanced Technologies, Microsoft

Linda Walton, IICS Executive Office

Lisa Brown, Interactive Services, AT&T

Lucille Bliss, Voice-over Artist

Marius Coomans, Producer/Publisher, Firmware Publishing

Mark Gavini, Console Cowboy, Apple Computer

Mark LoParco

Maya Daniels, Voice-over Artist

Mike Hawkes, Technical Director/Broadcast Consultant

Miles Gilburne, Attorney

Mitch Kapor, Founder, Electronic Frontier Foundation

Mitchell Yawitz, Interactive Designer, daVinci Time & Space

Mitsu Hadeishi, General Partner, Open Mind

Nina Zolt

Nova Spivack, VP of Innovation & Strategic Development, EarthWeb, Ltd.

Paige Hynes, Assistant, Sony Imagesoft

Pam Lovell, Acting Director, San Francisco State University

Pam Sansbury, Marketing Consultant

Pat Hanlon, Co-author, *Voices of the 30s*

Patrick Milligan, Programmer

Paul Saffo, Director, Institute for the Future

Peter Bickford, Interface Designer

Peter Lundholm, Designer/Engineer, Datadesign & Multimedia AB

Red Burns, Director of ITP, New York University

Rich Slim, Attorney

Richard Thompson, Attorney, Silverberg, Katz, Thompson & Golden

Roger Stewart, Publisher, Prima Publishing

S. Joy Mountford, Project Lead, Interval Research

Scott F. Lanes, Interface Designer

Scott Willoughby, CEO, Illuminated Media

Sean Lord, Recruiter, Interactive Development

Sheryl Hampton, Video Producer, RPM

Spencer Nilsen, Director, Sega Music Group

Stewart McBride, President, United Digital Artists

Susana Craig, Third Party Marketing Manager, Apple Latin America

Terry Winograd, Instructor, Stanford University

Thomas Dolby, Composer, Musician, and Sound Producer

Tim Oren, Vice President, Future Technology, CompuServe

Todd Power, Producer, Weldon Owen

Tom Livaccari, Online Publisher

Tony Mechin, Producer/Publisher, Media Technology

Vincent Grosso, ITV Project Director, AT&T

William Schwartz, Attorney, Morrison & Foerster

Table of Contents

Look for these icons throughout this book—they'll guide you to places of interest.

Introduction

"I want to get into multimedia."

It's a phrase heard often—at conferences, in conversations among friends, and especially by people already in multimedia. The reasons for getting into multimedia are many. For some, it's because they keep seeing words like "information highway," "cyberspace," "interactive games," "Internet," or "World Wide Web." With this much press, the reasoning goes, this area has to be the next big thing. For others, they've played with some of the CD-ROM titles. They've watched their children or someone else's children sit in front of a computer, captivated by an interactive storybook. For others, it's because they've got a story to tell or a product to build. Many of these, the best ones, can only be done on a computer, within a non-linear format, or with a technology that connects one person to another, independent of time or space constraints. All these reasons are sensible ones (some a little more sensible than others).

Interactive media projects are transforming almost every activity in society today. Some evidence of this is in the explosion of new words and terms to describe the activities and interactions people are having these days. But there is more to it than just words. There are products and services that are providing real enjoyment and tangible value to people and companies around the world. Video games today bring in more revenue than the entire film industry. One half of the Dow Jones & Company's $2 billion in revenue is derived from electronic information.

And so, there are lots of **opportunities**—opportunities to learn new skills, create innovative products, launch new services, design new games, tell stories that haven't been told before, and find jobs. But there are so many companies, so many projects, and so much information available that it is hard to know how to take advantage of these opportunities. A year or two ago, it took only a single credit on a multimedia project to be considered an expert and to move from one project to another. Now, with so much activity, it is much more difficult. It takes passion, skills, knowledge, and a plan. Only you can provide the passion and the skills. This book, though, can provide much of the knowledge and most of the plan.

For many, the first hurdle to getting into multimedia is understanding what the heck people are talking about. Something that is undefined always seems more complex than it really is. The world of interactive multimedia is no different. Part of the goal of this book, then, is to define things. We define what the roles are and what people do when they walk into the workplace in the morning. We describe what projects people are working on and the types of companies they are working for. But in the face of all these minor definitions lies the bigger one of what *multimedia*, or better yet, *interactive multimedia* means in the first place. Without a definition of that, it's hard to begin anywhere.

Multimedia ▶ 50, at a simplistic level, can be defined as the combination of more than one medium—text, graphics, sound, animation, and video—commonly assumed to be in digital format. The first generation of multimedia products

> We're really on top of the second wave of the information revolution and it's going to make the PC revolution—which was very substantial—look like we were playing with TinkerToys.
>
> —Anthony Perkins,
> Publisher,
> The Red Herring

Interactivity

To me, interactivity is about generating new kinds of experiences that aren't available through traditional media. In most CD-ROM books, I click the right arrow and turn the page, knowing the kind of thing I'm going to see on the next page. It's when you can be surprised that it starts getting interesting.

The Seventh Guest is an example. The use of video is really interesting. Eventually, it not only becomes surprising, but something you couldn't have done in a book. You expect one kind of image and you get this beautiful ghostly apparition. The use of sound succeeds on a couple of levels because it's a new kind of experience. It creates a sense of place that is strange and foreign and involving.

Myst is the same way. Whatever you feel about puzzle games or Myst's style of presentation—which is basically a slide show—they have successfully created a sort of gestalt. There's a coherence to the experience. Everything is in frame. They use this beautiful ambient sound track to create this total experience that is different from a book. And then there are surprises. Ultimately, it's still a page turner, but it's a different kind of page turner.

—Mitchell Yawitz, Interactive Designer, daVinci Time & Space

"Nobody knows for sure"

clearly shows these discrete media forms. Most of these products have some variation on the theme of "Click here for a QuickTime movie, click here for a sound clip, click here for text." The second generation of products is showing more subtlety and more artistry. Future products are bound to be even more seamless, as designers learn and evolve the art of transparently integrating media forms. A look at the art of filmmaking shows a similar development history—of integrating sound into movies, of using lighting and camera techniques. Multimedia is evolving in much the same way, but in a much shorter time frame. The *multi* in multimedia will likely become unnecessary in the future because the assumption will be that just about every form of communication—especially digital products—involves more than one medium.

A definition of **interactive** ▶ 171 is more difficult, primarily because it is still being defined. At this point, there is no taxonomy to point to, no step-by-step procedure, and no chart to use to describe how to go about turning a movie into an interactive game, or a story into an interactive narrative. Game designers speak of first-person interactions and game play. Creators of virtual communities talk about ways to represent various social constructs online. Interactivity can probably best be seen as a spectrum of experiences from passive to interactive. Where a project falls on the spectrum depends on what kind of outcome the designers—or more precisely, the audience—desires. Interaction is characterized by audience feedback and control—the more of each, the more interactive the experience. The difference, therefore, between a passive product and an interactive one is similar to the difference between a lecture and a conversation. Interactions can also be productive and creative and not just entertaining.

New technologies and new ways of thinking are allowing more people to create experiences different from traditional ones. Everyone who is involved in creating, designing, or publishing interactive products should know that they are not creating just products, but experiences for other people to share. Refining the levels and forms of interactivity is one of the ways to create richer experiences.

Transcending the Original Material

My notion of multimedia is basically the notion of the integration of a variety of types of media. What you end up with in good multimedia is something that transcends the original material that made up the separate parts. When you bring together images and video and text and sound and music, you have something greater than the individual components taken separately. Usually, the place where that value is added is in the interactivity. I think you can have multimedia without interactivity, but it's not as interesting as the stuff that is interactive—once you explore and navigate this space that the developer is trying to present.

—Patrick Milligan, Programmer

Organization of the Book

This book is specifically designed to give you the insight you need to land a job producing, designing, writing, developing, or distributing interactive products. In doing this, we applied the principles of **information design** ▶ 170 to take a disorganized set of data and transform it—through organization, presentation, writing, and editing—into information that has customized meaning for each reader. The goal of this book is to answer the question, "How do I get into multimedia?" The structure of the book and the materials inside were then chosen specifically to support this goal.

The main body of the book defines the roles that people play within the development of interactive media. The material in the **Roles** ▶ 118 chapter provides you with immediate access to the disciplines that best fit your current or desired skills. Interactive media is no different from a film, or any other project for that matter, in that each project has a project team comprising different but complementary skills and responsibilities. Each person performs a unique set of tasks that contribute to the project as a whole. Each role describes what these people do on a project, where they fit, what their process is, and the tools and techniques they use. Also included are the qualifications they typically need, how they get hired, and a discussion of the important compensation issues. Alongside are statements from experts describing issues related to each role and role models that describe how they got to be where they are.

Breaking the paradigm means that in almost every instance that I've had in the last four years, the best and most successful things have happened when we've decided to do something different from what was already being done.

Whenever we came at a problem in a traditional way, tried to solve it, and move it onto interactive TV—it wouldn't work. It was when we tried to solve it in a non-traditional way that things started to work—like involving people on the creative team who you wouldn't necessarily see there.

—Vincent Grosso, Interactive TV Project Director, AT&T

Have your own voice, whether it's in a content area or an artistic voice. Take risks creatively. There are a lot of people out there who are going to replicate the already-known genre. There are going to be many annotated music products and animated kids' storybooks. That's a safe place to be because somebody else has already put together the framework. The genre's established. You're punching out variations. You need to take a little more risk. It's too early in the medium to coalesce around those few understood pieces.

—Tim Oren,
Vice President, Future
Technology,
CompuServe

But just defining the roles and the tasks that people do is not enough. The world of interactive media is so large and complicated that talking about roles without talking about the types of platforms or projects gives an incomplete picture. The **Platforms** ▶ 12 and **Projects** ▶ 18 chapters will help define what people are doing and why. They present possibilities that you might not have thought about and they help you focus on those areas that interest you.

Related to the Platforms and Projects chapters is the **Industries** ▶ 50 chapter. Every industry has an infrastructure that describes the types of individuals or companies in that industry and the ways that they interact with each other. Just as the roles describe how people work together on a project, the **infrastructure** describes how the types of companies work together within an industry. The term "multimedia company" has little meaning to it because it is too general. Within the world of interactive media, there are hardware companies, multimedia production studios, game developers, publishers and entertainment companies, interactive advertising firms, and many more. Describing these types of companies and the things they do will differentiate one company from another and allow you to know better what type of people they need.

The **Global Hot Spots** ▶ 66 chapter provides a global perspective of multimedia, identifying the hot spots, the types of projects being done in each area, industry tie-ins, and any localized organizations or training centers. The **General Work Issues** ▶ 76 chapter provides information on contractor and employee issues and equipment concerns. It also walks you through a process for identifying opportunities, positioning and marketing yourself, approaching companies, signing work agreements, working, and wrapping projects. At each step of the way, we offer advice specifically tailored for multimedia. The information in this chapter will not only help you get a job in multimedia, it will help you get one that is rewarding, profitable and, above all, enjoyable.

The **Roles** ▶ 118 chapter describes many of the career paths in multimedia, and finally, the last chapter of the book contains a set of **Resources** ▶ 278 for finding opportunities, learning a discipline, and staying informed about the world of multimedia. Also included is a combined **Glossary/Index** ▶ 294 that helps define many of the terms that are tossed about with abandon by those practicing a trade within interactive media.

Categories and Distinctions

One of the hardest parts of producing this book was categorizing the various groups within each chapter. For example, in the Projects chapter, should a children's game go under Games or should there be a separate category for Children's projects? (We chose the latter.) When does a reference product become a special interest title? Is interactive music a separate category? Other decisions were more philosophical. What is a game? What is narrative? What is art? What is music? In confronting these questions, we were forced to make distinctions, to define patterns, and to draw lines where there are only indistinct boundaries.

This book, therefore, is meant as a guide, not a bible. You should read it as a reference and trust in your own experiences and viewpoints. In trying to take a snapshot of one of the fastest growing areas in all of human history, we have done so with the understanding that the best decision is the correct one, the second best decision is the wrong one, and the worst decision is no decision.

Hard Work

This book can go a long way toward answering your questions and pointing the way to new opportunities. But the most important element about becoming successful in multimedia is that it takes **hard work**—especially at this stage of its creation. It's difficult to position and market yourself. It is difficult to identify companies to work with. It's difficult to become expert in skills that put you in demand. Choosing a job as a programmer on a complex project can mean a yearlong commitment with no guarantee that

Sleep is for amateurs

the product will sell well, or in some cases, even ship. Designing or co-writing a major game can mean subjecting yourself to the criticisms of anyone with a computer and access to the Net.

Behind almost every success story are stories about taking great risks, of changing careers, going back to school, or believing in a product or market when others didn't. Stories of years spent developing games when only a few cared, or worse, of products with years of effort in them and never making it to market, are common. Brøderbund's Living Books, one of the more successful children's storybook series, is an overnight success that took five years.

The point isn't to discourage you from trying to fulfill your goals and desires. It is to get you to visualize what you want so that adversity and misfortune are seen only as obstacles and not deterrents. It is to remind you that motivation and self-discipline are your greatest assets. Passion, devotion, and a career pathway seen in years as opposed to months are more important than knowing the hottest authoring tool or understanding the latest in sound compression algorithms. A sense of humor, integrity, and a willingness to put the past behind you can move you forward faster than almost anything else.

Terra Incognita

Daniel J. Boorstin, in his book *The Discoverers*, once wrote, "The most promising words ever written on the maps of human knowledge are *terra incognita*—unknown territory." If someone were to create a map of interactive multimedia, it would have these words printed all over it. And in those places you would find people taking risks, seeking challenges, meeting with success and failure, and striving for creative, financial, spiritual, or other rewards. These people may have a few more skills and a little more knowledge than you—but perhaps not for long.

In a recent interview in *Wired* magazine, Bill Gates made the point that the people trying to predict the PC revolution in 1980 wouldn't have been talking to him. They would have been talking to Ken Olsen at Digital and the people at Hewlett-Packard. The same is true for interactive multimedia. While many of the people you read about in these pages will be heard from again and again in the future, there will be many new voices that have yet to be heard. A year from now, five years from now, ten years from now, that voice could be yours.

What are you waiting for?

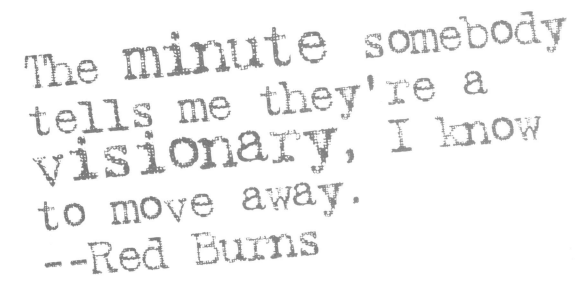

The minute somebody tells me they're a visionary, I know to move away.
--Red Burns

1. Platforms

The term "platform," as it is used here, loosely describes the operating system, hardware components, and delivery media used for playback and interaction mechanisms.

The bulk of this book is about the roles people perform within a multimedia project. To understand the roles on a project, though, you need to understand the types of projects. And to understand the projects, in turn you need to know the most common platforms for multimedia.

A few years ago, the boundaries between computer systems were clearer. Now, intense competition, rapid advances in technology, and increasing consumer influence on development cause innovations in one platform to quickly spread to others. Still, among all the components—microprocessors, compression algorithms, sound, video, and graphics cards, monitors, keyboards, controllers, drives, and communication wires—some general groupings can be made. The most common of these major platforms are **game players**, **desktop computers**, **television set-top boxes**, **personal digital assistants (PDAs)**, **kiosks**, and **presentation/performance set-ups**.

Platforms, though, are more than just collections of technology. The money and effort to create a platform and to develop a large number of products for it means that it needs a strong validation from consumers. This acceptance takes time, investment, marketing savvy, and some amount of luck. The fight to become a "standard" happens at both the micro level, between specific companies, and at the macro level, between groups of companies and industries. This struggle can be seen with game machines as Sega, Nintendo, and others vie for the hottest machines and the most popular titles. It can also be seen between platforms as the computer industry competes with the television industry to become the primary domain for the information superhighway. The platforms used in multimedia will continue to change due to technology, industry, and market influences.

There is a delicate struggle between co-operation and competition among companies within major platforms. The intense competition arises as companies try to outdo each other on pricing, features, and content. At the same time, there is often a need to cooperate by adopting standard protocols and components in the face of pressure from others. There is probably a balance between the two somewhere but history shows it is difficult to reach and easy to upset.

Distance of Experience

*One meaningful way to look at platforms is in terms of the **distance** at which experiences occur—experience being a discrete and meaningful event. The distance at which experiences occur help determine their structure and dynamic. These experiences in turn determine the level of interactivity, the balance of interaction between parties, and its context. In multimedia, distance influences the balance in the media types used, as well as many of the hardware components used, such as keyboards, remote controls, and projection screens.*

*In general terms, there is a 2-foot experience, a 14-foot experience, and a 50-foot experience. A **2-foot experience** is like a conversation: a one-on-one interaction with another person or a computer. These include dialogues that balance listening, viewing, talking, and*

*interacting. **14-foot experiences** include business meetings, dinner parties, and watching TV with friends. The distance is greater and the balance in dialogue is less controllable. A **50-foot experience** is like a lecture, a performance, or a movie. It occurs within the context of a large audience which is on the receiving end of material and has less opportunity for input. Using a computer or PDA is mostly a 2-foot experience, watching interactive TV is a 14-foot experience, and multimedia lectures and presentations are 50-foot experiences.*

There are exceptions; an online chat session with several people resembles a 14-foot experience in structure but a 2-foot experience in interaction. However, no distance or form is better than another—each provides unique opportunities for interaction and experience.

Game Players

Game players are specific electronic devices almost always attached to television sets for the express purpose of playing video games. **Games** ▶ 16, 52 for these players are primarily delivered on cartridges and CD-ROMs. At the end of 1994, there were more than twice as many game players in homes (37 million) as personal computers capable of supporting CD-ROMs (16 million). The entire market for video games and game players is bigger than the market for movies in the U.S. Sega and Nintendo have been the pioneers in making game players with significant market shares, and as a result of this effort, they own almost all of the market for game players.

Game players are essentially low-cost special-purpose computers. The first players relied on processors a generation or two behind those found in personal computers at the time. The most recent machines and those currently in development, however, have state-of-the-art technology developed for the sole purpose of supporting game play. Game manufacturers are battling each other on performance issues, with the result that terms such as 16-bit, 32-bit, and 64-bit are now a standard part of most advertising campaigns.

16-bit, 32-bit, and 64-bit refer to the transfer rate of the main processor, which loosely corresponds to the quality of graphics in a game and the responsiveness of the game play. Additional co-processors are being added in newer machines to support faster animation renderings or better sound and graphics quality. In addition, the introduction of **CD-ROMs** into the game player market has brought more sophisticated sound and graphics than **cartridges**. Some manufacturers build add-ons that fit into the cartridge slot or into the back or side of players for things like game acceleration, networking, or special features. Other companies, such as 3DO and Philips, license technology to companies such as Goldstar, Sanyo, and Panasonic, who in turn manufacture and sell game players.

Nintendo and Sega, the two dominant game manufacturers, face competition from other game manufacturers and technology licensers such as Atari, 3DO, and Philips, but so far these companies have not been able to threaten either of them. Collectively, game player manufacturers are facing competition from the personal computer market. The expanding market of Macintoshes and multimedia PCs are prompting most game developers to support game players and personal computers.

In addition, personal computer manufacturers and third-party hardware vendors are building products to support gaming technologies. For example, Apple Computer has announced an MPEG board for a line of its Macintosh computers that will turn Apple's CD-ROM drive into a CD-i player as well as a separate, portable CD-ROM game player. Philips has also announced it is developing CD-i cards for CD-ROM-equipped PCs.

As a result, some industry analysts feel that the growing number of PCs in the home and their multi-purpose nature are slowly outweighing the lower cost of game machines. Others, though, see the large numbers, the lower cost, and recent advances that allow inexpensive networked game play over telephone lines, and feel that the most popular game players will have a long shelf life. There is also a fair chance that the newer technologies might migrate into interactive TV set-top boxes.

At the cartridge level, you have a very limited palette. You only have six to eight voices to deal with at a time. It is imperative to concentrate on melody, harmony and rhythm...if you can get away with anything beyond that, great! On the other hand, Sega CD, 32X, and Saturn systems are capable of very sophisticated music and sound effects, delivering audiophile quality and total flexibility. At that level, planning and production become even more crucial.

—Spencer Nilsen, Director/Executive Producer, Sega Music Group

CD-i - 200,000 households
3DO - 250,000, Sega CD - 2 million
Sega Genesis - 16.4 million,
Super Nintendo - 18.7 million

13

CD-ROMs

Diskettes, CD-ROMs, hard drives, Syquest cartridges, and almost all other storage media can contain multimedia (i.e. more than one media form). Network and online connections support multimedia, mostly in the form of text and graphics, and in some cases, sound, animation, and video. For distribution however, only CD-ROMs make economic sense since they cost around a dollar or two each to manufacture.

A CD-ROM is a way of having a large chunk of very large media objects already present and accounted for in the customer's home. The CD-ROM just went into fast growth and it will probably continue to grow heavily for two more years. Where it's exploding is in the entertainment domain. The information-heavy stuff is already rapidly going onto the Net. I predict a fizzle for information-heavy products on CD-ROM because customers want that kind of information in a timely and relevant fashion.

*—Tim Oren,
Vice President,
Future Technology,
CompuServe*

Many people equate multimedia with **CD-ROMs** ▶ 53 on a **personal computer**. Though the other platforms in this section show this is not necessarily true, what this does say is that the CD-ROM title market is one of the most visible multimedia markets and it is growing fast. Although the sales of CD-ROM titles are not public knowledge (unlike the sales figures for movies and videos that are ever-present in the public eye), the combined sales of the top 20 titles are very large, relative to the production and marketing costs for producing and distributing the titles. These figures have encouraged the rapid development of many other titles.

Today, there is an abundance of materials on CD-ROM to suit almost everyone's tastes. There are art titles, reference materials, education titles, games, and children's titles. Many more will be developed in the coming years. Whether they will ever be as abundant as books in a bookstore is debatable but, regardless, the market has only just begun.

Many computers sold today include a CD-ROM player. A personal computer is considered to be a multimedia PC if it is capable of displaying high resolution graphics and playing sound and video at acceptable levels. For some computers such as the Macintosh, these capabilities are built into the system so that they are capable of playing multimedia programs "right out of the box." Many PCs these days are billed as multimedia PCs and have all the components necessary for multimedia. Whether these components and the configuration will work with all CD-ROMs on the market is another story.

The components needed for multimedia include a microprocessor fast enough to handle the large processing demands of graphics, sound, and video, a monitor and

graphics card capable of displaying an acceptable level of colors, hardware and software support for playing sound and music, and speakers. Many computers have inexpensive speakers built in while others come with free-standing desktop speakers.

CD-ROMs are formatted according to standards that designate what platform and type of CD-ROM player can be used to play them. The formatting must be done properly to meet the requirements of specific operating systems such as UNIX, Windows, or Macintosh. Many CD-ROMs can be made to play on more than one operating system so that a larger audience can be reached. These types of CD-ROMs are referred to as "hybrid" or "ISO 9660" CD-ROMs.

A CD-ROM can hold over 600MB of data. In the early days of multimedia, that figure was looked at with awe and promise. It was a fantastically large number when compared with the 1.2MB size disk. Today, that figure has less importance. Where the notion once was to fill up the CD-ROM with as much content as possible, the belief now is to stop when the information is shared or the story is told.

The future will show faster drives, better compression for sound and video playback, and better authoring tools. The CD-ROM format was originally designed to operate at a comparably low speed (now called single-speed) but technical improvements have increased that speed so that double-speed and quad-speed drives are currently the most commonly sold. Better compression and playback algorithms will improve the quality of sound and video and will make "full-screen" video a reality at some point. Better **authoring tools** ▶ 247 for the consumer will mean more seamless and better performing titles, while for the developer, they mean less production time and expense.

Online Systems

The **online world** ▶ 61 is a mix of the Internet, the World Wide Web, bulletin board systems, large online systems, and local online systems. It may seem to be a leap to equate this with a "platform," but if you look beyond just the desktop computer and consider the network connection, communications software, and peripherals, you will see a unique combination of capabilities. In fact, the communications software can almost be seen as a new type of operating system that lets numerous third-parties create products that work on top of this software. These third parties, though, are creating not only applications but also a rich assortment of information, entertainment, and communication services.

The Internet and online services both began with email and simple file transfer protocols using command-line interfaces. Other features have been added over time to support richer forms of interaction. Within the **Internet**, these features include the http (hypertext transfer) protocol, which is the underpinning of the World Wide Web. The World Wide Web is so named because it allows users to jump easily from one area to another through the use of hypertext links. The Web consists of an ever-increasing set of **websites**. Each website contains a set of **webpages** which are separate screens, each of which is individually downloaded.

These pages are created using Hypertext Markup Language (HTML), which started as a restricted subset of a document publishing markup language but has begun to grow in response to specific online needs. The current language supports text and graphics, but not all users are able to see the graphics. A **web browser** is an application used to navigate to websites and view webpages. There are many commercial, shareware, and freeware browsers in existence. Within the last couple of years graphical web browsers have appeared, reducing the need to know cryptic commands in order to navigate the Web. The most popular graphical browsers are Netscape from Netscape Communications and NCSA Mosaic. The appearance of these and other browsers are a large reason for the dramatic growth and popularity of the Web within the last year.

Online systems, which include large commercial services such as America Online, CompuServe, and Delphi and local online systems such as The WELL in San Francisco, are much more sedate than the Internet and the World Wide Web. They are similar to shopping malls with fixed enclosures and tenants. (Not all the activity, though, is shopping-related.) The Internet, on the other hand, is more like a street market or a district like SoHo in New York with little oversight and authority for the products within.

The competition between online services is causing them to quickly add features and content areas and improve their interfaces. Most offer email, conferences, and chat services. **Email** ▶ 84 lets users send and receive messages to and from specific users. **Conferences** let users read and post comments within public forums. **Chat** lets users communicate within a public arena in real-time. (The Internet allows these features as well but the software for them and the structure of the areas themselves are not as readily accessible as they are in online services.)

The tremendous growth in memberships to online services and in the World Wide Web shows that online activity is more than just a passing fad. The technology is rapidly evolving, partly in response to these market changes and partly as an agent of these changes. Two issues receiving a great deal of attention from businesses and government are better security and a stable form of electronic money. Together, these two elements will allow for secure and automatic transactions, which will dramatically increase trading activity.

Also receiving attention from a variety of sources are innovative navigation and communication tools and higher bandwidth transmission mechanisms allowing for easier navigation and better handling of large data sets. These developments will make sound, animation, and video more prevalent in online activities, as well as allow for more real-time interactions with people and data sets throughout the world. The opportunities for creating network-based games and innovative personal and business services, among other things, are enormous, which should help explain why so many companies are involved in online activities.

People who think about the information highway largely as a one-way conduit for delivering goods and services electronically are going to miss out on the most interesting, compelling, important aspect of it—which is that when you get people connected up with one another, they want to communicate with each other. They don't want to be couch potatoes. They want interaction, they want community.

—Mitch Kapor, Founder, Electronic Frontier Foundation

The Internet describes the estimated 2.5 million computers and over 17 million users connected to a decentralized backbone. It started years ago as a loose collection of interconnected federal, regional, campus, and foreign networks and has grown to include "gateways" to many other public and private networks. No one really "governs" it and where it begins and ends is difficult to define. Online systems, on the other hand, are primarily private enterprises with readily definable borders.

15

Interactive Television

Interactive TV ▶ 65 as a platform is more real than anybody would have thought two years ago, but much further away than many would like to admit. While many predict the 500-channel universe will not be seen for years, more than a few companies are hard at work developing technology, hardware infrastructure, and programming to make this vision a reality. An enormous amount of money has already been spent on test trials around the U.S.

The technology hinges on several key parts. These include set-top boxes, remote control devices, servers to provide the programming and respond to communications from the user, and network infrastructures. The most critical of these technologies, the server and the infrastructure, have not yet been developed and are extremely expensive. Even if the switching technology existed to keep up with viewer's real-time demands, the cost of upgrading the infrastructure is astronomical (billions of dollars per region). Not mentioned but certainly foreseen in the future by many are microphones and video cameras in conjunction with set-top boxes supporting video-telephony between users.

The **set-top boxes** currently available or in development look like a cross between cable boxes, game machines, and VCRs. Compression decoders, on-board computing power, recordable memory, and add-in slots are only a few of the issues still being resolved. Current **remote controls** also show similarities with game controllers and VCR and cable remotes. There may be a standard remote for a system or there may be many attachments such as trackballs, joysticks, keyboards, and others. These issues are still being refined and will continue to be for a while. **Servers** are looking to incorporate hardware and software relating to parallel processing and transaction processing, databases for video storage, and switching systems for routing and delivering individual streams of data.

A number of interactive trials are taking place across the country. Everyone in this industry is eagerly awaiting the feedback from these trials. Each trial is testing a different combination of services including video on demand (VOD), home shopping, home banking, classified ads, restaurant reservations, theater and movie ticket purchases, and news, sports, financial, and other information services.

Results from these trials and the continued development of advanced technologies will help shape the future of interactive TV. How long the process will take and what it will look like in refined form is a hot topic of debate. Many of those interested in providing programming for interactive TV are currently developing CD-ROM products or online service projects with hopes of moving them to interactive TV—if and when it becomes a viable platform. The growth of multimedia and online capable PCs in the home, though, is causing many people to think that interactive PC will become a more viable platform sooner than interactive TV will. Technology and market prices are also allowing the PC to become a television much faster than the television can become a PC.

Other Platforms

Personal Digital Assistants

Personal digital assistants (PDAs) are small hand-held devices used primarily for organizing business and personal activities. Examples of PDAs include Apple's Newton and Sony's MagicLink. Although many people think of handwriting recognition when they think of PDAs, most interactions are touch oriented, meaning users fill out forms and select icons using a stylus, pen, or finger. Handwriting recognition is also used, but it still has some problems. These will likely be resolved in the future, though how long it will take is hard to tell. The biggest growth area for PDAs, though, is in communication and transactions as wireless technologies become a standard feature. The creation of electronic cash combined with email and send-fax capabilities will open up new ways for people to be productive and stay in touch with others without being stationed at a desk.

Kiosks/Point of Purchase (POP) Displays

An electronic **kiosk** is a free-standing computer system, usually with a touch screen, in a public place to provide information and assistance. A kiosk often takes the place of an information booth. They can be found in malls, museums, car dealership showrooms, and exihibit booths at conferences. The hardware can vary, though there is usually a touch-screen monitor, an external housing, a reasonably fast computer, and a hard drive, CD-ROM, videodisc player, or other large storage device. A Point of Purchase (POP) display is a type of kiosk most commonly found in retail stores and used specifically for helping to sell a product or family of products.

Presentations/ Performances

The hardware and software components for interactive **presentation** ▶ 48 and **performances** ▶ 39 are the hardest to define because they vary widely from event to event, depending on the size and location of the space and the nature of the information or entertainment featured. A sample list of such equipment might include lights, multiple monitors, large screens (including rear-screen projection monitors), overhead projection equipment, microphones, and audio speakers. You may also need one or more computer set-ups as individual stations for hands-on demos. Many presentation software packages exist that let users easily create self-running demos or manually operated slideshows.

Others

There are other platforms or technologies that have a significant influence on the type of projects created and the roles needed on a project team, including location-based entertainment setups, video discs, highly specialized, high-powered computers, and high-end audio and video equipment. Since technology and markets rarely stand still, in the future there will certainly be new platforms and consolidations of existing ones.

There's a real need for people who understand the integration of video signals and audio signals coming out of the back of the computer for staging. The kids that come in and say, "I rewired my dad's old Macintosh to include a video card that didn't fit, resoldering it in the process," are a lot more interesting. We're constantly swapping out boards. It's the real screwdriver-in-the-hand skills that count, not how many command-option keys you know. We like to hire people with screwdrivers in their hands.

—Scott Willoughby, President and CEO, Illuminated Media

Magic Edge Entertainment Center, courtesy of Magic Edge, Inc.

2. Projects

A wide array of interactive products and services are being created by development teams around the world. This section examines established project categories, as well as emerging ones.

Several factors went into determining the organization of this list. One of the most important ones is the **market** a project is created for. These markets include children, home users, business users, and educational users. When developing projects for these particular groups, the characteristics, needs, and expectations of the audience will largely determine the scope, content, and form of the project.

Closely related to the market is the **goal** or **purpose** of a project. In some cases, a project is created primarily to entertain; in others it is intended to educate or let people communicate with each other in new or different ways.

Developing a list of project types is difficult because there is still much experimentation going on. New technological capabilities are allowing developers to incorporate many forms of interactivity into their work, which leads to new project types. For example, adding transactional capabilities to an online advertisement turns the ad into a catalog. When access to an online discussion area is offered as part of a CD-ROM title containing baseball statistics, for example, the nature of the product shifts from being a one-way transmission of information to a two-way experience with other baseball aficionados.

In spite of all these developments, there are certain types of projects that can be isolated. The list of project types covered in this chapter includes:

- Reference
- Children
- Games
- Narrative
- Virtual Communities
- Digital Periodicals
- Special Interest
- Erotica
- Music
- Performance
- Education
- Business
- Training
- Marketing and Sales
- Presentations

Weaving Media Together

My approach to any area or category would be to build out many different areas for that category—a community side, an entertainment side, an information retrieval side, an experience side, a service side, and so on.

Branding allows you to position for an audience, to really wrap an identity or a culture around a person and create something that resonates with who they are.

What if I could buy a health book, get a set of videos that related to that, and a CD-ROM that related to it too? I might have in my mailbox for my online service everyday tips or encouragements or a support group that I could later experience either through broadband interactive or narrowband interactive. There is a way in which all these different types of distribution and media can link together to weave a web around people.

—Linda Stone, Director of Advanced Technologies, Microsoft

Reference

Reference titles are comprehensive information providers, styled after traditional encyclopedias. They provide bits of information about everything from A to Z, to give readers a snapshot of a huge range of topics. The CD-ROM versions add video, animation, and sound to the text, graphics, and photos of their print ancestors. These discs usually hold more text than bound print versions can, but the quality of print images is not as great.

CD-ROM encyclopedias are organized as large multimedia databases, with search engines that take readers to topics quickly and easily. Some search **engines ▶ 253** allow users to customize what they're looking for with several queries at once. For example, if you want information about a particular flea specific to the Indian elephant, you can enter "elephant and Indian and flea," and the engine will only bring up references in which all three of those terms appear. This is much more useful than a larger, less precise list of every occurrence of each of the three terms on its own. The goal of the encyclopedia is to educate and inform readers, and to give them as much freedom as possible in cross-linking between topics. The wonderful thing about them is their size and ease of use—there is no need to hunt through heavy volumes.

The family market for the traditional encyclopedia has expanded with the dramatic drop in price and the improved utility of the CD-ROM versions. Professionals who might not have been inclined to stock their shelves with a set of encyclopedias are much more likely to own digital versions. The sales of print encyclopedias have actually plummeted since the introduction of CD-ROM versions. The enormous bundling deals that manufacturers have negotiated with scores of computer manufacturers also serve to put an encyclopedia in nearly every multimedia equipped home.

There are very few digital encyclopedias on the market, probably because they are so involved and time consuming to produce. In some cases, the development is a cooperation between a print publisher and a multimedia developer, as is the case with Microsoft's *Encarta*. It was built from the Funk & Wagnalls encyclopedia, and updated and redesigned for its new format. In other cases, print publishers develop the electronic versions on their own, as is the case with the *Grolier Multimedia Encyclopedia*.

Digital encyclopedias lend themselves well to constant revision and updating, especially when they are maintained **online**. Some of the encyclopedias are available in text-only form through private online service providers. CompuServe and Prodigy, for example, give members access to the *Grolier Multimedia Encyclopedia*. This is clearly a viable direction for multimedia reference when the limits of the fixed format CD-ROM become too confining.

However, few digital reference products take much advantage of interactivity. One that does points to the possibilities of more refined forms of interactivity. *Voices of the 30s*, an educational reference title about the 1930s in the USA is actually a living database that allows readers to not only record their own comments and annotations about the materials shipped on the CD-ROM, but also add new materials themselves. This creates a new dimension to reference works and makes a place for the inevitable personalization of information. Other features allow users to create and save their own pathways through the materials, in effect creating their own multimedia book reports.

Development budgets, as might be expected, are usually very large and can reach upwards of $1 million. Project teams can range from 20 to over 100 people. Testing, licensing, and fact checking become critical and costly due to the vast amount of information to be processed. Still, as the market expands, demand for multimedia reference tools is likely to grow.

If there is a killer app in CD-ROM, it is the large multivolume reference set—the multimedia encyclopedia. CD-ROM encyclopedias, with their unmatched depth and breadth of information, are the undisputed stars of the CD-ROM format. As the format matures, the challenge is to apply new and exciting multimedia techniques to the existing core content without exceeding disc capacity. Also as publishers we are continually seeking ways to add large amounts of value—content, connections, information display—all within the short time frame of producing annual editions. Because of the proliferation of new reference titles, competition in this category is becoming quite intense.

—David Wicks, Executive Producer, Grolier Multimedia Encyclopedia

Children

When kids sit down with a standard picturebook, their behavior is to read it from front to back. They read the words from left to right all the way through, but there's not a lot of reinforcement on a personal level.

With multimedia and interactivity, what the kids can do is blown wide open. They can click on the words individually in any order they want. They can see and hear what they sound like in association with what they look like. They can interact with them in the context of the story. Animated characters add a lot to the story. They open it up so kids can make freer associations with the words and have a lot more fun.

—Todd Power,
Producer,
Weldon Owen

Anyone who doubts the potential of multimedia might think again after watching a child read an interactive storybook or play a game. The enthusiasm and comfort they show will make almost anyone a believer in the ability of interactive media to entertain and educate. A well-designed interface draws children into new worlds, where a click on a mailbox makes a frog jump out and dance or a letter read itself out loud. A program that lets them paint or arrange objects gives them new ways to express themselves.

While the market spans children between 3 and 12 years of age, there are distinct and important submarkets within this range. Children between the ages of 3 and 8 have received the most attention so far (excluding video and arcade games), although more companies are beginning to create products for older kids. Most publishers and developers are acutely aware of the capabilities of children at each **age** within a range. For example, children near the age of 3 naturally have less developed perception and higher thinking skills. They tend to enjoy simple goals and repetitive events—features that would bore older children.

Gender plays a role as well in determining elements that go into a product. Boys typically tend to enjoy solitary challenges of speed and skill. They seem to be very competitive against themselves and others. In contrast, many girls prefer products that allow them to meet and interact with others. They may be more interested in making choices based on feelings than on competitive instincts.

A common misunderstanding about children's preferences involves the use of color and characters. While infants and very small children respond best to bright, highly saturated primary colors (because their eyes are not yet fully developed), most children have **color** experience and preferences that are much closer to those of adults. They can appreciate rich color schemes and fine illustrations.

As for **characters**, as children age, their expectations become more sophisticated. Younger children may not demand too much realism or originality in characters when presented with simulated actors such as small animals or cute, anthropomorphized objects. But older children will expect their actions to represent personalities and motivations (which is much more difficult for developers to do). This knowledge of children is usually the result of in-depth user studies, watching children of all ages play with interactive media products.

Aside from games, this category probably has the largest selection of titles from which to choose. So far these titles have primarily followed three basic forms—games, storybooks, and learning products.

Games

Most children's **games** are built around the same three game elements as adult games: goals, obstacles, and challenges. Combinations of these elements, presented in conjunction with sound and animation, primarily provide entertainment. The biggest distinction between games for young children and those for older kids or adults, however, is that younger children are not expected to ever truly fail at a task or lose the game outright. They are often protected from failure and disappointment by carefully structured game flow and positive reinforcement for incorrect guesses.

Storybooks

Interactive storybooks take children through a story with sound, graphics, and hotspots to explore. Stories are read aloud, with each word highlighted as the narrator comes to it. Ever since the Living Books Series from Brøderbund set the standard for storybooks, multimedia savvy children have come to expect every object on the screen to come to life in some form. The best part of the Living Books series is that by hiding wonderful little animations around the screen waiting to be activated, they reward curiosity and exploration.

These storybooks are mostly created within the paradigm of traditional narrative structure. They have beginnings, middles, and ends. Building satisfying non-linear narratives for children may be a challenge. Younger children who have simpler expectations may not respond well to complex jumps, preferring repetition and consistency instead. Older children, however, may want to participate in the creation of the story more and are likely to want more tools and choices to do so.

Learning Products

"Edutainment" is an unfortunate word. It has come to mean anything that can be remotely linked to learning, which tends to include every children's product on the market. There are few products targeted for children that are not educational in some way, or at least marketed that way. There are, however, products that are specifically designed with learning or creating in mind. Examples include models of museums such as Knowledge Adventure's *3D Dinosaur Adventure* and lively encyclopedias like David Macaulay's *The Way Things Work* from the Voyager Company.

Some titles are adaptations of creativity or productivity toolsets for adults, simplified and dressed up with animated characters, sounds, and bright colors. Microsoft's *Creative Writer* is an example

of this. Brøderbund's *Kid Pix Studio*, another example, lets kids create multimedia presentations on their own. It functions as a model, template, and toolset all in one, providing not just inspiration but methods of exploring.

In the Future

In the future we can expect the boundaries between these three subcategories to blur even more. For example, all titles may ultimately contain tools that let kids build, play, learn, and create. Also, new genres of products for children

will be developed targeting more specific age ranges and developmental goals. Online products in particular are being developed to connect children over local networks (in a hospital, for example) or over wide networks with telephone lines to let them play and learn in collaboration with others.

Multimedia presents an opportunity to give control of learning and play back to children. Just as a child with a stick is stimulated into far more creative play than another with a very specialized plastic toy, a handful of the newer children's applications are taking that evolution a step toward turning the stick into a magic wand. Allowing kids to integrate their own ideas and interests will be more interesting and fun for them and ultimately result in more successful products.

Wacky Jacks and Travelrama USA, courtesy of Zenda Studio

Children as a group extends from three to eighteen. Obviously, the cognitive ability of children varies enormously over that age range as do the content interests and formats. Young kids don't read. They also have some difficulty with fine motor skills with the mouse; they don't easily double-click objects. Young children have difficulty following a narrative, so adventure games have to be more limited and more goal directed. Children like different types of exploration activities and enjoy repetition more so than adults. Mowing the lawn endlessly in *Putt Putt Joins the Parade* is a drag for an adult but a delight for many children.

—Dr. Cheryl Weiner, Director of Product Development, McGraw Hill Home Media

One of my heroes is Jim Henson. He and everybody else with the Muppets succeeded in creating something that is entertaining for adults as well as for children—entertainment that is highly educational. That was one of my goals in writing Freddi Fish.

—Larry Kay, Co-designer, *Freddi Fish and the Case of the Missing Kelp Seeds*, Humongous Entertainment

Iron Helix is a registered trademark of Drew Pictures, Inc.

Games

Interactive **games** are arguably the most popular of all interactive products. A game is a structured entertainment activity characterized by three basic elements: goals, obstacles, and challenges. A **goal** is some final result that ends the game and symbolizes victory. It can be anything from finding some sort of Holy Grail to simply being the last competitor standing. It might include heroic deeds, a solution to a puzzle, or the defeat of evil. **Obstacles** are constraints or impediments to the progress of the game. They may be rules for using tools or moving pieces, or they may be opposing objects such as fire-breathing dragons, broken bridges, or thugs out for blood. A **challenge** is a call to arms to overcome the obstacles and reach the goal. A player may be motivated to this challenge by teammates or competitors—live or virtual—or by their own competitive instincts.

Interactive games are often built around **first-person** ▶ 189 interactions with each player acting as a protagonist in the game. Players breathe life into the games they play by interacting with them. Many games may rely on third-person narratives to set the stage for the game or guide the play along in the middle of the story. The defining element, however, is not narrative. It is the **game play** ▶ 178. Titles that are long on narrative but short on game play are more apt to be called interactive movies. Game play is a term used throughout the game industry but it is an exceedingly difficult one to define. In general terms, an interactive game must be addictive, challenging, and fun. It should provide a significant amount of entertainment hours. A common measure used is that an entertainment product should cost $2–4 per hour of entertainment provided. Therefore, a $40 product should provide 10–20 hours worth of enjoyment.

Games vary widely in structure and implementation. Anything from a shoot-em-up to a sprawling mystery or a night trek into the unknown becomes a game as soon as it incorporates the three elements mentioned above. Games are built around a few seminal models. The major

frameworks challenge the player to beat the clock, beat another player, or simply survive to the highest level possible. Strategy is a variable—game designers can embed as much or as little complexity into their game structures as they wish. Some games might have richer storylines or more deeply challenging puzzles, but bear in mind that games with simple rules like chess inspire strategies that are infinitely complex.

The budgets for producing games can be large—many approach the $1 million to $2 million range. The marketing budgets for games are also large, often exceeding the development budgets by factors of two or three.

Following are the types of games that are the easiest to define. Classifying games is difficult because there is still a lot of experimentation taking place. Some game developers, around since the days of Atari and the first computer games, are taking advantage of better sound and graphical capabilities to add life to existing paradigms. Others, such as entertainment companies looking for ways to extend their film properties, are bringing their sensibilities to bear on developing new formats.

Twitch Games

Twitch games are essentially pattern-recognition games built around stimulating intense physiological responses through rapid-fire gaming experiences. Many of these games feature some sort of shooting metaphor, but that is not a prerequisite. Violence and gore levels vary but high speeds are a constant. Twitch games constantly focus a player's attention on the immediate moment using a continual barrage of low-

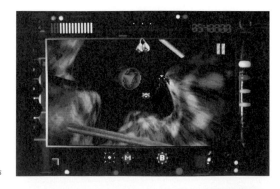

courtesy of Psygnosis

intensity information and high speed movement to keep adrenaline levels high. Reactions are physical rather than mental, primarily challenging a player's hand-eye coordination. The overall goal is simply to survive to the highest level the game has or to successfully complete some sort of mission.

Twitch games are generally built into series of interconnected **rooms** or **landscapes**, allowing freedom of movement and plenty of space for the battles. Thugs, monsters, or creatures of any variety attempt to prevent players from reaching any of their goals. These games may have introductory setups that describe the gaming situation, but once the game play begins, little information is presented that requires higher order processing such as spoken or written language beyond grunts or exclamations of pain. There are usually clear depictions of a player's status such as the energy levels and ammunition stores. Players can battle the computer or use multiplayer options to let more people into the action. Often, books are published that provide strategies and secret moves or tricks to help players win.

Acclaim's *Mortal Kombat* and Id Software's *Doom* and *Doom II* are three gold standards. Id Software has seen dramatic sales without major marketing investments since they uploaded a fully functioning first chapter of *Doom* to several Internet sites for free distribution. The word about the game spread like wildfire across the Internet and thousands downloaded it within days of its posting. A majority of these ended up ordering the full version of the game.

The Surrealistic Adventure That Will Become Your World

The market for these games is largely the infamous adolescent boy. The games may appeal to adult audiences as well, but far more men play these games than women. Nintendo and Sega have a large influence in this category but numerous other developers and publishers are gaining name recognition and market share.

Mystery/Adventure Games

The **mystery/adventure** game represents a broad range of larger-than-life experiences, from science fiction settings to mythical castle fantasies. It represents the middle ground between twitch games and narratives. The game play is less intense than a twitch game but the player is usually wrapped up in a first person interaction within the story.

Popular mystery adventure games include *Myst* from Brøderbund and *Seventh Guest* from Virgin Interactive. These games produce an impressive level of realism and immersion in the story. Mystery/adventure games are often centered around a building or region with the direction of play depending on the player's movements and performance. There is usually a **grand mystery** to solve coupled with **smaller puzzles** along the way. Since many games require hours or days of continuous play to reach any sort of conclusion, a "Save Game" feature is standard. This allows players to stop playing, save their progress, and continue from the same point at a later date.

Players generally enter a deserted landscape to find a set of **instructions**. These instructions describe a tale of intrigue and suspense, leading

Game players want to go to a place they can't really go in their normal lives, they want to do things they can't really do, and they want to be someone they aren't — just for a little while.

—Tim Schafer, Project Leader, Full Throttle, LucasArts

The best game to me is a completely interactive network game with multiple players, where each one starts off in his own virtual world. As he reaches the edges of his world, as he advances, his edges touch other edges. Throw a little reality ingredient in there. Tie it to some news service. Have the world change. Have parts of it that are changing daily so that it never gets boring. Have all the graphics available so that you can choose your character, who you are, where you are, what you do, and then have that interact with other people who have made their own choices. That would be a cool game. I don't know how you would do it but it would really be cool."

—Clifford Lau, Animator, Sega

SimCity is not a game—because no one wins or loses. It's more like a toy that you play with to have fun. People who use our software are more interested in experiencing something that doesn't talk down to them or require quick reflexes. We give people the opportunity to express their creativity through simulation. Each person is able to create their own life form, farm, city, or earth, and grow it and change it in any way they want. … With our stuff, there's no right or wrong, good or bad, it just goes. And I'll tell you what, it's working because no one wants to be told what to do, I don't care how old a person is.

—Jeff Braun, CEO, Maxis, in The Red Herring, *December 1994*

up to the present moment. The player becomes the lead character in the central drama and is charged with a specific goal. The path toward the goal might take any form—from a trek through a jungle, to a flight through time, to an exploration of a detailed setting. The obstacles between the player and the goal will be many and varied, but no player goes without a bag of tools of that can be used to defeat evil and achieve the goal.

The market for these games is large and is likely to grow still more. Many of these games appear to have broad appeal for young and old, men and women. Almost every fiction genre in book publishing is potentially open for creating products of this nature. While science fiction, fantasy, and crime dominate at the moment, nothing precludes someone from creating a deconstructed spy adventure.

Flight Simulators

Flight simulators date back to the original (and classic) Flight Simulator built in the early 1980s. Its graphics and its level of sophistication set a new standard for what the personal computer could do. The flight simulators of today bear little resemblance to their ancestor, but their emphasis on genuine flight procedure and practical authenticity have not changed. They represent a game genre well placed to exploit the multimedia resources becoming available. In some cases, there may not be a clear cut set of goals because the main appeal may be to simulate realistic flying capabilities of civilian planes. Other simulators such as those involving warplanes may have specific missions to fly and opponents to battle.

A cousin of the flight simulator is the **driving simulator** which provides the experience of driving a motorcycle, automobile, or other form of wheeled transportation. Simulators are a specialized form of entertainment. Full-screen displays mimic cockpits of military aircraft or high speed automobiles that would not be available to the general public. Some flight simulators, primarily those providing sophisticated motion control, are deemed so realistic that hours spent at play on them count as flight hours toward completing a private pilot's license. Born of military flight training simulators, these games are quite serious and difficult to master.

Simulation Games

Simulation games put players into representations of complicated scenarios, asking the player to coordinate the various factors. They are strategy games generally centered around business, social, or wargame scenarios requiring a player to maintain a city or create a plan of attack, for example. The games typically have rich graphics and complex **calculation engines** underneath.

The extremely successful *SimCity* and the other Maxis SimGames are examples of simulation games. In *SimCity*, a player is cast as the mayor of a city and must handle everything from managing the city's budget to coordinating the response to a natural disaster. The challenges range from the pragmatic to the bizarre—industrial sectors die because they lack adequate plumbing, or alien robots begin demolishing parts of the city. The game is organic, meaning that the city grows or dies based on transparent algo-

rithms constantly being calculated. This organic nature adds complexity and a certain amount of open-endedness to the clear-cut goals most games feature.

Role-Playing Games

Role-playing games are the online offshoots of Dungeons & Dragons style gaming. There are many different games and types of environments, but they share a focus on character building and maintenance amid a sea of strangers. Players enter the world and choose or build an identity for themselves. Their digital alter egos become central to their performance in the game. Weapons, abilities, and cures for ailments are available along the way, and interactions with non-player characters (NPCs) are crucial to uncover the final goal.

Zork was one of the first significant role-playing games. It was tremendously popular, and is currently being resold as a CD-ROM along with two other titles. Although it is completely text-based, it has a richly textured storyline and background. More recent role-playing games are all graphical, but insiders insist that storyline cannot take a back seat to graphics. Clearly, the opportunities here are to offer players a better blend of graphics and compelling storylines to immerse them into their worlds.

Sports Games

Sports games mimic professional sports in some form and, in many cases, have official sponsorship from an individual athlete or a league. In fact, games that are endorsed by a league are often permitted to use actual team rosters within the game. This level of realism can significantly boost sales. These games follow actual sports formats and rules, letting players choose team rosters and play the game from their desktops.

Sports games are one of the most popular genres in the established software marketplace. They can be found in retail stores, catalogs, and online services. They can be found on game cartridges, CD-ROMS, and are making their way to online systems and interactive TV. As with other prod-

ucts, celebrity appeals are attractive attention-getters but experience has shown that star power alone is not sufficient to sell a game. It must still offer a rich gaming experience.

Location-Based Entertainment

Location-based entertainment (LBE) refers to special interactive media centers typically located in public spaces that offer some type of **virtual reality** ▶ 220 experience. These centers can be sophisticated flight simulators with motion and multiplayer capabilities or rides based on the setting and characters within a movie. Since virtual reality technologies are likely to remain expensive to build and maintain for a while, these gaming centers are clearly the major focus for the near future.

Location-based games simulate reality by immersing players into the game environment. This is done not only with the game technology itself but with the setting and environment of the entire center. There is often a larger story context for the game that is established in the background, and players are usually "briefed" by live actors before their missions or rides.

Development teams are usually quite large, as are the requisite budgets for creating such integrated environments. These games are developed by teams of pioneers looking toward future virtual reality gaming possibilities. Whatever limits such systems face today, they are clearly set to improve dramatically.

Let's think ahead a few years about what something like Myst *might become. To me, its attraction—which is one of the very few graphical adventures that's held my attention in a long time—is that it really does have a sense of place. They did a great job putting together a synthetic environment that was interesting just to be in. Then they messed around with the puzzle so that you had to spend a certain amount of play time being there. If you did the same thing and then populated it with people and computer constructs, that could become very interesting. The early experiences with* **Habitat** ▶ *31 point to a mixture rich in social terms, artistic, and graphic values.*

—Tim Oren,
Vice President,
Future Technology,
CompuServe

Narrative

Narrative is a project type that includes all forms of fictional storytelling, including interactive movies and interactive fiction. As a specific category, however, its definition is hazy at best and non-existent at worst. Many products have some narrative component to them. Some games in particular rely heavily on interesting characters and setups to make them engaging. Several virtual communities have also created rich role-playing environments, but there are few popular interactive products that are based solely on narratives without some form of gaming or communication to them. Several people have tried building branching stories using video while others have used text and images. So far, few have managed to captivate an audience, leaving an ongoing debate among developers about narrative and its place in multimedia.

Oral Tradition

Written narratives are descended from the oral tradition, in which people tell stories to each other. The oral tradition can have mythological overtones, carrying cultural information through the ages, as a sort of organic memory. Novels, theater, and movies are three more contemporary western forms of storytelling. Each one tells a story in a different way. The author's goal is to present a story in a way that entertains, moves, or engages the audience emotionally. Stories can be very powerful when they touch on universal themes with which every reader or viewer can identify. William Gibson's *Neuromancer* is successful not just because it describes a sinister new cyberworld—it also addresses issues of loyalty, identity, survival, and relationship.

Narrative Elements

Traditionally, fictional stories have a few basic elements in common. **Characters** and **plots** or **storylines** are built around a framework of **con-**

flicts and **resolutions**. Conflicts add depth and richness and instill a sense of urgency in events. Resolutions provide closure. They are essential to a good story.

Common film structures typically include two "turning points" or conflict/resolution pairings—as do hour-long television dramas. Half-hour television dramas typically have time for only one turning point (soap operas excluded). Novels do not have formal guidelines, largely because their form is more wide-ranging, but a detailed diagramming of the structure of a novel would show not only conflicts and resolutions but also exposition, climax, denouement, and closure.

Another aspect of narratives is **perspective** ▶ 187, which is often separated into "first person" and "third person." It refers to the perspective the story is told from. Although books may be written in first person, they are largely third person experiences—the actions described are not the reader's but the main character's. A few movies and television shows have tried a first person approach in which the actions of actors and the camera give the perspective that the camera is the eyes of one of the main characters.

Related to perspective is the technique of following multiple characters. The modern day novel typically jumps from a variety of characters and substories, detailing events experienced by each one until the threads tie together in some form or another. Movies also commonly follow different characters but each scene usually relates to the previous scene so that abrupt jumps are less common and the threads converge more quickly.

Pathways through narratives can be **linear** or **non-linear**. Linear narratives are extremely common while non-linear ones are comparatively rare. The most common of the linear methods by far is chronological, where a story follows a main character through a specific sequence of time.

Non-linear works are difficult to define because they can take so many different shapes. There are no laws that state stories must center around a main character or setting, or a forward movement of time, for example, but it can be difficult to create a non-linear narrative that does not follow these conventions and is also a satisfying entertainment experience.

The film *Pulp Fiction* is an example of a non-linear story structure. It is built as an integration of several short stories, tied together by several central characters. One of the main characters is killed midway through the movie but is seen alive in a subsequent episode that had actually occurred earlier in time. The final scene turns out to be the opening scene of the movie, retold from another character's perspective. While the stories are not entirely disjointed, they progress from moment to moment from several different perspectives. The film *Six Degrees of Separation* shares a similar sense of non-linearity both in looking through several different **points of view** ▶ 55, 176, 192 as well as mixing the order at which events occur.

Interactive Directions

Multimedia developers have previously explored interactive storytelling by basing their stories around **branching structures**, presenting players with options at certain junctures for deciding the way a story should go. These products have met limited success. Part of the problem with them is that layers of options make them grow to unwieldy sizes very quickly. Unless some options can loop back to others, the story begins to look like a pyramid with a few beginnings and far too many possible endings. Another problem is that stories with this shape tend to stop making sense sooner or later. The very choices intended to make the audience feel like participants intrude into the experience, constantly reminding the audience that they are an audience.

Many people now are actively exploring the middle ground between author and subject. They are providing structure and tools and letting the audience determine its shape. Jaron Lanier, noted

virtual reality pioneer, characterized this century as a "weird" one because it has been dominated by one-way media. People are naturally two-way communicators, but our ability to respond to television, print media, and radio is indirect at best.

No other century has seen such distance between hearing and response. Interactive media forms, however, are slowly bridging this gap. Works like Abbe Don's *Share With Me a Story* present players with a template that leads them through building their own stories. The future of the narrative might well lie here, in taking the authorial role and giving it to the audience. Once the consumer enters a truly interactive world, they become "prosumers," in Don's view—active consumers, able to participate by defining the communications channels and the products involved, for themselves as well as for others.

Some people feel that interactive narrative is a contradiction in terms. While there may be titles that provide interesting stories, they will have more in common with linear media forms such as books and movies. Others feel, however, that interactive narratives will develop a form of their own. They point to the opportunities to describe events through multiple viewpoints and the ability to randomly order pieces individually for each viewer. They believe the world is just waiting for a groundbreaking example to show the way.

It seems to me the book has not just aesthetic values—the charming little clothy box of the thing, the smell of the glue, even the print, which has its own beauty. But there's something about the sensation of ink on paper that is in some sense a thing, a phenomenon rather than an epiphenomenon. I can't break the association of electric trash with the computer screen. Words on the screen give the sense of being just another passing electronic wriggle.

—John Updike, Author, Atlantic Monthly, *June 1994*

Where Is the Author?

We are working with a medium where one can no longer have an authorial voice. Many of us may not know that yet, but it turns out that we are no longer in the business of authoring narrative, or even of predisposing people to construct a particular narrative, or to find the right path through anything. I think that is true in general and it's going to become more true over the next few years.

Anything that relies on a storyline that has been produced by a content provider is not interactive. It's bottom-feeding on an old paradigm. If you wanted to draw two columns, on the one hand you've got content providers, and on the other hand you've got content traders, content makers, content merchants, and gifters. But the second column isn't about content—it's about relationships, tool providers, environment providers. It's about community instead of information.

What you get to do as an "author" is to provide materials, tools, and interesting environment suggestions. What we're talking about is introducing imaginary objects, images, and multiple media into conversations and the way communities relate to each other.

—Brenda Laurel, Member of Research Staff, Interval Research

Virtual Communities

We need to find these different genres of online places, some of which will be for recreation, some of which will be for work. We've got a good century's worth of work ahead of us. I think that's pretty exciting, actually.

—Mitch Kapor, Founder, Electronic Frontier Foundation

Humans are social beings, with a fundamental need to communicate. Communities help satisfy this basic need. They create a feeling of membership, a safety net of friends and friendly institutions surrounding a person. That feeling of community and mutual understanding is now extending across time and place as the computer, in combination with telephone lines, allows the formation of **virtual communities**.

A virtual community is a group of distant people who associate on a continual basis through some computer facilitated means. As Howard Rheingold defines them in his book *The Virtual Community*, "Virtual communities are social aggregations that emerge from the Net when enough people carry on those public discussions long enough, with sufficient human feeling, to form webs of personal relationships in cyberspace." A feeling of connection is the most difficult thing for the postmodern communities of today to maintain, but people seem to be turning to virtual communities more and more to make up for real-life losses.

The main goal of any virtual community is to inspire people to **interact with each other**—to communicate, exchange ideas, and get to know each other. Interaction in conjunction with computers can mean two things. It can mean interaction between a computer and a human, and it can mean between two people in ways that are facilitated by the computer.

Virtual communities largely provide the second experience. They are too experience-oriented to be games and too free-form to be narratives. Games are defined by an overriding goal, a set of obstacles to overcome, and a challenge to go forth and play to the end. There are no ends in virtual communities, there is no princess to rescue. There is just a set of people who know each other, and who share "a place where everybody knows your name." Likewise narratives, no matter how interactive they try to be, must have predefined story threads to take viewers from beginning to end. Here again, virtual communities just spin on endlessly, like a story with no beginning and no end, just an infinite middle.

People seem to form their online affiliations in three principal ways: geographical, topical, or demographic. **Geographical groups** are rooted in a specific physical place. They share in common a city, country, or region. These associations are no different than those shared in the real world, in towns and neighborhoods, on main street, in cafes, and in pubs.

The other two are more difficult to replicate in a real world perspective. **Topical groups** are formed around in a specific subject area such as biochemistry, stock trading, or Melrose Place. The Motley Fool is an example. It is a stock portfolio that an analyst keeps and updates every day online. The Fool explains Wall Street Foolishness in plain language, and presents the real numbers behind every transaction. It explains commissions and all the other transactional costs that deflate otherwise beautiful numbers. The Fool also has forums for discussions between readers about their own questions and thoughts. Services like these that cater to specific markets and interests are likely to become incredibly successful over time.

The Third Place

The book The Great Good Place *by Ray Oldenberg suggests that there are three essential places in people's lives. These are the home, the workplace, and the "the third place," an informal public place with which to be part of a larger social setting. Oldenburg points out that strip mall culture erodes many people's abilities to go for a drink, a cup of coffee, or a walk through the town square. "The problem of place in America manifests itself in a sorely deficient informal public life. The structure of shared experience beyond that offered by family, job, and passive consumerism is small and dwindling," Oldenberg observes. "The essential group experience is being replaced by the exaggerated self-consciousness of individuals. American lifestyles, for all the material acquisition and the seeking after comforts and pleasures, are plagued by boredom, loneliness, alienation, and a high price tag."*

Many online pioneers postulate that more than a few people's response to this increasing lack of third places is to find a point of contact with other human beings in online worlds. These pioneers note that every time a member of a virtual community refers to a community, they refer to it as "here"—a place, a little corner of cyberspace.

Cyberspace wins.

```
▇▐ Ken Fromm, 6:57 PM 2/1/95...,GovAccess.094: grand juries; $2 legis; ▐▇
  □  Subject: GovAccess.094: grand juries; $2 legis; CA budget; GOVMANAG; ed

"I know of no safe depository of the ultimate powers of the society but the
people themselves, and if we think them not enlightened enough to exercise
that control with a wholesome discretion, the remedy is not to take it from
them, but to inform their discretion."
  - Thomas Jefferson, 1820   [via Stanton McCandlish <mech@eff.org> ]

Mo' as it Is.
--jim

GovAccess is a list distributing irregular info & advocacy, maintained by
Jim Warren, columnist, MicroTimes, Government Technology, BoardWatch, etc.
  345 Swett Rd., Woodside CA 94062; voice/415-851-7075; fax/<# upon request>
  jwarren@well.com (well.com = well.sf.ca.us; also at jwarren@autodesk.com)

&    To add or drop the GovAccess list, email to  jwarren@well.com .    &
& Past postings are at  ftp.cpsr.org: /cpsr/states/california/govaccess  &
& and by WWW at  http://www.cpsr.org/cpsr/states/california/govaccess . &
```

Demographic groups form around age, culture, religion, or other characteristics. There are online places set up specifically for teenagers, Harvard Business School graduates, and business executives. SeniorNet is a huge network of information, resources, mail, and chat rooms devoted entirely to senior citizens. Forums discuss medications, death and probate issues, and individual retirement accounts (IRAs) as well as the usual get-togethers, vacations, and jokes. Users can access it through America Online or call it up independently. In the future, almost every demographic group may have some form of online representation.

Time-Shifted Communications

There are two major types of virtual human-to-human interaction. The first is the **time-shifted communications**—where the sending and receiving of correspondence are delayed in time. One person sends an email message to others or posts a message to a conference area. Others send an email response at their convenience or post their own comments to the conference area to be read at a later time.

Mailing lists or **aliases** are groups of addresses for people to carry on conversations with a large audience via email. This way, people with similar interests can reach a larger group, getting more information to more like-minded people. There are mailing lists for everything from environmentally concerned scuba divers to private family nets that let members post letters to a central address that sends them to everyone else. There are two kinds of mailing lists, unidirectional and bidirectional. Unidirectional lists usually have an editor or set of editors that create the material that gets posted. They are similar to a digital periodical. *GovAccess* put out by Jim Warren is an example. It contains information on actions of various government entities in areas of online access.

Bidirectional lists act more like bulletin boards. Anybody can post a message which then gets distributed to everyone on the list. Family nets are a good example of bidirectional lists, as is the list for environmentally concerned scuba divers. These types of lists show a tendency to split after they reach a certain number of subscribers. (This number can be as low as two dozen.) The bigger they become, the more they become unmanageable in terms of both the number of messages and the themes of the discussions.

Newsgroups, or **conferences**, are ongoing discussions about a particular topic. USENET is a popular place to find many newsgroups. It is a subset of the Internet that is used to host newsgroups. Newsgroups center around a particular topical interest and usually contain up-to-the-minute information supplied by regular participants. There are newsgroups about technological or scientific breakthroughs, bugs in programs, football scores, and the famed joke group, rec.humor.funny. The latter group is moderated, meaning there is an editor that determines what gets included. The jokes do tend to be funny. (Honest.) Newsgroups are based on participants responding to postings by others. The postings are done through email, and they often do not happen in real time. The groups are separated into different types using abbreviations for identification.

Real-Time Interaction

The second form of human-to-human interaction takes place in **real time**. You correspond as others are corresponding, sometimes in reference to you and sometimes in reference to others. Time-shifted communication is usually longer, more involved, and requires people to wait for a

Programs like Majordomo *and* Listserv *dominate the mailing list creation market. They are free for downloading from the Internet, and very easy to use. Essentially, they are nothing more than a bit of code that organizes subscribers in databases and reroutes mail sent to the program's host machine to all the people on the list.*

Moderated lists require a human moderator to review all mail sent to the posting address and choose which letters get reposted to the list. Currently, most moderators do it for fun but these will likely be paid and highly influential positions in the future.

A New Renaissance

Today, there's a renaissance of writing that's going on with the Net because the common medium is text-based electronic mail. Therefore, your power and persuasiveness is a function of how well you can write. That is shaping a lot of people. When the bandwidth gets higher on the Net and you can do not just voice messages, but video messages as easily as you can do email, there will be a lot of talking and less writing. This renaissance of textual literacy will have been a short one. That would be unfortunate because I am not one of those people who celebrates the arrival of the world of post-symbolic communication, where everybody is just waving their virtual-reality gloved hands at each other and communicating. I still believe in text but its future is not clear.

—Mitch Kapor, Founder, Electronic Freedom Foundation

courtesy of the Internet Roundtable Society
(http://www.IRsociety.com)

response. Real time "chat sessions" focus on a group of people communicating in short bursts. They are more like inexpensive global conference calls. Chat sessions can revolve around a specific topic, like the stock market or parenting, or about nothing in particular. They are famous for being the cyberspace equivalent of the fern bar, where singles go to check each other out. In many cases, people in chat groups can invite others into "private chat rooms" to get to know each other better, and perhaps engage in a little "hot chat."

Multiple User Dimensions or **Dungeons (MUDs)** are the ultimate form of real-time interaction. They are currently text-based worlds where users go for role-playing entertainment. The general goal is to bring people together in a fictional environment and let them bring it to life. If people are given a scenario full of objects and other people, they tend to spin their own stories. This is truly interactive because the players become just as creative as the authors of the environment itself.

MUDs resemble role-playing games at first glance. Players enter an environment that is described in detail, and direct their characters with a short list of commands. However, just like any virtual community, there is no real beginning and no end. Most MUDs have an entry screen that outlines the fictional history of the land, but this history has very little to do with what's going on in the MUD itself. MUDs are focused on the experience itself, not on any particular game goal. Even the stories lose importance next to real-time conversations, in character, that spin around the player. From the point of entry,

players are asked to describe their characters so that other players who know something about them can **identify** them at any time. The descriptions cover a huge range of animal, vegetable, and mineral, from hermaphroditic cyborgs to "squirreloid" animals, to anything imaginable. Players are not expected to keep to a single identity, species, or gender. Experimenting with your identity is a big part of the fun.

Players can wander around, using basic compass and common-sense commands such as "go north" or "open door," and can manipulate objects in the environment and see the results. The intricate settings just provide backdrops to inspire more creativity from players. The MUD administrator is part scriptwriter, part sysop (system operator), and part programmer/author, creating a world and responding to the players at the same time.

Net Issues

Currently, cyberspace is largely a social frontier. The appearance of digital cash, however, is likely to alter that landscape very significantly, metaphorically stripping away one last layer of innocence. Many net users are insistent that advertising and merchandising have no place in cyberspace. Still, commerce is definitely on its way in. How this will transform the net, or if commercial applications will exist peacefully alongside social aspects, remains to be seen.

Censorship is a major social issue. Private online services have been accused of having a "guards at the gate" mentality, limiting the nature of the discussions and policing the actions of members. In some cases, messages written in foreign languages were automatically deleted. These actions are often taken because of the desire to create a more hospitable environment, and additionally because of the fear of legal liability for the content contained in their systems. There is current legal debate occurring with online systems. It pits the idea of being simply a conduit for communications (like the phone system) against the idea of being responsible for the content that passes through the computers (like radio, television, and cable TV). Nobody is sure whether the more permissive Internet model or the more restrictive private online service model will prevail in the future, but groups like the Electronic Frontier Foundation are lobbying for broad electronic civil rights.

What happens when people are free to respond to the message of the medium of the Internet is that things take off in totally unanticipated directions. If you really want to harness the medium, you have to listen to that. It isn't Republican. It doesn't respect family values. In many cases, it respects the interests and desires of marginalized groups that find themselves together for the first time in a critical mass.

*—Tim Oren,
Vice President,
Future Technology,
CompuServe*

Virtual Communication

People in virtual communities use words on screens to exchange pleasantries and argue, engage in intellectual discourse, conduct commerce, exchange knowledge, share emotional support, make plans, brainstorm, gossip, feud, fall in love, find friends and lose them, play games, flirt, create a little high art and a lot of idle talk. People in virtual communities do just about everything people do in real life, but we leave our bodies behind. You can't kiss anybody and nobody can punch you in the nose, but a lot can happen within those boundaries. To the millions who have been drawn into it, the richness and vitality of computer-linked cultures is attractive, even addictive.

—Howard Rheingold, Author, The Virtual Community

Habitat

Habitat was a real-time graphical user environment—essentially the first virtual world. It was developed over seven years ago by LucasArts in conjunction with another computer company. The three primary designers at LucasArts were Chip Morningstar, Randy Farmer, and Aric Wilmunder. At its peak, the online system supported over 15,000 users. Fujistu recently purchased the technology after licensing it for several years. Habitat is important because the design and the technology allowed for many interesting social interactions. It was years ahead of its time and, as a result, has provided many seminal idea about online human behavior. These ideas hold many keys to the design of future systems.

Habitat was a 2D graphical environment where users were represented by **avatars**—human or animal character representations. Dialogue between users was represented in text balloons that appeared above each character. Avatars were customizable. Users could choose a character's gender, height, and clothing. The system was originally designed to support six different heads—three female and three male. All told, there were a few thousand permutations of appearance. In the course of playing around with the animation engine, though, one of the designers realized they could separate the heads from the rest of the animation. As a result, avatars could support any head that anybody could design. At some point in its operation, people were walking around as wind-up penguins and spiders.

One of the things soon learned in developing and managing Habitat was that it was impossible to keep up with the demands of the users. A maze that took a week to create would be solved in a few hours. And so at some point, the developers realized they had to turn the world over to the users. "Turning the world over" meant creating tools and objects with which users could develop capabilities on their own. Users were given the ability to modify much of the artwork in the system. The world also contained over 120 objects, such as doors, chess pieces, boomerangs, balls, and even guns. The idea of currency was introduced and through the simple combination of objects—a door that took currency would turn into a turnstile—interesting places and capabilities were created.

Turning the world over also meant identifying key users who could help moderate the world. These people were called super users or demigods and they would create and manage regions within the world. People reacted to authority in a very community-oriented way. They would make requests, such as not allowing guns to work in town. Everyone would vote and the wishes would be carried out in ways that tried to preserved the rights of both the majority and the minority. In the case of guns, they were reprogrammed so that they would not work within the city limits but would still work outside the limits. If people wanted to venture outside the city limits, they were essentially on their own. (At one time, people asked to hire a sheriff to patrol the badlands.)

One of the most important lessons learned in creating the system was that people essentially wanted to interact with each other. Some wanted to play games such as chess and checkers, others wanted to hand out drinks, and still others wanted to use magic wands to change people's heights. The designers found that certain objects took on value. They created mazes whose winners were awarded unique heads, something akin to the yellow jersey in the Tour de France. There were vending machines where people could purchase containers to hold items or cans of paint to decorate their bodies. But most important of all, they realized that people needed to have the ability to modify their world. They needed to make changes, to design things, and to have a voice in its creation and direction. By providing the ability for users to do this, the designers created a rich, vibrant, and ever-changing environment.

Digital Periodicals

*It's very credible to think about a world where you have a news agent that has the synthetic point of view of a Walter Cronkite—if you like having a reliable grandfatherly figure to tell you about the world from his perspective. Or someone else might decide that they want their news agent to have a differ-ent **point of view** ▶ 55, 176, 192, a "Generation X" point of view, or a "rocker" point of view, or whatever. Some people may actually license not only their personalities but their changing point of view.*

—Paul Saffo, Director, Institute for the Future

Why substitute a famil-iar, inexpensive, por-table and visually tan-gible media for nonde-script silver discs? Why not? New digital magazines are freed from the conventions of the printed page. These are magazines where images expand into video, illustrations transform into anima-tion, and typography leaps into motion. Even advertising is now seen and sold in terms of megabytes of space and levels of screens.

—Rhonda Rubinstein, Principal, R Company, an editorial design studio in New York

Digital periodicals are newsletters or magazines published in **CD-ROM** or **online** formats. There are many different kinds of electronic periodicals, focusing on a huge range of topics. The advan-tages to a digital format are many. They include increased access to archived versions and active search engines for finding areas of interest easily. Additional interactive capabilities can be added in the form of rich navigation schemes and cre-ative and productive features for making the information or entertainment more personal.

CD-ROM periodicals offer the ability to use sound, animation, and video as part of the content. Online periodicals offer immediate access to past and current information. They also offer the potential for a rich two-way communication dy-namic between author and reader and between the readers themselves.

In terms of distribution, CD-ROMs offer more controlled access, while online distribution offers low-cost delivery and the potential to reach a huge and wide-ranging audience. **Copyright protection** is a serious problem for all, but espe-cially for those that are online. Because copying may become difficult to avoid, some people argue that publishers may have to develop mod-els that generate revenues for published informa-tion in other ways.

The major types of digital periodicals are newspa-per forums, newsletters, news wires, digital maga-zines, and zines. Some are advertiser-supported while others are subscriber-supported, while still others are free of charge. Digital magazines are the only types that currently publish on CD-ROMs. The others are distributed exclusively online. In the future, most will likely have some form of online element even if it is only a place where subscribers can communicate with each other. There lies the potential for reaching every group and individual on any topic, provided the right structures and revenue models are determined.

Newspaper Forums

Newspaper forums are sites set up by newspa-pers to reach their readership online. Small news-papers nationwide have set up their own online services and many more have cut deals with private online services to carry their stories. Li-braries of back issues, search tools, and easy access to the editorial staff are the major benefits here. Their interfaces vary from the basic text presentation to the graphical interfaces that pri-vate providers and World Wide Web sites allow. Their content is roughly equivalent to the con-tent of the print versions. Some carry selections that include extra pieces, but the primary value is access to the content.

Newsletters

Newsletters are periodicals containing informa-tion on a specific topic, typically from an expert's point of view. They usually do not accept adver-tising and consequently are expensive. Their value often lies in the summary of news and description of trends from an experienced view-point. There are newsletters on almost every aspect of trade and business. Many of these, especially those related to covering high technol-ogy issues, are offering the text via email. A fear that many newsletter publishers have, however, is that the ease of forwarding the newsletter to non-subscribers will dramatically reduce the num-ber of paying subscribers.

Newswires

Newswires are summaries of news stories drawn from a wide variety of sources and sent in the form of email messages. They are offered by news services and can be free of charge or subscription-based. They are targeted at people who want to stay informed about events around them and generally focus on areas such as multimedia, high technology, or business.

Edupage and *Innovation* are two examples of newswires. They are prepared by the same two people. The first is free (it is sponsored by Educom, a consortium of colleges of universities). The second is a for-profit venture that costs a nomimal amount per year. Both focus on high tech and business information from numerous media sources. *Edupage* started about two years ago from a mailing list of 300 and has grown to about 35,000 unique addresses, many of which re-post to other addresses. All told, approximately 300,000 to 500,000 people see each message.

The CompuServe Executive News Service lets users enter keywords that correspond to their interests. Every day the news server searches databases from AP, Reuters, UPI, and several print newspapers, and delivers articles to subscribers' mailboxes containing the specified keywords. Subscribers pay per-article download charges for this service, in addition to monthly membership fees.

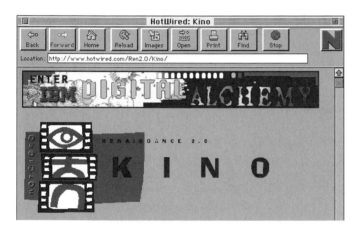

Digital Magazines

The **digital magazine** or "digizine" is an attempt at translating print magazines into digital form. It may be distributed in CD-ROM or online formats. Traditional reporting techniques may be updated to take on novel interactions—a click from the table of contents might take you to an interview, an expanded set of photographs, a relevant website, or a panel offering several points of view. Graphics tend to be lush in CD-ROM digital magazines. Art, animation, video, and sound are thrown in as features all their own or to accompany text. Content varies widely, featuring the same cross-section found in print media.

There are news magazines, avant-garde magazines, techie magazines, and many more in planning on every topic imaginable.

The World Wide Web is the major distribution point for most of the high production magazines, with text-only versions available by gopher or email in some cases. Graphics and sound are restricted by bandwidth and software limits, but can still be impressive. *O'Reilly Online* and *HotWired* are two major online magazines. They are available through the World Wide Web and are bound to the framed graphic windows characteristic of the Web. The high production values offered by CD-ROM magazines are not yet available over the Web.

'Zines

The word "'**zine**" is taken from "fanzine." 'Zines are net-based political, cultural, comic-book related, or open-ended diatribes. They represent a chance for people to express anything they want. The distinction of being part of a cultural mainstream or even a specific elite has no value to an activist. 'Zines have specific audiences and still more specific goals. They say what they want, in no uncertain terms. Many of them do not even try to convince readers of anything; either they're believers already, or they're not. The classic 'zine is usually based in plain ASCII text, hidden somewhere on the Internet.

'Zines are usually built by very small teams or even just one person working alone. They are usually labors of love and not intended to make money. This usually frees them from worrying about offending subscribers or advertisers or even putting out a cohesive package. Audiences can take it or leave it. 'Zines are a living symbol of freedom of speech on the net. It is not clear whether a highly regulated net would be threatened by them or have space for them, but their presence and their roots are strong enough that any movement to inhibit them would encounter serious resistance.

There are a few significant differences between digital magazines and 'zines. The primary distinction is that digital magazines are supported by advertisers and subscribers, while net-based 'zines are generally supported by donations or by nothing at all. 'Zines charge nothing and do not expect advertisers. Their aim is simply to communicate a very specific view, political or not, and serve as an oracle for their creators. Digital magazines are far less subversive. They will probably charge for subscriptions as soon as they reliably can and many already carry advertising.

Special Interest

Special interest titles are **nonfiction** works that focus on a particular field or some aspect of art, history, culture, language, or science. The nature of these titles lets them explore the sweeping range of information just under the surface of any subject. Beyond the surface reference information, almost any topic explodes into a million routes to explore. These titles capitalize on the variety and color that underlie all aspects of life. They are usually distributed on CD-ROM. They bring topics to life by weaving together images, sound, animation, video, information, and stories.

Part book, part photo essay, and part film documentary, these works explore the intersection of the three genres as well as the world around the reader. Other special interest titles weave stray threads of narrative into their fabric, presenting a less formulaic account of the topic at hand. Live Oak Software's *Four Paws of Crab*, for example, lets users choose from conversations between Americans and Thais, a trip to the market, and a sampling of Thai recipes, with accompanying video clips of how each dish is made.

Dorling Kindersley's *The Way Things Work* explores basic scientific principles, and the rules of mechanics and force. It explains numerous kinds of modern devices, using audio and animation to detail and clarify the principles and issues behind the machine. Filled with humorous explanations, *The Way Things Work* represents one of the vast array of design options at hand for the special interest producer.

The collection of genres is similar to that found in non-fiction shelves of bookstores or the documentaries seen on cable television. The list below is just a short sampling of some of the more popular genres. This collection is sure to expand in the future.

• **Art:** Art gallery collections and installations will be an expanding force in the CD-ROM marketplace. These can bring both the tangible and the esoteric to readers. Already, online galleries are sprouting up via the World Wide Web offering constant access to global audiences for every type and quality of artistic expression. Many companies are busy licensing rights to artwork. Some are interested in creating art encyclopedias while others have plans focusing on art criticism and instruction.

• **Health:** There are a number of health reference titles on the market and many have been extremely successful. Titles like *The Mayo Clinic Family Physician*, *The Mayo Clinic Family Health Book*, and *The Total Heart* from IVI Publishing explore common medical problems, and have suggestions on what to do. These titles commonly contain highly graphical drawings of the human body. One in particular, *ADAM* from ADAM Software, contains detailed drawings of almost every layer of the human body and major organ system.

• **History:** Historical journeys like the *Haldeman Diaries* from Sony Imagesoft, *Normandy: The Great Crusade* from The Discovery Channel, and *America's Civil War* from Software Marketing Corporation present exciting new ways to understand history and breathe new meaning into it. Survey products might cover vast ranges of dates,

A Faith for Living CD-ROM: courtesy of Enoptika Productions ©1994

realize the value of including tools to let people personally interact with the information and advice they offer.

• **Religious:** Numerous multimedia Bibles are making religious study more rewarding, letting students explore and compare texts and translations. Some religious documents seem ideal for interactive media. The Talmud, for example, is already a multilevel hypertext document in printed form.

• **Self-help/Spirituality:** Self-help and spirituality titles interactively address the spirit within every person. Just like their print-based cousins, this market has seen exciting growth over a large array of topics. Everything from personal fulfillment, crisis intervention, goal achievement, and spiritual enlightenment will provide for an important market and innovative products.

• **Sports:** Sports are clearly an area of interest for many publishers. Microsoft in particular has made its mark in this area with titles on baseball and basketball. These are largely statistical resources on the history of the games. Expect to see more titles in this area, along with online components to these types of products to keep them up-to-date to feed into Rotisserie League activities.

• **Travel/Maps:** There are numerous map collections on the market now that offer a variety of views of land, sea, and space. There are street-level collections, primarily designed for business use, and regional maps, often adapted from existing paper-based atlases. Although there are fewer travel titles on the market, expect to see more in the future as developers combine existing map resources, photo collections, and personal viewpoints to build interactive vignettes on cities, regions, and countries.

while other products shed light on specific periods of dramatic historic importance.

• **Language:** Language tutors on CD-ROM have already proven to be effective ways for people to learn languages quickly and well. Sound and video can be used to help test for listening skills, and other interactions can test grammar and understanding. Berlitz, as might be expected, already has a critically acclaimed series of language instruction CD-ROMs.

• **Nature:** Titles on animals and the environment have received lots of attention. Dinosaurs, whales, and sharks seem to be particularly popular. These titles typically feature stunning drawings, photos, animations or video of each animal or plant, and descriptive information and statistics. They usually feature video interviews with noted experts on the subject matter.

• **Personal Finance:** Intuit, creators of the renowned personal finance package, *Quicken*, have produced a *Quicken CD* that incorporates material such as financial advice and information on tax codes. More products of this nature are likely to be seen as software developers learn to extend their products with additional content. At the same time, book and magazine publishers will

Erotica

In the erotic market, some degree of interactivity is attractive to the consumer, but the bottom line is that too much can be a distraction. The consumer is buying the title for one reason, and that is that it's erotic. Interactivity is secondary.

—Larry Miller, Creator of the erotic game The Interactive Adventures of Seymour Butts

As in other media, erotic and pornographic titles represent a significant portion of the market. Most lists of top sellers do not include pornographic titles, but if they did, these titles would consistently appear in them. For example, a recent sales list compiled by Virgin Records of CD-ROM titles sold in its stores shows pornographic titles taking four of the top ten slots in the Windows market, two in the Macintosh market, three in the DOS market, and the number one slot for the 3DO platform (of only three titles listed).

Erotica and pornography should not be confused. **Pornography** is the graphic depiction of sexual acts (in any medium) while **erotica** is the description of sexual and sensual situations without necessarily the depiction of these situations. In general, erotica is intended for the mind while pornography is intended for the eyes. The distinction, however, can be vague and often lies with the beholder.

While there is almost no multimedia erotica yet, there are quite a few different kinds of pornography. The largest by far is **digitized video.** Most of the CD-ROM titles available now are simply porn videos, edited and digitized for presentation on

CD-ROM. In these, the video clips are presented in small windows on the screen, generally at poor levels of quality. (Full-screen video at television or movie standards is a bit beyond what current technology can deliver.) This low quality makes these titles a poor substitute for magazines or videotape or, of course, the real thing. This has not seemed to deter the market, however.

Sexually explicit **computer games** ▶ 22 have been around since the early days of PCs but are taking on new dimensions through the use of added

net.sex

graphics and sound. These games most commonly offer lewd depictions of women but products are beginning to appear that offer a more intelligent outlook with richer forms of interactivity. Advances in other product categories will undoubtedly spawn new genres in this area.

Hybrid products mix traditional computer software features with erotic photographs. For example, some desktop calendars feature pictures of naked or scantily clad models. This area is a fair reflection of the mix found in printed calendars.

Another significant part of this market can be found **online** ▶ 15, 61. The Internet allows access to a huge supply of sexually explicit images. There are several places containing compressed images of everything from supermodels to girlfriends. Also, many erotic magazines, journals, and discussion groups can be found in the USENET groups and on the World Wide Web.

Net culture is mirroring society as consumers and interest groups come together to discuss topics and interact with each other. The model for 976 and 900 phone numbers already exists online as "hot chat" rooms on most major private online services. These rooms let users participate in real-time erotic discussions. Users can also enter private cyber-rooms where they can shut out others and personalize an encounter. Newsgroups like

Twenties

This is a time when many people move away from their parents' homes and have their first major committed relationships. As their priorities change, many young adults find their sexuality becomes a more integrated part of their life and less of the all-consuming, hormone-driven need of adolescence. They also feel more comfortable expressing their sexuality the further they distance themselves from youthful peer pressure and the more they perceive themselves as individuals and adults.

Earliest Memories
Childhood
Puberty & Adolescence
First Sexual Experience
First Long-time Affair
Marriage
Twenties
Thirties
Forties
Fifties
Sixty to Eighty
Eighty & Beyond

History Experiences Fantasies Feelings Resources Index Diary

Disc One, Sexual Pleasures CD-ROM, upcoming title produced by Media Schmedia.

alt.sex and soc.singles offer places to go to discuss all these issues and more. At least one group is already providing nude video-conferencing via the Internet for those with credit cards and the right equipment (a video camera, a fast workstation, a fast phone connection, and the necessary software).

As there is no shortage of pornographic images and video available for repackaging, source material has not been a problem. The major issue has been distribution. While there is obviously a large market, developers have found most distributors reluctant to carry these products. The few who do face the same regulatory issues that traditional purveyors of pornography face. Many communities and countries define what is acceptable along very different lines. These regional definitions create particular problems for products that are available online. Even though the computer hosting the online activities may be in a tolerant area, someone connecting to the host may not be.

In addition, developers and publishers of sexually explicit interactive products are facing hurdles within the industry itself. Most industry conferences do not permit adult titles to be exhibited on show floors, or allow publishers to appear at all in some cases. Some provide special guarded and roped-off sections for these titles, but most would prefer not to acknowledge the market at all. Most magazines do not publish reviews or information about this market but, as noted above, most sales figures do include its revenues. More than a few people find this attitude a little hypocritical. They point out that these groups do not make similar distinctions about the use of violence in multimedia products.

Pornography rises and falls with each new technology. Sales and quantities of erotica tend to do extremely well in the beginning of a technology.

Initially, they can dominate the market, but as the market grows and more "mainstream" titles become available, their market percentage naturally drops. This pattern applied to the VCR when it first came out—the explosive sales of VCRs were fueled in large part by the new ability to rent or buy pornographic videos to watch at home.

As the CD-ROM market matures, the production quality of the average pornographic title is likely to rise, while the quantity of adapted video titles will probably decline, to be replaced with video on demand or other online features and forums. Also, developers will begin making better use of interactivity and create new genres that are more interesting and promote innovative uses of multimedia technologies.

Pornography Revisited

What happened after the invention of the printing press was something very similar to what's happening today in new media—a bunch of entrepreneurs with crazy ideas, shoestring budgets, and not a lot of adult supervision tried to figure out what they could do with the printing press. It turns out that there is a constant pattern in the history of media. What did we do after we printed the Bible? Cheap sensationalism, pornography, and unselective collections of "useful" information. The 1470s were filled with this stuff including medieval smut, like The Canterbury Tales *which, if you speak Middle English, is pretty hair-raising stuff.*

All successful media go through a pornography phase on their way to success. It happened with films, it happened with audio, and everybody knows the story about videotape. The good news is, we passed through it pretty quickly. People seem to be curious about pornography, but there's a high novelty factor. They tire of it really fast. The industry leaves it behind, and becomes genteel and respectable.

—Paul Saffo, Director, Institute for the Future

Music

We know that people like to sit at home and listen to music. We know that they like to have music on in their cars. We've found that, up to a point, they like to watch an evening's music videos of some of their favorite stuff, see pictures of some of the musicians in different settings playing their music, and some of the abstract ideas associated with the music. We've proven that there's a market for all of that. [But] there's a different level of enjoyment that comes from the ability to get behind the scenes.

Up to a point, music is a passive rather than an interactive form of entertainment. As interactivity becomes possible, what will the public really want? Will they want to go behind the scenes and get to know the star from all different angles, or will they want to become the star themselves?

—Thomas Dolby, Composer, Musician, and Sound Producer

Many in the music industry are beginning to look at **interactive music titles** as a new frontier. Several noted pop musicians have begun working with developers to create interactive CD-ROMs featuring music, music videos, and discographies. Peter Gabriel was one of the first to explore the interactive music market with his 1994 title, *Xplora1*. This title included not only music and discography but interview clips, tours of Gabriel's studio, and videos and lyrics for many of his hits. Since then, David Bowie, Prince, Thomas Dolby, Yes, and many other artists have produced interactive titles.

These types of titles differ from other CD-ROMs on music in that they focus on creating an entertainment experience with the music and performers at the core of the title. They are similar to music videos, using the nature of the media to create an interesting musical experience. Titles such as Micosoft's *Musical Instruments,* on the other hand, are more special interest titles about music.

A few titles have built storylines that tie all the individual songs on a CD-ROM together into an overall vision. Gabriel himself has noted several times that he wanted it to be more of a pure exploration than technology and time permitted. The Residents have integrated graphics and storylines deeply into the music in their *Freak Show* and *Gingerbread Man* titles. Future titles are likely to be built around original material that fits with the concept of the title as a whole, taking advantage of the strengths and weaknesses of an interactive CD-ROM format.

Currently, most CD-ROMs cannot be played in audio CD players, thus limiting the appeal of many interactive music titles. A new **mixed mode** CD format has been announced, however, that integrates CD-ROM information with CD audio tracks to support both computers and audio CD players. This dual functionality promises to offer expanded liner notes, creative outtakes, rich graphics, as well as pure CD-quality music in a multipurpose format.

courtesy of Graphix Zone

All digitized music comes in two flavors—sampled music and MIDI (musical instrument digital interface). The quality of **sampled music** is determined by the sampling rate and the sample size. Stereo CD sound quality has a sampling rate of 44kHz and a sample size of 16 bits. Lesser qualities have lower sampling rates and/or smaller sample size. **MIDI** is a standard format for communicating sound information between electronic instruments and computers. It is a language that describes how to recreate sounds from a variety of instruments. It is a much more compact and efficient way to store music. One limitation however is that voice and sound effects cannot be translated into MIDI. A sampled file will play back the sound of music exactly as it was recorded, whereas a MIDI file will recreate music as notes and timing information.

Nearly all mass-market multimedia hardware systems include high quality sound cards, and small but capable desktop speakers are commonplace. While playing back full-screen animation and video are likely to continue to pose problems in the short term, playing back high quality sound is easier to do, less demanding of bandwidth, and more powerful in effect. In time, computers are likely to come standard with CD quality sound and more sophisticated speaker technology.

Budgets and team sizes vary tremendously, depending on the artist's popularity, the scope of the project, the vision, and the market. The market itself is uncertain at the moment, unsure of what the technology might actually deliver and what would be worth buying. The mixed mode CD format is likely to open up the development market, which will mean tremendous opportunities for artists who want to build something wonderful within its constraints.

IUMA, the Internet Underground Music Archive (http://www.iuma.com)

Performance

Interactive performances can be found where theater, music concerts, performance art, and multimedia presentations come together. Some performances are enhanced musical shows, others are 3D theater shows, and still others are explorations of bodies in motion.

Most shows feature combinations of live talent, sets, lighting, music, computer animation, and real-time video. Artists begin with a message they want to communicate, and set about choosing the appropriate technologies and forms to get this message across. One approach to using technology is to let it coordinate carefully timed arrangements in the presentation of the various media. Certainly, this limits the space for interactivity but it provides precise control of orchestrated effects.

The second model is the participatory model, where the artists start with something and let the audience modify or alter it completely during the course of the show through their participation. Perhaps the best model for this form comes from improv theater. Few other performance forms require such split-second creativity, lightning response, chutzpah, and training in order to handle input from the audience. Interactive performers can learn from this area, potentially taking it to further extremes through the use of technology.

George Coates, the visionary behind the George Coates PerformanceWorks in San Francisco, has been developing innovative multimedia performances for more than six years. His troupe presents wry, insightful commentary on the effects of technology on our lives using the same technology they refer to in the pieces. He mixes live actors with prerecorded video and audio, live mixing, and layers of projection systems. His

latest work, *The Nowhere Band*, includes live input from the World Wide Web and other Internet sources as well as audience members on the net.

Audiences are seeing the beginnings of interactive performances, as artists try to conceptualize how to include the audience in the show itself. There are no defined ways to do this just yet—theatrical structures need to be revamped in order to handle audience input, just like narrative structures do. There is a great deal of space in the field for more artists to test out their own reconceptualizations of theater.

The vast majority of development is done on Macintoshes, as a flexible, low cost alternative to high-end workstations. Artists rarely have any kind of realistic budget to work with, and often an artist's vision requires that an object be completed before it can be sold. This means that income is by definition scattered and sparse. While this fits with the stereotype of the starving artist, there are success stories that can inspire new legions of artists to express themselves. Digital artist Mark Petrakis insists that there's plenty of room for new artists to come together and try to define the new structures that will embrace interaction between performers and audiences. The first step is always a thought and a pencil.

We do a certain amount of interactivity using the MIDIBall [a large inflatable ball that uses radio controlers to trigger sound and graphics when the audience hits it]. We're planning on doing much more in-depth interactive shows using technology as a means to bridge the gap between performers and the audience. Basically, the whole nature of it is finding ways where people can be together and do things together. That's what we mean by interactive. Our model is looking at other cultures that we've been involved with, in things like drum circles and dancing.

—Candice Pacheco, Co-founder, D'Cückoo

Real-Time Performances

In the live presentation environment, you have everything from sporting events to teacher-student classroom situations, seminars, the conference experience in hotels, etc.—any time there's a point-to-many relationship in a real-time live moment. In the subset of theater, you find interactivity in what is called improvisational theater. The audience will be asked to throw out the name of choosing, and the actors are supposed to spontaneously interact as if they had no idea that they were going to hear the audience's suggestions...The audiences, right now, are limited in their opportunities to enter into the dramatic narrative, or in the discourse. Audiences have been kept at bay for lack of an interface. I would like to develop a means for audience participation in providing content, not just choice, not just choosing outcomes or subjects—but to interact with characters in a drama by helping to advance the narrative. For example, to help a character out of a jam, or participate as a group to change the conditions of the stage environment so that the actors' experience is altered fundamentally.

—George Coates, Writer/Director, George Coates PerformanceWorks

Education

The next five years will be critical for schools and for technology providers. Schools are facing key issues in terms of reform, management shifts, and continued concerns about overall funding. They are ready for new technologies, but are cautious about investing heavily in unproven teaching tools.

Similarly, publishers and content providers are cautious about jumping into markets or formats that are unfamiliar to them. Without firm sales histories, publishers are leery of hefty development costs for a market that admits its reluctance to purchase. Those publishers that ally with savvy school marketers and producers of successful curricular materials will be the most likely to fare well in establishing themselves in the K-12 market for electronic media.

—Claire Schoen, Editorial Director, SIMBA Information Service, from The Red Herring, December 1994

Interactive educational products are designed and built specifically for sale to the public and private school market, from kindergarten through college and beyond. There are several subcategories in the education market. These include preschool, kindergarten to third grade, fourth through eighth grade, ninth through twelfth grade, college and university, professional training, and adult continuing education. Each category represents a different market in itself, with distinct demographics, interests, and approaches.

Educational products are mostly distributed through **public** or **private school system** channels, though there is a market for parents teaching their children in "home schools." Because of these highly structured distribution channels, the content is usually governed by school boards at local, county, and sometimes state levels. What goes into products can become a serious political issue. The official goal is to educate, but exactly what to teach and how to teach it to them represents a philosophical question. What is taught in school tends to reflect the prevailing winds of culture. Educational software has tended to follow the large textbook model—it is produced on a huge scale, sent through countless boards and bureaus for approval, and purchased by the thousands during the process. If it is approved, thousands more will be purchased. These quantities are attractive to publishers, but this is not a market for the uninitiated.

Interactive educational products can be found in three major forms at the moment: electronic textbooks, speaker support materials for instructors, and educational online networks. These formats parallel special interest titles, interactive presentations, and virtual communities, respectively.

Titles for young children teach basic skills like reading and arithmetic and are organized in discrete lessons at traditional grade levels, using common testing models. What goes into a title depends heavily on what grade level it is built to address. Titles for high school students might apply to any topic the curriculum covers, from history and social studies to physics, using any level of interactivity.

There are two models of educational title development. First, independent producers create titles that address specific topics and grade levels, and pitch them to large textbook publishers. Second, many of the publishers have in-house multimedia development departments. Smaller packages focused on elective courses can cost under $100,000 to build, but typical products range from $300,000 to $700,000 in development costs, and full mixed media curriculum packages can cost millions, even for print media.

Many textbook publishers are reluctant to invest in CD-ROM titles when they are not convinced that schools have the computer setups to adequately support individualized multimedia instruction. Some of these companies are creating **multimedia presentation packages** for instructors instead of individual student packages. They hope to establish a presence in the market for

Instructional Electronic Media Forecasts, 1993–98

Media	1993	1995	1998	1993–98
CD-ROM	$46	$115	$325	606.5%
Standalone Software	295	450	600	103.4%
Videodiscs	60	90	120	100.0%
Distance Learning	70	90	120	71.4%
Videocassettes	125	146	174	39.2%
Online Services	3	3	4	38.7%
Satellite/Cable/Interactive TV	112	131	153	36.6%
Integrated Learning Systems	310	346	420	35.4%
Total	$1,021	$1,371	$1,916	87.6%

$ in millions

Electronic Media for the School Market, 1994–5. SIMBA Information, Inc. (Wilton, CT)

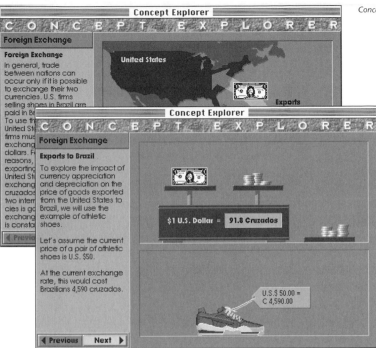

Concept Explorer, courtesy of Jennings & Keefe

interactive products and be in a position to expand when electronic textbooks become more viable.

Education networks are appearing at universities and within several states. The electrical engineering department at the University of Illinois at Urbana-Champaign, for example, has built an interactive system to connect students, teaching assistants, and faculty in a campus-wide virtual classroom. Students use computers wired through their residence halls to turn in homework, take exams and go over problems with professors or teaching assistants. More experiments in learning and communication can be expected, though who will fund and operate these remains a question in many people's minds.

The market is immense—every child is required by law to be educated, using some sort of classroom materials. Multimedia tools offer ways to make the learning process easier for both teacher and student. Educators are increasingly turning away from the older educational paradigm, where "fun" was out of place in the classroom, to accept and even build joy into the curriculum. New technologies promise to let students follow their own interests and do their own research. Educational products are likely to include not only content but also independent activities, challenging them to make the material their own.

A big part of the problem is, of course, **delivery platforms** ▶ 12. Few school districts have the resources to install banks of CD-ROM equipped computers, let alone consider putting one on every desk. Still, multimedia technologies have impressed parents across the country with the possibilities of engaging and teaching children skills and knowledge. Many of the consumer titles are sold for use in schools as well as in the home. Developers like Jennings & Keefe and Mindplay are building everything from kindergarten reading titles to full multimedia courses for high school students. Teachers' editions, lab packs, and network packs are all available at separate pricing structures. The range of titles is enormous, and includes unexpected bonuses like bilingual titles.

The SIMBA Information Service predicts that the CD-ROM boom in educational media has just begun. The markets for electronic media in schools will grow by leaps and bounds as the prices on hardware drop, and more importantly, as teacher resistance to new methods falls. Many teachers in fact see educational reform as a high priority, and technology as a means toward achieving it. There are tremendous opportunities for developers to build compelling educational applications—the market is preparing itself for significant high-tech restructuring. At the same time, developers can build titles for both educational and consumer markets. In this way, development costs can be leveraged against income from consumer title sales, though the pricing systems for these two markets have little in common. From any perspective, this market is set to explode, and it is likely to make numerous new developers successful.

However, the real success in this market will depend on developers who address the entire realm of education. Teachers cannot be expected to use CD-ROM titles effectively without teachers' guides that explain how to integrate the material and the experience into the class curriculum. The processes of learning and capturing children's interest will always take precedence over the elegance of any new form of technology.

One of the gratifying things about using [Voices of the 30s] is that students can become immediate authorities on a subject. They become immersed in a particular area of Voices of the 30s *and they develop a vocabulary of concepts very quickly, in ways that they don't do if they're only relying on the text or if they're only relying on listening to a teacher.*

Even in a full class discussion, if you can immediately see those images and tie it in with text and get a sense of what the time was about, almost intuitively you then develop a vocabulary of concepts that deal with what the issues are.

I always think that kids can learn more and faster than we can teach them and I hope that computers will allow us to do that. It's almost impossible for a teacher to do the depths of research needed. If I'm teaching five classes a day, I can't do that level of research to really bring kids to the subject in a way that they can absorb it. I hope that computers will grant them that opportunity.

*—Patricia Hanlon,
Co-author,
Voices of the 30s*

Business

The key is you can't sell tools to people that are building mass-market products because there aren't enough of them. You have to be able to get into the marketing communications enterprise information. You have to get into the part of the triangle that's not trying to just create CDs to be sold over the counter.

Look at where Macromedia's biggest marketplace is and where all the creative professionals' marketplaces are. It's not necessarily in doing those things that you buy in the bookstores but it's in doing the everyday commerce—the brochures, the annual reports.

—Miles Gilburne, Attorney

The business market is interested primarily in straightforward tools and useful and relevant content. The average businessperson is not terribly interested in a lot of multimedia bells and whistles unless they directly support the goal at hand. They are less interested in products with entertainment or educational value than in open-ended toolsets or tightly focused training applications.

As a result, time to market, ease of use, and compatibility with other business tools are the key issues for people developing successful interactive business products.

Business Tools

Productivity tools are the many software applications that have been developed since *VisiCalc* and *Lotus 1-2-3*. Their defining point is that they provide a specific tool to business professionals in the workplace. They are generally character-based, allowing users to organize and manipulate text and numbers in various ways.

Productivity tools can be general or task-specific. Word processors, spreadsheets, and databases are general tools. Documents created with these tools typically start out blank to be customized and then populated with information. Most business people primarily use these three general tools, coupled with a few more specialized tools, to run their businesses.

In the future, these are likely to support more media forms. Most word processing programs now support graphics, and most spreadsheets allow data to be viewed in many common charting views. These forms, plus time-based media such as sound, animation, and video, are likely to find their way into these tools more and more. Data represented in these formats will likely be directly accessible and modifiable as opposed to just viewable. For example, a spreadsheet might allow manipulation in a graphical view as well as in the typical row and column view supported now.

Another area likely to see growth is the **task-specific applications**. More and more business users are looking for tools that allow them to quickly and easily complete a tightly focused task. A business plan builder, for example, has a specific purpose, namely, to help an entrepeneur create a business plan. Its value lies in how well and how fast it can help the entrepeneur create a cohesive plan.

These products will likely be hybrids of both tools and content. The tools will allow business people to accomplish important tasks with their own information—as opposed to hypothetical tutorials—and the content will provide rich case studies, notes, and advice about how to follow the task processes and why different steps are important.

Groupware is software used over a network that allows people to share resources and notes, work together on projects in real time, communicate over distances, and trace versions of past work. These tools can be designed around any task or function. The most innovative of these is *Lotus Notes*, a kind of multi-user database and discussion system that allows users to build "knowledge" databases that can be searched within context for user information about corporate activities and processes. Project management, schedule management, and virtual meeting soft-

New Forms of Business

Companies have always had structures that resembled their communications infrastructures. The companies' organizations resembled the conduits they used, and the information sources they accessed. Our shift from the monarchy model of the 1850s to infant corporations at the turn of the century was triggered by the arrival of the telegraph and reliable postal service. Each subsequent complexification of corporate hierarchy was triggered in turn by things like the arrival of long distance phone networks, the telephone, and, as Peter Drucker was first to observe, the arrival of mainframe computing. Corporate structures reached their high point in the mid-1960s when the General Motors hierarchy of the time became as complex and as complicated as a Swiss watch, not unlike the guts of their mainframe computers. Now organizations are beginning to look like webs. No surprise at all since we're using web-like networks to communicate. We're going to see those kinds of changes just continually tumbling through the Zeitgeist.

—Paul Saffo, Director, Institute for the Future

ware are more examples of groupware applications. These too will evolve as relevant new media capabilities are added.

The budgets for developing business tools are almost always extremely large, on the order of millions. This is primarily due to their complexity. It takes enormous development and testing resources to create tool-based applications.

Tools are open-ended both in design and in implementation—there must be space to let users push the limits of the package with their own designs and there must be enough strength in the framework to withstand that strain. Developers must decide from the outset whether their priority lies with adaptability or with tight structure and ease of use. Testing can consume up to 40% of the development budget and, in the end, there is often little hope of eliminating all the bugs. Technical support and marketing also require huge expenditures.

Information Storage and Retrieval Systems

The online revolution has been compared by many to the revolution set off by the printing press after the 1450s. People are confronted with more and more information, not because it was not available before, but because it was so inaccessible. It was difficult to find and use, much less assimilate into corporate processes. For example, SEC filings were once buried within file cabinets, and accessing them cost a lot of money because someone had to physically open the files. Now, these filings are available over the **Internet** and are suddenly in demand.

Businesspeople increasingly need information organized logically in order to make the best use of it. They need information, both about their own corporation and about the rest of the world. This can be delivered on CD-ROM, at regular intervals, or online, constantly updated and available. Several companies such as Dow Jones & Company and Knight-Ridder Information Services generate enormous revenue by providing businesses with up-to-date information electronically. Many online services have content areas for business purposes provided by research companies and business magazines. Many of these companies are creating custom tools and pricing mechanisms to further expand their services and markets.

Christine   David   James   Frank

Some of the trends that make it easier to get started:

- Increasingly sophisticated technology available at ever lower costs
- Major corporations are subcontracting
- Market data is more accessible
- The acceptance of low-overhead operations is rising

Go Forward   Go Back   Next Topic   Auto Play   More/Help   Info Map

At the same time, organizations that can streamline their information sources and concentrate them by topic are finding new savings in overhead and operations. Well-designed search and organization applications—true information tools—that can take both internal and external information and help organize and present it in more knowledgeable ways will be some of the most important business tools in the next decade.

Content Titles

Content titles are basically CD-ROM adaptations of books about business issues. While there are few to look to as examples, many feel that this will be a growing industry. They point to the large number of successful business books and audio and video products and see them moving to interactive formats over the next decade. Also, they see the increasing number of home-based computers and the need for interesting and valuable titles for adults.

These products can be interviews with noted experts, animations to convey complex concepts, quizzes to test retention, and tools to help personalize the knowledge and advice. These titles are likely be targeted to individual consumers looking to improve their business knowledge and skills.

The dirty little secret in the information revolution is that consumers never want information for its own sake. Ever. When you see people who want information, it turns out that it's to satisfy some higher desire. The stock page on the Wall Street Journal *is appealing to people only because it supports their transactions. Telephone books are amusing only because they support communications or entertainment or transactions.*

—Paul Saffo,
Director,
Institute for the Future

Training

*Many current corporate video training programs are likely to be converted to desktop multimedia training programs. This transition will provide opportunities for **video producers** ▶ 238 and editors with knowledge of digital tools. Additional opportunities will be available for instructional designers who can add features such as quizzes, scenarios, and customizable content.*

Multimedia training promises to be one of the largest areas of growth in the corporate world. Part of the reason is that the growth of multimedia computers and broadband networks in business will allow greater access to training programs regardless of their location.

Another reason is that interactive training programs increase learning efficiency. People learn differently. Some are visual learners, while others learn more from reading or listening. Some need explicit, step-by-step directions, while others need only the outline and a clear purpose. Training programs are most successful when they let people learn in ways that are natural to them. Interactive multimedia has the promise of supporting all kinds of individual learning methods.

Also, current training programs usually interrupt work schedules. They are often treated as special events occurring in special rooms at specified times. This makes it difficult for workers to integrate new knowledge into their present work environment. To make matters worse, training products often use generalized processes and hypothetical data and situations rather than material relevant to specific problems people encounter within the daily context of their jobs. This generalization may be easier to program, but it makes training even more difficult and arcane for workers.

Newer products are being developed that allow new users to access procedural knowledge while they work instead of during training sessions. Even specific training programs are beginning to offer more realistic services that workers can complete at their own pace and in more realistic settings.

Product Training

Many software toolmakers are beginning to incorporate training components into existing **business applications**. Ideally, every application should not only make its purpose apparent to the user but also describe the relationships and connections between the content and features within it. In this way, training becomes embedded in the use of a product. There are several different kinds of information about a product that can be taught. The first is the use of the software or hardware product itself. This instruction might take the form of an overview of the options or a task-based review of the process in which it works. In either case, the goal is to teach how to use the product to complete specific tasks. The next level is helpful information about how to use the product effectively and efficiently in a real-world situation.

A third level of information is the larger context in which the process is used, including why the process and knowledge is important and relevant. It may seem obvious, but even seasoned professionals occasionally need to be reminded of the relationships between various processes and data. At this level, case studies and rich simulations can be very effective, because their concentration is usually not on the mechanics of the process, but the cause and effect relationships that govern why things work or do not.

CRUSH™, from Hands On Technology, is an example of a next-generation business product with embedded training. The product lays out a process for creating a marketing strategy. Procedural knowledge, case studies, and anecdotes are available at every step in the process. This adds a dimension of reality for those who want context-oriented help instead of merely help in using the generalized features of the product. A guide is available at all times to offer this procedural information, which in this case is in the form of video interviews with Regis McKenna, an acknowledged industry expert in the field of marketing.

In addition and most importantly, the entire product is carefully structured to build a cognitive model in users' minds that describes the relationships between various data in their own projects. Users enter real data from their own relevant work, and CRUSH helps them to organize and discover the meaning within that data and their relationships. This model persists even when users are not working with the product; this is why it is such a powerful training application as well as a productive work tool.

Computer-Based Training

Many issues and processes lend themselves only to localized solutions—solutions that take into account a company's particular environment and set of issues. Training managers on a company's personnel practices, for example, usually requires custom solutions that reflect the company's management beliefs and structure. Most people refer to these types of programs as **computer-based training (CBT)**. They are likely to resemble corporate video training products in the beginning but progress to more integrated systems within a company's information system.

Development Issues

Teams for developing training applications tend to be large because there is so much to analyze, describe, and plan for. This makes some training products fairly expensive. To add to this cost, many training programs need to be integrated into a company's existing computer facilities. This requirement can mean putting on added pressure to create training programs that take advantage of the latest in interactive media technologies and yet still support existing computer setups.

Also, because processes and localized issues are difficult to discern and describe, they usually rely on experts to help define and illuminate them. These experts may be experienced instructional designers or people that are knowledgeable in a specific area of business management. They can be extremely helpful in analyzing the work flow and decoding a process or method of training that makes sense. Ideally, these experts should work with a team to verify the observations, assumptions, and decisions about the work environment as a whole.

Marketing and Sales

*Numerous businesses are working to set up an Internet **presence**. This means that they build strategies that phase them in through relevant USENET newsgroups, to ftp and gopher sites, to World Wide Web sites, to finally market their products on the net.*

Experts recommend caution when moving online. Businesses are increasingly welcome online but people need to be aware of how products and services are appropriately marketed on the net. A well-managed entry onto the Net can be very good publicity. A poorly managed entry can create a negative backlash, however.

Interactive marketing and sales applications represent a huge, undefined area. Businesses are going online in record numbers. As a result, the opportunities for net-savvy marketing people are immense. There is also a significant market for various kinds of fixed format advertising such as demo disks, interactive annual reports, kiosks, and press kits. These forms of marketing are likely to grow as more people have better access to multimedia-capable technologies.

Online Marketing

The major **online media** ▶ 15, 61 include the Internet (the World Wide Web in particular) and private online service providers. These two have their advantages and disadvantages from a marketer or vendor's point of view, but they also hold a tremendous amount of promise. The Internet does not charge for space as a commercial online service might, but at the same time, the Internet does not offer the service and support a commercial service might.

The World Wide Web is a global collection of websites containing "pages" of text and graphics. There has been a booming business for third party information designers, specializing in the creation of corporate webpages for clients, while individuals tend to create their own pages. Corporate webpages include marketing information, company and product line profiles, and contact information, while individual pages are generally artistic outtakes, resumes, and professional portfolios. Many are betting that the World Wide Web will become the graphical information system of choice, partly because it works so well,

and partly because it has experienced such astronomical growth. The Web is accessible 24 hours a day, 7 days a week, anywhere in the world.

Electronic catalogs are other obvious online marketing tools. These catalogs originally started as CD-ROM-based but quickly migrated to online areas. There are many on the World Wide Web as well as in many large commercial online services. Developers found people were not as interested in high production values and huge amounts of data on products as they were in more salient information provided by online access. They wanted current pricing and inventory and they wanted to order easily.

Catalogs do everything you would expect a print catalog to do in terms of promoting products. Added advantages can include tools to help determine whether the products are suited to a certain face shape, hair color, body type, or lifestyle. One shortcoming is that nothing can be purchased online yet with absolute security, although this capability is likely to be only months away. Shoppers must call 800 numbers to confirm their selection and complete the transaction.

The Whole Earth Catalog, found at the GNN Home Page on the World Wide Web (URL: http://www.gnn.com) contains a large selection of software and high tech gadgets. You can access descriptions and pricing information, but you cannot purchase anything online yet.

Electronic malls are cyberspaces devoted to facilitate retail transactions. They are similar to what you might expect in a shopping mall although usually devoid of sales clerks. Shoppers typically "enter" stores through rendered doorways to see lists, images, or even walkthrough maps showcasing the products. Emalls are largely still under construction but plans are in motion to get them online and available as soon as possible. Many Internet tool developers and commercial online services are creating tools to let retailers create custom spaces and gain direct access right from the desktop.

Online help and support systems are combinations of marketing tools and customer service.

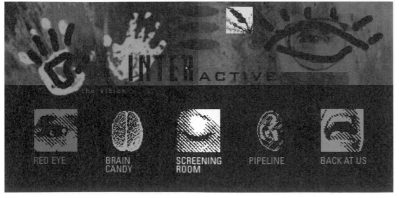

courtesy of Sony Electronic Publishing

Some of the most common forms are technical support forums, pre-established lists of frequently asked questions (FAQs) or real-time discussions between consumers and **technical support personnel** ▶ 274. Online help systems are commonly included in installed software packages. As static information tools, they cannot respond dynamically to specific user problems, but they are easily accessible from within most applications and fairly comprehensive. The overriding goal of all these forms is to inform the consumer about usability issues and resolve problems as they happen. This can be done by email, fax, or telephone—the method is unimportant as long as the consumers feel that their problems have been addressed.

Fixed-Format Marketing

Interactive demos are abridged versions of an application or title designed to give viewers a tour of software or a multimedia product. They can be found as stand-alone diskettes or CD-ROMs or can be included in interactive catalogs or as a sort of trailer within a shipping CD-ROM title. Demos can contain guided tours, a slightly disabled application, or specialized presentations designed to entertain and excite. Ads are similar in intent, namely to interest buyers, but usually smaller in size. They can include anything from startup screens to sound clips and company icons.

Interactive annual reports are designed to present financial information and the state of a company to stockholders in the best possible light. Although most stockholders are accustomed to glossy paper shareholder reports, an increasing number of technology companies are creating interactive annual reports to take advantage of time-based media such as sound and video. Multimedia annual reports can create a colorful and impressive presentation of a company's fiscal well-being.

Interactive press kits (IPKs) are digital assemblies of business plans, product announcements, funding projections, and other information that present a company's desired image to members of the press. They usually accompany major press releases or herald new entrants into the larger arena of any field. Press kits are short, detailed, targeted packages meant to present and enforce a specific image of a company or product to potential clients and journalists. They can be created on diskettes or CD-ROMs.

Kiosks are interactive installations in public places that offer information. Many companies use kiosks at trade shows, in retail stores, and on company premises to provide product and company information. These kiosks are often organized as multimedia databases and typically feature touch screens as opposed to a mice and keyboards.

These formats can be created by an internal marketing department but many companies at the moment are working with multimedia production studios. The technology and the complexity of the process often requires the contributions of many skilled professionals.

Mass Media vs. New Media

The mass media business was dominated by a small number of business models. In contrast, the emerging new media world will see a species radiation in new models. We are entering an environment where there will be no single "right way" to do business, and the art of media entrepreneurs will lie as much in creating novel business structures, as in creating novel content. And the crux of this art will lie in finding the right match among structure, content, and an ever more fractured audience. The challenge in advertising will be to find the right level of specificity and the right approach that hits this group and not that group, and not trying to do a one-size-fits-all ad.

That said, mass audiences will not disappear entirely. Even as mass media is breaking up, there are moments where the audiences are bigger than ever, but the moments are ever briefer and more volatile. We are trading mass audiences for "mass moments" where ever larger audiences coalesce around a specific event. Examples are already occurring—one billion people watch the Academy Awards and the World Cup soccer finals regularly shut down small countries while citizens drop everything to watch the TV.

—Paul Saffo, Director, Institute for the Future

Presentations

Presentations are live events with computer-based graphical and auditory support and are a specialized form of marketing. They are one of many project types that have always been based in multimedia, using the literal definition of simply relying on more than one form of communication. Technically, a slide show with a person speaking amounts to a multimedia presentation, because visuals and sound each represent one medium. The consolidation of multimedia onto the digital format simply gives the presenter a lot more flexibility and power.

The goal of any presentation is to convey information from the presenter to the audience. This can be information on a new product, a new sales strategy, or the current state of a business. Tests of audiences have proven that multimedia assisted talks raise retention rates two to three times higher than lectures where a person simply intones at a lectern.

There are a number of **presentation software packages** on the market. Packages like *Adobe Persuasion* and *Microsoft PowerPoint* organize information for users, from printed slides to charts, graphs, photos, and video clips, typically in linear fashion. The basic goals of these packages are to streamline the creative process and integrate media quickly and easily. They are tightly structured tools, intended to be easy to learn and use.

Presentations can be run straight out a portable computer to an input-ready projector. There is often no need to print materials or use traditional slides. Transitions between slides can be graphically beautiful, fading into one another slowly or using splashes of color for emphasis. Sound and video can support more conventional arrays of bullet lists, organizational charts, and graphs. Remote point-and-click devices permit presenters to walk around onstage and in the audience, which can often add another level of drama to the show.

There's a real need for people who understand the integration of video signals and audio signals coming out of the back of the computer. There's also a need for onsite graphic artists to go to conferences and set up slides for speakers right there. There are never enough freelancers that you can trust—there's just not a huge database of those kinds of people. It's kind of a live-out-of-the-suitcase lifestyle, but knowing what I know now, if I were a student, I would focus less on how many Kai's Power Tools filters I can put into backgrounds and more on how to import scans and graphics from other packages into the rudimentary programs like Persuasion *and* PowerPoint *to make clean corporate slides.*

—Scott Willoughby, President and CEO, Illuminated Media

Created and produced by Mindsphere, Sausalito, CA

Creating large complex multimedia presentations, however, is still a bit of a problem. The business market contains a fair number of basic, solid presentation packages from well-known developers. These packages have simple interfaces and fairly limited capabilities. Sound and video capabilities are often new and handled a bit inconsistently. To make things more difficult, the normal presenter usually cannot just sit down and immediately start recording CD-quality sound.

As a result, there is a growing group of **third-party presentation contractors** that have the integration skills to make it all work. They often create the presentation, set it up, test it, and run it during the show. They will travel to distant locations and stage large presentations for corporate executives, company sales forces, conference attendees, and others. Their knowledge of the technology, the tools, and the process allows them to elude many of problems that inexperienced people typically encounter.

Shortchanging Sound

One hears people talking about multimedia and new media in the same sense, if not the same word. Really, what they're referring to is the use of video on the computer or playing back video. We've shortchanged sound. After having made a career out of doing multimedia presentations around the world, you ask for AV help and you spend your life getting V help, but no A. You ask for a plug out of the Mac into the projection system and you never get it, so you mike it with a separate mike off the Mac. That gives me a sense of what's going on in the industry. We're not really thinking about this.

—S. Joy Mountford, Project Lead, Interval Research

3. Industries

Many people when talking about multimedia refer to it as "the multimedia industry." While this is a convenient and catchy phrase, it is not entirely correct.

Multimedia is a set of technologies that can be used to bring various types of products to market or to enhance various existing types of products. Unfortunately, we like to label things and put them in neat little categories and say, "Oh, multimedia is an industry now." And so, people talk about multimedia products when, in fact, I believe very strongly there is no such thing as a multimedia product. Instead, there are products that use elements of what we think of as multimedia.

—Frank Boosman, General Manager, Virtus Corporation

Part of the problem in creating and selling interactive media products is not in the technology, design, pricing, or packaging, but in the lack of structure and understanding between companies at every step along the way. The problem does not stem so much from self-interest as it does from not knowing the economic picture of the other party along with not having clearly defined lines of responsibilities. Time and experience will likely bring the relationships of companies in interactive media to a plane that everyone understands better.

It is extremely hard to find a clear division between multimedia and any of the other industries mentioned in the same breath—namely, the entertainment, computer hardware, software, publishing, communications, and music industries. Also, the types of projects and the different markets create several new industries with little resemblance beyond the word "multimedia."

A better way to look at **multimedia ▶ 8** is not as an industry but as a set of **technologies and techniques** that are used by a variety of people and industries to do things that have not been done before. The technologies affect platforms and peripherals. The techniques affect process and include non-linear structures, features for creativity or productivity, and capabilities that let people communicate with each other.

Many of the areas in interactive multimedia share aspects from a number of established industries. Interesting infrastructure models include the film, advertising, publishing, and software industries.

The following pages contain short descriptions of these. Each offer different ways of dealing with people, products, and distribution. Also included are descriptions of a few up-and-coming industries. Some are more established than others such as games, while others, such as online systems and interactive TV are still emerging. While there are jobs in these nascent industries, there is less diversity in the types of companies and, correspondingly, in the types of opportunities.

The structures outlined on the following pages are not as clear in the real world. Even a basic structure, however, can help point the way to what types of jobs are available within each industry and what the influences are on these jobs. Knowing which companies produce CD-ROM titles and which ones do not can reduce the amount of time spent chasing lost causes. Likewise, knowing where the financing is coming from and going to can point the way towards where the hiring will be.

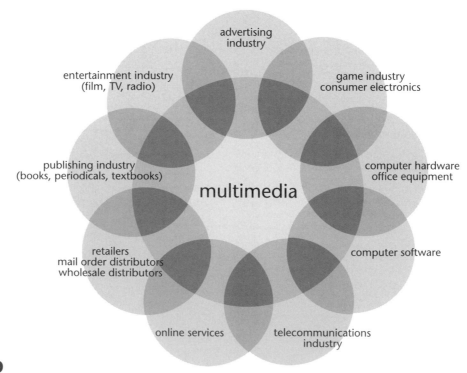

The Film Industry

The creative talent in the **film industry** probably has more control over compensation and production issues within their industry than any other. With that influence, however, comes competition as many people try to get into movies as either actors, directors, or scriptwriters. Part of this is due to the creative aspect, part the glamour, part the money, and part the power.

On paper, the development of a film starts with a script created by a **scriptwriter**. The script catches the interest of someone in the industry, many times the result of an **agent** shopping it around. Scripts can also happen to fall into someone's hands who takes an interest in it, though legal concerns often prevent many people from looking at unsolicited works. In some cases, a script might be commissioned by a producer, to be based on a novel or some real-world event, for example.

The party interested in the "property" might be a **producer**, a **director**, or an **actor**. Their interest then brings in others. This package is then shopped to **studios** for financing. If one studio is interested and agrees to fund it, then development work begins. The studios will provide small amounts of financing to reach certain milestones. If the film project is still of interest to the studio once the milestones are met, the film gets the "green light" and goes into production. Most films, however, never go beyond the development stage. These films are said to be in "turnaround." Films in production often take on a life of their own. A director could walk out at the middle of filming and the film would still likely get made.

In reality, the process is not this simple. Production is usually much more dynamical—even chaotic—as all the elements come together at or near the same time. Relationships are critical because the level of trust between people is so much higher than in other ventures. There is a risky phase when the elements are being put together, where people need tacit approval from one person in order to get another person interested. Because of this ambiguity, people will only deal with people they know. One bad film could be a major career setback for most of those involved. This is part of the reason why agents and business managers play such a prominent role.

The studios may or may not make the films themselves. There are a number of **independent production houses**, many of which are affiliated with producers, directors, and actors. These production houses will manage the production of the film.

Almost no film goes into production without first having a distribution deal. Anti-trust laws prevent movie studios from owning theaters (although it was not always this way) but there is still only a limited number of **distributors** that put movies into the theaters. Without the cooperation of one of these distributors, a film has little chance of being placed in the channel. The release of a film has gained significant importance within the last decade. For a "wide release"—where the film is publicized widely and appears in many theaters nationwide—the first three days of the opening either make or break the film. Films that do not attract a significant number of movie-goers in the first week or two of

It's like when you were a kid and you went to your mom and you asked her for the car. You told her dad said that it's okay with him if it's okay with you. And then you went to your dad to tell him that mom said it's okay with her if it's okay with you. Putting a deal together is all about that twelve second window of approval between the elements. Only in Hollywood, instead of twelve seconds, you've got three weeks, but the principle remains the same. That's how a deal is assembled.

—David J. Ores, Interactive Writer

Hollywood vs. Silicon Valley

In the movie business, everything is negotiable and people will ask for everything. There will be four or five drafts of the contract. Paragraph 25 will get beaten to death. The movie business is like the rug bazaar. People will throw something in there just to negotiate it.

People in the software business, though, don't like to negotiate as much. They come closer to the attitude of saying, "Take it or leave it." Now, it's never like that because there's always some room to negotiate, but there's a big difference of degree between Hollywood and the software industry. If I want a $200,000 deal in Hollywood, I might go in at $600,000 and settle for $250,000. That's just how things are done here.

In software—first, let's ratchet the numbers down a bit—say I want $25,000, I'd better not go in above $35,000 or else I won't get the phone call returned. You can't negotiate in the software industry like you would in the movies. At the same time, you can't negotiate in the movies like you would in software. You go in at $250,000 and they'd smell blood and get you down to $100,000 in no time.

—Richard Thompson, Attorney, Bloom, Dekom, Hergott & Cook

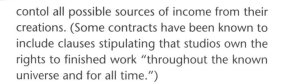

The film industry has been a pioneer in new funding models for media properties. Splitting foreign distribution rights is the latest in an evolving financing and distribution picture. This type of deal is where two or more studios split distribution rights to various territories in return for sharing the cost of development.

a film release often get pulled. Some studios have been using a "platform release" to great effect. A platform release is where a film opens in a few theaters and expands as the word of mouth builds. *My Left Foot* and *The Crying Game* are examples of this type of release.

The numbers of outlets and opportunities for additional revenue increase with each passing year. The VCR was first thought to be a competitor to the movie theater. Now, the sale of video cassettes is just another form of release for a movie. Foreign sales, cable movie channels, broadcast TV, and now interactive games are other additional forms of distribution. By managing

contol all possible sources of income from their creations. (Some contracts have been known to include clauses stipulating that studios own the rights to finished work "throughout the known universe and for all time.")

Many of the large film studios are already deeply involved in interactive media. These companies are creating games based on many of their movie themes and characters and are rapidly beginning to use the Internet and online systems for promoting and merchandising their properties. Because film production is an enormous expense (even small films can cost several million dollars), studios are not fazed by the comparably low costs of CD-ROM and online development. This industry is probably the only one that has this belief.

these outlets effectively, the right property can turn a modest film success into a financial blockbuster.

Entertainment companies understand how to leverage their properties and are careful to secure the necessary rights to do so. They often wish to

The first generation of interactive products, like most film and broadcast properties, tended to offer little interactivity and provided few places for users to participate. Newer products, however, are beginning to provide truly engaging experiences. The film industry has been one of the fastest of the traditional industries to evolve new understandings of interactive experiences.

Unions and Guilds

*The film industry has the strongest presence of **unions** and **guilds** of any industry involved in interactive media. A union or guild represents almost every role within the film process. Some of the more noted groups are the Screen Actors Guild (SAG) and Writers Guild of America (WGA). These organizations arose long ago to counter the power of the large studios and prevent the widespread abuse of individual talent. Today, these groups are extremely powerful in their own right.*

*One of the prime functions of the film industry unions is the establishment of compensation rates for members. These rates, often referred to as **union scale**, are usually listed in several payment formats such as hourly, daily, and weekly rates. People are eligible to join unions once they have worked at a job at union rates. Once they become members of the union, they cannot perform in non-union venues. A non-union venue is an organization that has not signed a guild's contract to use only union talent.*

Many of the film industry unions and guilds have created divisions that are focusing on establishing agreements with interactive media companies to use union talent for the roles already represented by the unions. Current interactive agreements are typically binding for only a single project. Some companies are signing these agreements but many with roots in the software industry or that began as start-ups have been reluctant.

The Advertising Industry

The **advertising industry** has a relatively simple structure, consisting of advertisers, advertising agencies, and media outlets. It is primarily a service industry. Most ad agencies receive their revenues not for designing and producing ads but as a percentage of the ad space they purchase for their clients.

Advertising agencies can be very small (a few people) or very large (thousands of people and worldwide offices.) The primary assets of these agencies are the minds and talents of the people that work in them. People in the software industry or the film industry will leave behind technology or film properties whenever they leave. But in the advertising industry, there is little of value that does not reside within a person's head. There are many cases, in fact, where people have left and started up their own firms taking their previous clients with them and, overnight, becoming influential agencies.

Advertisers will typically go through a lengthy decision process in order to choose an advertising agency. These accounts, which often run into the millions of dollars, are periodically put up for review. When this happens, several advertising firms are usually invited to develop concepts for new advertising campaigns with the winner receiving the ad billings for a certain period of time.

Although there is a lot of excitement about interactive media in advertising circles, there are few people who are truly knowledgeable about the technology and the techniques for producing it. Many agencies are still oriented towards traditional media (such as television, magazines, and billboards), both in terms of development process and compensation from advertisers. Only a few have built compelling paradigms for advertising in new media, although there have been many attempts. Until more examples exist, advertisers may continue to be unwilling to take chances.

Interactive Advertising

If you were to examine how advertising works today in a 60-minute program on television, you might find 18 or 21 slots. Advertising in interactive TV will not have the same boundaries of temporal linearity. In other words, there may be many kinds of advertisements embedded in various applications that you will either choose to take or not choose to take. But the whole idea of how you pay for the advertising is going to change. What's the value of an advertisement going to be in an interactive world? It probably will be very much weighted to whether it ended in a transaction. There's no reason why if you advertise something and someone wants to do something about it that you couldn't transact right then and there. One way to look at advertising is to look at interactive TV as another channel, another direct relationship to the customer. Then you begin to understand what advertising really means for interactive TV.

—Vincent Grosso,
Interactive TV Project Director, AT&T

ADWEEK

There is incredible potential for work in this area, however. The individuals who understand interaction are in key positions to affect the future of the industry. Until advertising agencies establish their own internal interactive divisions, most will be looking to work with **multimedia consultants** or partner with **multimedia production studios**.

The Publishing Industry

The **publishing industry** is one of the oldest and most established models for selling information. It is largely dominated by a few constituent groups—authors, agents, publishers, and bookstores. Key features of the industry include a large number of products in the market, tight margins, and a relatively well-defined cost structure.

Paul Saffo
Director,
Institute for the Future

vivid: Between the publishers and the film industry, do you see there being one particular model that's going to prevail? Or are we going to be looking at a compilation of different business models?

I believe that the publishing industry is an especially rich place to look for new media business models. The publishing industry's already very diverse. You've got small presses, large press houses, controlled circulation magazines, every variation on the commercial models of the magazine—from magazines where the consumer pays the entire cost of the magazine, to magazines that come free to the consumer in exchange for a promise to look at the ads. It's a really rich place to look for ideas. And for small startups, it's a richer place than Hollywood to look for models.

The problem with Hollywood is that it is an industry dominated by big players, and the small startups are forced to exist in the big boy's shadows. Thus, the small company models from Hollywood aren't likely to work as well in the wide-open uncertainty of the new media industry. Also, there is a dark side to Hollywood culture that new media players would do well to avoid. For every Hollywood innovator, there are a dozen shallow, content-less hangers-on, hoping to get in on whatever's happening. God save us if new media is invested with these types as well. The result is an infuriating superficiality to Hollywood despite the great things it produces.

But even absent the problems of the Hollywood models, I think that the publishing business is a good match for small players. If I were a small new media developer, I would be going toward the publishing end of the medium. They are people who really love ideas and learn.

Unlike films or software where a marketing budget is allocated directly to a title and approximates or exceeds the development costs, the marketing budgets for books are commonly grouped around a catalog of books and approaches 4–5% of gross revenues. Many publishers release books on a seasonal schedule such as spring/summer and fall/winter. Much of the marketing budget goes into preparing and distributing the catalogs. Only a few in each catalog receive money for individual marketing efforts and usually it is only after they show strong sales in the first few weeks of release or are from established authors.

Another difference between books and other publishing industries are comparatively low sales volumes. Most books sell less than 25,000 copies per year (or ever). With software, games, and even CD-ROM titles, those numbers are not nearly enough to cover the development, marketing, and support costs. Book publishers, however, are able to show a profit from these numbers because of the tightly controlled development and production costs and the less expensive technologies involved.

Large publishers publish books on almost every fiction and non-fiction topic imaginable. **Smaller publishers** often concentrate on a single market and specialized topics such as computers, business, art, or cooking.

Authors or their **agents** ▶ 148 usually approach publishers with an outline, a draft of the first chapter, or, for many first time authors, a completed manuscript. A publisher may offer an advance on royalties which, for most authors, is usually less than adequate compensation for the amount of effort entailed in writing the book. A few select authors receive advances in the hundreds of thousands and million dollar ranges. **Royalties** ▶ 91 may be non-existent for some types of work, but for trade books the royalty rates typically range between 7% and 15%.

The **bookstore** has changed markedly over the past decade. Large chains are beginning to dominate the retail channel. The quantity of purchases that they make gives them increased influence with publishers over content, cover design, and even marketing issues. In fact, many publishers base book publishing decisions on the reception from book buyers from these few companies.

Publishers often work with major **distributors** to move books through the retail channels. Distributors will typically ask for an exclusive arrangement and a discount of 45–60%. The publisher is responsible for printing and delivery while the distributor warehouses books and fulfills orders. Most distributors have direct sales forces actively selling products into bookstores and other retailers.

Alternative routes exist outside the publisher/distributor model, but these take more time and money on the part of the publisher/author. **Wholesalers** differ from distributors in that their arrangements are typically non-exclusive and they often lack a direct sales force. Some may work on consignment, meaning they pay only on sales of the book as opposed to on delivery from the publisher. Beyond wholesalers lies **self-publishing**, where the author/publisher handles warehousing, fulfillment, and distribution. Few authors choose to go this route.

Traditional book and magazine publishers are only now beginning to seriously invest in interactive media. They have been wary of new technologies, put off by the cost of productions, and unsure of the means of distribution. CD-ROMs have let the publishing industry feel comfortable distributing digital information without fear of unlimited copying, but only a few have figured out how to create rich interactive experiences. Many in the past have viewed CD-ROMs as a new way to repackage and distribute materials they already own or publish.

Most large publishers are implementing strategies for interactive media, from setting up divisions to assist in turning out interactive products to creating separate business units to develop interactive products. Still others involve partnering with **multimedia studios**.

Linda Stone
Director of Advanced Technologies, Microsoft

vivid: What is your view of the traditional print publishers? How are they going to fare with these new media?

A lot of people think they're going to be passed by but I don't think that's going to happen at all. There are actually very few large publishers who are only in print. All the large publishers have migrated into audio and video already. They've migrated into other media just fine. They've just done it in their own good time.

If you look at the expertise that these large media companies have, it has everything to do with finding, courting, and channeling creative people and creative energy, and packaging projects, marketing, positioning, and distributing those products in ways that are effective and that get the products to the greatest number of people. Developing brands is another skill that they have which is directly transferable.

What they don't have is a real strong sense of the technology, which they will need to learn. Those companies will begin to understand and they'll also buy or invest in companies that understand. You'll start to see all sorts of relationships. Sometimes, you wonder if these companies know what they're buying. Some know better than others but I think that there's a way for these companies to keep their talent close to them.

If you're a Penguin Books, you want to keep Stephen King close to you. If you're Random House, there are certain children's authors you might want to keep close to you. In every single one of these cases there is a pool of talent, an understanding of packaging, an understanding of markets, and an understanding of people.

When publishers think problems through, they think through the trends, where people are going, and what people need. They think about how to build a product list that provides information or entertainment for people. [They] think about how people are going to spend leisure time.

When I go to a book store to buy a book, there are some things that jump off the shelf at me. There are other things that don't come near but they jump off the shelf at someone else. The publishers know something about what's going to jump off the shelf and at whom. It's different from doing these really broad-based things that are meant to appeal to everybody. Maybe you can do that in certain reference areas, where you don't need a point of view, but not in everything else.

Point of view is key in media. Memorable music, movies, and books have a point of view. At this point, we are still learning what point of view means.

The Software Industry

The **software industry** has developed a relatively unique approach to developing ideas and growing companies. Although many predict the heavy consolidation in the software industry will continue, new business opportunities on the Internet and in other areas of technology promise a continuation of the entrepreneurial start-up model that so richly defines Silicon Valley in particular and the multimedia industry as a whole.

At the center of this process lie **entrepreneurs** and **venture capital companies** ▶ 121. In the past, the typical entrepreneur was an engineer with an idea and a crude business plan (sometimes not even the plan). Venture capital companies were run by a few former executives at engineering companies who understood what technology could do and what its economic potential was if managed and marketed correctly. This was a time when few even knew what a microprocessor was.

This quaint model is all but legend these days. Rare is the lone engineer with the idea. Now, that engineer requires a stronger business background and is more savvy to what the marketplace needs. It also is more likely to be a group of engineers rather than one. The way that information on new ideas and new companies travels and the dramatic shortening of the time allowed to bring technology to market means that venture capitalists are less forgiving of early mistakes and look for tightly focused and complete business plans.

The venture capital community is also no longer made up of a bunch of independent investment cowboys and cowgirls blazing new trails in innovative investment models. These companies are now run by portfolio managers with eyes continually watching the **return on investment (ROI)**. The venture capital community has become much more professional and, many argue, more colloquial.

(The typical model is for a single venture capital company to lead the investment but to bring others in to share the risk.)

One of the more noted differences between software companies and the film model is that most software companies develop and **distribute** their own products, regardless of their size. In the entertainment and publishing industries, there is much more separation between those who create the products and those who market and distribute them. Software companies, though, are not known for having many dependencies or partnerships with other companies or using outside talent. Historically, everything from the initial idea to development, from marketing to customer support is handled by employees of the software company. Part of the reason is the long-term nature of a software product, a reflection of the slower acceptance phase of software and the extension provided by the development of new versions.

Another reason is that software has traditionally been tool-oriented and not information-oriented. This change is requiring software companies to cooperate with others to create new products. The tool orientation at least helps software developers build more interactive products since tools are highly interactive. What they often lack is an understanding of the sophisticated level of media production quality necessary and a feeling for what subject matter will find a broad appeal with consumers.

Software companies commonly budget as much for marketing a product as they do for developing it. On top of that, a significant percentage of annual revenues is allocated towards providing **customer support** ▶ 274. Although many companies are beginning to charge for customer service, these revenues usually do not begin to cover the costs.

Software commonly gets to the customer by way of retailers, distributors, and mail-order houses. This pathway has gone through a number of changes in the past several years, with each wave bringing mail-order companies or retailers dramatic rises in profits, followed by steep losses. There is often little that retailers can do to differentiate themselves beyond competing in price, so software retailing has become mostly a commodity business. Software companies advertised for many years only in computer magazines, but that is changing more and more as computers become part of the mainstream.

Law firms play a role equally important in the software model as the venture capital companies. A few large law firms dominate much of the work. This structure differs dramatically from Hollywood where smaller law firms are typically the powerhouses. The Silicon Valley law firms represent startups and established companies alike. They help create and maintain the corporate structures of these companies and play significant roles in IPOs and other investment activities. Security and tax law, **intellectual property** ▶ 142, and patent and trade secret litigation are also important areas for law firms working for software companies.

Investment banking companies such as Montgomery Securities and Morgan Stanley also are a part of the software industry. Venture capitalists speak of the **exit strategy** of a company, in other words, how to recoup their investment in a timely and profitable manner. The most common forms of software companies' exit strategies include getting bought out by another company or going public. Going **public** means offering stock to the public in the form of an **initial public offering** (IPO), managed with the cooperation of an investment banking company. In the past, companies going public had to have a couple of years of strong revenues. In the last two years, however, several companies have capitalized on the publicity surrounding high technology, and have gone public before any products have been shipped or revenues created. Whether the people who purchase the stock will be as fortunate as the founders and the initial investors remains to be seen.

Venture capital companies play a large role in the initial or seed investing of technology companies. A few venture firms have invested in the early stages in game developers, multimedia production studios, or multimedia publishers and, depending on the returns over the next few, may continue to do so.

Common Terms

Below are a few common terms found in a number of media industries:

Property – *A tangible work that has value, or a person or group whose future work is valuable. A property can potentially be leveraged in many ways for creating additional value.*

Talent – *Individuals who apply their skills to a particular area in the development of a project.*

Content Provider – *A generic term used to describe an individual or company that provides material for creating interactive products. It is usually the copyright holder of a body of work.*

Production Studio (Developer, Author) – *A production studio is a company that has the knowledge of the process, access to talent, and technical resources to create products. A production studio usually works with a publisher to obtain funding and distribution. Production studios may or may not retain the copyright to the completed work.*

Publisher (Studio, Label) – *A company that manages the funding and distribution of a product.*

Distributor – *A person or company that buys, or accepts on consignment, products from a publisher and then resells them to retailers.*

Retailer – *A store or company that buys from distributors or publishers directly and that resells to customers.*

The Game Industry

The interactive **game industry** is one of the few areas of multimedia that can rightly be termed an already viable industry. Many people creating interactive products make an effort to distinguish between games and other types of multimedia. At the core of this industry are the dedicated **game hardware manufacturers**, the established **game companies**, and **small game developers**. The hardware manufacturers include Sega, Nintendo, 3DO, and Atari. The game companies include Acclaim, LucasArts, and ElectronicArts. Numerous small game developers are working as production arms of large publishers creating games from existing characters and storylines. Others are creating original games and selling them to the highest bidder.

Within the last few years, more and more **entertainment companies** have entered the market with interactive games. These companies include Sony, MCA, Time-Warner, Fox Interactive, and others. Many make use of existing characters to leverage these assets across multiple media types hiring established developers to create the games. The entry by the entertainment companies has also encouraged many of the **talent agencies** to open interactive divisions. The principal focal points for most agencies, which include CAA, William Morris, and ICM, are games and children's titles. So far, these agencies represent interactive scriptwriters, producers, and a few game designers.

One of the unique features of the cartridge game industry is the royalty that is paid to the hardware manufacturers by game for each product sold for that platform. This royalty is a large reason why the costs of dedicated game machines is so low in comparison to PCs. Game developers make their profits on the royalties, and not on the sale of equipment. This royalty and the resulting high margins are the primary reasons for the growing competition in this area. One open question here is what happens to the profits of these companies if PCs become the dominant game platform.

While the distribution of games software follows the electronic consumer products distribution model, CD-ROM title development follows the software distribution model. The **retailers** for games are mostly toy retailers such as Toys-R-Us and many of the consumer electronics stores that dot the American landscape.

Game companies are already oriented toward interactivity since games are some of the most interactive media products ever developed. The biggest change in the market is that the production qualities are raising quickly as game machines become increasingly more capable of supporting demanding sound and graphics and as both audiences' and manufacturers' expectations become more sophisticated.

The CD-ROM Title Industry

CD-ROM title development has a lot in common with the game industry because they share the same technology and interactivity issues. But since games have sold more successfully, the infrastructure for these types of deals tends to be more developed. At the heart of any CD-ROM production is a project team. The project team can be within the **publishing house**, in an independent **production studio**, or in some combination of the two. For example, the publisher might retain editorial control and the production studio might supply the media production and the programming.

But before a project can get to this point, many things have to happen. In the past, a few people with an idea could get together and create a product that they could then sell. This is no longer a realistic option. The number of titles is growing faster than the shelf space available for them, which creates intense competition. Without access to distribution, few projects can hope to recoup their production costs.

In addition, the dramatic increase in the level of production values of CD-ROMs in the last few years has correspondingly raised the **budgets ▶ 126** for all titles. The typical range for a special interest title is $200,000–$700,000, and for a game or reference title upwards of $1 million. The size of the budgets, combined with marketing costs that can approach three times the production cost makes it extremely difficult for small publishers to create and distribute products without large financial backing. A few years ago it was possible to create and market products for much less. Several of the companies that did so have been able to grow large enough to become CD-ROM publishers in their own right. Examples include Maxis and the Voyager Company.

These days, most production studios are looking to **entertainment companies**, **book publishers**, and **software companies** for financing and distribution. These potential publishers are, in turn, looking for new titles as well as production facilities to turn their own properties into titles.

The relationships between these types of companies vary greatly. Some deals may include only production fees with no royalties, while others may feature royalties ranging from 10% to 25%. The economic models for CD-ROM development are still evolving, partly because of sporadic sales in the marketplace. A few dozen titles may sell hundreds of thousands of copies, but the rest sell only in the thousands or tens of thousands.

Besides the production studios (or developers) and the entertainment, multimedia, publishing, and software companies that fund and market the titles, there are several other types of companies as well. **Private investors** may provide seed money for the development of projects that can then be taken to publishers for the remaining production funds. At the moment, few companies are interested in funding projects without some type of prototype—especially for companies without a proven track record. As the industry grows and more wildly successful titles appear (outside of games and children's titles), these companies may be more willing to invest in projects backed only by ideas on paper.

The **distributors** for CD-ROM titles are currently the same distributors found in the software industry. These include Ingram, Merisel, and Baker & Taylor. While a publisher can start production on titles before lining up a distributor, most publishers line up the distribution channels before committing a large amount of money to production. Many of the packaging and distribution decisions are dependent on the choice of distributor.

*An **angel** is a private investor who agrees to provide funding for a company or product in return for equity in the company or royalties in the product. Family and friends are often a source of this type of funding.*

The new media revolution is too important to be left to gearheads, which is why we're trying to get artists involved. It's not about bells and whistles, it's about content, vision, and talent. The artist is the most important part of the new media equation. Our belief is that the lifeblood of this industry is coming from the multimedia garage bands, the guys who live on credit and answer their own phones and don't get a lot of sleep. This is where its all going to come from.

—Stewart McBride, President, United Digital Artists

The **retail channel** for CD-ROM titles is a mix of software retailers such as CompUSA and Egghead, music retailers such as Tower Records, bookstores, and newer media stores such as Virgin Megastores that combine all of them. Although the price for many consumer titles are consolidating at the $30–60 range, many other distribution issues are still in flux. For example, the packaging for CD-ROM titles is a mix of software-like packaging and music packaging. On the one hand, software retailers tend to want the big shelf presence, regardless of the ecological or economic implications, whereas book and music retailers are more comfortable with more ecological packages that do not take up as much room.

Distribution is the most difficult part of the multimedia equation. It is even harder to secure than financing.

Mail-order companies, while not considered retailers, are a significant channel to customers. Some mail-order publishers buy from distributors while others buy from publishers directly. Several publishers are even experimenting with direct sales through online channels, but their success has yet to be proven.

Creativity vs. Clout

Independent production companies driven by creative talent, I think, are premature because you're not going to get the positioning that you really need. You can't cut an interesting deal with the major distribution companies that now control the channels for retail CD-ROMs. You don't have clout with the America Onlines that take most of the revenue from narrowband services. You don't have clout with Nintendo and Sega. As creative talent, you don't really have the leverage that you will later.

—Miles Gilburne,
Attorney

The Online Industry

Although many people perceive the publicity about the Internet and **online systems** ▶ 15 as a lot of hype, there is enough activity taking place and revenue already being generated to legitimately view it as a functioning industry. The primary constituents of this industry, online services and their members, have been around for a long time. The sudden interest in online areas has many of the early pioneers mystified about the timing but not about the results.

The **Internet** is not so much a network itself, but a term for the collection of networks connected to each other. The Internet started when a few networks, some private and some government, were interconnected so that they could share email and transfer files. Because they began supporting a common communications protocol, they began to function as if they were a large network. This loose collection of networks has grown over the past few decades to include several million computers which are in turn gateways to other networks and users. (A common way to estimate the number of people using the Internet is to count 10 users for each computer hooked up to the Internet.) The Internet is growing at a rapid rate, meaning that more and more people around the world are gaining access to the networks, resources, and each other via the Internet.

Some of the biggest and better known companies in the online industry are the large **commercial services** such as America Online, CompuServe, Prodigy, and Delphi. Much of the industry is awaiting the influence Microsoft may have with its new Microsoft Network. For much of their existence, these services have largely been independent of the Internet. But starting a few years ago, they began allowing email access to and from the Internet and now recognize the need to offer more access to other Internet services such as the World Wide Web.

Commercial online services not only offer features for people to use to communicate with each other (such as email, conferences, and chat), they also have extensive libraries of information.

CompuServe, for example, has a vast list of corporate forums where users can get technical support and feedback from just about any hardware or software company. Several contain flight schedules for most major airlines. These large online services also serve as meeting places for groups interested in specific topics such as senior citizens and business executives.

The economics of providing content or creating meeting spaces are changing quickly. Those providing content or wanting a meeting space in the past often had to pay online services for the privilege to create these and access to these features was strictly controlled. Now, online services are offering to share revenues with organizations in hopes of attracting their customers and constituents. Smart **content providers** and organizations, however, are using the fierce competition between the online services to get greater coverage and better deals. Many online services are hard at work developing capabilities to allow organizations to have greater control over the access, appearance, and interaction of their areas.

Online services are beginning to pay "bounties" to companies and organizations whose customers, subscribers, members, or constituents sign up for online service as a result of direct promotional efforts by these companies and organizations. Current bounties are reportedly in the $20–$30 range.

The cost for phone service is not an issue when dialing an online service or service provider with a local number. Long distance phone charges can be huge, however, when a local number is not available. Whether local phone companies will modify their pricing in response to increased phone traffic caused by electronic communications will be an interesting question in the years to come.

Internet service providers ▶ *84 are companies that provide access to the Internet. A company that wants to establish its own domain can sign up with a service provider who will manage the registration of the domain name and set up and manage the connection between the company and the Internet. The speeds of the transmission lines between the company, and the service provider and the service provider and the Internet are a big deciding point in choosing a service provider.*

Many see these local service providers as a new version of the early cellular phone service providers. Several companies are buying up providers trying to establish regional or national presence. One company, Netcom, went public at the end of 1994 and within a month, its stock price had almost doubled, valuing each subscriber, or "pop," at $3,600. Even in the heydays of the cellular phone and cable industries, the value of a subscriber did not even come close to that amount.

Besides large commercial online services, there are also **regional online services**. Many of these started at the same time as the larger services but decided to cater to a specific membership and grow a strong and vibrant community instead of a large size. Membership is not limited by geography, but members tend to be residents of the region they are located in. These services tend to offer stronger discourse and more in-depth communication about local or regional issues.

The WELL is a San Francisco Bay Area–based regional net that specializes in building strong community ties between its members. It was one of the first online service to open, starting back in 1985 when almost every other network on the Internet was a government or university site. The WELL is a very loosely structured service, acting almost as an co-op. The Vine is a Los Angeles-based regional net specializing in making connections between people in the film business.

Another form of online system is a **bulletin board system** (BBS). These have existed for a long time and many thousands of them are in operation all over the world. Most are privately run by individuals and organizations. For example, some people may run a BBS as a hobby from their home or to serve an interest group. Many BBSs are migrating to the **World Wide Web** since graphical web browsers are now widely available, allowing non-technical people to have greater access to the Web. In addition, many people and companies are extending the capabilities of the Web to include features found in many commercial online systems such as conferences and threaded discussions.

The World Wide Web has seen explosive growth in the last year because it allows individuals to easily share graphical information as well as text. Sound, animation, and video can be shared but not with the immediacy or intergration found in other media forms. Because the Web is relatively easy to navigate and is accessible 24 hours a day, 7 days a week, from anywhere in the world, companies view it as an ideal way to make their products and services available, contact customers, and eventually conduct business. Advances in the capabilities of web browser software will eventually allow commercial transactions, secure communication, and richer interactions. In turn, these will allow more varied forms of communication with fewer limitations that frustrate both users and developers.

Multimedia studios, **design firms**, and **advertising agencies** familiar with multimedia issues and online technologies are already helping to design and build websites for their clients. As more sophisticated technologies augment the Web's present capabilities, the firms that truly understand interactivity and are capable of extending these technologies are going to be the winners.

Europe Online

The growth of online services has not been as fast overseas as it has in the U.S. Many experts are predicting this will change dramatically in the next several years. CompuServe boasts 200,000 subscribers in Germany, and Great Britain, and a number of services are preparing to debut, including Europe Online, a Luxembourg-based service backed by British, French, and German publishers. Market researchers are predicting some 500,000 Europeans going online in 1995 with as many as 15 million by 2000. Other regions promise similar growth, though several years later.

The Interactive Television Industry

The **interactive TV industry** ▶ 16 is still in a rudimentary stage. It would not even be qualified as an industry if it were not for the amount of money being spent on test trials and the potential size of the industry. The technology and the structure are still being created and the economics have yet to be determined. As a result, only a few types of companies are working in this area. As the technology becomes more refined and the economics more profitable, this will change and it will likely be more competitive and more dynamic in as short a period of time as any development in the last half century.

At the head of interactive TV development are the **cable and telephone companies**. Each see interactive TV as a logical extension of their businesses, and are moving aggressively, both technically and politically, in order to keep up with other cable and telephone rivals. Since there is no direct revenue from any interactive TV venture at this point, most of the investment is coming from these benefactors. The cost of the trials going on across the country is in the hundreds of millions of dollars. The money is going towards wiring homes, building the set-top boxes, purchasing and configuring large media servers, developing navigation tools and interactive programming, and building a high bandwidth responsive two-way network.

In partnership with various cable and telephone companies are computer hardware and software manufacturers such as Apple Computer, Silicon Graphics, Microsoft, and Oracle Systems. These types of companies are building set-top boxes, computer chip sets, media servers and databases, relays, and operating systems that run these new networks. There are still daunting technological problems to solve in creating the networks that may not be solved satisfactorily for a while.

Working in conjunction with cable and telco companies and computer and hardware manufacturers are several **production studios and developers**. These companies are designing and developing interface technologies for navigating through programming options, performing transactions, and communicating with others either through text or two-way video. These companies and a handful of others are developing original programming content for the interactive trials. At this point, not too many broadcasters, publishers, entertainment companies, or multimedia publishers are porting their traditional products, CD-ROMs, or online service products to interactive TV because the economics do not justify the effort. Also, the tools are not as seamless as most would like, currently requiring a significant amount of additional work before they can be used.

Once the technology and the economics are worked out, services will begin to appear. This roll-out will still be somewhat slow, due to the costs in retrofitting the network infrastructure. Then a variety of companies will become heavily involved in this industry. These include cable and network television channels, television stations, entertainment companies, publishing companies, advertising agencies, information services, retailers, and many others. The sizes of companies involved and the relationships between companies may be dependent on the political and economic environment that is created. A closed-access structure like the cable industry is likely to make interactive TV the domain of large companies with access to lots of capital. A structure that is more open to access, like the telephone companies, is likely to offer opportunities for companies of all sizes.

Right now, some of these companies are participating, but not significantly. Each company has hired a consultant or two or assigned one or more people to attend interactive TV conferences, read the trades, gain visibility, and essentially accumulate a base of knowledge, resources, and contacts so that when the time is right they are positioned to move quickly. People with a background in marketing and technology and who can communicate to upper management will work best in these positions.

Used with permission, Electronic Media, 1995

Ray Smith
CEO of Bell Atlantic Corp.

A large component of the interactive TV trials largely overlooked is the service end—the installation and maintenance of the lines and set-top boxes in the homes. Though this work may be unglamorous and falls directly into the domain of the cable and telephone companies, it is likely to be a potential source of new jobs.

Upside: Do you think the standards will come about in the next year?

Yes. It is to everybody's advantage. Period. The manufacturers, all of the providers, everybody. We have a rough set-top guidelines standard with every telephone company. They aren't specific enough yet, but at least we have the general standards. One of the interesting battles that's going to take place between the cable and the telcos is the open systems vs the closed system. The cable systems are closed. They want to make money by trading carriage for equity. I'll let you on my system, give me 20 percent of your company cheap.

Upside: That's what TCI did.

Yes. There's nothing wrong with that. That's a bargaining chip. It's perfectly legitimate and legal. It irritated a lot of people; clearly, it irritated Sumner [Redstone, chairman of Viacom Inc.] and others. My god, I've been in forums in which Rupert Murdoch [CEO of The News Corporation Ltd.] said: "Ray, with your new systems, are you going to open them to people like me so I can start another CNN in this country, I want to start a news service in this country, but I can't get on. I can't get on anywhere. Are you going to open it up to me?" "Yes, Rup." "Really? Promise?" "Yes." "Why would you do that?" "It's the law." "Oh."

Upside: What if it weren't the law?

We wouldn't open it up [laughs]. No, no—that's off the record [laughs]. Of course we would [he says sarcastically]. We understand the nonlinearity of information and how it becomes more valuable...

No, I think the days of closed systems are passed because we are going to open them up.

Upside: Because you have to?

No, we are opening them up because we got into the cable business by challenging the law and so we are actually going to build it. We happen to be a common carrier, but even if we were not, the days of channel shortage would be changed substantially, because you would have all of our channels, as well as the cable system's. We are going from a period of totally restrictive capacity to one of substantial capacity for unaffiliated programmers. Completely different trade-offs; money will be made in completely different ways.

Upside: You believe that common carrier rules will continue?

Yes. One of the keys here is the point of indifference for us. You ask what would we do if we could restrict it? We probably really would not. We can construct a system with more than sufficient capacity that the point of indifference is 600 channels. Meaning, if we have 600 channels, we don't care whether our stuff's on there or not. If we can sell 600 channels, we're home free. How many channels are there in Philadelphia, in the telephone system? Two and a half million. There are two and a half million channels. They happen to be voice channels, not video channels. Are we upset? Do we say we want only certain voices on there? No. The more voice channels, the better. That's the business we're in. That's why we have 20 million of them, 1.4 million. The days of restricting speech in that way are ending.

—Ray Smith in an interview in Upside *magazine, October 1994*

Technology of itself doesn't create anything. It's simply a tool and its no more inspired than Rembrandt's brush.

--Stewart McBride, President, United Digital Artists

4. Global Hot Spots

Wondering where the opportunities are? Here's an overview of multimedia activity around the world.

Want to make the leap into multimedia but uncertain where to begin? You don't have to move to a major city—knowledge of the tools and access to equipment is reaching the far corners of the globe, launching a flurry of new industries. You may find your skills in demand in your own hometown.

Of course, major metropolitan areas have distinct advantages. Proximity to universities, research facilities, and key industries such as publishing, entertainment, and software/hardware development have given San Francisco, New York, Los Angeles, Atlanta, Miami, London, Tokyo, and other major metropolitan areas an edge over other regions, both in terms of the size of the industry and the quality and innovation of the work being produced.

We talked to writers, designers, artists, programmers, producers, students, and educators in more than 20 countries to compile this look at how the industry is growing in different regions. However, because this new industry is growing and changing so fast, we can't make any claims to completeness. To find out more about multimedia in your region, contact your local library, universities, computer companies, and design studios. Or look for a local chapter of the International Interactive Communications Society (IICS) or professional organizations in related industries, such as art, graphic design, or sound and video engineering (see Resources).

Our thanks to the many people who helped us gather this information.

San Francisco

Welcome to Multimedia Gulch, the Cradle of Interactivity and Cyber Civilization

San Francisco, renowned for its colorful, sometimes off-kilter populace and life-loving pace, is the kind of city that encourages risk-taking and entrepreneurial spirit. For years it has been a magnet for creative professionals, particularly in the design industries. This critical mass of talent, combined with the close proximity to Silicon Valley's entreprenuers, has created a rich mix of companies that venture beyond the borders of traditional disciplines.

Popularized in the 1970s and 1980s as the center of computer hardware and software development, the Bay Area, spanning from Sonoma County in the north to Silicon Valley in the south, to Berkeley and Oakland in the east, has gained new fame as the birthplace of multimedia. Nowhere is this more apparent than in the eastern half of San Francisco's South of Market (SoMa) neighborhood (dubbed "Multimedia Gulch"), where literally hundreds of developers and producers have set up shop in sprawling warehouses and rehabbed Victorians.

The Gulch is brimming with creative energy and technical savvy. Some of the brightest stars include **Wired** magazine and their online counterpart **Hotwired**, published on the World Wide Web (http://www.hotwired.com). **Macromedia**, producers of the authoring tool Director, has become one of the most widely known and respected suppliers of tools for the industry. **Colossal Pictures** push the bleeding edge of desktop video with their animated commercials and serials for MTV's "Liquid Television" and the Nickelodeon channel. Major corporations, seeking to be close to the action, are setting up shop as well: **Sega of America** and **Sony** have divisions here too. Telecommunications giant **Pacific Bell** and companies offering pager service and Internet connections have made a home here as well.

But by far the most significant growth is in the number of small developers found here. From online world builders to CD-ROM producers to point-of-purchase kiosk designers, practically every kind of foray into the digital realm is happening somewhere in this land of lofts and (relatively) low rents. In addition to the more popular genres—games, educational, reference, and children's titles—emerging areas are gaining ground as enterprising developers focus their attention towards interactive narratives, productivity titles, and online services—networked gaming, real-time teleconferencing, and network-based transactions.

As expected, educational resources are plentiful in this region—**San Francisco State University** draws on the local talent pool to teach classes in their Multimedia Extension Program. To the south, **Stanford University** offers undergraduate and advanced studies in everything from interactive communications to digital typography. Dozens of regional and community colleges offer courses in media tools and theories. Practitioners and professionals looking for a career change will find **weekend workshops** and evening seminars are plentiful, covering everything from using the latest tools to pitching a story idea to a producer.

In addition to being home base for developers and hardware manufacturers, San Francisco and **San Jose** also host some of the most important trade shows in the field, including MacWorld, Intermedia, Multimedia Expo, and VISCOMM—good excuses to visit and possibly job hunt if you don't already live nearby.

North America

pacific northwest

Seattle, Washington is known for strong coffee, great bookstores, and a growing multimedia industry. Industry kingpin Microsoft has produced several top-selling CD-ROM titles, but the field is large enough for plenty of other developers—although Microsoft's formidable presence gives Windows an edge over the Macintosh as the preferred development environment. Small start-ups and established design firms are turning out websites and titles in all areas, from games to educational titles. Local schools are putting together programs in multimedia to train the next generation of developers. Professionals seeking kindred spirits turn to the Washington Software Association, a large and active organization of developers from all over the state.

Further south in **Ashland, Oregon,** a small but established industry is flourishing in this region of 100,000 residents, thanks to the presence of Trilobyte, Inc., makers of the CD-ROM *The Seventh Guest,* and Open Mind, an artistic and technical research firm delving into interactive entertainment, object-oriented software engineering, and neural networks. The largest local industries are entertainment and education. Not surprisingly, the most common projects are education or entertainment-oriented. Development studios and artists are major players in the field.

san francisco
See page 67

los angeles
See page 70

las vegas

Gambling capital of the U.S., **Las Vegas** is also the destination for vacationers who want to attend some of the largest and glitziest trade shows in the world. COMDEX, the twice-yearly show (the autumn show is here, the spring show is in Atlanta) draws hundreds of thousands of attendees from around the world, all eager to view the latest hardware and software, as well as preview what's coming. The National Associaton of Broadcasters' annual convention takes place here too, as does the Consumer Electronics Show in January and several hardware/networking shows during the year.

texas & southwest

Austin, Texas boasts a thriving multimedia industry, fueled by the presence of an iconoclastic art and design community as well as Apple Computer. Smaller design and media production companies abound, and the **University of Texas/Austin** is developing a curriculum in interactive media. Educational projects are particularly important here. Elsewhere in this region, **Dallas** is carving out its own niche with computer hardware manufacturers and major corporate and financial institutions looking for ways to use multimedia.

mexico

Mexico is one of the largest computer markets in all of Latin America: Together with Brazil, Mexico accounted for over 60% of all PCs shipped into Latin America in 1993, according to a report published by Apple Latin America. Mexico's ratification of the North American Free Trade Agreement (NAFTA) eliminated hefty tariffs on imported hardware (20%) and software (10%), making it easier for developers like **Mexico City's** Macware to set up shop (Macware created a series of multimedia kiosks for a children's museum).

ontario & quebec

Ottawa Valley, aka "Silicon Valley North," is home to over 500 high tech companies employing more than 30,000 people, and accounts for 45% of all Canadian research and development spending. Many of those companies are involved in multimedia. For example, Future Endeavors develops interactive CD-ROMs for children's adventure and learning games as well as edutainment titles aimed at adults. A video director in **Montreal** predicts that the entertainment industry and the government will be quite influential in spurring multimedia activity. Although the industry in this region is relatively young, it is growing. Some of the better known companies include Tune 1000, Astral, Thoughtworks, Megatoon, Buzz, SoftImage, and Discreet Logic. Advertising agencies are also getting involved by setting up consulting facilities. CD-ROMs, games, and cartoons are among the most popular products. Those who seek to learn more about multimedia go to The NAD, a training center, and Concordia University, which has one of the best communications and media programs in Canada.

chicago & the midwest

Chicago, Illinois, famous for its architecture and corporate headquarters, is home to numerous design studios. The **University of Illinois/Urbana-Champaign** is turning out designers at a rapid pace, many of whom stay in the area to launch their own multimedia and web design firms. Other regional cities, including **Milwaukee and Madison, Wisconsin**, and **Lafayette, Indiana**, have their own infant industries. Even tiny **Canton, Ohio** has gotten its fingers in the pie, with InterBold's foray into designing next-generation ATMs.

boston

Boston, a traditionally conservative city with a strong hold in the computer industry, is not particularly active in the multimedia world. Despite the high profiles of MIT's Media Lab and a handful of organizations that thrive on the Internet, notably BBN and Delphi, there just isn't a whole lot of interactive design going on here. Notable exceptions include **Cambridge** publisher O'Reilly and Associates, whose web-based Global Network Navigator was one of the first (and is still quite popular) online magazines. The MacWorld show in August always draws crowds, as does the well-designed and enjoyable Computer Museum—worth it just to view the walk-through computer.

washington, d.c.

Washington, D.C., is the nation's capital, the birthplace of the Internet (it began as a Department of Defense project to link research facilities and decentralize information in case of nuclear attack), and home to many important advancements in science and technology, such as virtual reality. Washington is also the premier repository for information in the US. Thus, it is only fitting that government agencies would explore multimedia as a means of making information more accessible to the public. Websites are one of the most popular methods for distributing information to a widespread audience: the site for the Library of Congress (http://www.loc.gov/) contains information about exhibits, selections from the stacks, pointers to legislative information on the Internet, and searchable online catalogs and databases. The National Library of Medicine (http://www.nlm.nih.gov/) contains research findings and a gallery of unusual photographs (not recommended for the squeamish). One of the most useful sites found anywhere comes from the Internal Revenue Service (http://www.ustreas.gov/treasury/bureaus/irs/taxforms.html), where visitors can download the latest federal tax forms. It may not be as much fun as other websites, but it fulfills a vital purpose. Outside of the government, however, there are few other multimedia clients or developers in the region.

new york

See page 71

southeast

Other than Ted Turner's cable television empire, the biggest media player in **Atlanta, Georgia** is IBM's Multimedia Studio. The development community here is relatively small, which can mean lower production costs than in other metro areas, but also less intense competition. Much of the development activity comes from Georgia Tech, ADAM Software, Crawford Communications, and Floyd Design. Farther south, **Miami, Florida** is becoming the multimedia capital of Latin America: numerous developers have set up their U.S. bases in this subtropical town, and Apple Latin America manages its Central and South American distributors and subsidiaries out of its offices in Coral Gables. In **New Orleans, Louisana**, a small group of developers including Bent Media are creating interactive training programs for one of that region's major industries: petrochemical companies. Many "artist/musician types" are drawn to multimedia in the Crescent City, says one producer. Many developers here studied at the Electronic Imaging Laboratory (EILAB) at the University of New Orleans, and have set up shop downtown or in the city's funky warehouse district.

Los Angeles

If San Francisco is the king's court of multimedia development, then Los Angeles is content queen. Home to the largest film studios, television production companies, and record labels in the world, L.A. is eagerly devising new ways to create and repurpose content for new media, in part by hosting conferences like Digital Hollywood and the Interactive Media Festival.

The odd coupling of Hollywood and Silicon Valley has spawned the term "Siliwood," meaning the meeting place between L.A.'s glitz and power and the Bay Area's technical expertise. Although these alliances have yielded several success stories such as Universal Studios' hit movie *Jurassic Park* owes a lot to the Silicon Graphics jockeys who created the stunning effects—most of these relationships are still quite young and susceptible to the risks that accompany any dealings between parties with very different business models and working styles.

The major industries determining the path of multimedia in Los Angeles include the following:

• Film and television studios, many of whom are turning to northern California for special effects wizardry such as that coming out of George Lucas' Industrial Light and Magic, located 20 miles north of San Francisco. Disney, Fox, and Universal have all launched interactive divisions, and studios are eagerly looking for ways to tie in feature releases with interactive games and online projects. Actors welcome the additional opportunities that live-action video games are presenting; expect to see more familiar faces turning up on your desktop in the near future.

• Record labels, always looking for new and innovative ways to promote their artists, from offering downloadable songs on the Web (check out the Internet Underground Music Archive, http://www.iuma.com) to having bands "tour" chat rooms in the online world and answer fans'

questions. One of the trendiest new acronyms is IPK (interactive press kit), a digital package containing press releases, animated logos, videos, and audio clips from interviews and songs. Interactive CD-ROMs from musicians are also quite popular, not only for repackaging songs and videos, but also for presenting the artist in a new context (check out the exploration-based game CD-ROM from the artist formerly known as Prince). In some ways, CD-ROMs are the boxed sets of the 1990s. And more than a few well-known musicians have written scores for computer games.

• Location-based entertainment. The leader in this industry is the vast Disney empire, but smaller companies are making their mark. Everything from 3D movies to virtual reality goggle-and-glove games to themed amusement parks and game franchises are springing up in shopping malls across the country.

• Computer science. When the aerospace industry downsized in the 1980s, many programmers turned to other fields for work. However, many found that they hadn't kept up with the new tools. One multimedia recruiter in L.A. claims he has more producers than he knows what to do with, but is always short on qualified programmers who know how to create digital media. His advice to job seekers in L.A.? "Go learn Photoshop, Director, and Premiere—then we'll talk."

• A host of related players are finding themselves involved, however peripherally, in the interactive media industry. Talent agents, lawyers, publicists, scriptwriters, set designers, makeup artists, and cinematographers are realizing that they need to know about electronic rights, non-linear navigation and compression ratios, and how colors appear on monitors as their clients move into the desktop world.

New York

Multimedia is alive and well in New York City, and growing rapidly; so much so that many people now point to SoHo as the East Coast's own Multimedia Gulch.

By far the major industry driving multimedia here is publishing—the biggest publishing houses in the U.S. are headquartered here, and many international firms have U.S. bases in Manhattan as well. Heavyweights such as Time/Warner, Viacom, Grolier, Random House, and HarperCollins are all testing the interactive waters by launching their own new media divisions and expanding their catalogs to include CD-ROMs. Some, such as Time/Warner and Viacom, have established their own media empires covering a vast range of territory and are laying tracks for future technologies, such as interactive television.

Periodical publishers are already a step ahead of the game, making their publications available online. Commercial services, such as America Online, offer digital versions of dozens of popular magazines and newspapers, including *@Times (The New York Times)*, *Spin*, and *Business Week*, while the Internet is home to websites for *Time* and *Vibe*.

Developers aren't all massive corporate entities, however—smaller shops such as Byron Preiss and Thinking Pictures are carving out their own niche in the market. Probably the best known of all these firms is the Voyager Company, an organization dedicated to digital products that has taken the industry by storm and carries an impressive number of best-selling interactive titles in its catalog. Voyager's CD-ROMs are among the first to really explore the dimensions of interactive, non-linear narratives.

New York has also been a major center for art and design of all types, so it's only natural that many local practitioners would turn their attention toward interaction and interface design. Local universities, including Columbia and the School of Visual Arts, offer many courses in all phases of media development and production, as well as in programming, design, writing, and theory. As one producer put it, "Everybody and his second cousin twice removed teaches a course on Director." The best, and best known, of these is New York University's graduate-level Interactive Telecommunications Program (ITP). ITP turns out some of the leading interface and interaction designers in the world.

As expected, hardware, software, books, and professional training are easy to come by, and all the major bookstores have sections devoted to multimedia products.

Job seekers, networkers, and media junkies seeking kinship turn to online services, such as ECHO (the East Coast Hang Out) to post resumes and swap stories and job tips. In real life they flock to places like the News Bar, a trendy coffeehouse with machines set up for public access to the Web and USENET newsgroups, or they join professional groups like the New York New Media Society or the New Media Group (a special interest group within N.Y. Women in Film & Television).

Like most other major cities in the U.S., New York hosts its share of conferences and trade shows. Also, New York has terrific resources for other kinds of gatherings, such as film festivals, museum exhibits on communications and broadcasting, lectures by leading theorists and producers, and professional workshops led by top designers and artists at institutions like the School for Visual Arts and New School for Social Research.

U.K. & Europe

british isles

Multimedia is exploding in some parts of the U.K., but is still relatively quiet in outlying regions. Public awareness of the technologies and capabilities is limited, although the news media is helping to generate interest. Most development happens in major cities like **London**. No project types dominate the market, however U.K. schools are making good use of multimedia, and computer games are leading the current technology. Hardware, software, and books are easy to acquire in cities throughout the region. Small developers with strong ties to the educational system are among the major players in **Cambridge**. Here, resources for the general public are limited, but Hampshire Microtec Centre (CITE), Cambridgeshire IT Education, and the Leeds Computing Centre all offer training and software libraries to educators, many of whom are eager to explore the potential for putting information online. Among the institutions already doing that are Trinity College at the University of **Dublin**, where the computer science department has put up a website with information about network security, data exchange, and payment mechanisms over the net (http://ganges.cs.tcd.ie/), and C.ENT.I. (Computer Entertainment of Ireland), an online catalog of CDs and audio samples from Irish artists (http://www.centi.ie/).

france

People don't flock to **Cannes** just for the film festival; they also make the annual pilgrimage to attend Milia, a major international publishing conference. **Paris** is home to Apple Computer's European headquarters and also hosts several large media conferences, including MacWorld, Seybold Europe, and Interactive Television.

sweden

Multimedia has been warmly received by the techno-savvy cultures of Sweden. The multimedia industy is established and growing, particularly in larger cities like **Stockholm**, where universities and publishing houses play a major role in shaping the industry, as well as large corporations such as Scania and TetraPac. Advertisers and developers are the driving force behind the industry, and company presentations, educational works, and information kiosks are among the most popular projects. Hardware and software are easily acquired, but training resources are lacking. Production companies like Datadesign & Multimedia AB in **Umea** are helping to cement the foundation of a small but growing industry in other areas of the country. One programmer/sound engineer says that media attention is helping to create interest, however many people have different conceptions of what multimedia is.

germany

Germany, long a center for design and technological innovation, has spawned its own multimedia gulches in **Frankfurt, Munich, Cologne**, and **Berlin.** Small ateliers and research facilities are producing CD-ROMs, kiosks, interactive presentations and educational tools, and investigating new applications for virtual reality. However, as in much of the rest of Europe, most of the titles available on the market are from the U.S. The monthly magazine "Inside MULTIMEDIA" reaches more than 200,000 readers eager to read reviews of the latest CD-ROMs and learn about new developments in software and hardware. A sister publication, "PC Spiel," covers the gaming market and is distributed with a CD-ROM of games, demos, and shareware. Action and adventure games like **Myst, Doom,** and **Rebel Assault** are immensely popular with kids and adults. Internet access is still relatively limited to universities and major commercial organizations. However, many smaller businesses and private citizens are eager to go online. CompuServe is quite popular, as more and more people are realizing how important email can be for business and personal communications.

finland

In **Helsinki,** multimedia is highly visible and thriving. Several universities and polytechnics offer multimedia-oriented programs and media research centers, and smaller development companies are blossoming. Current areas of interest include multimedia telecommunications, company presentations, computer-assisted learning software, interactive television technology, and electronic newspapers. Websurfing is a popular pastime, and Helsinki is home to two computer cafes offering games and multimedia software. In addition, several public libraries offer free access to the Internet, as well as hardware and titles for their patrons to play with. Many Finnish schools and universities offer multimedia training courses and programs, including The University of Arts and Design in Helsinki and The Helsinki University of Technology; Espoo-Vantaa Institute of Technology, The Tampere University of Technology, The University of Tampere, and Tampere School of Art and Communication, The Lahti School of Art and Communication, and The Lappeenranta Institute of Technology. The industry is partially driven by established software production companies, such as Tietovalta Oy and Media Company Sansibar Oy in Tampere, I ja piste Oy in Pori, To the Point Oy in Espoo, and Rec Button and CD-Queen in Helsinki. Major publishing houses WSOY, Otava, and Painatuskeskus Oy are experimenting with multimedia production as well, and the Finnish Broadcasting Company is about to launch its first multimedia program in connection with a language teaching program (Working English). One place where multimedia hasn't made much of an inroad yet is in entertainment. The number of consumer products is still fairly small; during 1994 seven Finnish multimedia titles were available for consumers and schools. The majority of titles available in the stores come not from European but rather U.S. publishers.

russia

Moscow's multimedia industry is in its infancy, but growing rapidly. The number of multimedia computers in the city grows by more than 1,000 per month, and although there are few producers in Russia, many of them exhibited at the Softool Trade Show in September of 1994. Trade shows are in fact one of the best resources for learning about the industry. As one producer points out, Russia is undergoing profound change. There are many highly talented people from universities and research institutes whose financial support from the government has effectively vaporized. Many Russian programmers have been recruited by U.S. and European firms. However, he feels that with additional training, they will be able to develop a strong multimedia community (and in fact, the top-selling astronomy title *Red Shift* was developed in Moscow for U.S.-based Maris Media). Currently, most people rely on networking and the Internet to learn about multimedia. Top-notch schools, such as Moscow State University, are popular places for meeting others interested in this field.

Asia & Oceania

far east

Japan is one of the most technologically advanced countries in the world, and nowhere is this more apparent than in **Tokyo.** The largest consumer electronics manufacturers are based here, and the local market is filled with next generation equipment unavailable anywhere else. Frequently the setting for cyberpunk novels, Tokyo eagerly embraces the new and unusual: everything from the latest in titles and high-end game players to location-based entertainment like VR arcades and indoor artificial beaches (with piston-driven waves suitable for surfing). Many of the major conferences in multimedia, virtual reality, and interactive design are held here. **Hong Kong** is very active in CD-i development efforts, and with good reason: although few people on the mainland have computers, nearly everybody has a TV. Hence, there's a sizable installed base for CD-i players. Given the prevalence of major financial and manufacturing institutions, this city is ripe for all types of interactive development projects, particularly those that serve the needs of the business community. **Taiwan** and **Korea** are both major manufacturing centers for computers, however, most of the equipment built here is intended for export.

india

India's world-renowned technical institutes produce some of the finest computer scientists and programmers in the world—many of whom turn up at leading-edge software companies and research facilities. Although home computers haven't made nearly the imprint here that they have elsewhere, the country's huge film industry is setting the stage for future multimedia endeavors.

southeast asia

Multimedia is growing quickly in **Malaysia** and **Thailand,** spurred by the commercial and advertising markets, and competition is heating up. Advertising is the primary product, and major players include the software industry, publishing, and media outlets. Hardware, software, and books are easy to come by, however, software is reportedly expensive. Training is scarce, so developers rely on industry magazines to educate them about the tools. As one developer put it, "Everybody is trying to make a quick buck, especially the computer dealers who sell [products] without knowing what the major uses will be."

australia

Multimedia has been making headlines in **Melbourne, Victoria;** in late 1994 the government launched major policy initiatives to encourage the development of a local multimedia industry. Their vision is to get Australia involved as a major producer right from the start. This, along with the recently launched Australian Interactive Multimedia Association (AIMIA), has been a boon to existing multimedia producers in this rapidly growing industry; AIMIA has over 300 members, chapters in most states, and holds an annual conference in July. Although the market is currently dominated by U.S.-produced titles, entertainment and education products are coming out from Down Under: notable CD-ROMs include the historical 'expanded book' *Long Time Olden Time*. Hardware and software are readily available, as is information from several excellent technical bookstores, however, good production assistance is less apparent. Journalists at local paper *The Age* are wired up and provide good coverage of the industry in a weekly computer insert. **Sydney**-based Firmware Design offers training courses in Director and other products; their publishing division is one of the few in Australia to have more than one title to their name. Firmware is doing its part to develop a social culture around the industry through a newsletter and professional-level user support club, and one local publisher reports that an active social scene exists for both suits and t-shirts. A few small conferences have been organized by the local multimedia society, however most of this activity has been Sydney-centered. Academics, artists, and interested professionals are creating an online version of the cafe culture found in other cities; participants share information and techniques primarily via email and the Web.

South America

peru

Multimedia courses are taught at the Pontifica Universidad Catolica del Peru in **Lima**, but training and educational materials are expensive and not widely available. One developer reports that multimedia is still generally thought to mean CD-ROMs and not much else. However, interest in the field is growing, and conferences such as 1994's First Andean Multimedia Forum are fostering the public's understanding of the technologies. As in much of South America, presentations, tourism and educational projects are the most prevalent project types in Peru; reference tools on CD-ROM are very popular in the universities. Most of the titles available here are imported, primarily from the U.S., but the number of Peruvian developers is growing. Active local developers include ASIX S.A., specialists in interactive kiosks, Phantasia Multimedia, and EOS. IBM and Apple both have a strong presence here as well.

brazil

Brazil's computer industry is thriving: More than half a million people attend Fenasoft, the annual computer trade show in **Sao Paulo** (believed to be one of the largest shows in the world) where an estimated $2 billion changes hands. Not surprisingly, a significant portion of that interest is directed towards multimedia. IBM has a multimedia studio here, and Apple Computer is ramping up its own offices. Apple currently has a developer program in Sao Paulo, where every six months the local developers can take courses and workshops in such technical areas as learning how to integrate multiple authoring systems. "People have the products," says a third party marketing manager for Apple Latin America. "They just aren't getting the full use out of them and integrating them." She adds that some enterprising Brazilian musicians are using Macs to develop courseware (interactive classroom materials). Corporate training projects are also growing in popularity.

argentina

Multimedia has been eagerly accepted in **Argentina,** a very technologically advanced country and the fastest growing computer market in all of Latin America. Many state-owned industries have been privatized, opening the doors to entrepreneurial and technological innovation. For example, most of the television stations here now use Macintoshes for desktop video editing and effects.

chile

As in Colombia and Brazil, educational titles are the big hit in **Chile**, where the World Bank provided a grant to wire schools for computer networks, allowing students to create and share their own works about art, culture, and history. Although games sell fairly well through South America, most local development efforts are in information-based titles, such as tourist guides. U.S.-produced titles sell well. Softel, the annual computer trade show, attracts more than 60,000 dealers; however training and access to hardware and software is rather limited. Ample opportunities exist for professional trainers in this region. Although many universities are offering courses in digital media production, developers wanting to learn more end up traveling to the U.S. to attend major trade shows.

Africa

zimbabwe & south africa

Multimedia is practically non-existent in **Zimbabwe** — practically. Hampered by the lack of skills and high import duties, this infant industry is growing slowly. A producer in Harare claims that although the traditional media covers technology as best it can, this region (and other small countries) suffers from the "invented here syndrome;" If it's local, it's not as good as the imported stuff. However, local advertising agencies are starting to use desktop systems for special effects, and the University of Zimbabwe has launched its own multimedia program. **South Africa** seems to be building an interesting multimedia business, with nearly a dozen companies making interactive software, and rumor has it several universities in that region are developing multimedia curricula of their own.

5. General Work Issues

The number of opportunities available is both a blessing and a curse. The sheer variety and range of what can be done in multimedia is often daunting.

The process of finding and managing job opportunities includes the following steps:

- *identifying the type of work you are suited for*
- *positioning and marketing yourself*
- *finding available opportunities*
- *approaching companies*
- *qualifying companies*
- *signing a work agreement*
- *working*
- *wrapping a project or job*

Where do you start? How do you make decisions? Should you leave your current job and move to another area? Should you go back to school? Not surprisingly, the answers to these questions are going to be different for each person.

What is needed for creating a career in multimedia is a plan—a plan that takes into account a person's skills, interests, temperament, and the current state of an industry. This plan focuses on both short-term issues such as finding opportunities, and long-term issues such as managing jobs correctly. This section addresses the issues that go into that plan, presented in the form of a process of finding and managing job opportunities.

How to Get into Multimedia

In general, there are four approaches to get into multimedia. The first is to **develop** a multimedia title, a website, or an interactive portfolio on your own or with others with little or no funding. If it's a title and you're lucky, it may get picked up for distribution. If it's a website, it may be seen by others in need of development help. Regardless of the profitability of the project, it will give you knowledge that is hard to get elsewhere and provide you with something to demonstrate to get hired or to get funding for another project.

Another way to get into multimedia is to develop multimedia products as part of your **current job**. A person in marketing could get involved in a project at a traditional company to develop an interactive marketing piece. Starting with something small, refining it, and increasing the sophistication is a common, and safe, approach.

The third way to get into multimedia is to get a job at a **multimedia company**. The hard thing here, though, is to know what type of company to pursue and, then, which company in particular. Working as an assistant or an intern on a single title can get your foot in the door for work on additional titles. Working at a nominal wage as a digital artist, programmer, or tester can give you the portfolio and credits to take to other companies for higher wages.

The fourth way to break into multimedia is to **write about it**, preferably getting paid in the process. Many leaders of companies producing or distributing interactive products got their knowledge and contacts by working as a reporter, analyst, or by writing books or magazine articles. There are many newswires, newsletters, and magazines covering interactive media in part or in total.

Expert vs. Generalist

Many people ask if they should become an expert in one area of multimedia or a generalist in all areas. The answer is that you need to become an expert, period, but that expertise can be tool related or it can be process related. People who are great at programming in Macromedia Lingo or HTML, or who are experts with Adobe Photoshop and Macromedia Director, can walk into almost any production studio and stand a good chance of getting a job immediately, or at least on the next project that gets staffed. Experienced multimedia producers, art directors, and other experts who know the steps in a process and can choreograph others within that process also stand a good chance of finding opportunities, though maybe not as quickly as tool experts.

Identify Your Goals

Consider Your Passions

The first thing to do before you begin a career change or a job search is to look inside yourself and seriously analyze your capabilities and desires. What are your **passions**? Where do you spend your money or your time? What do you like to do at your present job? What don't you like to do? These answers should give you a starting place. Not all people can make a living at what they love to do, but most who do cannot imagine how they could live otherwise. In looking to change careers, why not choose something you love?

Most employers look for people with passion, though some may not be aware that that's what they are looking for. At a recent conference in New York, the new media marketing manager for a large music company stood up and made a request for someone that had a passion for music and a knowledge of interactive media. One without the other would not do. That comment has been echoed many times in different ways by producers, creative directors, art directors—in short, almost anyone who has responsibility for hiring people. In fact, passion and enthusiasm can many times outweigh a lack of specific knowledge.

Once you have an idea of what subject matter and activities really drive you, the more difficult part then becomes finding a way to combine that passion with an opportunity in interactive media. Fortunately, almost every activity has, or is beginning to have, some interactive component. That component can arise in CD-ROM title development, online place activity, custom applications, or other types of development projects. It could be for eventual sale to consumers, for advertising to clients, or for internal operations. Matching a passion with an opportunity requires research on companies in any number of industries.

Karen Burch
Producer, Synapse Technologies

vivid: You said once that Bob Able took a chance on you because it was something that he saw in your eyes and that he looks for certain things and that you do something similar. What is it, then? What do you think it was that he saw in your eyes and what is it that you look for in other people's eyes?

I think it goes back to that drive, that need to do this stuff that we're now calling interactive multimedia. We're certainly defining it better and further than we were two or three years ago even, but I still am not convinced that we know what it is or maybe will ever know what is—at least within our lifetimes.

A young man came in about a month ago and there was something in his voice. I don't think I could put words to it but I invited him in and we sat and looked at some of the products we've done. I watched him and, you know, his heartbeat was racing and his eyes were going. When we were through with it, he said, "I was a structural engineer for a long time and I did it well. I was making a good living but something told me that that is not what I needed to be doing."

vivid: That something that appeals to you, when you're looking to hire someone or work with someone, is it excitement? Is it a sense of courage? Is it a sensitivity or curiosity or energy?

It's all of the above, but I think it has to do with risk-takers. That might conjure up, in some people's minds, the image of the person who goes bungee jumping or parachuting, but I'm talking about life risk-takers. We're in an area that is still defining itself. There are a lot of sacrifices being asked and made to advance this field into what I think we all hope it will be.

vivid: It sounds to me like you're saying to anyone out there who is looking to get into the industry—especially in the context of a job interview—not to be afraid to show their personality, to show themselves, and their energy.

If I wanted to be a doctor, there's a specific path that I would have to follow and certain commitments that I would have to make in order to be a medical doctor. It's really clear-cut and defined. The same goes for a lawyer or a teacher. However, this industry is calling people with very eclectic backgrounds. It doesn't put you at a disadvantage if you've done one thing all of your life or if you're just fresh out of school and you studied fine art....I look for people who have had lots of different kinds of experiences because that says to me, they weren't afraid to change courses.

Consider Your Skills

After assessing passions, assess your **skills**. The two are not necessarily connected. A passion for reading science fiction doesn't necessarily mean that you could write the next Star Trek movie. The skills a person has directly correlate to the activities they are suited for. For example, a person who leaves their desk spotless before leaving at the end of the day might not be suited to a role as an agent or sales person. Though organization skills are an asset to any job, the nature of these two jobs involves dealing with constantly dangling loose ends. A job in sales means hearing "No" many times and leaving messages that do not get returned. This lack of completeness in the job itself, not necessarily in the approach to the job, may not be satisfying for someone whose nature thrives on a sense of closure.

Discovering how your skills relate to activities can be elusive. One producer looks for people with a musical background when she hires programmers. She has found over her ten years in the software industry that many of the best programmers have an affinity for playing music. That may seem a strange connection, but music has a strong connection to mathematics, and mathematics in turn have a strong connection to programming. Theater skills might, at first, seem hard to relate to interactive media, but those who are creating online places and interactive TV programming are searching out people who know what it takes to capture an audience's attention within a dynamic environment.

It may be important to work with others who balance your skills. A producer who puts off preparing budgets or schedules, preferring to focus on bringing the idea, team, and funding together might look to hire an assistant producer that can do the numbers work. A programmer who likes solving interesting problems but often leaves many loose ends might try to get in on projects early to prototype and lay the framework, as opposed to being involved in the completion and testing phases. A word person might look to collaborate with a visual person in order to find innovative ways to communicate ideas.

Thinking Strategically

Since interactive media in some form is likely to touch every industry at some point within the next several years, it is not necessary to change industries to find new opportunities. What it takes is awareness of the companies within an industry that are working with new media. Companies currently involved in interactive projects already have many of the roles and structures in place. Companies that do not will be looking for knowledgeable and enthusiastic people. The people who can fit into these positions are those who can advise upper management and build relationships with key parties. Once a strategic plan is in place, companies then either build structures internally or rely on external sources.

I've found that the most effective way to get a job is to seem focused in the eyes of an employer. The way that you seem focused is to use your own motivations. Look inside yourself and ask yourself what am I really good at? What products do I really like? Once you understand why you like them, use that motivation to list specific companies you would want to approach. Get a list of all the relevant companies creating products in the area you're interested in and then, literally, approach these most-favored companies.

—Sean Lord, Recruiter, Interactive Development

Choose Projects Carefully

I think [making it in multimedia] will turn out to be the same way that it's turned out to be in the film industry—you look for projects that meet your expertise. You have to be willing to work either for free, or below market, and believe that many projects can use any expertise that anybody can bring to them. You have to choose those well, believe in, and have a passion for the project. You have to build a resume and take the forces you have to network.

The growth path will turn out to be exactly the same thing, which is, you work on other people's projects and build credibility. Eventually, if you're good enough, have creative ideas, and you've networked enough visibility and marketability for yourself then you can probably find anything. I can't tell you how many times I saw that over the years I was in the entertainment industry.

—Nina Zolt, former Los Angeles Attorney, former Manager at Kaleida Labs

People interested in these opportunities can find and get these jobs if then have knowledge of interactive media, if they position themselves correctly, if they do the research, and if they take the chance.

While many areas in interactive media are wide open, people who do the hiring still look for basic skill sets and then map them to a particular role in their company or on their project. A mistake many people make is to try to change both industry and role. For example, a programmer in the software industry who wants to move into video production on interactive projects might have a better chance of reaching that goal by making three moves spaced over time instead of making one all at once. They might consider first programming on a multimedia project and then after a few projects transitioning into video editing, and then finally into the video producer role. Though a single move should not be discouraged, a **slower transition planned over time** might ease the headaches and the sacrifices involved in the change. (Finding a job as a video producer without prior experience or credits often means working for very little money and on risky projects.)

Another example is trying to move from customer support at a hardware company into marketing in multimedia. Aside from the fact that finding a marketing job is difficult without first focusing on a specific area of marketing (such as product acquisitions, public relations, distribution channel coordinator), there are hundreds of people with marketing backgrounds and experience competing for these jobs. An alternative strategy is to recognize that **customer support** ▶ 274 is a potentially huge area of opportunity in multimedia. Sending a letter and a resume that shows passion for a company's products and knowledge of the customer support process will get more phone calls returned than any number of faxes, letters, or calls with the stated goal of "finding a job in marketing at a multimedia company."

Also, intelligently combining interests and skills and strategically approaching well-qualified companies can be more valuable than sending out hundreds of letters or meeting tons of people. For example, Adam Curry, formerly an MTV video jock who started MTV's Internet presence under his own initiative, has parlayed his knowledge of music and his net experience into building and managing an Internet domain for BMI, a music performing rights organization that represents 150,000 songwriters, composers, and publishers.

Improving Your Skills

Refining current skills and developing new ones are great ways to position yourself for new opportunities within multimedia. There are a number of schools that provide training in interactive areas. These include university extension programs, art school programs, and film and video study programs. Also, a number of conferences are beginning to add week-long seminars for learning digital tools and techniques. A good thing about these programs is that they usually feature the latest tools and technologies and, often times, offer hands-on training.

These programs are good not only for developing skills but also for finding jobs. A number of the instructors work at companies in interactive industries and can provide numerous leads and recommendations. When selecting a course, make your decision based as much on the teaching ability of the instructor as on the subject matter.

The other day I was speaking to a girlfriend of mine who works in "interactive" and is looking to relocate. She asked me how to begin the process of selecting a new city and company. I told her to get out a map and pick a place where you want to live. Then find a corporation within those city limits, and position yourself as their interactive expert. There are headquarters for retailing, publishing, and media companies all over the world. In these evolving times, you can find a group where you can walk in and say, "I can take your existing assets and move them into the digital world. Hire me as your technical evangelist or new media guru." So that's basically what she's going to do. She's a big windsurfer and she's interested in Portland so she's writing a letter to Nike right now.

—Lisa Brown, Director, Offer Development, Interactive Services Downtown Digital/AT&T

79

Positioning and Marketing Yourself

Positioning refers to the strategy a person or company uses to frame what others think about them. **Marketing** refers to the process of implementating and verifying that strategy. Most people view positioning and marketing as being important only to companies, but everybody in the workplace, regardless of experience or occupation, needs to position themselves and market themselves effectively. The difference between doing these two things and not doing them cannot always be seen by the outcome of one deal. It can, however, be seen over the course of several deals or a career by the way people hear about you, by what they already know about you, and by how often they call with opportunities within the scope of what you do.

Positioning Yourself

The way you position yourself should reflect your passions and skills as well as match those of your potential clients or employers. You do not want to position yourself for something you have neither the skills nor the desire to do. At the same time, you need to position yourself in such a way that potential employers are attracted and impressed.

One of the most common problems that new people have when they try to get a position on a multimedia development team is that they position themselves too broadly. For example, a lot of people call production studios or developers and say they can and are willing to do almost anything. A better approach is to narrow the role down to something that fits your skills and is specifically needed on a production team.

Almost every producer would love to have someone handle the day-to-day routine of tracking people's progress and continually updating the budget and schedule to reflect the progress.

Many producers often do not make the effort to find someone for these tasks, either because they soon become overwhelmed or they have trouble finding someone that is capable of this job. Someone who specifically asks for this type of role stands a much better chance than does someone who simply says that they want to get into multimedia. By narrowing the focus of what you are looking for, you let the other person better visualize how you can fit into the production team. Ultimately, you increase your chances of getting a job.

Positioning yourself properly means plotting your strengths and weaknesses and your competitor's strengths and weaknesses against the significant trends in your particular environment. These trends can include social, technological, legal, political, or economic issues. This exercise will help you find ways to differentiate yourself from others and play upon your strengths.

Ideally, everybody should be trying to position themselves as an **expert** and as a professional. Even those who do not have specific experience with interactive projects or digital tools can position themselves as an expert within the realm of their current skills. It is, therefore, not necessary to take a subpar wage in order to break into an area of multimedia. For example, someone who has written children's books and who has explored thoroughly the current children's offerings can position themselves as an expert in children's storybooks. Working with an interaction designer, this person can function very well on an interactive project.

Positioning yourself not only means coming up with the roles you are capable of performing, it can also mean positioning yourself with regard to a **platform** ▶ 12 or a **project** ▶ 18 type. A person that presents themselves as a multimedia producer may not be nearly as effective as someone who positions themself as a multimedia game producer or multimedia producer specializing in

Demo Reel
Kathleen Egge
(415)978-2643

reference products. Although the first title may cover the other two, the other two specifically call out to employers looking to produce games or reference products. Any type of positioning needs continuous attention, however. Focusing yourself too narrowly or too rigidly can mean concentrating on a limited set of opportunities or on trends that have quickly become outdated.

Marketing Yourself

The marketing process and materials used in multimedia are no different from those in other industries such as the film, music, book, software, and advertising industries. The main difference is that there are no established standards for representing and describing your work. These materials include resumes, credit lists, portfolios, demo tapes, and demo reels. What they look like and how they are used will largely depend on what your positioning is and the people or companies you are approaching.

The primary purpose of marketing materials is to get you to a **personal contact**, which is an interview or some other form of personal interaction with someone who has hiring authority. There are some recognized guidelines for how things should look and what they should have in them, but within that framework there is a lot of freedom. For example, a voice tape should be no more than 2 to $2^1/_2$ minutes but the material on that tape can vary according to the industry and types of work it is targeting. A resume should list common elements such as work history and education but the layout and organization are subject to personal preferences.

Spending a lot of time and money is not a requirement for effectively marketing yourself. Your materials need to reflect your current positioning but recognize that these will change over time as your positioning changes and as you find out what does and does not work. Just as a company must evolve their products or services as the market dictates, you should evolve your marketing materials according to the ways that others respond to them.

Resumes

In many areas of multimedia and for many roles, a **resume** is very valuable. The roles for which it is less important are design-oriented roles and free-lance opportunities. People looking to hire someone full-time will likely be interested in seeing some form of traditional resume. This, along with a cover letter, will help a potential employer decide whether or not to agree to an interview. Few people make a hiring decision based solely on a resume. They use it to filter the many applicants down to just the most suitable ones.

The importance of a resume varies. For some roles such as scriptwriting, animation, and sound production, a credit list or demo tape carries much more weight. Producers hiring creative talent are more interested in the type of work a person has done in the past with regard to multimedia. An interactive writing credit on a successful game is going to be more convincing and relevant than a resume containing a list of unrelated jobs and mention of a liberal arts education.

Experience is not what it used to be. Compared to intelligence, ethics, communication skills, and team spirit, experience is a shallow measure. Basing hiring and promotion decisions on experience can be as dangerous to a business as using age, sex, religion, race, politics, national origin, or disability.

Traditional approaches to candidate evaluation should be expanded to reveal deep thoughts, like personal philosophy. People who believe in something and can explain it to someone else are generally worth having.

—Dennis Coleman, Technology Marketing Center, in "Who Needs Experience?" Upside, February 1995

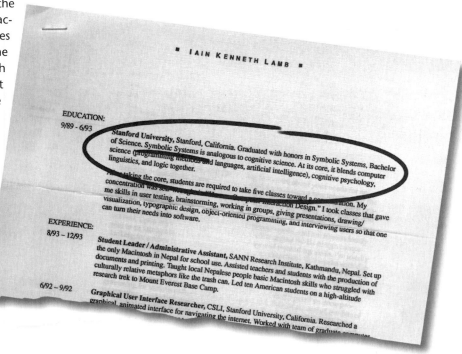

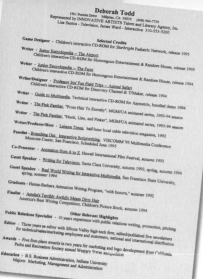

*Resumes and credit lists are two sides of the same coin. In a **resume**, the prominence is often given to **companies** whereas in a **credit list**, it is given to **projects**. The role and the industry often determines which has more relevance in a hiring decision.*

*A recent trend is the development of personal **webpages** ▶ 15. Many companies are encouraging or allowing their employees and contractors to create webpages specifically for themselves and placing them in the company website. Some universities and conferences are also beginning to include webpages for faculty or speakers. A few savvy freelancers are beginning to develop their own websites to list their biographical information and their capabilities.*

People that hire in multimedia look at resumes in order to understand a person's *experiences*. This is not the same as looking to see a person's *experience*. In most industries, a resume gives a prospective employer an idea of how experienced someone is for a job, using the common assumption that experience is the defining factor in someone's ability. In the interactive market, experience does not matter as much as experiences since there are so few people with experience anyway. These experiences can include paying jobs, non-paying jobs, jobs in school, jobs on the side, formal education, informal education, clubs, classes, membership in organizations, hobbies, and many others.

Not many people have experience at producing, creating, developing, or distributing interactive products. And even if they do, it is likely to be within one small area of a continually developing larger domain. In talks with many producers and others in the field, a frequent comment is that they want to see lots of different things. They want a resume that shows diversity, versatility, and an ability to adapt.

The form, content, and layout of your resume are up to you. Everyone has their preference and there are no set standards. These decisions depend on the person who will read the resume, the industry and companies you are approaching, and the role you are looking for. A resume for a marketing person will be much different than a programmer's resume. The marketing person's should show extra care in structure and layout. It should be well designed and well written. A programmer's resume, however, does not need a fancy layout, icons, or other design elements. It needs a list of platforms and languages and some indication of how good a programmer they are. Ultimately, a resume should reflect you, as if it is an extension of you.

Credit Lists

A **credit list** ▶ 190 is a list of projects that a person has been a part of and the roles they have played. Its popularity is much bigger in industries where there are discrete projects, definable roles, and highly visible products. In Hollywood, a credit on a successful film largely dictates a person's earnings for the next three years. A credit is a big deal and the standard contracts for the Screen Actors Guild, the Writers Guild of America, and other guilds specify the appearance and placement of credit. Actors, directors, producers, and other talent considered "above the line" have their placement in the product, in advertisements, promotional material, and packaging determined by their standing in the industry (and by the negotiating skills of their agent).

A credit list should primarily reflect acknowledged credits (projects where there is documentation that a person played a relevant role). Projects that have been written or produced but never published or distributed can be included but should not be given the same prominence as the others. Producers, art directors, visual designers, programmers, sound producers—in short, anyone playing a significant role on discrete projects should maintain and make use of a credit list. Currently, the practice is largely confined to people with a film or music background as well as many creative professionals. This practice, however, is starting to carry over to programmers and other technical people and is likely to continue.

Portfolios

Every art director, visual designer, and media professional should have a print or electronic **portfolio** of past work to bring to interviews or send ahead of time. People in these positions must be able to show high-quality examples of related work in multiple media and in a variety of formats. They should prepare presentations of their work in at least print form and possibly video and interactive forms as well. Also, different companies may have different capabilities to preview interactive work. Some have expensive, high-end presentation or demo machines in both Windows and Macintosh formats, while others may have poorly maintained systems with low memory requirements or more obscure platforms that you may not have prepared for (CD-i, Sega, and others). Be prepared to demonstrate your work in as many different ways as possible. Call ahead to find out the type of equipment available and bring as much with you as is convenient. For example, when bringing a hard drive, bring all the necessary cables and adaptors.

An important part of showing a portfolio is explaining all the issues and constraints within each project. An amazing 4-bit graphic (16 colors) may not appear so great if the other party is looking at it from a 16-bit perspective (thousands of colors). Patiently explain what the client wanted, what the goals of the project were, and the process you used to get to each result.

Demo Tapes and Demo Reels

A **demo tape** ▶ 228 is an audio cassette containing audio samples that represents a sound professional's work. The audio samples can be musical scores, voice tracks, sound effects, background sound, or any other form of sound. Tapes should be clearly labelled on the case and the cassette itself. They are commonly handed to producers, sound producers, and/or art directors to demonstrate the capabilities of a musician, sound producer, voice actor, or other sound professional.

A **demo reel** is similar in concept but it contains animation or video samples (often with accompanying audio) as opposed to stand-alone audio samples. Demo reels are prepared by animation or video professionals and handed to producers, video producers, and art directors for conveying the type of work that a person can perform.

Due to the constant decrease in the expense of making audio CDs and CD-ROMs, it is increasingly possible to use these media for holding portfolios and audio and video samples. One advantage is their random access structure that lets viewers navigate the contents at will. Also, they show a certain familiarity with the current media and technology. An animator, video producer, or video editor, especially, can show their talents at making material look good and run well on a CD-ROM. Another advantage is that this media may be more convenient for some people to preview. Some producers and art directors may have better access to CD players and computers than they do cassette players or VCRs (at least in the workplace). At the same time, CD-ROMs may be a disadvantage since many sound and video producers may still wish to see traditional media forms. This is especially true in the film industry.

The purpose of a demo tape or reel is to showcase your capabilities. Ideally, the work on the tape or reel should demonstrate some variety but it should always contain only your best material. They should be short and dense. **Voice artists** ▶ 230 recommend keeping demo tapes to under 2 minutes in length. Demo reels can be longer but they should move quickly from example to example.

There is more to handing out demo tapes and demo reels than just dropping them by a studio or sending them to a multimedia producer. These materials need to get to the right people with the right positioning in order to be effective. Sound, animation, or video professionals need to find out which companies need sound or video work, what kind of material they are looking for, and what time frames they are working under. Because of the technical constraints, sound work for a video game cassette, no matter how good musically and technically, is not going to impress an art director for a CD-ROM featuring the greatest golf courses in the world. Likewise, a demo tape containing tracks of music to kill aliens by might not go over too well with a sound producer working on a preschool title. Just like all marketing materials, demo tapes and reels need to be placed in context for them to be effective.

Business Cards

A set of **business cards** is a must for anyone that contracts or consults. There are as many schools on the look and format of business cards as there are opinions on the economy. They can be simple or they can be elaborate. Some people suggest business names even for companies of one. Most suggest some sort of title or tag line, though they debate on the generic versus the highly specific. For example, should it be "programmer" or should it be "HTML programmer"? A point few debate is that the card should contain as many forms of contact as possible because its main purpose is to provide potential employers or clients with the means to get in touch with

The main problem with unsolicited video tapes is that they take up too much space in the trash can. I prefer to get unsolicited audio cassettes because they make this really pleasant sound when they hit the video tapes in there.

—anonymous entertainment agent

All email addresses should be listed in collateral materials in forms that are recognizable and accessible to everyone. This sometimes means including two formats, the native format and the Internet format.

you. Cards should contain any address, phone, fax, and email address (or set of email addresses) you are reachable at.

While the appearance of a business card can help with the initial impression someone has of you, it is not going to be that significant in terms of a final decision. In general, create marketing materials that are reflective of you and that fit your time frame and budget.

Email

Anybody who wants to communicate effectively with people in interactive industries needs access to **email** ▶ 29. This is especially true for those who do not work on site. The written dialog helps make correspondence more clear and more effi-

cient than leaving voice mail messages or faxing requests. These forms of communication are still important because it can take longer to type and send (or receive) a message than it does to pick up the phone and call or fax. Most mail programs also let senders enclose documents. This feature lets you and others exchange files and work in progress and can be very important when working on a project.

One of the issues with email is the use of personal email addresses versus company addresses. The current legal thinking is that email accounts administered by an employer belong to the employer. As a result, the contents of an email account can be searched and used as evidence against an employee. Also, many employers have

Four Ways to Get an Email Account

Getting an email account means contacting a service provider, opening an account, and then receiving and installing the necessary software for sending and receiving messages. Below are several common ways of proceeding.

1 Commercial Online Services
For most people, the easiest way to get an email address is to sign up with one of the larger online systems such as America Online, CompuServe, or Delphi. The prices for these and the installation and use are straightforward. Most of these services offer more than just email, including conferences, chat, and many third-party content areas.

2 Local Online Services
Another way to get email is to join many of the smaller regional online services such as The WELL in San Francisco, the Vine in Los Angeles, or ECHO in New York. While these services have fewer content areas than larger online services, they do have active conferences and bulletin boards, with many postings relevant to local work issues.

3 Local Service Providers
For low-cost no-frills email service, the best choice might be to use a local service provider. These will differ from city to city much like the service providers in the early days of the cellular phone industry. Netcom, however, is one of the more common services and has offices nationwide.

4 Setting up Your Own Domain
One of the best ways for companies or individuals who wish to establish their own identity on line is to set up their own Internet domain. A domain is a specific place on the Internet. It has a unique name that is registered with a private Internet agency. For example, vivid.com is the domain name for vivid studios. Having your own domain usually means having a computer on-site dedicated to maintaining it.

policies against the private use of email accounts, though few bother to enforce them. These issues may justify obtaining a personal email address.

An argument for using a personal email account as a primary point of contact is to continue relationships beyond a stay at a particular company (salespeople take note). Email addresses have a permanence that few people's residential or business addresses can ever hope to achieve. A personal email address can, therefore, last longer than that person's duration at a company. Email addresses also let you foster and maintain a permanent independent identity. Continually using an email address and propagating it through email messages and bulletin board postings helps position you as an individual as opposed to an employee of a company. The greater the presence you have outside your company, the greater your value in the marketplace. A consistent and recognizable email address can help foster this visibility.

Speaking, Teaching, and Writing Engagements

Companies are not the only ones who should market themselves within an industry's infrastructure. As an individual, you will benefit tremendously by positioning yourself within a specific role and then actively seeking opportunities to leverage that positioning into publicity and name recognition. A big part of this type of marketing can include **speaking** at seminars, **teaching** at educational institutions, and **writing** articles for magazines and newsletters. It can take a long time to develop the necessary credibility and visibility to do this (unless, of course, a product or service you are involved in becomes an overnight success). But fortunately, once this type of exposure starts, it tends to grow by itself. One speaking engagement can lead to others, which can lead to an article in a newsletter, which can lead to an article in a magazine.

These opportunities, however, rarely land in someone's lap. A large part of being able to join panels at **conferences** ▶ 291, teach courses, and write articles involves actively soliciting these opportunities. It means preparing biographical materials and outlines and sending them to editors and coordinators of conferences and teaching programs—in short, it takes the same type of process for finding a job that is described in this chapter.

[newspaper clipping]

...ng. Collectively ...cts appear on maga-...oards, films, on ...-ROM multimedia ...p will demonstrate a ...g software such as ...p, Fractal Design ...ive Picture.

...director for Adobe Systems and ...shop, Adobe's powerfully versatile ...t imaging workshops through...

...t photographer and graphi... ...le, Adobe, and Leaf System... ...blished as posters, calendars, ...er, Omni, Audubon, Sierra, and

...ait photographer whose work ...ated, and New York Magazine. ...ransformed his celebrity portraits ...l by HarperCollins. ...computer artist and interface ...work on Star Trek, the Movie. He ...of HSC Software which distributes ...ary imaging software, Live Picture. ...grapher and the art director of ...he effects of high technology on

SESSION 302

...ending the ...gn Food Chain

Clement Mok
CMd

Claire Barry
CMd

Michael Patrick Cronan
Cronan Design

...lia world, conven... ...studios and jobs ...ns have been...

dio. At SuperMac she created "VideoSpigot Interactive," the first CD-ROM to include QuickTime movies. For other clients she has created multimedia projects ranging from corporate training kiosks to rich interactive music CD-ROMs.
Michael Patrick Cronan is the president and principal designer of Cronan Design, a multi-disciplined firm whose work includes image development, corporate communications, print graphics, and exhibits. He is on the board of the American Institute of Graphic Arts (AIGA).

THURSDAY 11:30 AM–1:30 PM SESSION 3

**Multimedia Demystified Part 1:
A Creative Guide for Beginners**

Jeff Burge...
The Desktop Mult... ...ible

Stephen Johnson
Photographer

Jim Lanahan
Multimedia Producer

Stewart McBride
United Digital Artists

Nathan Shedroff
vivid

This workshop is designed for creative professionals—photographers, designers, videographers, and other visual thinkers—interested in the profound impact of multimedia and interactive technology on their professions. Panelists will decipher industry "buzz words," survey the latest multimedia tools and techniques, then sketch each of the necessary steps in the process of creating interactive multimedia—from initial concept, team selection and storyboards, to design, production, and packaging. The workshop will consider graphic design, authoring tools, development of visuals (pho-

THURSDAY 11:30 AM–1:30...

In Your interFace,
The Design Profess...
90s: Designing Info...
Screens and Intera...

Living B...

This workshop con... design challenge of r... tive experience as ric... presenting informatio... fashion. Good interfa... a delicate balance betw... communication needs,... the information, and c... communicate. The u... help users navigate th... relevant to them. Inter... out screens, create icon... paths, choose fonts,... Finally they must als... their work will appear... kiosk, a computer, or o... **Steve Gano** manages the Media... Inc. which is developing guidelines an... cross-platform multimedia description... the lead designer at Apple Computer's... **Kai Krause** see Session 301 for... **Brenda Laurel** is the editor of... Interface Design" and currently a rese... Company. She previously worked as... Systems, and co-founded Telepresenc... development of virtual reality syste...

85

Finding Opportunities

Keeping Current

Professional bicycle racers know they need to drink water before they become thirsty. If they wait until they're thirsty, they have compromised some of their performance. The same holds true in looking for new job opportunities. Regardless of whether you are a contractor or an employee, if you wait until you need (or want) new work, it may be too late. This guideline does not mean you need to be actively searching for a job when you are working, but it suggests that you should always be positioning yourself so that you are in a better situation if and when the time comes.

Being prepared means keeping track of trends and important companies and individuals. It means finding trusted sources (friends in the business, favorite columnists, a set of periodicals, or online areas) and then establishing a routine that makes it easy to monitor these sources. Saving articles and keeping an eye out for new resources (like this book) is also a part of the preparation process. **Casual research** completed over time greatly increases your productivity once an active search begins. It lets you filter information better and make quicker decisions on what is or is not important.

Another step in keeping abreast of changes involves **socializing with people in the business**. While people often refer to this process as "networking," many that use this term tend to do so with a mercenary connotation. This connotation, however, is not how it should be approached. In almost every industry, relationships are ultimately the deciding factor in decisions. Most producers are reluctant to hire art directors, technical leads, sound producers, or others with significant responsibilities on a project without first knowing that person. In the film industry, getting a script in front of someone is based on a relationship. In the book industry, it is much the same. Multimedia is no different. In many areas of multimedia—and especially in San Francisco—the talent community is so close that little passes by without others quickly noting it. For example, the Director programming community will probably hear about the status of a project faster and in more detail than the board of the company doing the project ever will.

The purposes for building relationships with people include direct business opportunities, indirect business opportunities, and using people as sounding boards for advice. **Direct business**

Relationships are everything. As soon as you treat people as commodities, they dissolve into nothing. Look to meet interesting people that you get along with and forget about meeting "important" people. This is particularly important at industry events where people tend to get hyped up and out of control. Put the person first and any opportunities second. You'll be am-azed at how your effectiveness grows and your stack of business cards shrinks.

—J. Sterling Hutto, General Manager of Technology and Solutions, Electric Classifieds

New Jobs for New Media

People are hoping that multimedia is going to be the next wave of employment and that if you are trained in these skills, you will have a job. I'm not saying that there won't be multimedia jobs available, but it's just that the tenor of their search, of their quest, is intense. You know, multimedia is not God.

But with that said, the SFSU Multimedia Studies Program has a student advisor who assists our students with choosing classes and locating jobs. We have a BBS with job listings on it. We still have it in the old-fashioned paper format, too, for those people who don't have the technology at home. Anecdotally, our self-forming alumni groups report that 40 to 50 percent of their membership are getting jobs after taking classes here. Now, part of this is that they're learning the tools and another part is that this place is an incredible place to network.

—Pamela Lovell, Acting Director, San Francisco State University Multimedia Extension

usually refers to employment (where you hire them or they hire you). **Indirect opportunities** might include sharing information or resources. The information could be about a job lead, a new division opening up at a company, a new hire, or any other type of news that might be of use. A **sounding board** is useful when you need someone to listen to your thoughts and advise you well. Other career books refer to finding a "mentor" although this may be too formal a term for an area that thrives on its informality. Having someone to talk to and confide in is as important in work situations as in personal life.

Searching for Opportunities

Looking for work and positioning yourself for new opportunities often go hand in hand. You have to know what opportunities are available to best position yourself for them. At the same time, you must somehow indicate to others where you fit in an industry (your interests, skills, roles, and experience) in order to hear about many of the opportunities.

Some people can have opportunities fall easily into their hands, but for most it will take hard, coordinated work to find them. There are passive and active ways of searching. **Passively searching** means looking for information posted by others. It can bring forward opportunities from far and wide that might never have been found by actively searching for them. On the other hand, **actively searching** means announcing to friends and acquaintances that you are looking for work and calling companies to ask if there are available opportunities. It can be far more precise because it is in response to information you are posting.

Most people think of looking in newspaper classified ads when they think about looking for job opportunities. For interactive media and for most other industries, newspaper classified ads are, in fact, one of the least qualified sources for finding good opportunities. The majority of multimedia companies are increasingly turning to **online areas** ▶ 15, 61 to announce job openings. There are many local as well as national forums for placing job ads online. Many of these services have only recently become available and there will likely be many more in the future. There will

Four Ways to Do Research Online

1 Search and Post Questions in Bulletin Boards
USENET newsgroups (on the Internet) and private bulletin boards (local BBSs, content-specific BBSs, and others) are widely read and can be a great source of information. Find a group related to your topic of inquiry (e.g., if you're researching television programming, look for groups like rec.arts.tv). Be sure to read the board before posting to make sure that it contains the kind of discussions you're looking for.

2 Surf the Web
Surfing the Web is a fairly randomized approach, but it can often be successful. If you don't know of a site in your interest area, go to a site that has a search engine for finding appropriate sites, such as Yahoo (http://akebono.stanford.edu/yahoo) or O'Reilly's Whole Internet Catalog (http://gnn.com) and start surfing. You may not find exactly what you want at first, however you may discover other useful information you hadn't even thought of.

3 Dig into a Gopher Server
Gopher is a menu-based tool for browsing through resources on the Internet. With gopher, you don't need to worry about domain names or paths—you simply connect to a gopher server and start looking around. To run gopher, either telnet to consultant.micro.umn.edu or gopher.uiuc.edu and at the prompt, type "gopher" or use a utility like TurboGopher to connect to a nearby gopher site. You'll receive a menu of choices and can search from there.

4 Dial in to a Commercial Online Service
America Online, CompuServe, and other commercial online services offer access to searchable databases and specialized places, such as Associated Press (CompuServe), Reuter's News Service (AOL), Dow Jones News (CompuServe), @Times (New York Times daily edition on AOL), Morningstar Mutual Funds (AOL), and Sabre travel information (CompuServe), to name only a few. In addition, these online services have their own discussion areas (sometimes called forums or chats) arranged by topic, in which you can ask questions and respond to other members.

probably be a lot of change and consolidation as some become more popular for people both advertising jobs and those looking for them.

Meetings of multimedia-related organizations are other good places to learn about job openings. Many companies that have immediate needs send someone to these meetings to make an announcement. The more closely an organization is tied to a discipline (such as design) or a technology (such as parallel-processing), the more likely these announcements will be valuable.

Finding and signing with an agent follows the same process outlined on these pages.

The keys to a successful job hunt in multimedia are looking at multiple sources, being flexible, and listening to what people are saying so you develop the best possible skill base, maybe not today but maybe in a year's time.

—Sean Lord,
Recruiter, Interactive
Development

It's amazing to go to meetings like the IICS or the Macromedia Users Group and see people stand up and say, "We want twelve programmers. We want twelve graphic artists. We need 3D modelers. We need people." This is a real opportunity for people with ambition who have a sense of commitment and some basic talent. How long will this window last? I don't know, but I suspect it won't be over in a while because there's so much going on.

—Dana Atchley,
Interactive Storyteller
and Performer

One of the first steps in any active search should be let to your **friends** and **acquaintances** know that you are looking for work. This cannot be done haphazardly, however. It must be done in a focused manner. Your friends and acquaintances should know what you are looking for and what they should tell others about you. Do not expect others to pass out resumes and actively promote you for a job. No one will be more motivated about getting you a job than you. You should expect to do much of the work on your own.

Another part of actively searching for a job is knowing the companies that are performing work within an area of multimedia that interests you. There is so much going on within interactive media that it can easily become overwhelming to try to stay continually informed. It is better to focus on a particular area that fits your interests and your skills. Within that area, find out the types of companies within the total industry infrastructure. Not all companies are creating products. There are an equal or greater number of companies supporting the development of products. These companies include talent agencies, law firms, publishers, distributors, financial institutions, magazines and newspapers, and many others. Finding out the role a company plays will let you know what types of skills they need. For example, trying to get a programmer's job at a publisher that does not have any in-house development is largely a waste of time—unless you can get the names of their outside developers. Trying to get a job in customer support at the same company, however, may not be so frivolous.

When looking for information on companies, try to find out more than just what they do and where they fit. Find out how they are structured, who they have done work for, and, most importantly, who the right people are to contact for information or for a job inquiry. For designers, these people might be the creative director and the art director. For composers, it might be the sound producer. For a sound producer, it might be the producer and so on.

There are a number of ways to get information about a company. There are written **directories**, online directories, newspaper and magazine articles, and the company's own marketing materials. Most companies will have brochures, catalogs of their products, and descriptions of their services. Many have also put webpages on the Internet that can be a single source of information about a company, its products, and its people. **Trade shows** can be another good way to find out what companies are doing. A morning or afternoon spent walking around looking at products and picking up materials can present as clear a picture of an area within multimedia as three or four months worth of reading magazines on the topic.

The hardest part of using directories to find and research companies is that they quickly become out-dated in a rapidly growing industry. For example, the tremendous growth of the popularity of the Web in late 1994 spawned the creation of hundreds of web developers almost overnight. Trying to get a directory of these companies would be impossible. Nobody can react this fast. Directories can be of use at times though, and when combined with other sources, they can be a powerful tool in finding available opportunities. Online sources tend to be more current, but recognize that any source, online or printed, can be out of date or inaccurate.

"I wish I had known. I would have put you in touch with people."

Approaching Companies

There are two ways that people commonly approach multimedia companies in terms of job opportunities. The first is in direct response to a job opening and is relatively self-explanatory. The second is based on beginning a relationship that might turn into something later. Timing is a big part of getting multimedia jobs. The second approach lets production studios and talent look for each other before they have an immediate need. This scenario is common for people that have exceptional and/or specialized skills. It also fits into the needs of production studios that have a number of projects in various stages of development and will need immediate staffing if they are funded.

Contacting

The goal of approaching a company is usually to obtain an **interview** with someone that has hiring authority for the type of role you are looking for. Needless to say, it is best not to go through the human resources department at a company. (Fortunately, not a lot of companies in multimedia have human resources departments.) The hiring authority on a development team usually rests in the hands of someone that manages others, namely the executive producer, producer, creative director, art director, technical lead, sound producer, video producer, or test manager. The final authority may rest with one person, typically the producer, but one or two others may have a role in making the decision.

When researching a company, find out who the people are that have **hiring influence or authority**. For immediate positions, a contact person is usually listed on the job posting. For an informal interview, the person who is best able to judge your skills may be the most appropriate person to contact. For example, a visual designer might want to approach the creative director or an art director. Play off the natural affinity that people have for those who do similar things. Targeting someone too high up can result in meeting with a person who has little time or interest. Targeting someone too low can mean meeting with a person that has little influence.

Calling, writing, faxing, or emailing is dependent, again, on whether it is in response to a posted job opening or not. For a **posted job opening**, there is probably a method of contact suggested. If not, call and ask what their preference is. For an **informal interview**, calling, writing, or emailing are all appropriate where you know the person or have a reference from someone that knows them. In cases in which you have no connection to the person (a blind lead), an initial call probably has less chance of being successful than a well-written letter or email message followed by a phone call.

When contacting someone for a posted job opening, ask what materials they would like to see and in what form. Follow their instructions closely and provide them with the materials as quickly and as professionally as possible. A resume and/or credit list is usually standard. Samples of writing, artwork, audio and video work, or code development may be requested. Preferably, these samples should be theirs to keep (although the person hiring may not look at the materials again). If the materials must be returned (as with a portfolio), make it as easy and convenient as possible.

When contacting someone to see if they have any job openings, it can sometimes be beneficial to do so indirectly. Asking them, "Do you have any job openings?" is likely to receive a "No" answer as a reflex action. Asking if they know of any companies that may be hiring people with your skills, however, does not necessarily put them on the spot. They may be more likely to think about where and when you might be able to fit into their company or they may provide leads to several other companies. Approaching the topic of job openings indirectly also gets around embarrassing situations such as calling people that do not have hiring authority or where your skills or interest do not match those of the company you are contacting.

"I asked for his resume and he gave me his URL..."

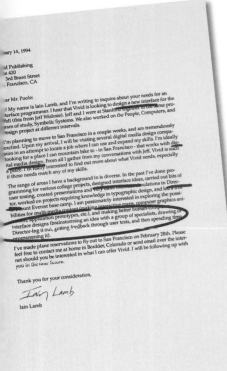

Job Description

For posted job openings, see if a **job description** has been prepared. Hopefully there is one in writing. If not, ask that one be prepared. A job description is important for any role, but especially for those with significant responsibilities to them.

The job description is important not only for understanding at the outset what the job entails but also, after accepting the position, to make sure that the job turns out to be what it was supposed to be. Having something in writing can put you in a better negotiating position should there be problems with the position or the company.

Interviews

Interviewing for a job is an art in itself. There are numerous books on the topic that will do it more justice than these few paragraphs here. Nevertheless, a few simple guidelines are worth mentioning—especially considering how many times they are disregarded.

The foremost rule is to **be prepared**. Know what the company does and the relationships they have with other companies. No one likes to interview someone not deeply interested in their company. Also, have the **necessary materials** to demonstrate your capabilities. These materials can include additional copies of your resume and credit list, a paper or electronic portfolio, demo tapes or reels, and work samples. If there is an electronic portfolio, make sure that you or they have the equipment necessary to view it. Keep the materials simple and well packaged.

Keep in mind that you are interviewing the company as much as they are interviewing you. While you are trying to impress upon them your capabilities, take the time to judge the people, the project, and the company to see if they meet your expectations. There are lots of opportunities available, and when you consider how much time you might spend on a project or with a company, it pays to make the right choice.

Pay particular attention to the people on a project or in a company. The success of a project is directly related to the skills of the team. Also, your enjoyment of working on the project is related to how you get along with others on the team. Success and enjoyment are independent, unfortunately. One can happen without the other just as easily as they can happen together.

Plan the direction you want the interview to go, but react to the signals from the interviewer. **Adapt** what you are saying to how it is being received. Listen to what they are asking and provide them with the information they need. In multimedia, there are so many new people in positions of responsibility that many are not familiar with interviewing others. If this is the case, consider leading the interviewer gently to the areas you wish to cover. Some interviewers may try to put you in awkward positions by asking you unusual questions or asking you to solve difficult problems. Play to your strengths, but above all command respect.

Non-Disclosure Agreements

Many companies will ask you to sign **non-disclosure agreements** ▶ 130, 135 before sharing confidential information. Most agreements are straight-forward with their primary intent being to insure that you do not share with others what is not public knowledge. Non-disclosure agreements should ideally be mutual, meaning that both sides are bound from disclosing confidential information provided by the other party. Most are innocuous but beware of agreements that are longer than a page, have language in them that you do not understand, or ask for guarantees against **copyright infringement** ▶ 102.

Avoid saying anything negative about any product, company, or person, especially in initial meetings. It not only reflects poorly on you, but in an area with so many different types of connections, there is a good chance the other person may be on good terms with some of the people you are talking about.

A good job description contains the following:

- *a list of duties, responsibilities, and possible deliverables*
- *what the expectations and/or requirements are for the position (such as good telephone skills, expert HTML programming skills, or the ability to handle many projects at once)*
- *who the person reports to*
- *a description of the work environment (such as in a large office, working at home, and work hours)*
- *a framework for priorities (such as completing work on time, meeting several specifications, or satisfying the client)*
- *the tools available for completing the work*

Follow-up

In traditional interviewing circles, following up means writing a letter or email the day of the interview thanking the other party for the chance to speak with them. This gesture should be applied in this area as well. But since much of the work in multimedia is project-related and there are often continual needs as new projects arise at unpredictable times, following up also means staying in touch with the other party throughout the year. Send periodic updates of your credit list, call and see how things are going, make a point to say hello at industry events, send Christmas cards—in short, build a relationship over time.

If You Don't Get the Job

Remember that just because you do not get hired that it does not mean that you are not qualified or that you will not get the next job. In this business, team dynamic is extremely important. Two notes of music can be beautiful independently but they don't always harmonize. Chances are that the person who is interviewing you went through ten interviews to finally make one offer. It is often a matter of timing, numbers, instinct, and luck.

The word "internship" is derived from the Latin root intern, meaning "a cause of great suffering," and ship, meaning a boat. Other words derived from intern include "internment camp," "internal bleeding," and "international terrorism." The word was first used in English to refer to slave galleys, hence internship.

—Jonathan Chait, "Interns of the World Unite!" from The Wall Street Journal, *9 January 1995*

Internships

*An **internship**, in theory, is a non-paying or low-paying position typically offered to students or other aspiring but inexperienced people. Students may or may not receive school credit for their efforts. The expressed intentions of an internship are to offer insight into an industry as well as opportunities to learn and practice relevant skills. An internship can be an excellent way to acquire new skills and/ or refine existing skills within a real-world setting. It can also turn into a job at the company or at a similar company. In some cases, an internship has a specific job description and assignments that are relevant to a professional discipline such as interface or visual design. In others, it might be to cover anything and everything that comes up.*

The term internship is often used as a euphemism for hiring eager, low-priced talent to perform menial tasks for a set period of time (commonly 1–3 months). After that period, the company may decide to hire the intern on a more permanent basis for more professional and higher paying tasks. Tasks at the beginning might include answering phones, photocopying materials, or taking notes at meetings. The advertising industry and book publishing industries have strong traditions of using interns in this manner and some companies in multimedia are following this tradition. To be honest, these opportunities are not necessarily ones to turn down out of hand. Most people in certain industries start in this manner, especially those that do not have experience or training in a certain field or in areas where there is a lot of competition and few opportunities. With hard work and fast learning, menial tasks in multimedia can quickly grow to include prep work such as scanning or minor digital image manipulation or production work helping to develop and manage budgets, schedules, and proposals. Ultimately, internships can lead to valuable skills and full-fledged positions on project teams. However, if you are not finding opportunities to grow, learn, and create, you need to move on to opportunities that allow you to do so.

Any person considering an internship should first of all find out if the program is affiliated with a university or if it is a program that is used more as an initiation rite into the business. Knowing the type of intern program will offer a better idea as to what a day in the life of an intern is like. Potential interns can better prepare themselves by getting a written job description and by talking to previous interns. It is important to try and avoid bait-and-switch tactics—programs, for example, that on the outside look like they involve interesting and challenging tasks but, in reality, require work in lesser tasks for the majority of the time. Whenever possible, avoid working at non-paying internships or ones that pay extremely little, even when school credit is available. Wages are often negotiable and faced with losing a more-than-qualified candidate at a bargain price, companies may agree to pay more than they had originally intended.

Qualifying a Company

Becoming successful in multimedia starts with choosing the best companies to work with and the best projects to work on. A big part of making these decisions lies in researching companies and making decisions based on the information you find. Below are some guidelines to use when qualifying companies.

Products or Services

A company's **products or services** are probably the first thing you are going to come in contact with and will likely be one of the primary reasons you are interested in them. Ideally, the products or services a company produces should appeal to you both in terms of subject matter and approach. You should try to find companies whose products you are proud of. One caveat here, especially in an area where the products are changing so rapidly, is that it is possible to have an immediate and direct influence on the form and the quality of a company's products or services.

When interviewing with a company and looking at the products they've produced or are producing, try to find out who is responsible for the various pieces. Pay attention to the structure of the project team. Some teams are very centralized with the producer making most of the decisions, including design decisions. Others are more de-centralized, with art directors, sound producers, scriptwriters, and others having more influence on the creative direction of the product. Still other teams are driven by the technical people. Patterns that you see in project teams within a company should give you an idea of how much influence you will have on what the company does.

Reputation

The **reputation** of a company is defined by many things. There may be one reputation for their products or their customer service and there may be another for what it is like to work at the company. Do not confuse one reputation for the other. Talk with employees and former employees. Also, reputations can change. They can change as a result of business conditions forcing a company to be leaner or improve short-term productivity at the expense of long-term goals. Managers and key talent can come and go, changing the environment and attitude overnight. Most importantly, trust your instincts. Few people or companies are completely blameless and even the most principled people have bitter enemies. Balance carefully a company's reputation on the street with the reality seen in the eyes of people working at the company.

Management

Since the sizes of companies in multimedia range from two people in an apartment to large public companies, it is difficult to give any specific guidance on what a **management structure** should look like. Some general advice, though, is to look for a structure that makes sense. There should not be too many layers of management nor any duplicate roles. There also should not be any "status" positions. Small companies that have grown into larger companies in particular often have a few management positions that have little relevance to current business conditions. These positions are often there because one or more founders may not be qualified for a direct management position and so another one is created to provide some form of status.

What to Look for in a Project

- *well-defined market*
- *well-defined product*
- *well-defined process*
- *talented people that are fun*
- *imagination and precision*
- *a clear project team organization*
- *a good producer*
- *an art director that listens*
- *a realistic budget and schedule*
- *funding and distribution in place*
- *an opportunity to learn*
- *great tools*

Also, management and leadership are two different things. Managers are those who direct what others do. Leaders are those that people look to for guidance. Hopefully, the managers in a company are also leaders but that is not always the case. Look for people in responsible positions that you respect.

Goals and Market

The **goals** of a company and the **market** they are targeting will provide one of the best clues as to what a company's long-term prospects are. Whether they are too narrow or too broad, too ill-defined or too focused needs to be determined case by case. They also need to be weighed with the idea that few people can predict whether an idea will be successful or not. What can be predicted, though, is whether all the other aspects of a company are in place to meet those goals. Becoming a dominant publisher of health and fitness CD-ROMs is an ambitious but not necessarily unrealistic goal. It is a bit presumptuous, however, to think it can be done with $250,000 in the bank and no distribution deals.

Financial Position/Funding

In a perfect world, you should not even consider working for a company that is not in a strong **financial position**. If that were the case in multimedia, however, over 60% of the companies would be out of consideration. The current financial position of a company needs to be balanced with what its promise is. An agreement to produce one game can move a production studio from annual revenues of zero to revenues of $1.5 million. At the same time, the list of multimedia companies that have gone out of business or run into financial difficulties is a long one. There are no guarantees.

The things you want to look for are either long-term contracts, a steady stream of short-term projects that are highly profitable or funding to last beyond the length of time they think they will need it for. A company should also not be dependent on a single client or publisher. If the client or publisher runs into trouble or backs out, the company can be at great risk. Also, too much funding can be as big a problem as too little cash. The software industry is filled with stories of companies receiving venture capital and then seeing much of that money go into luxury offices and lavish parties. Not surprisingly, few of those companies ever met with much promise.

Growth/Exit Strategy

Common business convention usually dictates that a company continues to **grow**. That may or may not be the case with many companies in multimedia. Most publishers and online services will certainly need to grow in order to fund the development and marketing of new titles or content areas. As the costs for these grow, many of the smaller companies will either go out of business or be bought by larger companies. Companies that create products, though, may not need to grow in order to make money and stay in business. The economics and the talent may be such that they can continue to create products or perform services that are in demand and that have few competitors.

The term **"exit strategy"** refers to the way a group of investors or shareholders convert their equity in a company into cash. The most common ways include going public or selling a portion of the company to another company. The right growth strategy or exit strategy is entirely dependent on the type of business a company is in, the market conditions, the desires of management, and the desires of the shareholders. Anyone looking to become an employee of a company should try to find out what the plans are for these two areas. The answers here can be compared against what the mission and goals are of a company to see if they match. If they don't, then something funny may be going on.

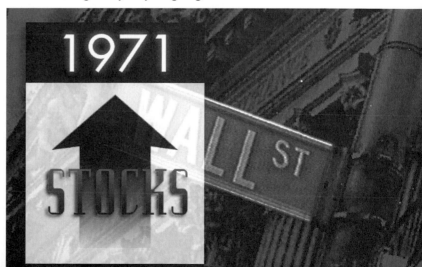

How to Check a Company's Vital Signs

• Strong values and beliefs

A healthy organization has strong views about what is good or bad, right or wrong. These are guiding principles about how business is done, a set of beliefs that the organization holds sacred and on which it bases all of its policies and actions. How successful an organization is in the long run depends largely on the strength of its basic beliefs and how well it adheres to them.

• Common purpose

The healthiest organizations are composed of people with a strong sense of purpose. It is crucial, therefore, for an organization to have a clear and powerful overall aim: a shared vision, inspirational cause, creative ambition, or supreme objective that unifies the organization and becomes a focal point of effort—a "guiding star."

• Exceptional people

You want to see people who are good at what they do, hard working, and dedicated to fulfilling their commitments. You want to see the type of people who simply don't like to have their names associated with poor work—those who, even under pressure, will not cut corners. It is particularly important to see that management is not threatened by good people. In fact, you want to see a management team that hires the best possible people, even if they are better than the managers themselves. You also want to see that the organization seeks the best possible professional services (legal, accounting, advertising, etc.).

• Customer driven

Behavior throughout the organization should demonstrate that all employees know the simple truth: "Ultimately, we work for our customers, not for management."

• Attention to business fundamentals

Every organization needs to pay attention to the nuts and bolts. As a corporation grows, it needs to implement such things as budgeting, accurate and timely financial reporting, cost accounting, schedules, and planning. In particular, you want to see that the organization forecasts and manages its cash flow with care. Cash is the lifeblood of a company. Keep in mind that roughly half of all business bankruptcies occur because of a shortage of cash after a year of record sales.

• Creativity and innovation

Most great organizations can trace a large part of their success to creative contribution. Some of the things to look for in assessing whether a company is creative are

1. *Willingness to experiment and take calculated risks.*
2. *Continual flow of innovative products or services.*
3. *Tolerance for diversity and uniqueness in people.*
4. *Resourcefulness in overcoming problems.*
5. *People aren't afraid to make mistakes.*
6. *People enjoy themselves at work—they have fun.*
7. *People have a high degree of freedom to act, combined with high levels of responsibility.*

• Mutual trust, communication, and teamwork

There can be fierce disagreements in even the healthiest organizations. But these disagreements should take place within a context of trust, mutual respect, and common purpose.

• Willingness to see and act on reality

Management must be willing to relentlessly seek the truth about any situation whether it is "good news" or "bad news." The risk of wearing rose-colored glasses is that reality has a funny way of making itself known. As soon as I see people afraid to present brutal truths to top management, I know the organization is on a path to certain difficulty.

• Strong and effective leadership

How can you tell if a company has effective leadership? One could write a book on the topic—there are multiple dimensions and complexities—but the primary things to look for are

1. *The ability to instill strong values and beliefs.*
2. *The ability to instill a sense of common purpose and to motivate people to work toward that purpose.*
3. *The ability to set a cohesive strategy.*
4. *A willingness to see reality.*
5. *Widespread enthusiasm and affection of the leader.*

- **Commitment, convictions, confidence, and pride**
- **Superior products or services**
- **Good economics and solid financial condition**
- **Clear and well-executed product and market strategy**
- **Non-bureaucratic, lean, and decisive**
- **Long-term orientation**

—Jim Collins, Co-author of
BUILT TO LAST: Successful Habits of Visionary
Companies, *HarperBusiness, 1994*

Signing the Contract

Although it can be tempting to begin working on a project before all the details of the working relationship have been agreed to, do not begin work on a project, or say yes to an offer, until that relationship has been clearly stated, in writing, and you have had an opportunity to ask questions and make changes. Almost everybody ignores this rule at one point or another, for better or worse. For example, a client might need a sample specifically created in order to make a final judgment. Or, the relationship may be a continuing one where the expectations of the future work correspond to previous engagements. Nevertheless, there is a fine line between winning business and being taken advantage of. Approach an offer for a job, regardless of whether it is temporary, project-related, or permanent, as you would a personal transaction. Understand what the offer is and hold people to their commitments.

The offer should be presented in written form in either a **work agreement** or an **employment contract**. The first is typically used for contractors while the second is used for employees. Although many employers and clients will present the agreements as being standard, there really is no such thing. Agreements can vary according to industry, geography, management philosophy, role, task, and project type, as well as according to your work skills and negotiating skills. All points are negotiable. Whether a company is willing to negotiate, however, is another story. Again, certain industries and companies are used to dealing with agreements on an individual basis. Others are more reluctant to involve their lawyers in approving amendments. Plus, for small contracts or entry-level positions, aggressive negotiations might make the other party think twice about hiring you for fear that the risk and effort might be greater than the reward.

Deliverables

A **job description** ▶ 90 will usually describe what is expected in a job or role. It will include the name of the role, the responsibilities, the reporting structure, and the **deliverables**. Many times, though, the deliverables are only loosely defined. This is fine for preliminary discussions but before signing a deal, make the effort to define the deliverables in writing and with clarity and detail. Many make the mistake of leaving the deliverables hazy, putting them at risk of having to do an enormous amount of additional work near the end of a project or risk having to get into a disagreement with the client.

A description of the deliverables should contain some indication of the size or length of the work (a 150-page script or 50 minutes of music), specific parameters for judging completion (C++ code modules that conform to the functional specification), or some other quantifiable measure for deciding completeness. In some cases, an **acceptance procedure** is established that formalizes the hand-off. For example, the client may have a certain number of days to review the materials and then either accept or decline. The contractor may then be obligated to make revisions to remedy problems and conform to the specification. This type of formality is usually only seen on larger jobs where there is more distance and less communication between the client and contractor. For those jobs where the deliverables are reworked and then integrated into a product or where the work is performed until the project is complete, the hand-off is a less important issue.

The format and requirements for deliverables need to be described in detail. The format can include descriptions of the media form (such as paper, 44MB Syquest cartridge, or recordable CD-ROM) or the electronic file format (such as Word 5.1, GIF, TIFF, or QuickTime 2.0). These requirements can include style guidelines (such as a script that follows scriptwriting standards for film or source code that contains extensive comments), and any specifications that the deliverables should adhere to (such as 16-bit sound sampled at 22kHz or 15 frames per second video with an image size of 240 x 180 x 240). Not coming to an agreement on the details in the beginning can cause conflicts and nasty surprises at the end of a project, costing time, money, and potentially the work relationship.

The following pages contain a list of items that can be issues in a working relationship. They are presented within the scope of a project as opposed to a full-time employment position, but most are relevant to employees in some form or another.

Related to deliverables are the milestones for intermediate and final deliverables, the copyright ownership of the deliverables, the number of reviews and revisions, and possibly termination procedures in case the relationship is not working out or the deliverables are not being met.

Payment

Payment ▶ 109 for work can only be determined after the work is well defined. The type of payment and the amount will again vary according to working arrangement, role, and level of talent. For contractors, work is usually performed on a fixed-price basis or a time-and-materials basis. A **fixed-price** bid refers to a set price for performing the deliverables. A **time-and-materials** bid typically refers to time-based rate (hourly, daily, weekly, or monthly) plus the cost of materials that go into the work.

With interactive media, materials may include stock photography, voice talent, run-time licenses, or other similar costs that are incorporated directly into a product. These are viewed differently than expenses, which are indirect costs incurred in pursuit of the deliverables. Both materials and expenses should be reflected, and recovered, in any form of bid. Ideally, these should be listed ahead of time either as individual items or as a lump sum. If the exact costs are not known, then estimates can be given with provisions for receiving approval if the actual costs begin to exceed the estimates.

There are advantages to both forms of payment. A fixed-price bid gives you the opportunity to earn higher than average margins than under a time-and-materials agreement. A group or a person that has experience performing the work and is more talented and faster than is normal can do the work in less time and earn more money. A disadvantage is that a fixed-price bid can be risky if the work is difficult or not clearly defined. Budget overruns may not be covered by the client, which will not only erase any profit but can also entail a loss. Clients often like fixed priced bids because they can be budgeted more easily. They also hedge against work that may be subpar or overproduced. Under a time-and-materials agreement, these types of situations could incur serious costs unless a manager was on top of the

billings and taking steps to prevent serious overruns or missed expectations. Fixed-priced bids can also be far less expensive than the same work performed at an hourly rate. For example, negotiating an agreement with a lawyer to prepare a non-disclosure agreement for anywhere from $100–$300 can avoid getting a legal bill a month later for three hours of work at $220/hr ($660). A fixed price can help focus the amount of work to be done by the contractor and keep a tight rein on the effort and the cost.

Hourly rates are best when the work is hard to define or has never been done before. Inexperienced people are often better off working under hourly, weekly, or monthly rates as opposed to fix pricing work because they are not usually in a position to make reasonable estimates of what a job will take. Even people that are experienced in performing certain tasks are unable to accurately estimate the time and effort involved in a set of tasks. It can only be done by diligently recording time on previous projects and reviewing them extensively.

Working on an hourly basis on a project can be a safe and lucrative way to work since there is no financial danger of underbidding on time. Lawyers, for example, can earn fees billing at hourly rates ranging from $100–$250/hr. A C programmer working on a rush job might be in a position to get $70–$175/hr. Hourly rates are also good for small jobs and for modulating a contractor's work load. As an example of the second case, a higher than normal rate can be used during busy periods. If the client agrees to the terms, the higher rates can provide the motivational boost to complete the work. Likewise, at times of little work, using a lower rate may increase the odds of getting work.

Arriving at an hourly rate involves a few steps. One is knowing what others are getting for similar work in the same geographic location. Finding this information is easier in jobs where there are **unions** ▶ 52. The union scale will provide the minimum rate for union-affiliated talent. In multimedia, however, not all production studios hire union talent and there are no unions for many of the roles. Some may use non-union talent and pay less or in ways different than

Many people have difficulty dealing with confrontation, especially in a business situation. Over time and with practice, you can overcome this hesitation. Sometimes it can be to your benefit to have someone else available to help negotiate a business relationship, allowing you to focus on performing the best work you can. Agents ▶ 148 are a possibility for some roles and projects, lawyers ▶ 134 advising on a contract for many others.

Always be prepared to walk away from an offer at any point in the process. Do not throw your heart and soul into a project or a job until an agreement has been reached.

prescribed by union contracts. Standard union rates, however, will provide a starting point.

The task is harder, but certainly not impossible, for roles not represented by unions such as programmers, testers, interaction designers, and game designers. A variety of multimedia related organizations as well as organizations for specific professions provide up-to-date salary and wage information. For example, there are compensation guides available from the Software Publishers Association and from accounting firms such as Coopers and Lybrand containing wage information for programmers. Unfortunately, while this type of information is valuable as a rough start, it has limited usability due to regional and project differences, especially in an area that is changing so rapidly. A year or two ago, there was nowhere near the demand for Macromedia Director or HTML programmers as there is now, so salaries for these are not going to be reflected accurately in any publication. Rough estimates can help but it needs to be substantiated by other factors.

The more information you can find on actual wages, the more confident you will be in **negotiations** ▶ 136 about compensation issues. Many experts suggest holding off on discussing salary until there is interest on the part of the employer. They also recommend letting the other party make the first offer. For free-lancers, however, holding off on discussing pay issues may not be wise. In fact, it is important to qualify prospective clients at the beginning in order to prevent investing a lot of time pursuing a client only to find that their budget for the work is far below what a realistic budget would be. Experienced free-lance talent are typically up-front about their rates and often use it as a positioning tool. Sometimes, high prices command more respect from potential employers who figure that they must be good if they charge that much.

It is important to know what the costs of service are in order to arrive at a reasonable rate. **Contractors** ▶ 110 that use their own equipment, provide for their own health insurance, and pay their own self-employment tax will have overhead costs far greater than someone working as an employee and who is provided with a computer and health care benefits. Many beginning free-lancers neglect to figure these costs when pricing themselves and are surprised and disappointed to find themselves struggling to make ends meet and pay taxes every quarter.

A variation of an hourly rate is a daily, weekly, or monthly rate. Using a rate with a longer time frame is usually more of a benefit to the employer than the talent. In other words, a 14-hour day costs the same as an 8-hour day, whereas with an hourly rate, the cost would be 75% higher. At the same time, a weekly or monthly rate can eliminate the need to rigorously track hours and always have to feel productive. It allows more freedom to focus at the task at hand, reducing the guilt that can sometimes arise for spending a lot of time on something but not having a lot to show for it.

The length of the pay scale usually relates to the length of the project. For projects under a few weeks, daily rates may be better. For projects under a few months, weekly rates may be better. Hourly rates often factor in the cost of not having work for approximately half of the total work hours in a year. As a single client begins to fill your work schedule, the rates to this client can drop to reflect the increase in steady work.

Royalty

A **royalty** is typically a percentage of the gross or net revenues for a product that is paid by a publisher to an individual or company who participated in creating the product. Companies receiving royalties in turn can pass along portions of their royalties to their contractors or employees. Royalties for authors and musicians are common in the book and music publishing industries but not as common in the software and film industries. Software industries prefer to hire employees and compensate them through equity and profit sharing plans. Although film studios do pay royalties to certain stars, they prefer to pay higher fees if given the opportunity. (Production companies as opposed to individual stars often do receive a percentage of the gross.)

Multimedia shows a wide variety of royalty and non-royalty relationships. Most royalties at this point are allocated to production companies as opposed to individual talent. The royalties can range from a few "points" to more than 20%.

Royalties should be calculated off of gross revenues as opposed to net revenues. The royalty is often based on what the other party receives, which in the case of a publisher is usually the wholesale price. Deductions against gross revenues should be clearly defined. Some, such as returns and a limited amount of promotional copies, are reasonable; others, such as commissions for sales representatives and marketing costs are less so.

Employment Issues

The terms of employment between you and an employer can be described in the form of a letter, but ideally it should be contained in a **contract** that makes the accord binding. While most transitions into new positions are straightforward, some are not. Business conditions sometimes cause the employer to withdraw the offer or change it significantly between the time of acceptance and the beginning of work. A binding employment contract will leave you in a more protected position should this happen.

Job Responsibility

Most people inexperienced with the job market think that compensation is the most important issue. Those that have been in a miserable job that paid well know better. Get a clear understanding of what the job entails, who makes decisions, who reports to whom, what the work environment is, and what the expectations are.

Compensation/Benefits/Vacation

For full-time employees, compensation typically means a *salary* or *wage* and benefits. Bonuses, raises, and overtime pay are related issues that either are negotiable or dictated by law. Bonuses can be awarded upon signing, upon completion of certain milestones, or on some periodic basis according to market conditions or company profits. Raises are usually rewarded in conjunction with reviews. Although companies may have policies with regards to either bonuses or raises, it is usually up to the employee to negotiate for these items on a regular basis.

Benefits are usually dictated by company policy. Government policies can limit the ability of organizations to offer special benefit packages but only in the sense that they are not considered taxable income. Special arrangements can be negotiated in this area, though there may be tax consequences for both the company and employee. *Vacation time* is another area dictated by company policy, but this can be negotiated. One way is to reduce or waive any initial vesting period for vacation time. Another is to restructure a vaca-tion plan based on number of years with the company. Essentially, workers should try to receive the same or an improved version of the vacation policy they had at their previous job. Exceptions can always be made to company policy but it is up to the worker to negotiate these exceptions.

An issue that becomes more important as the responsibility of a position increases is *severance pay*. Most companies will have a standard practice either contained in writing or established by actions with previous employees that have left. This area is usually negotiable and can be a fixed sum or tied to the length of service at a company.

Equity Compensation

Equity compensation is similar to royalty except that it is tied to the success of a company as opposed to the success of a particular product. While companies in many industries provide equity to upper management, the practice is more widespread and more distributed within high technology companies. Many offer stock to almost all of their employees although the amount will vary between those considered key talent and others. Also, how early people start at a firm can also factor into the amount (and value) of the equity.

Equity compensation is usually considered to be a form of "golden handcuffs," meaning that employees are encouraged to stay at a company to realize the value of the compensation. Most forms of equity compensation have vesting periods in which portions of the equity are accrued over a period of time. A vesting period means that portions are awarded over a period of time. Typical vesting periods are four and five years. For example, a newly hired president of a year-old start-up may be awarded 5% of the currently issued stock with a five-year vesting period and a one-year initial vest. In other words, the president must stay at the company for five years in order to get the full 5% of the stock. If an employee leaves before that period, the stock percentage is reduced accordingly. The president, however, must be at the company for at least a year in order to realize any stock compensation.

There are several forms of equity compensation such as stock options, restricted stock, employee stock purchase plans, and stock bonus plans. Each form has its nuances in terms of securities, accounting, and tax issues, both for the issuing company and the receiver, and are continually adapting to keep pace with federal and state legislation. Anyone putting these types of plans together for a company should work with a qualified law firm to set them up properly. Anyone on the receiving end of such a plan should know the full implications of the compensation.

A *stock option* is the most frequently used form of equity compensation. In short, it is an agreement between a corporation and another party (called the optionee) which allows the optionee the chance to purchase a predetermined amount of stock at a predetermined price within a specified period of time. That period of time may be the length of employment plus three months, for example. This option locks down the price of the stock so that even if the market value increases, the optionee can purchase the stock at the price fixed in the agreement. There are three stages of stock options—the grant by the corporation, the exercise by the optionee, and the sale or transfer by the optionee.

The benefit of stock options is in the difference between the purchase price and the market value of the stock. In other words, a person could exercise the option months or years later at the fixed price and then sell the stock at the higher price (assuming, of course, that the stock price has risen). The difference between the purchase price and selling price is profit for the individual (and subject to capital gains taxes). They are called options because the optionee is not obligated to purchase the stock, which an employee would not do if the stock is valued at a price below the option price.

Deferred Compensation
Deferred compensation commonly refers to retirement plans. These can be administered by a union, corporation, or other entity on behalf of an existing or former member or employee with one or more parties contributing to the plan. Qualified plans refer to plans that meet certain requirements of the Tax Code, thereby providing tax benefits to one or more contributing parties. There are a number of variations in plans. These include

- Profit sharing plans
- Simplified employee pension plan (SEPP)
- 401(k) plans
- Stock bonus plans
- Employee stock ownership plan (ESOP)
- Traditional pension plans

Equipment
In the case of an employee relationship, the employer usually supplies the **equipment** ▶ 114 needed for an employee to perform their job. Ideally, an employer should create the most productive environment for its employees. This commitment might include installing lots of RAM and allocating two monitors for programmers and visual artists, and video boards and high-end video editing software for video producers and editors. In reality, many employers either are unaware of the productivity improvements that can be made or choose not to make them in order to reduce capital expenditures at the expense of labor costs. The place to negotiate for the most effective equipment is before becoming an employee. One of the negotiating points should be the type of equipment that will be assigned to the position. You can talk about the type of computer, its speed and memory size, the size of the hard drive, the size and number of monitors, type of peripherals, and software that is needed. A budget to cover software can be negotiated as well.

The range is dependent on where the ideas come from as well as the negotiating capabilities of the production studio.

Very few free-lancers receive royalties. Part of the reason for this is that there is less of a division between experts and practitioners. Unless a company has a policy of rewarding all project team members, most are reluctant to offer royalties and prefer to use less expensive (and possibly less skilled) talent or offer higher rates.

Do not count on royalties to pay any bills. The number of projects that make any significant royalties are few. They are a nice thing to have but do not spend any royalty money until you have it in hand.

The individuals that are receiving royalties are typically those that are closely affiliated with the properties that are being developed. The way to get into the royalty stream is to help conceive an idea, find a publisher, or play a key role in producing or creating it. A programmer who starts just before production probably should not expect to be given a royalty. They can ask, but it is probably not even negotiable. The types of individual contributors who might receive royalties include producers, art directors, lead designers, scriptwriters, and lead programmers. They may be awarded anywhere from a fraction of a percentage to 1.5%.

Payment Terms

The payment terms for a job refer to the frequency of payment and the duration between invoice and receipt of payment. This is an important issue for a contractor and can mean the difference between running a successful business and having a tough time making a living. Too many free-lancers run into problems and stretch their finances too thin because they do not give proper attention to getting prompt payment from clients.

The place to address the payment terms is in the **work agreement**. In most business relationships there is a power struggle between one party wanting to delay payment as long as possible and the other party wanting to receive payment as soon as possible. Most companies, if given the chance, prefer to pay 30 or more days after a project is completed and an invoice is received. There are three primary reasons why companies ask for 30 or more days after the invoice is received. The first is, not surprisingly, because they want to hold on to the money for as long as possible—in a sense, getting free financing from

the vendor for that period of time. The second, and more understandable, is because most companies batch their payments together and only cut checks at certain times. This time period is anywhere from weekly, bi-weekly, semi-monthly, to monthly. The final reason is that many businesses try to leave as little money in checking and savings accounts as possible because it earns low interest rates. Most of the cash reserves are invested in higher interest bearing vehicles that are less readily accessible. As a result, companies spend a lot of time and effort balancing receipts with outgoing payments and prefer a longer period between invoice and payment to manage that balance.

Clients are not the only ones who can influence the payment terms of a contract. A contractor can get more favorable terms depending on the negotiating position they are in. Smaller companies are often more flexible because their departments are not as distinctly separated. One technique for managing the payment for a project is to break the payment up into portions and distribute those over the length of the contract. These payments are usually tied to reaching milestones and handing over intermediate deliverables.

For example, a two-month project to create a website might have major milestones tied to deliverables. The first payment may be at the signing of the contract. The second may be at reaching a state where the functionality and content are complete (sometimes termed an alpha or beta state in reference to stages in software development). The third may be upon final completion of the project. Even with the structuring of payments this way, the payments may not arrive until a certain period (30 or more days) after each delivery. One way of speeding up payment within large companies is to have the lead contact issue a purchase order which gets the payment into the system so that it will be closer to being ready when a delivery has been made.

Outside Equipment

Any use of **outside equipment** ▶ 112 should be factored into the rate or wage for the service. The cost can be calculated by taking the expected life of the equipment (2–3 years for most equipment including upgrades) and dividing by the number of hours of billable work per year. This cost should then become a line item to be added or subtracted to the fixed priced bid, the hourly, weekly, or monthly rate, or any other type of compensation arrangement. Too many contractors ignore the cost of equipment and continually struggle when it comes time to buy or lease better equipment. In cases where it is clear that a contractor will use their own equipment, the contractor might want to avoid itemizing the cost of the equipment because it might only provide room for the client to negotiate the rate lower based on their estimates of the equipment costs.

Reimbursed Costs/Expenses

One way that profits can evaporate is to not include clauses that recapture **expenses** on a contract. These expenses can include research materials such as books and magazines, travel, media costs such recordable CD-ROMs or Syquest cartridges, photocopying, delivery or mail charges, and many other out-of-pocket costs. Clients are often reluctant to agree to open-ended expense clauses, however. Sometimes, costs can be identified and estimated beforehand and included in a bid. Otherwise a ceiling can be determined relative to the total cost of the job with approval of the client needed to exceed the ceiling.

Schedule

One of the more valued qualifications for anybody working on multimedia development is their ability to estimate the tasks correctly and deliver materials on time. Although a producer may be willing to put up with late deliverables, especially for those that are highly creative or those who the producer has worked with before and know how to pad their estimates correctly, most experienced producers rank reliability as one of their highest priorities.

A **schedule** ▶ 126 can mean a detailed list of deliverables tied to specific dates, or it can mean a schedule of days, weeks, or months when services are needed. Schedules are usually developed by carefully plotting the tasks and deliverables needed for a job. Novices are often tempted to pull dates out of the air and try to fit the work to those dates. This approach usually leads to frantic scrambling throughout the project, chasing these ever-elusive target dates. A better approach is to break the work down into discrete tasks plotting them on a calendar, accounting for dependencies on others, building in time for reviews and revisions, and then leaving generous room for errors and contingencies from all parties, client included.

Any provisions that include a schedule should address what happens if the schedule is not met. For work that is being done for a fixed price, you should avoid signing contracts that contain heavy penalties for not meeting a schedule. Most contracts withhold a substantial amount of payment until a job is complete and this should serve as the primary incentive to complete as soon as possible. Also, fixed-price bids that go over schedule usually mean less profit, if not a loss. Time-and-materials bids, however, can and probably should (if the client is smart) have provisions that limit the amount of hours that can be spent on a task and include some penalty such as significantly reduced rates for not being timely.

Contractors should also make their clients act responsibly in terms of meeting schedules. For rates based on time such as weekly or monthly rates, you might want to include a provision that increases the rate if a project extends beyond the length stated in the work agreement—effectively giving you a raise—provided, of course, that you have not been the cause of the delay. Many contractors can use schedule limitations on upcoming projects as leverage to get rate increases.

Reviews

Reviews ▶ 162, 211 are an important part of any working relationship but especially so in any client-contractor relationship. There are two rules for reviews. The first, and most important, is to include them as a part of any and all work. Even when schedules do not seem to leave room for reviews, put them in regardless. Otherwise, changes will still be made and the project will inevitably slip. Accounting for changes in the beginning simply makes the process run more smoothly. These reviews should be planned and the costs of possible changes resulting from these

*Roles such as **3D animators** ▶ 214 and **video editors** ▶ 245 often have several rate levels. One rate is for when they are actively working at the computer and another rate, usually $1/2$ to $2/3$ less, for when the computer is processing on its own. Using two rates provides a good way to balance both the work time and the processing time, reducing the risk of underbidding a job.*

Flexible payment terms can help contractors win jobs. By lowering payments at the front and pushing more towards the end, a contractor can help companies that get the majority of the money from their client after the project has been completed. Consider this an option, though, only for people that you trust and for projects that are well managed.

reviews should be reflected in the bid. Not putting a cap on reviews can cause a project to continually diverge between opinions. This guideline holds true for any project regardless of whether it is fixed-priced or time-and-materials work.

The second rule for reviews is to put emphasis on the earlier ones. It is in the beginning stages that the direction and tone of the work will be established. Being too lax in preparing materials or waiting too long to get client input are easy ways to perform work that has little value to the client. In a perfect world, clients would take the time to look at materials provided by the contractor and create a detailed list of comments and suggestions. In the real world, though, clients are often too pre-occupied to offer relevant feedback until the project is further along and they have more to react to. As a result, it becomes the contractor's obligation to **force** the client to provide feedback.

Make any materials for review highly presentable. They should be as professionally prepared as possible. These materials also have to be placed in context with the whole project. Clients may not understand the development process or have a design background and, as a result, may not know what the purpose of the materials is. You should explain how the materials fit into the project plan. Try to get the lead client contact to consolidate the input from all parties representing the client. Also, limit the number of undecided or extraneous elements since they tend to draw issues away from the relevant topics. For example, clients might fixate on a preliminary color scheme or the look of a character at the expense of looking at the navigational structure or the set of creativity tools. If they wait to review these other issues until the color scheme or the character is fixed, a lot of work in the interim on the structure or tool set may need to be redone.

Changes/Corrections

Related to the number and schedule of reviews is the allocation of the costs for **changes** and **corrections**. A change refers to an alteration while the work is still being undertaken. A correction refers to a repair made after the work is considered finished. Changes occur in the course of almost every project, with some being more extensive than others. It is important that a contractor, when negotiating a work agree-

ment with a client, include a provision for handling changes in the project regardless of whether the changes are a result of client requests or unforeseen circumstances. One of the more common ways to handle changes not included in a review cycle is for a contractor to provide an estimate for the work (fixed-priced or time-and-materials), and the client to either accept or reject the additional charge. Being consistent and tough with the client is just as important as a formal process for handling changes. Letting changes go by early without formally acknowledging them sets a bad precedent for the future.

Copyright Ownership

A **copyright** ▶ 107 is an exclusive legal right granted by a government that protects original works of authorship fixed in any tangible form of expression. It gives the owner of the copyright the exclusive right to reproduce the copyrighted work, distribute copies of the work, perform and display the work publicly, and prepare derivative works.

A copyright comes into existence by the act of creating an original work of authorship. The first owner of a copyright is the creator, unless 1) the creator is an employee of a company in which case the employer is the owner, or 2) the work is considered a **"work for hire"** ▶ 136 in which case the client is the owner. Owners of copyrights may assign or license them to others. (Assignment is a legal term indicating a transfer of ownership.) Owners may also license one or more specific rights within a copyright. For example, a client who owns the copyright to a work created by a design studio might grant the design studio the right to display a copy of the work in conjunction with promoting the studio's services.

Copyrights can be confusing—especially for those who are learning about them for the first time. The first thing to realize is that copyrights are valuable. They should not be assigned or licensed without arriving at some fair compensation. Also, copyrights are owned by the creator of a work unless there is an employer-employee relationship or a contract that specifically calls out copyright ownership issues to a work.

The copyright to an original work immediately becomes the property of the owner as the work

Few large CD-ROM projects ship on time. In fact, most projects ship more than five months later than originally intended. This situation, though, is likely to change in the upcoming years as the film and publishing industries exert influence in completing projects on time in order to coincide with expensive marketing efforts.

A single work can have multiple copyrights to it. For example, a song may have a copyright to the lyrics, another for the music, and a third for a particular rendition by an artist. In addition, there are mechanical reproduction rights, synchronization rights, performance rights, derivative rights, and others. These copyrights, or portions of copyrights, may be held by one or more people. They may be the original creators, heirs to the creators, or some guy named Bo living in a houseboat in the Florida Keys.

is created. A copyright has a fixed duration to it after which the work becomes part of the **public domain**. Works that are in the public domain can be used by anyone in any form and in any manner. Interpretations of works in the public domain, however, may have copyrights associated with them. While the score for a symphony by Beethoven may be in the public domain, a recording of the music by the New York Philharmonic is not. The recording is a unique expression and most likely under copyright protection.

An original work is a form or expression of an idea that has not been copied from a work under copyright protection. Since many ideas are based on existing ideas, what constitutes original work and what is a non-original reinterpretation is often the central conflict of many copyright infringement lawsuits. Most people avoid using work that they do not have the rights to, no matter how much they change or modify the previous work.

In the case of work created by an employee, the work is presumptively considered to be owned by the employer if it is created by the employee within the scope of their employment. Most employee agreements have a clause that specifically states this. What constitutes "within the scope of employment" should be defined in the work agreement. Many companies consider all work within a related field created by employees to be theirs unless the idea or technology is specifically listed in the work agreement as being exempt. Whether a work created during private time does actually belong to the employer is often up for individual interpretation.

In the past, companies that used contractors under conditions of "work made for hire" commonly owned the copyrights to the work performed. (The copyright statute contains a specific definition for "works made for hire.") In 1989, however, the U.S. Supreme Court ruled

that it may no longer be enough to cause a work to be created for it to be considered a "work made for hire." The court ruled that freelance artists and writers retain some or all of the copyright ownership to their works unless a written agreement expressly assigns the copyright over. To resolve any disagreements, employer-contractor agreements should explicitly state who has ownership of the work. Many experienced contractors try to negotiate agreements that let them retain the rights to all or parts of their work. In cases where they cannot negotiate ownership, they typically charge a higher rate to reflect the loss of the copyright. Assigning the rights to the final deliverables but retaining all rights to the intermediary deliverables is another hedge many use to preserve the ability to reuse their work in other projects.

Indemnification

Indemnification refers to who bears the liability for infringing on someone else's intellectual property rights. One party to a contract will typically ask the other party to indemnify them or, in other words, hold them blameless against any claim of infringement. Such guarantees are important parts of doing business and are a part of almost every contract. Production studios and publishers will want guarantees from a scriptwriter or game designer that the script or game are original works and do not infringe on other people's copyrights. A producer will want guarantees from a contract programmer that any code resources used in a product by the programmer, again, does not infringe on the rights of another programmer or company.

Ideally, indemnification clauses should be **mutual**. If both parties create content and/or programming for a title, each party should indemnify the other for the materials they respectively create. Making changes in indemnification clauses can be difficult for parties that are at a disadvantage in the negotiations. Most large companies are going to be very reluctant to assume any more intellectual property liability than necessary, especially since the frequency of infringement suits against filmmakers, software companies, book publishers, and music labels are on the rise.

Lawyers ▶ 134 can be consulted to help explain indemnification clauses and help rewrite them to be more balanced. In general, you should try to limit indemnification provisions wherever possible. One way of doing this is to limit what type of intellectual property right will be indemnified against, the most notable ones being patents, copyrights, and trade secrets. Also, intellectual property rights are enforced by countries and so you should clearly define the countries to which the indemnifications apply.

Another component of most indemnification clauses are the conditions that should be met once someone makes a charge of infringement. These conditions may include who controls and pays for the defense and whether there is guaranteed cooperation from the other party. Many companies will want to control the defense but have you pay the legal costs. As to what the remedies should be in the event of an infringement ruling, they can include repairing or replacing of the material to make it non-infringing, or refunding the money received for the purchase or license of the infringed materials. These remedies are important because open-ended agreements can hold the indemnifier responsible for any and all damages.

On Indemnification

Indemnification's a thing that blows everybody's mind. Lawyers argue about it because they're haunted by the possibility that in years to come, their client is going to be drawn back into the dispute over this thing.

For example, if you create a "History of Jazz" disc, you might sell or license that disc to a company or a publisher. The publisher is going to make you promise that everything in that disc is okay to use. But then the publisher will say, "Okay, don't just promise to me. I want you to indemnify me." To say, in essence, that if some jazz musician sues me because you didn't get permission, that you will pay the costs for me, the publisher, to defend that lawsuit. So it's not just that the company that created it has to defend themselves; they have to defend the person who they sold it to. And if they lose the suit, depending on how the indemnity's drafted, they will have to pay all of the damages that result.

Where it's important that the developer pay attention is in what you're indemnifying for. In my mind, you should only have to indemnify them that the object is original to you and that you have a right to transfer it to them. But some people try and get the developer to indemnify them for everything. That the mail's going to be delivered on time—to anything— so that it becomes so inclusive that any third party lawsuit that results, the developer has to pay. I would urge people to really read that section and pay attention to it, especially if they're on their own. Because those are the things from the past that come back to you and you go—Aaaaaahhhh!

—Rich Stim, Attorney

Non-compete and Exclusivity

Many companies will include a **non-compete clause** that prevents a contractor from performing work that may be considered competitive. Publishers also tend to want assurances that developers and production studios will not create competing works. Many states have laws that govern the use of non-compete clauses but regardless, most individuals and companies should avoid signing an agreement with a non-compete clause in it. Often times non-compete clauses can be negotiated from being non-competitive to non-conflicting. This subtle change means that a contractor has not and will not undertake work that would conflict with their obligations to the client. For those who develop ideas and where non-compete clauses might prevent them from creating new works, offering the other party the right of first refusal or the right of first negotiation to a new work is a common substitute.

In cases where equity or royalty positions make it difficult to remove a non-compete clause, you should try to limit its application. This can be done by putting time limits on the term (one year limits are typical) and by narrowly defining what is considered competitive. Also, a non-compete clause should not apply in the case of a lay-off or termination.

A form of non-compete clause is an **exclusivity** clause. This type of clause is standard in almost all agent/client relationships, but there are ways to structure them to allow for certain flexibility. One way is to limit the term to a year or less. Another is to limit the representation to a particular venue or market such as CD-ROM games or theatrical-based films. A third is to limit the representation to a set number of works instead of all work.

Credit

Many areas of multimedia development, especially title development, are quickly adopting Hollywood standards for providing **credit** for individual talent. While most credits in Hollywood are dictated by individual contracts or union agreements, the credits in multimedia projects usually do not have such legal backing for individual talent. Production studios are increasingly negotiating prominent credit in press releases, on packaging, in opening sequences, in credit screens, and in closing sequences of the products.

Individuals, however, have been slower to negotiate these provisions for a couple of reasons. In many cases, people do not realize that these are important and that they are negotiable. In other cases, the talent may not be in a prominent enough position to command credit in more than just the credit screen and possibly the closing sequence. As individuals become more prominent in the eyes of consumers, more and more titles and online places will include displays of key talent. Roles that are likely to receive prominent credit in multimedia products are producers, scriptwriters, game designers, creative directors, and art directors. Noted composers are also likely to be featured.

Credits are much easier to negotiate before work begins than once the work has been completed. Negotiate the particular wording and the placement of the credit. Although a standard way of listing credits within multimedia titles has not yet developed, you can tie the placement of your credit to the placement of others on the team. Therefore, if you are a scriptwriter, you can tie your credit to the producer's credit so that wherever the producer's credit appears, yours has to be in close proximity.

Promotional Copies

One contract provision that is easy to get but often overlooked is the **number of copies** of a work that a project team member will receive. This issue is more relevant to mass-market products than for projects such as developing or maintaining content areas in an online system. Anyone who has ever had to buy copies of the work they helped create, even at reduced prices, to give to friends, contributors, or prospective clients will never again make the mistake of not asking for a suitable number of copies of the work in their next contract. Negotiating this number before the contract is signed is much easier than after the fact.

Demonstration Rights

Related to promotional copies is the right to **demonstrate** a work to others. This right is one of the rights specifically denoted in the U.S. Copyright Law and any assignment of the copyright to a work transfers this right to the new copyright holder. As a result, demonstrating a work whose copyright is owned by or assigned to another is illegal. Though most will not pursue infringement cases against contractors who demonstrate their work, it is in a contractor's best interest to include a provision in their work agreement giving them the specific right to do so.

In some cases, companies will not grant the right because the work is confidential and may not be released to the public for some time. While this is a reasonable desire for a company, it can put the contractor in a bind if they are unable to show a potential client any recent work. Solutions around this dilemma can include getting the right to show small excerpts that do not compromise the larger work, or by asking for the right to demonstrate a work on a case-by-case basis. Putting in a provision that allows for the right to demonstrate a work after it becomes known to the public through no fault of the contractor, much like the clauses found in non-disclosure agreements, is another solution.

Working

Try to overcommunicate, especially in written correspondence. There is a tendency to provide only the material that is new or only on a need-to-know basis. Train yourself to explain something as if the person is only vaguely familiar with it. Write and present the material well but let the other person share a portion of filtering what is relevant.

Signing a contract for performing work is only the beginning of a complete working relationship. There are many places for missteps, regardless of whether the relationship is as an employee or as a contractor. There can be a problem with the deliverables, or the work may be fine but problems might arise in the relationship, in the follow-through, or in the payment process. No relationship is easy and there are no rules that will work every time. Following a few simple guidelines, though, can prevent small problems from becoming bigger ones.

Showing Consistency from the Start

An important lesson for any working relationship is to show, and expect, **consistency** right from the start. There is often a tendency in the beginning to either miss minor milestones or be less demanding when receiving deliverables from others. No matter how tempting it is to slip the schedule a few days at the start, no matter how hard it may be to get tough with a client at the beginning of a relationship, it is important that early expectations and milestones on both sides be met. Meeting milestones at the beginning may not appear significant, especially in relation to a schedule, but they are paramount for setting the tone for the rest of the project. Be prompt for all meetings and do what you can to encourage them to start on time.

Continually communicate to others when you need deliverables. If you do not get them or they are handed over later than expected, communicate this fact to the other party immediately. If you have to, adjust the schedule to reinforce the importance of timely delivery. No matter how tempting it is to try to avoid any type of confrontation no matter how small, it is much easier to be open about expectations than it is to scramble and work faster in order to make up for the miscues of others.

Establish your own internal deadlines that are sooner than the deadlines you have to others for your deliverables. An internal deadline should be looked at as more than a wake-up call. The time between should be used for making additional passes at the material, testing it for accuracy and compatibility, and preparing it for delivery.

Establishing Trust

There has to be **trust** in a relationship for it to work well. Some of the things that can get in the way of trust are conflicts of interest, inconsistent actions, and changes in expectations. These elements are more likely in a client/contractor relationship because the boundaries in this type of relationship are less defined than in an employer/employee relationship. Before a working relationship begins, try to get a clear picture of what the framework for the relationship should be. There is the general idea that the client comes first but this can get confusing when a contractor has multiple clients. Know what can be said about a project and what must remain confidential. Develop a list of the goals for the relationship and continually keep these in mind. Discuss promptly any differences and be adept at reading any changes in a client's reaction.

Communicating Frequently

Part of establishing trust is frequently **communicating** to the other party. If it is an employee-employer relationship, these communications often occur through the use of weekly status meetings or status reports and in the natural course of the typical work environment. With a client/contractor relationship, this structure is not necessarily the norm. In most cases, a contractor works independently of the client's location and may not need constant interaction to

weekly time report

Name			Week Ending										
Susan B. Anthony			2/18/95										
Project	Name	Phase	Task	Role	Sun	Mon	Tues	Weds	Thurs	Fri	Sat	Total	
												0	
												0	
												0	
ABC.003	WWW Site	1	Architect. Design	Creative Director		4	2					6	
ABC.003	WWW Site	2	Graphics	Visual Designer					4	5		9	
MIC.015	Interface Design	2	Concept & Design	Sr. Visual Designer					3	4		7	
ROL.001	Book		Image Aquisition	Visual Designer			6	3	2.25			11.3	
XYZ.001	CD ROM	1	Graphics	Sr. Visual Designer				3				3	
XYZ.001	CD ROM	1	Client Meeting	Creative Director		2.5						2.5	
												0	
												0	
												0	
Internal.001	Internal		Marketing			1	1					2	
Internal.003	Internal		General	staff meeting				2				2	
Internal.004	Internal		WWW Test Patterns			2						2	
												0	
												0	
												0	
												0	
												0	
Total					0	9.5	9	8	9.25	9	0	44.8	

perform a particular job. It is important, however, to make a habit to check in periodically to make sure that there are no changes in the work and that the expectations on both sides are similar.

A good habit is to use the phone to maintain a social connection but to follow up some conversations with faxes or emails to record important details of the conversations. The purposes of these faxes or emails are not just to provide some written record in case something goes wrong during the relationship, but to provide a different spin on the explanation of events. What one person hears is not always what the other person has said. Saying something in a different form and in a different way can bring discrepancies to light that might not otherwise have been discovered.

Having Early Reviews

Get the work **reviewed** ▶ 162, 211 frequently at the beginning. Although it is tempting to produce something substantial before having it reviewed, not getting it right the first time can make it extremely hard to rework the material and meet the necessary deadlines. There can be problems with showing work too early, though. Sometimes the other party may not be trained enough to visualize what something in rough format will be like when its finished. This can happen with writing, sound production, or visual design. Consider showing several possibilities and make sure that any work that is shown is properly explained.

Keeping Records and Archiving Work

All workers should log their hours, the projects they work on, and the tasks they perform. This practice is especially important for contractors in the event that a relationship runs into problems. It is also important to **keep records** of all correspondence such as memos, status reports, agreements, invoices, and deliverables. This correspondence can be in the form of letters, faxes, email, and notes from phone conversations. Most people learn the hard way about the importance of keeping records on projects. It does not have to be that way.

Archiving work refers to both the creation of backups of digital (and paper) material at regular periods of time and the preservation of previous versions of a work in progress. In other words, a backup is for preserving work against loss due to accidental deletion of files or equipment malfunction, theft, or loss. A revision is for keeping material that might have been edited or changed in case it is needed in the future. This is commonly done by including version numbers within a file name or within a draft. Archiving work is primarily an internal insurance mechanism but it can also come in handy with clients in order to trace the progression of a project.

Diligently retaining previous versions can be an important precaution when there is a major change in a project team or within the client. These versions can be used to educate newcomers on the development of a project. This type of effort can also reduce the impulse of new people on the team to feel like making changes to already made decisions.

Keeping up to Date

There is often the tendency to get into a routine and relax. This is especially true when working on a long project or in a comfortable environment. Every employee or consultant needs to be continually **positioning** ▶ 80 themselves for future work. This process involves refining skills, keeping track of current trends, and developing or maintaining a certain level of visibility and independence outside of the current working relationship. All of these are pretty straightforward. The first can be done through classes, books, or learning from co-workers and friends. The second is a matter of reading a variety of magazines or belonging to a set of newsgroups or attending a few exhibitions, **conferences** ▶ 291, or seminars every year. The third can be done by staying in touch with friends and acquaintances, developing new relationships, joining organizations, teaching, writing articles, and promoting your work.

Any employee, contractor, or consultant should get in the habit of every Monday morning thinking about what they would do if they suddenly lost their job or all their clients walked away.

Two steps forward and one step back. Right from the start, no matter what your job is, you should be constantly retraining yourself—reading the trade presses, realizing what the current and forthcoming trends are, and schooling yourself on a continual basis. If that is not possible, as soon as you have been laid off or your job ceases, go back to school. You do not have to go to a school to teach yourself or to be taught the information necessary to get a new job. You can teach this yourself but what it takes is effort. Also, do not expect the same status as your previous job. You have to be fluid and flexible.

—Sean Lord, Recruiter, Interactive Development

Wrapping

*Right after completion of a project, a few steps should be taken internally by members of the project team to effectively mark the end of a project. These steps include some form of a celebration commemorating the end and honoring the participants, a **post mortem** either in a group or individually that goes over things that were done well and things that could be improved, and the updating of company and individual **portfolios** ▶ 82 to reflect the completed work. Not doing the first two especially tends to leave a project without a feeling of closure.*

Handing off deliverables and completing the finishing touches in a work relationship is referred to as **"wrapping."** How a job ends plays a big part in the perception of the other party as to the success of the overall project. The biggest components of this phase are the look and presentation of the final deliverables and the words and actions of the contractor in handling the endgame of the relationship.

Many jobs may not have final deliverables that mark the end of a work relationship. The work may be done when it gets done. For example, a programmer's work might be considered complete when the product ships. But for cases where there are distinct deliverables, the hand-off should be accompanied by more than just the paper or electronic files containing the work. You should create a package that ties up all of the loose ends and summarizes the project. There should be a letter restating the work relationship and the deliverables, listing what has been done and including instructions for use. You should act as if you are handing off materials to someone unfamiliar with the project and provide them will all the explanation they will need to understand the work.

Billing and Getting Paid
Most deliverables are usually tied to some sort of payment. When this is the case, **invoices** should be delivered once the deliverables have been accepted. Sometimes this means in conjunction with the deliverables, other times a day or two later after a confirmation of the acceptance.

The place to address payment is not upon handing over the work or sending over an invoice. It needs to be addressed before work begins. Most companies will try to get the most favorable payment terms they can. The more leverage a person or company has with the client, the better they can negotiate terms. It is important that the contractor act consistently to have the terms of payment honored throughout the duration of the contract. Just as the contractor has deliverables, so has the client or employer in the form of a check or series of checks. Many times, though, companies view payment as something

outside the terms of the contract, dealing with them as they see fit. It is often up to the contractor to see that the payment terms are honored.

Delays in payment are usually not because a company is intentionally trying to squeeze their contractors. Most times it is because the process of moving the invoice through the accounting system takes time or encounters delays. One way around this problem is to monitor the process and confirm that the invoice gets passed off to the accounting department and that the accounting department has it in their system.

As far as receiving payment when it is late, companies typically pay those that make their presence known. This does not mean that you should call and threaten a company. It simply means that you should call and ask for the **expected dates of payment**. You should do this continually until payment is made. Relationships matter so it is worthwhile to get to know people that make the payments and treat them with respect.

Following Up
Although the working relationship may be officially over by the terms in the work agreement or contract, it is important to stay in touch with former clients or employers. For clients, especially, it pays to call shortly after the final deliverables have been received and see how things are developing. These calls can sometimes lead to additional work on the same project or on future ones. If not, information gathered from the client about the project or about your skills can be invaluable.

Terminating a Relationship
Someone once said that almost everybody should be fired at least once in their career, otherwise they are not pushing the limits of what they can do. A related thought is that many of the best people have walked out on jobs not because they had other opportunities lined up but because they were extremely dissatisfied with the position, the project, or the company. Severing work relationships, whether it is an employer-employee relationship or a client/contractor relationship, is

a natural, though infrequent, part of every working person's life. These events should never be looked on as failures. You should learn from them but not fixate on the past.

The termination procedures should be established at the beginning in the **work agreement**. If they are not, then be prepared for a messy dissolution. It is inevitable that both sides will disagree unless a formal way to proceed has been established beforehand. In the case of an employee, the procedures and conditions of the termination are typically governed by state laws. Some states, like California, have employment at-will laws that give companies great leeway in hiring and firing. Some of the areas to pay attention to in terms of the termination of an employee are severance pay and health benefits. Also important for people in positions of high responsibility are indemnification guarantees that protect them from any actions performed as an employee. Unless termination provisions have been determined beforehand, you are typically at the mercy of state laws, the benevolence of the company, the severance packages for previously terminated employees, and your negotiating skills.

For contracting arrangements, terminating a contract in progress might include the drafting of a letter notifying the other party of the first party's intent. The process usually includes the payment and transfer of the work completed up to a certain date. Assessing the value of the work completed to date is often difficult and requires some give and take on both sides. If a fair value cannot be agreed upon and the contract stipulates an arbitrary clause, that will be the next step. If not, there may be little recourse.

Line Up New Work

The best chances for getting hired are when you are currently working. The second best chance is immediately upon termination of employment or upon completion of a contracting job. Many people make the mistake, however, of delaying the process of finding work for several weeks or months, taking time off instead. No matter how tempting it may be to just step away for a little while, recognize that if you do, you run the risk having to dramatically lower your expectations in order to find work when you finally start looking. Many careers have ended up in shambles be-

Tips for Receiving Prompt Payment

- *Establish reasonable terms with the client and have them reflected in the work agreement.*
- *Include an interest rate for late payment, not to exceed that permitted by law.*
- *Establish a primary contact at the client for all work-related issues including budget, schedule, deliverables, and payment.*
- *Find out how the payment process works. Know the route the invoice travels and who is involved in the process until the check is sent out.*
- *Create invoices and deliver them to the primary contact according to the invoicing schedule.*
- *Follow through the delivery of the invoice with the primary contact to be sure the invoice is in order and is being processed. Ask for a date for receipt of the check.*
- *If the payment is large or needed promptly, consider paying for overnight delivery service.*
- *If there is doubt about receiving payment as promised, contact others in the payment process to check up on the status of payment.*
- *If payment is late, contact the appropriate person in the payment process. (The primary contact often hands over responsibility to others once they pass along the invoice.)*
- *Contact this person regularly and ask for full payment or set up a schedule for partial payments.*
- *Repeat the previous step on a regular schedule until payment has been made in full.*

cause it took a person longer than they thought to find new work. And when they did, they had to settle for something they did not especially want to do.

If you find yourself out of work unexpectedly, your first goal should be to line up new work. The new work does not have to start right away—it can be delayed a few months—nor does it have to be full time. A person can consult or contract part time for a few months while looking for other opportunities. Also, many people that do leave jobs and become consultants make the mistake of concentrating on establishing an office and a market presence instead of doing what is the most important—lining up several clients as soon as possible. Fancy collateral materials and a nice office are not what win consulting jobs. Skills, hard work, and determination along with a lot of sales calls do. It's hard to get business while sitting behind a desk, much less when buying a computer.

Suing companies for wrongful termination is an expensive and lengthy process, and largely an unsuccessful proposition. While it can be tempting to threaten a lawsuit in the heat of the moment, avoid even mentioning the subject until you have consulted a competent lawyer in the matter and rationally thought it through.

Contractor vs. Employee

When establishing a contracting business, experts suggest taking several steps to make it as legitimate as possible. Local accounting firms or law firms are likely to have materials tailored to your state and local government. These steps include

- *registering the business at the local and possibly state level*

- *obtaining a federal tax ID number*

- *creating a distinct business name*

- *printing up collateral materials with the business name on it*

Employment regulations are determined by a combination of federal, state, and local laws. One of the thorniest employment issues in many areas of multimedia is the difference between a contractor and an employee. Though it may seem like there is a gray line between the two, that is largely because many people do not refer to the guidelines set down by the IRS in defining what constitutes a legitimate independent contractor. These guidelines appear on the next page.

The basic foundation of these guidelines is that an **independent contractor** has control over the means and end result of their work. Essentially, anybody that works on a company's premises without paying for the space or is given a lot of direction in their work qualifies as an employee and not an independent contractor.

There are several reasons why many companies prefer to hire independent contractors instead of **employees**. The first and foremost is because it allows them a way to fill specific needs that have only a limited duration. For small projects or for special work, hiring a contractor as opposed to an employee is much less complicated. When the work has been completed, the relationship is over.

Another reason companies might use contractors is because it allows them to reduce their payroll expense. Companies only have to pay a contractor's invoices. They do not have to pay the worker's Social Security taxes, worker's compensation or unemployment insurance premiums, or health and retirement benefits. They may also avoid awarding stock options or profit-sharing bonuses. A final reason is that it reduces a company's liability

in employment matters. Companies have fewer legal restrictions in the hiring and firing of contractors than with employees. This issue is significant considering many companies' fear of lawsuits for wrongful termination.

There are few penalties to a contractor that is later termed an employee by the IRS but there are stiff penalties for the employer. The exposure to the employer includes back withholding taxes (state, federal, and FICA), interest, civil penalties, and potential criminal liabilities. (The back withholding taxes are often due regardless of whether or not the contractor paid their taxes.) Also, contractors are not covered under the Workman's Compensation Act and therefore are not barred from suing for injuries suffered on the job. Not only might the fines for not providing workman's compensation be substantial, but the employer may be held liable for medical bills plus temporary or permanent disability.

There are advantages to being an independent contractor. The first is that business expenses are tax-deductible. Also, contractors, in theory, receive some form of worker independence and the freedom to structure their work environment and work schedule. Several disadvantages include self-employment tax, the potential loss of health and retirement benefits, and the lack of worker's compensation coverage. Most contractors rates are significantly greater than employment rates to reflect the costs of bearing these additional costs.

Entwined in the debate between contractor vs. employee classification is the issue of ownership of the **intellectual property rights** ▶ 142 of the work performed. The rights to most of the work performed by employees belong to the employer under the work-for-hire doctrine. Under that same doctrine, the rights to the work performed by a contractor many times belong to the contractor unless otherwise called out in the contract. As a result, companies that use contractors must make sure that they obtain the proper rights to the work. Contractors are in a position to charge more for the copyright ownership rights.

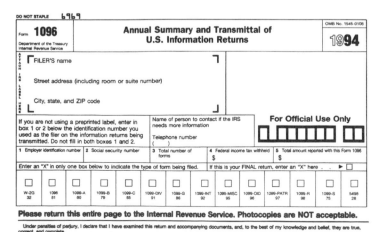

SCHEDULE C
(Form 1040)

Department of the Treasury
Internal Revenue Service   (U)

Profit or Loss From Business
(Sole Proprietorship)

► Partnerships, joint ventures, etc., must file Form 1065.
► Attach to Form 1040 or Form 1041.   ► See Instructions for Schedule C (F

Name of proprietor

A   Principal business or profession, including product or service (see page C-1)

C   Business name. If no separate business name, leave blank.

20 Factors for Determining Independent Contractor Status

The IRS uses 20 common law factors on a case-by-case basis to determine whether a worker is an independent contractor. The courts have not assigned weights to these factors but the factors most often used to determine are whether a worker offers services to the general public, supplies their own tools and a place to work, and controls the methods used to accomplish the work.

1. Receive No Instructions
Contractors can be provided with specifications for the work they are supposed to perform but they cannot be required to follow instructions to accomplish the job.

2. Receive No Training
Contractors should not receive training by the hiring firm.

3. Non-integration of Services
The services of contractors should not be integrated into the business operations of the hiring company.

4. Can Hire Others
Contractors are hired to provide a result and therefore can hire others to perform the work.

5. Control Their Own Assistants
Contractors should be free to hire, supervise, and pay assistants at their sole discretion.

6. Non-continuing Relationships
Contractors usually do not have an ongoing relationship with the hiring company.

7. Independent Work Schedules
Contractors should be free to set their own hours.

8. Not Required Full Time
Contractors should be free to work when and for whom they choose.

9. Not Work on Employer's Premises
Contractors should not work on employer's premises. If they do, they should not be under that company's supervision or direction.

10. Establish Order of Work
Contractors should be free to determine the order to perform work in.

11. Provide No Regular Reports
Contractors should not be required to submit regular reports.

12. Receive Payment by Job
Contractors should not be paid by time. They should receive payment for the job.

13. Pay Business Expenses
Contractors are generally responsible for their own business expenses.

14. Supply Tools and Materials
Contractors usually supply their own tools and materials, and do not use those furnished by the hiring company unless they pay a reasonable rental for them.

15. Make a Significant Investment in Their Business
Contractors should have an adequate investment in their business and not rely on the resources of the hiring company.

16. Realization of Profit or Loss
Contractors should be able to show a profit or a loss from the activities of their business.

17. Work for Multiple Firms at a Time
Contractors often work for multiple clients at the same time and should not be restricted from doing so by the hiring company.

18. Make Services Available to the General Public
Contractors make their services available to the general public through advertising and maintaining an active business license.

19. Work until Job Completion
Contractors cannot be fired as long as they are producing the results that meet the contract specifications.

20. Liability upon Terminating Work
Contractors incur potential liability upon ending a work relationship.

*There are special IRS rules for certain roles such as computer consultants. Individuals and companies should check with a qualified **financial advisor** ▶ 144 to clarify their particular situation.*

There are federal "safe harbor" rules passed by Congress that protect a worker's independent contractor status if the taxpayer treatment was in reasonable reliance on any of the following:

- *judicial precendent, published rulings, technical advice with respect to the taxpayer, or a letter ruling to the taxpayer*

- *a past IRS audit of the taxpayer in which there was no assessment attributable to the treatment of individuals with similiar positions*

- *long-standing recognized practice of a significant segment of the industry in which such individual was engaged*

Equipment

The first thing many people in multimedia do when they go into business for themselves is to buy a computer. While that might seem the most appropriate thing to do, it is not necessarily the first thing you should do. The first thing is to find clients. Once you have those, then you can go about getting computer equipment. Paying clients sometimes take longer to find than most people realize. Conserving cash until an agreement is signed is one of the smarter things people can do.

Most people that work on multimedia projects are provided **equipment** by the companies they work for. As a result, equipment decisions are usually handled by someone else. There are many, though, that either work full-time or part-time out of their home or office and periodically need to obtain equipment.

If you have made the decision to **purchase** a computer, peripherals, or specialized equipment (such as a video camera), you should be interested in getting the best price that is convenient. Consider the cost of the entire arrangement when comparing prices. There is a fine line between buying a computer that is powerful enough to grow with your needs and obtaining one with options and expandability you will never use.

Remember, however, that a deal that sounds too good to be true probably is. Beware of knock-off equipment, especially. It may have components of inferior quality—something you may not find out for months. Established brands are safe bets for quality, service, and resale value.

Leasing Equipment

Buying equipment is only one option. For some people and companies, **leasing** makes a lot of financial sense. There are plenty of companies that lease computer equipment. The primary advantage of leasing over buying is that it reduces the amount of money that has to be paid up front. A portion of the money received from clients over the course of a project can go towards paying the lease. Financing the purchase of equipment provides the same advantage, but financing for equipment is often more difficult to get outside of a leasing company. Another advantage is that it reduces the risk of equipment obsolescence by enabling you to simply return the equipment at the end of its useful life rather than keeping it.

A disadvantage of leasing equipment is that the implicit interest rate that a leasing firm will charge can be as high as 30%. This rate compensates the firm for the risk of obsolescence as well as maintenance costs they oftentimes bear. Another disadvantage is that is does not provide you with the asset base that purchasing equipment does. An asset base is one way to build value in a business and can be extremely useful when seeking credit at a later date.

Many leasing companies have **buy-out options** for leases that let people purchase the leased equipment after the lease is up. (Prices can range from $1 to 20% of the original purchase price.) Leases with buy-out options are called capital leases. Leases without buy-out options are called operating leases. The difference is significant because it can determine the tax deductibility of the equipment and the responsibility for maintaining it. Equipment that is purchased or obtained through a **capital lease** must be depreciated over time. This means that only a certain portion of the equipment cost can be deducted in any single year. Also, you may be considered the owner of the equipment and thus responsible for keeping it operational. An **operating lease**, however, can be deducted in full in the year that the expense occurs and the leasing company is generally responsible for repairs and maintenance.

Calculating Interest Rates

The easiest way to calculate the interest rate in a lease is to use a spreadsheet program. In a single row, list the price followed by the monthly payments. The monthly rate can be obtained by using the Internal Rate of Return function (IRR). The first argument is the column range between the price and the last payment and the second is a guess. (0.1 works fine.) The annual rate can then be determined from the monthly rate.

Price	Payment1	Payment2	...	PaymentN

Monthly rate = IRR(Price:PaymentN,0.1)
Annual rate = (1+Monthly rate)^12-1

Example

5000	-200	-200	...	-200 (36 periods)

Monthly rate = 2.23%
Annual rate = 30.35%

The tax advantages for leasing equipment, however, are less important for new businesses as the tax laws allow them to write off a certain number of capital expenses in the first year of business. Meeting with a financial consultant early when establishing a business can help you determine and pursue the best course of action.

What to Get

Regardless of the decision to buy or lease, it can be difficult to decide what to get. The type of machine and peripherals are largely determined by the roles you will play and the platforms for which you will develop projects. One piece of advice that many learn the hard way is not to fall in love with a technology at the expense of ignoring market trends. Think of technology as a tool. If the tools in the marketplace change, then change along with them—provided they assist you in your work.

Also, do not confuse the development platforms with the delivery platforms. The **development platforms** are the computers, operating systems, and peripherals used to develop an interactive project. The **delivery platforms** ▶ 12 are the platforms used by the audience to play or view that project. They do not have to be the same. There is a big trend for products to be cross-platform, meaning that they run on more than one platform. This is usually accomplished by using an authoring tool or a custom authoring system that allows projects to be quickly ported from one platform to others. For example, *Macromedia Director* is an authoring tool that currently supports Macintosh, Windows, and 3DO platforms.

As a result of these cross-platform tools and capabilities, more than one platform can be used as the development platform. Many of the multimedia developers creating mass-market products are using Macintosh computers for most of the routine work, and high-performance computers such as Silicon Graphics computers for complex 3D animation and video production. These platforms may change in the future or they may not, depending on what happens in the marketplace between the various hardware and software manufacturers. You must understand the technology but do not become attached to it to the point of blindness.

Finding Out What to Buy

The best places to find out what to buy are the many multimedia and computer **magazines** such as *New Media*, *MacUser*, and *PC Magazine*. Almost every issue contains advice for purchasing hardware or software as well as product comparisons. Many also have annual equipment and tool summaries that provide comprehensive information on what to buy. Since technology changes significantly every six months to a year, magazines are typically your most current and best resource. **Online sources** are rapidly growing as resources for product information, but make sure you ask questions in the proper forums.

Other sources for information about what to buy or lease and where to go are **other developers** or **professionals** in your area. These people should be able (and willing) to give you more details about obtaining equipment than you might wish to hear.

Developer Discounts

Many of the companies that are trying to create a standard in the marketplace either in hardware or software (such as Apple, Microsoft, Sun, Kaleida, and General Magic) have **developer programs** that offer equipment or software at reduced prices. Most of these programs, though, are targeted at companies as opposed to individuals. There is typically an annual fee, and though this fee can be recouped by the savings from the discounts, it usually exceeds the savings from the purchase of a single unit.

Student Discounts

Student discounts can be an affordable way for individuals to purchase hardware and software. Many of the same hardware and software manufacturers that have developer programs also have purchase programs for students. These programs are offered not only to high schools and colleges but also many times to extended education programs. The savings on software can be up to $2/3$ of the retail price. Savings on hardware, if offered, are substantially less but still attractive.

Make sure the value of the equipment in a buy-out option is clearly enumerated. Do not leave it as simply "fair market value."

Buy a computer model one or two levels beyond what suits you at the time of purchase. This guideline will help insure that your computer is still useful after your skills improve and the tasks you perform on it expand.

Equipment and Roles

Executive Producer
Producer
Lawyer
Financial Consultant
Agent
Recruiter
Marketing Manager
Sales Manager
Scriptwriter
Editor
Moderator
Content Expert

Management and Writing

These roles do not require very powerful computing capabilities, although, given the frenetic nature of some of them (especially producing, agent, sales, and marketing) it is nice to have a computer with the capacity to smoothly handle multiple applications at once. A CD-ROM player is recommended, as well as 8–12MB RAM. A 14-inch color monitor is sufficient (although a 16-inch is also a bonus), and a fax machine or fax modem is a must.

A laptop is a good call, especially for producers (giving demos to clients, working on the road), sales people, writers, and editors. An internal fax modem, especially in a portable machine, is ideal for checking email and sending faxes on the road. Internet access gives users a competitive advantage, as managers and producers can obtain instantaneous access to information resources around the world.

Design and Animation

Creative Director
Game Designer
Interface Designer
2-D Animator
Art Director
Photographer
Visual Designer
Illustrator

A powerful graphics machine is a requirement for all of these roles, as well as a CD-ROM drive and a large color monitor that displays at least thousands of colors. Having two monitors is ideal for switching between palettes and different graphics applications—one monitor should be 16 inches or greater. A scanner, or at least access to one, is essential for placeholder and final art. Many people find graphics tablets helpful when creating lines and shapes that are difficult to generate with a mouse or trackball. Serious photographers will want to investigate digital equipment; digital cameras are becoming more sophisticated and less expensive, and they speed up the process of original photographic image acquisition in multimedia. Twenty to thirty megabytes of RAM is recommended, and 500MB to one gigabyte of storage space is usually sufficient for storing the amount of data that artists and photographers work with. An additional drive, CD-ROM burner, or Syquest cartridge drive are recommended for archiving old work.

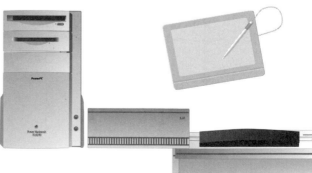

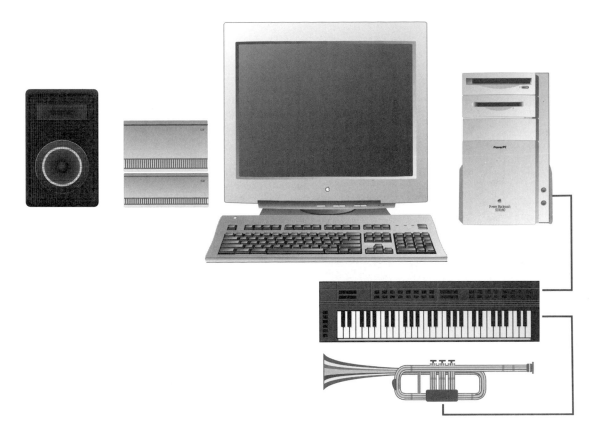

Musician
Composer
Sound Effects
Engineer
Sound Producer
Sound Engineer
Sound Editor
Video Producer
Videographer
Lighting Designer

Sound and Video

Lots of peripheral gear is needed for these roles to add their voices to a multimedia production. First, though, one needs a powerful computer with at least 20MB RAM. A CD-ROM player is important, as is additional storage space.

Sound work requires at least 500MB–1 gigabyte of disk space, nice speakers, connection to a MIDI system, and a large color monitor for running multiple applications and keeping track of palettes.

Video work requires more RAM (30–60MB), as well as more disk space (over 1 gigabyte). A video accelerator board speeds up digitization and rendering, and is highly recommended, though high-end ones can be expensive. While a Hi-8 camera will provide satisfactory video, most recommend using Betacam equipment whenever possible.

Programming

Technical Lead
Programmer
3D Animator

Programmers use a variety of machines for work, especially when creating multimedia titles. Macintoshes and PCs are perennial favorites, and authoring on both for delivery on multiple platforms is now common. Important things to look for are: one or two large color monitors (reduces eye strain and helps manage many open documents), lots of RAM (20–30MB), a CD-ROM drive, and a decent amount of disk space (500MB–1 gigabyte).

System administrator
Unix programmer
3D Animator
Website maintenance

Programming and Systems Administration

These power users need heavy-duty machines that can handle complex mathematical calculations, distributed computing, and multitasking (run multiple processes at once). Unix machines are ideal for many of these purposes—they are built for multitasking and can serve a network of users. Unix is the preferred platform for website administration and maintenance and other functions that require one machine to communicate with many users (e.g., serving as a mail server). Unix machines are also good for 3D modeling and rendering programs that require a fast processor and tons of RAM; 30-60 MB of RAM is recommended for 3D work. Deciding which system to buy can be difficult: some three dozen variations exist, each with its own idiosyncracies. Full-blown Unix systems, such as those from Sun, Hewlett-Packard, and Silicon Graphics, are considerably more expensive than PCs and Macintoshes; however, there are versions of Unix available for PCs with a 486 chip, such as the ever-popular BSDI and Linux. Apple has its own Unix flavor as well, A/UX.

Testing and Support

A test manager needs to have a machine that will help them manage multiple projects and resources, and communicate with the outside world via the Internet. A mid-range machine with 8MB RAM and a 14-inch color monitor is fine, and a CD-ROM drive is nice to have but not necessary. A fax machine is a must for the receipt of bug reports from beta sites. Internet access helps here as well.

Testers need machines which are capable of running databases, word processing applications, Internet access software and CD-ROM titles. A mid-range PC with 8MB of RAM, a 14-inch color monitor, a CD-ROM drive, and Internet access is ideal.

A capable, mid-range machine similar to that used by testers and test managers is also appropriate for use in customer support.

Test Manager
Tester
Customer Support

Test Suite

Test suites should have a wide variety of machines that enable comprehensive analysis of consistency, quality, and compatibility of work. It is good to have different model computers from the same platform, to test performance with different processors and RAM sizes. Also, a mix of computers, configurations, and peripherals is essential. In studios that develop and test websites, a test suite must have Internet access, preferably with variable bandwidth.

6. Roles

The film industry has a very structured format for the roles people play in creating a movie. The same can be said increasingly for many areas of multimedia.

It is critical for each person on a multimedia project team to know what role they play because that role will detemine their tasks and responsibilities. It will also help determine who reports to whom and who communicates with whom.

The roles can be separated into major disciplines. These disciplines include business and project management, marketing and sales, legal work, creative direction, media production, programming, testing, and support. If you are looking to break into multimedia, you should pick a single area to concentrate on. Focus on areas that correspond to your interests and strongest skills. Make sure you think about where you want it to lead. For example, taking a position as a production assistant for a group of designers can lead to role as visual designer, animator, or other media specialist. Someone with an interest in the tools and the process for creating artwork, sound, and video is likely to perform much better in this role than someone whose ultimate goal is to manage people or negotiate deals.

The roles covered in this chapter include:

Management

Support

Marketing

Testing

Project

Legal

Programming

Creative Direction

Media Production

Executive Producer	Sound Producer
Producer	Voice Artist/Vocalist
Lawyer	Composer/Musician/Sound Effects Specialist
Financial Consultant	
Agent	Sound Engineer/Sound Editor
Recruiter	
Marketing Roles	Video Producer
	Videographer
Creative Director	Performer/Actor
Art Director	Lighting/Sets/Costumes/Props
Interface Designer	
Game Designer	Technical Lead
	Programmer
Scriptwriter	
Editor/Moderator	Test Manager
Content Expert	Tester
Visual Designer	Sales Roles
2D Animator	Customer Support
3D Animator	

Executive Producer

What They Do

The executive producer's main responsibilities lie in managing a business, service, or series of titles. **Executive producers** are found in both publishers and in production studios. An executive producer in a publisher may create and manage an in-house production staff, look to outside studios for either production services or original works, or do a combination. An executive producer in a production studio is often the president as well, overseeing corporate direction in addition to leading a team of producers. The focus of an executive producer is outward on the creation of production deals and the oversight of a series of projects. The focus of a producer is inward, on developing and managing a single project.

Many people ask what the deals are like in multimedia and the answer is, "All over the board." Some developers are producing titles under work-for-hire arrangements and receiving production fees. Others are receiving production fees or advances, royalties between 3% and 20%, and possibly **copyright ownership** ▶ 102 to works, their characters, and/or code. Online work consists primarily of production fees, though some developers may receive licensing fees (for the use of technology), management fees, revenue sharing of subscription fees or advertising receipts, or equity in some online ventures.

Executive producers are valued for their ability to move projects into and through production. They may help develop product concepts as well as help decide which ones to spend resources on. In the case of a publisher, these resources might include funds for production. In the case of a production studio, they may include marketing and sales efforts for either responding to requests for proposals or pitching original ideas.

Once in production, executive producers have **oversight responsibilities** to ensure projects are on track and to step in in the event of any unusual circumstances. They need to continually assess the ability of producers to complete projects within the given budgets and schedules and take corrective steps as needed. Executive producers are ultimately responsible for the profitability of each project under their direction.

An executive producer's job needs to be considered within the context of the fiscal year. It involves how profitable a business or division has been and what leverage they have built in terms of products, programming, market share, brand name, or technology. It extends to the development of strategic relationships, the recruitment and retention of talented individuals, and the implementation of sound systems for finance, marketing, sales, design, media production, technical development, and quality assurance.

Executive producers are primarily involved in the early beginnings of projects. The executive producer's goal is to move products and services into production. Once this happens, the executive producer's role defers to the producer but may re-enter the picture in a more expanded capacity but usually only if something goes wrong with the production. In one situation, for example, the primary company funding the project went bankrupt, leaving the executive producer at a game developer searching for alternative financing. Finally after a month or two of scrambling, he was able to arrange the transfer of the production contract to another publisher. In another, a game machine manufacturer discontinued funding the outside production of a game because of unexpected low sales of a new machine. The vendor had to halt production, let go of several people, and look for other funds to complete the project.

Process

The process that an executive producer follows is similar for executive producers on both the publisher side and the studio side. This process looks at the **external development** and **funding** picture in a particular market. An executive producer needs to know about many of the available products or services within a particular category. They need to know what makes them successful, what the budgets are, and what the structures of

Late 1993 and early 1994 saw the rise of several CD-ROM-based catalogs ▶ 46. Over the course of 1994, that activity migrated from CD-ROMs to online services and the World Wide Web. This points to the need for an executive producer to be continually aware of the trends that affect their business.

the deals look like. The types of products and programming being produced for all platforms and markets can change dramatically in less than six months. The budgets and the production deals also change as quickly.

The process also looks inward at the recruitment and management of producers and/or studios. Educating and training producers and pulling together a close-knit team of designers and engineers are important parts of an executive producer's role. One executive producer pins his success on his ability to clone himself, or in other words, recruit talented people and transfer his knowledge of developing and producing projects to them. An executive producer focuses a company or a division on a particular market and leverages a few particular strengths such as publishing savvy, technology, or brand awareness. They put the structures in place so that the organization runs smoothly.

For original titles or online service ideas, an executive producer will work with a producer to package the concepts and then pitch them to internal or external funding sources. These external sources can be investors, publishers, cable companies, online services, advertising agencies, sponsors, lending institutions, or any other parties interested in investing. The executive producer helps locate and approach these funding sources and negotiate the production deal.

When pitching a title or series of CD-ROM titles, an executive producer may meet with an executive producer or the manager of **product submissions ▶** 155, 190 at a publisher, describe the ideas, and possibly demo a prototype. Budgets for CD-ROM titles range from $250K to $1.5 million. More often than not, an executive producer will try to find financing for several titles as opposed to one. These may be produced all at once or spaced over time. In many cases, two stages of funding are necessary. One to obtain seed money to option rights, develop a workable concept, and produce a prototype, and the second to fund the full production of the title.

For companies offering production services, an executive producer will coordinate the process for soliciting and responding to **requests for proposals ▶** 125. Most executive producers defer the **proposal ▶** 126 writing to others but often work on key parts or look through them before they are sent out. Once projects are in production, executive producers monitor them to be sure that milestones are being met and the budget and schedule are on track. The executive producer should be the first to notice the likelihood of any slips in the schedule or budget overruns. The producer may be too close to the project and blinded by overconfidence. Others on the project may have the same problem.

Tools and Techniques

The tools of an executive producer are those of a **manager**, **recruiter**, and **salesperson**. A prime technique is to continually know the types of deals that are available. Many trade magazines and newsletters list the deals that are taking place, and so finding out what deals are taking place is not hard. Finding out what the terms are, however, can be. Without the ability to move from identifying a funding or production source to signing a production deal, though, an executive producer will not get far. This is where closing techniques come in. A good executive producer shows enough of the package to gain interest but not enough to turn away. Their pace and tone will match the pace and tone of the other person, which is critical in an area where so many different industries and cultures are clashing.

Qualifications

The best qualification for an executive producer is to have a series of **successful deals**. A successful deal these days includes not only a project that makes it through production and into the hands of clients or customers, but one that is profitable for all parties involved and is well received by the audience. The fascination with multimedia within media companies is quickly fading. They are looking much more closely at the bottom line in any interactive media investment.

For a developer creating products, it is important to know which companies are in positions to fund projects, followed closely by knowing the pros and cons of the different funding sources. For

Henri Poole
President and Executive Producer, vivid studios

Henri Poole wants his team to get everything they deserve, from compensation to credit to copyrights. "As an independent contributor, I didn't have the negotiating power to get what my co-workers deserved," he says of his life prior to becoming the head of **vivid** studios. These days, Henri devotes his time to bringing in new business and poring over legal contracts, making sure his team gets a fair deal.

Henri's belief in people is strong: "Individual contributors to this industry will be the ones who discover innovations that may change the world and open up new forms of communication."

An artist and high-tech entrepreneur from age 16, Henri first began to develop multimedia technology at Apple Computer in 1988. Two years later he founded Spatial Data Architects, a multimedia consultancy, which he later merged with **vivid**. Henri suggested that **vivid** write a multimedia "cookbook" and began brokering a deal with Apple. In 1992, Apple funded the book now known as Multimedia Demystified.

In 1993, Henri led **vivid's** research and development effort for CRUSH, a productivity tool that allows marketing managers to analyze the environmental and competitive forces at work in their markets. Henri also led **vivid's** first online design team in the 1994 redesign of The WELL. This research and design effort gave **vivid** its first course in designing tools to enhance communications within virtual communities.

His business and technology savvy gave him an early start, but it is his skill in finding talented people and his abilitiy to guide their efforts that has propelled him to his current position. "I didn't expect to be involved so deeply in this revolution in human communications," he explains, "but I love it now." He is equally passionate when talking about his goals: "I want to help create a new business model that shows people it's OK to work and have fun at the same time. I want to help create tools that allow people to communicate more effectively with one another. I want to bring about new communities for people who had none before."

example, **venture capital** ▶ 56 is often pointed to as one source of financing, but people going this route should recognize that it is probably only appropriate for seed money to start a company or develop technology. By almost all accounts, using venture capital to finance titles is not likely. Many publishers and private investors are willing to, but taking this route can mean a long sales cycle and a lot of preparation.

How to Hire

Finding an executive producer most likely dictates one of three routes. The first is finding someone who has been a producer on a number of multimedia projects and has a working knowledge of deals and the players in the multimedia industry. Unfortunately, there are few people experienced enough with the production aspects as well as knowledgeable of the bigger picture. In addition, many of the potential candidates within production studios or developers are likely to participate in royalties on projects or have equity stakes and, therefore, are difficult to hire away.

The second route is finding someone who has business expertise in another form of media (preferably the film, TV, or cable industries) along with a working knowledge of the multimedia production process and practical experience with a good sampling of multimedia projects. If an executive producer cannot name what the top projects or companies are in a particular area, they are probably not the most appropriate choice. People that are close to the distribution end of multimedia can be excellent executive producers for product-oriented companies provided they are good managers and can select good producers and help assemble good teams.

The third route is to look to executive producers at multimedia publishers. There is a lot of change going on in interactive media and many companies are reassessing their direction or moving very timidly. There may be a number of people at these companies who are interested in working for companies with aggressive plans in a marketplace.

When looking for an executive producer, it helps to find one that has an open mind about projects and is willing to give up lots of creative control to the creative director, art directors, and producers. Someone that comes from a position that is more hands-on may be less willing to let others create, thus becoming a bottleneck in the development of multiple projects.

How to Be Hired

There are several ways to get hired as an executive producer. One way is to **move up** within an organization, for example, from producer of one project to executive producer of a series of projects. This pathway rests on helping to develop the business from a creative standpoint as well as a business standpoint. You may need to create a business plan that provides the strategy for proceeding. It also means lining up producers to work on each project, either training associate producers or finding ones outside the organization. This route can apply to any type of project or business area such as title development, kiosks or marketing presentations, or the creation of online places.

Another way is to **change organizations** in the same type of business within the context of moving from producer to executive producer. Since there are few executive positions available, you may have to look outside your organization in order to make the switch. When making this change, however, make sure you receive an employment contract that clearly states the offer

and makes it binding. Switching positions at this level should only be done in a secure and orderly way. Also, look to protect yourself in the event of a change in direction or problems at the new company.

Still another way is to **switch** from a publisher to a studio or a studio to a publisher. This strategy can have a large payoff because it means having the knowledge of how the other side works. It can also be filled with problems because the change in environments can be overwhelming. Moving from a free-wheeling small company to a larger company with many policies and procedures can be a shock. Likewise, moving from a larger company to a smaller company that may not have support staff and other office "perks" can be a humbling experience.

A final route is to **start a company** on your own. Many of the people at the head of multimedia companies got to be there this way. Recognize, though, that this is a risky proposition. Nobody ever bothers to count the number of people who tried but did not succeed. If you do go this route, focus on a particular market and a type of product or service. Whereas several years ago it was possible for a multimedia company to handle almost any project that came up, it is definitely not this way anymore. Look to separate development from distribution. At small companies especially, it is difficult, if not impossible, to do both. Also, conserve cash, keep a fair amount in reserve for unexpected occurrences, and avoid relying on a single customer or client.

Compensation

Executive producers are typically highly compensated. This compensation is usually in the form of a salary as well as possible **equity** ▶ 98 or profit-sharing in the company. Larger companies are likely to offer higher salaries, larger benefits, and better severance packages but less equity or profit-sharing. Smaller companies are usually the opposite.

Chris Thorman
Executive Producer, Times Mirror Multimedia

Unlike many of the newly minted "Vice Presidents of New Media" who come from the publishing, marketing, advertising, and entertainment worlds, Chris Thorman brings some serious technical skills to his position as Executive Producer at Times Mirror Multimedia. Beginning with a B.S. in Computer Science at M.I.T. where he earned a 4.0 average and worked as a researcher on interactive video applications at the Architecture Machine Group, Chris's career has provided the opportunity to work on some of the cutting edge products that have defined the very look and feel of interactive multimedia. After leaving M.I.T., Chris went to Apple's Advanced Technology Group, then helped engineer the software for QuickTime 1.0. At Macromedia he led the process of updating Director's 10-year-old code base, redesigned the interface,
and brought it cross-platform to create Director 4.0 for Macintosh and Windows. As engineering team leader of the development team launching Director 5.0, Chris led the writing of the technical specification, and balanced his engineering team's passion for excellence against a tight deadline, a limited budget, and the concerns of "a vocal user community."

At Times Mirror Multimedia, Chris oscillates between San Francisco and the headquarters in Los Angeles, where he is helping lead the publishing conglomerate's charge into CD-ROM production and publishing for the home computer market.

Bill Appleton,
President and Executive Producer, CyberFlix

vivid: Describe what roles you play.

My job as president of CyberFlix is to lead the company in overall business strategy and to provide the tools and technologies necessary to create our products. I've been personally involved in crafting our important relationships with Bandai and Paramount, as well as managing the creative end of the company. For example, right now we are working on a horror title, a western, and *Viper* for Paramount. I want to make sure that these titles have the CyberFlix trademark of high quality, hard-hitting interactive movies.

vivid: What skills are necessary to do your job?

Over the past year I've gotten lots of practice switching roles as necessary to keep everything moving. Some days I need to negotiate an agreement with one of our strategic partners. Other days I'm writing code for an IBM conversion or working on the new Dream Factory™ architecture. Still other days I'm helping with creative design, like a new logo or a box. I used to love to 3D model and paint

but there seems to be less time for that now. Luckily, I've got lots of help. Our vice president handles most of the negotiating details and legal work, not to mention managing company operations. Our producers track the titles that need to be developed. Our graphic artists are great in the 3D domain, we've got a sound producer who handles music and sound, and a designer who handles packaging, merchandising, and corporate image.

vivid: What off-the-shelf tools do you use? What tools have you created?

In general, we use a wide range of off-the-shelf tools, although I don't like to go into details about that for competitive reasons. The new proprietary tool set that we are using is called Dream Factory.

vivid: Can you make money selling tools or is content where the future is?

I've been in the tools business on the Macintosh for over a decade, longer than anyone. This is a very difficult place to

Bill Appleton, *continued*

work because there is such a limited audience for your work. CyberFlix has significantly altered that strategy because now we are using the tools internally for titles and they give us a great competitive advantage. We have also licensed the tool set to one of our strategic partners. All in all, this is a better way to use authoring tools in a business setting, but you have to be ready to handle the creative end of the content as well.

vivid: What's an interactive movie and how does it differ from a game?

If I'm trying to tell someone what we do, the "game" word often comes up—people don't have much experience with interactive movies. But we definitely don't want to be a game company. We want to take the issue from reflex to emotion, from game play to drama. This takes the medium much closer to a mass-market vehicle that many different people can participate in and enjoy.

vivid: What's the definition of interactive as it pertains to movies?

A movie is a linear thing. That's why the folks using live video are going down a dead-end street—it will never be very interactive, and storage problems are also a problem because the data is not very reusable. We have taken a really different approach here. We are trying to build the things that are needed to create worlds, set them up, teach them to behave, and see what happens. There will still be a role for linear things, or narrative, but the level of interactivity needs to go much higher. One important part of this is to put the artist in charge. If they can change things right there on the keyboard as needed, then we will get much better titles.

vivid: Describe some of the complexity that is involved in an interactive movie.

The total team effort for this type of work is staggering. Usually the title starts as a screenplay or some kind of concept piece. Then the visual style and logo are defined. Next important marketing lead time elements are developed, like a movie trailer, text description, and still graphics. Then the real work of game design and graphic development starts. There will be some real give and take between the lead programmer and the lead artist on format and architecture. Next begins the bulk of the work—generating the tons of content that go into the title. In our case, this includes puppet voice recording, airbrush work, scripting, compression, and massive rendering. The last days are the most difficult. This is where major elements of the title sometimes have to be reworked and this can cause delays. The final phases involve play testing and beta testing. Coordinated with all this is packaging and marketing and management. Later tech support and shipping are involved.

vivid: Does a script play an important part of an interactive movie?

Absolutely. Our latest title *Jump Raven* is based on a 200-page screenplay. The real issue is how to write an interactive screenplay in the first place. Right now we use innovative writing methods that allow the screenwriters to design things in interactive pieces. Dream Factory, however, takes us into more explicit control of the interactive narrative. The screenplay becomes hierarchically organized scripted handlers that define the interactive aspects of a given situation. This medium is the way that licensable properties will be created in the future.

Producer

What They Do

A **producer** has two main responsibilities. The first is to form a project and move it into production and the second is to oversee its creation once in production. These two definitions can peacefully co-exist in a single person or can be divided between two separate people. A skill at bringing an idea together or responding to a proposal may or may not translate into managing all the components that go into creating a consistent and functioning product in a predictable manner.

A common task for a producer is to develop proposals in response to **requests for proposals (RFPs)** from publishers, entertainment companies, advertising agencies, and other companies. For established studios, these RFPs may come unsolicited; for others, RFPs may only come as a result of actively looking for companies in need of production capabilities.

Another potential task is to develop an idea, package it, and with the help of an executive producer, offer it to various funding and distribution sources. A common saying in the film industry is that the producer is the person who holds the rights to an idea. Certain steps, both business and creative, need to be taken to develop that idea and move it into production and then into distribution (most likely through the use of a publisher).

Besides helping to form the concept, a producer is also charged with preparing a budget and a schedule, forming a project team, allocating resources, and moving the project from script to storyboards to finished product. Proper staffing and preparation will set the stage for smooth interactions between project members. Good management skills in the form of creating individual and team milestones and in overseeing the development progression will help keep the projections on target. Producers should have as little hands-on responsibility as possible. Instead, they should put people in the right places with the right tasks, establish communication pathways, oversee the performance of the team, and probably most importantly, inspire and motivate the talent on a daily basis.

Producers play a role before, during, and after a project. They are one of the few whose responsibilities last from the beginning conceptual phases to the end of the process. The final deliverable may be a **golden master** ▶ 259, 266 that is handed off to a publisher, though a few final tasks after this milestone are usually in order. In the case of digizines or maintenance of online places, a producer and a team may have ongoing responsibilities where there is no clearly definable end.

Because of the duration of the role, it's important for producers to pace themselves, in the concept and design phases, during production, and during testing to prevent burn-out. Also, not every proposal will result in work. Companies looking for production services often send RFPs to several production studios, and for original works, only a small percentage get picked up and even a smaller percentage make their way into production. In both cases, a producer has to be prepared for hearing, "I'm sorry. We're going with someone else." Once in production, either internal problems (conflicts between team members, difficulties with technology) or external problems (competing products, market conditions) can stop production. Having other projects and relationships in development and some prior planning for setbacks can make these situations less traumatic.

The Producer Hierarchy

*Producers typically manage one or possibly two large projects at a time or several smaller ones. An **assistant producer** is often a glorified intern performing many of the routine day-to-day tasks of a project. An **associate producer** typically has larger responsibilities such as helping to write proposals and create budget and schedules. They may also be given tasks involving interacting with the client and managing members of the project team. Associate producers are commonly groomed for the producer role whereas that may or may not be the case for assistant producers.*

Process

A producer has a large responsibility for developing new business. Marketing managers and sales people can help identify, qualify, and approach potential customers and/or publishers. Often, the producer formally takes over the contact when a proposal begins to take form. A **proposal** is a bid for work that outlines the budget, the resources, and the schedule estimated for the project. It is prepared by a company wishing to obtain business from another company. A request for proposal (RFP) is a document prepared by the company awarding the business that explains the project and provides an indication of its scope. Although a proposal can be developed on little more than a phone conversation, it is wise to ask for a written request for proposal to reduce the chance for miscommunication and wasted effort.

The request for proposal will often contain a list of items that should be included in a proposal. These will commonly include a budget and schedule, proof of technical capabilities, key talent, and past projects that are similar to the work requested. The last three should already be a part of any production studio's marketing materials and should be easy to provide. For CD-ROM development work, most people are going to want to see previous CD-ROMs. As a result, it is highly beneficial for producers to get credits on shipping CD-ROMs. The requesting company may also wish to see some ideas for the development of the project. The depth of these ideas will depend on how original the work is.

The budget and schedule are a core part of the resulting proposal. Often RFPs will not contain any indication of what a budget or schedule should be. A producer can save a lot of time and effort by trying to get an idea of both right away from the client. Not only will the answers provide an idea of what to build into the proposal but they will also indicate the amount of resources to spend creating the proposal.

Developing Original Works

The responsibility for bringing in projects can also extend to developing **original concepts** and pitching these to companies that will fund the production. While the selling and closing is often a part of the executive producer's role, the development and "packaging" of the concept lies in the hands of the producer. In the development of original works, a producer may locate and then option the rights to a story or a set of content, they may license ideas or scripts submitted to them, or they may conceive the work entirely within the confines of the production studio.

A few independent producers are able to walk into a publisher's office, pitch an idea with little or no supporting materials, and then walk out with money to hire people to develop the property. With little more than a treatment a couple pages in length, they have been able to move the idea into a formal project. Most publishers/distributors, though, are not actively funding under these terms and are looking only at more complete packages, which in many cases include working prototypes. At the least, these packages should include a project brief, scripts and descriptions of the product structure, designs of key screens, and biographies of key individuals on the team. These packages should also include proof of the necessary rights to produce the work. These assurances are one of the first things that an experienced publisher will look for.

Financing for initial development work can come from the developer themselves, family and friends, from private sources looking for investment opportunities, or from venture capital financing. All of these sources need some form of a presentation in order for them to put money into the idea, with some needed more than others. Venture capitalists in particular are likely to provide only seed funding in a company and not on a project basis.

Preparing a Budget and Schedule

In all projects, a budget and a schedule are two principal elements a producer uses to manage a product. A **budget** is a list of tasks associated with cost. A **schedule** is a list of tasks associated by time. These two, together with a concept, define a project. Any of the three can be a starting point with which the other two are then developed. For example, a concept can be broken down by tasks and then these tasks assimilated into roles. The roles can be plotted over time, producing a

Some prospects may be hesitant to provide a budget either because they do not have an idea what the budget should be or because they want to see if they can get a good deal. A producer can get around hesitancy by trying to target a range. The time frame can also help target the budget.

Whereas private investors are likely to need some form of an investment document, publishers are typically interested only in the concept and in the ability to complete the project. Given a concept, the audience, and a budget, a publishing house can put together its own financial picture.

"Are we talking $30,000 or are we talking $300,000?"

"I'm telling you. The budget's not going to work. We just can't do it for that."

schedule, and then the cost for the roles developed into a budget (with the inclusion of equipment and overhead). Or, a budget and schedule can be provided and then a concept refined within these constraints.

Knowing what roles to include on the project team is a skill every producer needs, as is knowing how much to allocate for each role, including profit margin, equipment costs, and incidentals. But knowing who to bring in is highly dependent on what you are building. The complexity of the product will quickly determine the number of visual designers, animators, or programmers needed, the amount to budget for sound or video production, and the amount of testing that will be needed.

A budget and schedule are typically needed early in the process of managing a project. The nature of some projects may not allow for exact budgets and schedules until later in the development process. For the creation of an online magazine, for example, there are few existing products to point to and say, "Let's do it like that." As a result, each project requires a lot of design work in the beginning, work that makes it difficult to budget anything that follows. A way around this is to leave room in the budget to bring in creative directors, art directors, interface designers, and writers to properly create the product concept. This can be done by isolating distinct phases in the development process and refining the earlier phases but including rough estimates or ranges for that latter ones.

Assembling a Project Team
Assembling the **project team** for a title consists of first identifying the roles that are necessary and when they are needed, and then finding people to fulfill those roles. The budget should provide an idea of what can be offered to prospective talent in terms of pay. In reality, it works in both directions, a producer has to know what people are likely to accept as well as what can be offered.

Key individuals should be staffed first. These roles can include art directors, interface designers or game designers, possibly scriptwriters and content experts, and technical leads. Once these

are chosen, the others should be selected so that all tasks in a project are handled by someone. Ideally, the art director and the technical lead should be charged with staffing their areas but it is likely they will need help locating and selecting candidates and in handling the legal and business issues of staffing. A skill that seems common to all good producers is the ability to evaluate talent, both when initially hiring and when managing.

Assembling Resources
Hand in hand with bringing a team together is finding space and getting **equipment ▶ 112** needed to do work. The cost of space and other resources need to be factored into the budget. Both of these are made tremendously easier by planning ahead. If a producer has to get space or equipment on the spur of the moment and they do not have prior arrangements with equipment vendors or leasing companies, then they had better have cash available to make things happen quickly.

The equipment needed should be determined on a role-by-role basis and should be done with an eye foremost toward productivity. A producer does not need a high-end machine and two monitors if they are using only email, spreadsheets, scheduling programs, and word processors. Visual designers working with *Adobe Photoshop* or programmers working with *Macromedia Director* need the fastest machines with the most RAM possible, and two monitors. Equipment is one of the cheapest ways to increase productivity for media production and programming. Not only does a slow machine or not enough RAM increase the time to do a job, it takes the artist or programmer out of their rhythm. Depending on which course a producer pursues when allocating equipment, they will win the enduring love (or hate) of those on the production team.

Managing Conceptual Design
Managing the **conceptual design** of a title is far different from that of the production. In the production phase, most things are known about the product. There are plans to follow with lists of

A producer should not be afraid to tell a prospective client that their budget will not cover the work they are asking for.

Going to publishers for financing is a more established process than raising funds from other sources. Not only are they knowledgeable about the business, an added benefit is that they have established distribution channels, which few of the other investing sources can offer. An advantage of the others is the opportunity to take a more developed product to a publisher or directly to market and, in theory, get a higher royalty rate.

Todd Power,
Producer, Weldon Owen

Todd Power reads children's books more often than most adults—it's his job. As former product manager for Living Books, it was his responsibility to ensure that their products were the best on the market.

Living Books are probably the best-known interactive children's titles on CD-ROM. Top sellers like Just Grandma and Me *not only tell charming stories but provide kid-friendly interactivity for young explorers. In these animated worlds, furry beasts talk and dance—and fenceposts make music, and clothing changes color with a simple click. Todd calls this type of non-linear, exploratory interactivity "perfectly appropriate for 2–7 year-olds, because that's what they're experiencing in the real world as well."*

Todd and his team put every title through rigorous testing: "If we want to see how a title will do in the hands of a 3-year-old kid, we'll bring a whole gaggle of them in and set them loose. We look to see what they like, what they don't like, and if they're getting bored with something." Frequently, kids will tell them, "Hey, we think that this little thing over here should have done something." Watching these users and receiving their feedback has firmly convinced Todd that "it's really important to underscore the fun and personal exploration" in learning.

But Todd's job isn't all hanging out with

happy children; he spends most of his time with the grown-ups who produce the titles, from the initial concept to the final product roll-out. "First, we find stories we like," he explains. "Then we secure the rights to do a multimedia version, which takes some negotiating but generally is getting a lot easier." Production begins with a storyboard: "When we adapt a book that's been printed already, we try to maintain the spirit of that book as well as the storyline. We give it an added dimension without taking away from the story." Once the storyboards are completed, the team animates the story and designs the sound. QA and user testing happen toward the end of production. Marketing and publicity plans are created at the same time.

"In my position I'm managing a process, and there aren't a lot of rules about how to do it," explains Todd. "I'm working with different types of people and information, looking two years into the future to see what technology and the market will look like. Being able to facilitate a creative process and have a fantastic product come out at the end is a real challenge. People really need to understand how to work with a lot of different types of people, how to facilitate different types of talents, and help it come to a good end."

What's the most important aspect of his job? "There are so many talented programmers, artists, and animators out there, but they need to be pulled together as a team to work. Making a successful business, helping them out, and getting their product to market is what the product manager's job is all about."

---

vivid: Can you walk through the process of developing a title?

Sure. I'll try and make it simple. There is a lot of very minute stuff but generally what we do is we isolate titles that we think will make good Living Books. For instance, we did our own original of *The Tortoise and the Hare,* **which was based on a story that we adapted. We secure the rights from the author or whoever owns**

them—in many cases, it's the author—to do a multimedia version, which takes some negotiating but generally is getting a lot easier. Then we go into our production phase, which starts with a traditional pre-production like you would do for a movie, where you've stripped it out and storyboarded.

When we adapt a book that's been printed already, we try and maintain the

media elements and technical specifications. In the design phase, little is known and so little can be measured. Things may fall into place very easily or they may be dragged kicking and screaming. Sometimes a product can be started by an **interactive scriptwriter** ▶ 184 and then passed to others to modify and develop. Other times, it takes an **interface designer** ▶ 170 working alone. At times, three or four people from a variety of backgrounds may be involved.

A producer needs to have a handle on how particular creative people work best and appropriate development time needs to be allocated. A producer should consult the **creative director** ▶ 158 for advice on the resources and time frame needed for the conceptual and design phases. One of the key points that many producers mention is that the **technical lead** ▶ 250 should be involved early in the process so that what gets designed can actually be built within the techni-

Todd Power, *continued*

spirit, feel, and characters of that book as well as the storyline. We also try and flesh it out. We give it that added dimension, without taking away from the story. We go through pre-production, map it out and design all the characters, and then go into complete animation. Most of our animators are traditionally trained. I think the computer was second for most of them to learn. A couple of them worked for Disney for a while.

We do all of our recording, composing, and sound design in-house in our own recording studio. We start off our sound designers as composers and immerse them in the realm of computers. We go through that big production cycle which takes x amount of time. Then toward the end, we start testing where we go into quality assurance, making sure that everything works properly. We do some user testing.

All along the production cycle we work on marketing and public relations. We'll start the marketing strategy for a particular title, gauge how it fits within the product line, what group we want to target with the title, any different spins we can put in the title, and any strengths we can leverage.

vivid: Typically, how big is the team that's involved on a particular title?

It depends. I can't tell you specifics but it is composed of a number of animators,

an art director, one or two sound designers, and then there are support people within that kind of work within the different teams. I work around and through, but not over them. I tip-toe around. One of the things that is fun about my job is working with creative people, being able to pull them all together—even though I don't lead them—and trying to facilitate that process in a timely fashion and on budget, which is very difficult with creative people.

vivid: In other industries such as TV production, writers will often move on to become producers. Is there a similar path in interactive software?

I see it trying to happen, but from my experience I think it would be difficult. You have to start on the ground floor. In software development, you're still bound by technology. In the film industry, you're bound by the story. Film is time-based and there are a bunch of people that know how to make the pictures and develop the film. Because software is technology-based, you have to understand the technology and the struggles of developing for quirky technology. With computers, it's very difficult to hammer it down and get it working on the technology that's out there. That's one of the biggest challenges. I wouldn't say that would limit somebody who was a writer and wanted to go into producing, but I don't see that as a natural progression for the software industry— right now at least.

cal, financial, and schedule constraints. Another point is to start with the goals of the project and the audience and then build in the technology, content, level of interactivity, and features.

Managing Production

Managing the **production** of a title means coordinating all the tasks that the members of the project team are doing and making sure that the product is being built in the way intended. This responsibility is made much easier by having everyone have a clear of idea of what is being produced and why. Several items are necessary to make sure this happens, including a clear and complete script and accompanying flow charts and storyboards, a well-documented **functional specification** ▶ 173, 251, and a series of milestones marked on a schedule for each individual, for each group, and for the team as a whole. Also needed is a clear delineation of the authority for various decisions. For example, a sound producer may be entrusted with collecting and choreographing all the sound for a title. Giving the sound producer a clear idea of what needs to be produced and why lets them be creative in the area they have their skills in. Ideally, the art director and producer should only step in if the sound does not do what it is supposed to.

Managing a production with the elements above is a matter of monitoring the progress that people are making and adjusting where necessary. In reality, the task is anything but simple because of any number of things that will happen. A common situation is where a task will take longer than thought. Either the project date can be slipped or alternatives can be put into play, such as simplifying the design or hiring additional people. A good producer can recognize the warning signs early and make adjustments without many people noticing.

Other unplanned situations can include conflict between team members. An art director may disagree with a video producer. Or, two of the programmers may disagree about the connections between their two parts. These types of disagreements are often a natural by-product of putting talented people together. A good producer puts in place a clear way to resolve conflicts. The decision-making structure mentioned above can help. A second help is a regular forum for bringing up disagreements and resolving them before egos get involved. Most teams have a meeting scheduled once a week to cover the status of the project and air differences in opinion. Groups within the project team may also have their own regular status meetings.

Tools and Techniques

The most common tools for a producer besides a telephone are spreadsheets, project management software, and/or scheduling programs. Essential resources include a database or rolodex of talent as well as lists of agents and recruiters. Other important resources for finding people to work on projects are popular online and print job listings and key multimedia organizations. Licensing agreements, employment agreements, personal service agreements, and **non-disclosure agreements** ▶ 90 should also be readily available for licensing content, hiring contractors or employees, or soliciting scripts or prototypes.

The techniques a producer uses are part sales techniques and part management techniques. The sales techniques include identifying, qualifying, approaching, negotiating, and closing, and are used for areas such as raising funding, licensing content, finding distribution, and hiring talent. The management techniques include creating a fun and productive environment, getting talented and creative people to work together, setting and reaching milestones, and resolving conflicts.

An important technique is to define a process that works for a particular project type and practice it consistently on each project of that type. This process should be communicated to all on the project team so that they understand what they do as well as what others do and how it all fits together. Related to this technique is assigning clear roles and tasks so that people know what is expected of them. Good producers use deadlines for individual tasks as well as collective tasks to keep people motivated and prevent them from getting lost on unimportant details. A producer should monitor the progress towards these deadlines continually to know when reality differs from plan and then adjust internal and external expectations accordingly.

Building into the budget an assistant producer and several production assistants can spare the sanity of many on the team. These assistants can take on basic tasks, letting people concentrate on what they do best and what makes them special. An assistant producer handling routine tasks can be the difference between a producer handling one project at time or two.

Karen Burch
Producer, Synapse Technologies

Karen Burch calls herself a producer/director/ writer/associate creative director. That kind of job description is more often the rule than the exception in the field of new media. Here, roles are loosely defined, and often flow from task to task on a single project. And, since most multimedia startups are woefully shorthanded, it is common for talented, energetic people to pick up the ball and run with it, in the process creating a new career for themselves.

"This industry is calling people with very eclectic backgrounds," she notes. "It doesn't put you at a disadvantage if you've done one thing all of your life or if you're fresh out of school and you studied fine art."

Karen, or Kiwi, as she is known to family and friends, should know from eclectic. Formerly an educational psychologist in Los Angeles, where her family roots go back 103 years, she was hired by Bob Able "on instinct" to work on the groundbreaking Columbus Project in 1990. With no track record, Karen quickly advanced from administrative duties to production assistant to producer of the African-American

storyline that ran throughout the database. "If you are getting into this late and you start off being a production assistant," she says, "there is a great deal of pleasure in that, because as I'm bringing somebody coffee or cleaning out the xerox machine, I'm also reading what they've written. It's the act of learning at whatever level you are that will propel you forward."

As a producer, Karen must maintain a coherent vision for her team, which she does by condensing it into a mission statement. "It gives all of us a touchstone, a place to come back to. Does [our work] make sense in terms of this statement. Does what I'm doing here make sense? I like to have something like that."

Qualifications

A producer needs to know how to efficiently respond to proposals or, in a related area, how to put together submission packages. While templates can help, nothing teaches someone as well as going through the process many times. The proposal process involves knowing how to qualify potential clients to know whether to, first of all, create a proposal and second to find an appropriate range for the budget. Next comes knowing how detailed the proposal needs to be. The budget should convey the costs for the various tasks being performed but not be so detailed that a client gets lost in the numbers. The delivery of proposals and then the follow-through are equally as important as the contents of the proposal. The executive producer is primarily responsible for getting a deal, provided there is an executive producer in the company structure. The producer, however, should be able to work comfortably in sales situations and help move a deal towards a close.

Management skills are the most important ones for managing a production once an agreement has been reached. These skills include preparing realistic budgets and schedules and managing the project team in meeting their targets. Many technical people working on CD-ROMs consider projects that are completed within four months of their initial ship dates as being a remarkable achievement. This belief is largely influenced by the software industry, which is notorious for shipping products late. To some extent, creating complex multimedia products often means working in uncharted territory, so it can be extremely difficult to estimate how long tasks may take. On the other hand, good producers are able to build into the budget and schedule enough room for unanticipated situations. They also keep the reins tight during development so that the tendency for work to expand to the allocated time is dramatically lessened.

Beware of adding people in response to missing milestones. This approach has a tendency to amplify problems as opposed to resolving them. More people mean more communication channels.

A common question asked about the producer role is if they need to be experts in every aspect of product development. The answer is no, but they need to be able to recognize who the experts are. Also, they have to have the **intuition** to know what is and is not possible. If a producer takes a programmer's word that a certain task will take two weeks, they had better have worked with that programmer on other projects to know how valid this response is. If not, then they had better check the dates with other programmers and, even then, be willing to pad the schedule significantly until the programmer's estimates can be tested against reality. Many producers have a technical background. While a producer can get around a lack of knowing technology by working with a qualified technical lead, it pays to know what can and cannot be done in interactive media. The biggest failings of multimedia producers are either overestimating the capabilities of technology or underestimating the time to develop the software components.

The ability to **judge talent** is another important qualification for producers. This ability extends not just to expertise but also to the ability to work with others in a collaborative environment. The type of people in multimedia crosses many boundaries. Many of the successful ones do not have traditional backgrounds. Good producers understand the skills that are needed for various roles and the types of experiences in life that provide those skills. A producer also needs to be quick in recognizing mistakes in hiring and take measures to correct problems. These measures may include changing or structuring tasks, bringing others in with supplemental skills, or replacing people.

Recognizing key ideas is another strength of a producer, especially for studios that are creating and pitching original ideas. It may not be essential for managing a project once it is in production but it is essential for bringing projects into the studio. Again, the producer does not have to be an expert in story structures, game designs, or character development, but they should recognize good ideas when they see them and be in a position to move quickly when they do.

How to Hire

A lot of producers prefer to work on a project-by-project basis for a variety of companies. Within the context of a project, they will likely be employees of the company producing the product (considering they be will be working on the project for five months up to a year or more.) Others are more permanent employees continually working on products, typically of a similar nature.

Finding out who these producers are is not as difficult as finding one whose schedule matches yours. Keeping track of producers even though you do not have an immediate need is highly recommended. It can be difficult to find one on a moment's notice so it pays to be prepared. You can gather the names of good producers by talking to people in the industry, especially those that work on multimedia project teams. Look at completed projects that you admire and find out who the producer is. More than one successful product or service is an excellent measure especially if they are in different genres or with different project teams.

Posting job notices for producers typically results in a flood of responses. While not necessarily a bad way to find people, it often results in having to filter through the accompanying resumes to find suitable candidates for interviews. Many will have experiences that are only partially related to multimedia. Others will have experience in different platforms or different genres. While you may not want to discount any of these outright, you might want to consider narrowing the experience or knowledge you are looking for to the project type, platform, and other significant constraints. Even though specific job postings will still result in responses with qualifications outside the requested ones, they may be fewer than asking for a generic "multimedia producer."

When interviewing prospective producers, try to learn what their development process and their management style are. While demos can be impressive, they may not give any indication of what the production was like or what influence the producer had on the project. Find out whether their previous projects met their budgets and schedule and why or why not. Find out how they find and hire people, how they motivate them, and how they reward them. The answers to these questions will form a good picture of whether they will fit within your company.

How to Be Hired

One way to be hired as a producer is to develop an idea and help package and pitch it to others in conjunction with an established production studio. Developers may be willing to agree to giving you a co-producer role in return for helping to move a project into production. While this may not be a common method at the moment, it may well be in the future as individual talent begins to gain more leverage over publishers.

A more likely way to get hired is to work on a project team in some managerial capacity such as a technical lead or **test manager** ▶ 264. Learning how to manager others and meet milestones coupled with direct experience in the conceptual development aspects are key to learning how to manage a multimedia production. Another way is to work as an associate or assistant producer and then graduate to a position with more responsibility over others. Making the transition from any of these positions to producer is more likely within the context of one firm as opposed to changing firms as part of this transition. Most companies will be unwilling to hire a producer unless they have prior experience in full capacity as a producer.

Compensation

The compensation for a producer will range widely across platforms, project types, industries, and geographic areas. The range for many multimedia producers lies between $40,000 and $60,000, though those near the entertainment or music industries may receive more. Not surprisingly, independent producers who help develop and manage innovative projects with strong funding and distribution are likely to receive more than producers working within a company on a genre of products that is well understood. **Royalties** ▶ 91 are possible but probably only as an independent unless you have a lot of negotiating power within a company. Profit-sharing and equity are possible, but again, dependent on your negotiating power.

Five Principles for Being an Effective Producer

1 Find the best people
Spend the time and money up front to find the most talented people. You will save months—even the entire project, based on your ability to find quality talent. I've had the privilege of working with some of the best people in the industry. However, finding the best is not always easy.

2 Fly high, dive low
Keep a high-level view of the project and people. Understand the details, but make sure this doesn't overwhelm your ability to take action on the bigger picture. Keep the projects' goals in view. Don't get bogged down in minutia.

3 Nurture your team, don't control
Let everyone show their strengths and be a star. Create the opportunities for everyone to be the best they can be. You have to be good with people to succeed. People will rally around you if you're fair, honest, and charismatic. Good producers have to be good with people.

4 Learn from your mistakes
Everyone makes mistakes, the key is to learn from them. Get coaching from your mentors. Write down what happened, what you learned, and commit yourself to changing your behavior.

5 Articulate, articulate, articulate
Repeat the project's vision and goals to everyone. Do this in writing. Do it often. Remember, you're the one who needs to keep the project on schedule. It's your job to make sure people don't forget or get sidetracked.

—Doug van Duyne, CD Producer, KidSoft, Inc.

As a producer, your value lies in your project ideas, contacts, process, and management skills. A wise producer leverages these assets with every new project. If one company is not interested in pursuing a project, a producer should always keep open the option to take that project elsewhere. As a result, it can be important to have a work agreement that does not preclude you from developing ideas on your own that the company does not wish to pursue.

Lawyer

What They Do

Lawyers perform work for all types of individuals and companies throughout multimedia. Their role is part advisor, part agent, and part contract writer. Their work is tactical on one end and strategic on the other. The tactical work involves drafting model releases, work agreements, and investigating trademarks—work that is relatively well understood. The strategic work involves licensing content, negotiating production and distribution contracts, and crafting strategy. An experienced and well-connected lawyer can help companies invest millions of dollars in companies and technologies. They can also provide advice on how to approach the right source for licensing materials. These, however, are more sophisticated, tricky, and unique relationships.

There are an increasing number of lawyers specializing in multimedia law. Off the record, however, many of these same lawyers will confide that there is really no such thing as multimedia law. There is **entertainment law**, **software law**, and **communications law**, and they all mix together within the domain of interactive media. This combination of legal disciplines, however, goes beyond mere legal language or knowledge. It extends into the way lawyers structure and negotiate contracts. As a result, the primary asset of a lawyer is not necessarily their knowledge of the law, but in their understanding of the way the law applies to each industry and across industries.

A lawyer can work for a company in a number of different arrangements. They can be a full-time employee for a company or they can consult as part of a law firm or as an independent attorney. The type of arrangement largely depends on the lifestyle that a lawyer desires. A full-time position offers security and the opportunity for more streamlined work. Working in a law firm can pay many times more than consulting, but at the expense of appearing as a virtual lawyer to a large number of demanding clients—many of whom may have vastly different ways of operating. Working as an independent lawyer will likely not pay as much as being a partner at a law firm, but those that work in this type of arrangement appreciate the flexible work schedule and the independence in dealing with clients. In fact, more and more lawyers are leaving large firms and setting up practices on their own.

It is not unusual for a single company to use several lawyers or law firms. One lawyer will commonly act as general counsel, but others will be brought in for specific needs such as litigation, patent, and trademark work. Also, companies may need lawyers with expertise in different industries or regions. A company might form a relationship with a law firm in Washington, D.C., for example, specifically to represent them in front of the Federal Communications Commission (FCC).

Lawyers are essential to every person and project in multimedia. They are usually involved even before a project or business begins and then continue their involvement throughout the project and course of the business. **Executive producers** ▶ 119 and **producers** ▶ 125 are the people commonly in contact with a lawyer. The executive producer typically helps leverage legal help across all projects, though individual producers may be in touch with concerns on a specific project.

At the beginning, a lawyer's help is likely needed to seal a relationship between parties. This might take the form of putting together financing such as venture capital, a private source, or as part of a production/distribution arrangement. It also might take the form of an agreement between client and contractor (individual or firm) or employer and employee. A lawyer is also recommended when licensing content. Some licensing can be relatively simple as in the case of stock photography or music and probably does not need a lawyer. Others can be particularly sensitive, the result of dealing with unsophisticated licensers or rights to a work that are in great demand or form a substantial portion of the project.

The size of a firm may or may not have a correlation to its prestige. In Hollywood, small law firms typically represent the most influential "players." In the software industry, a few large firms are the most influential, representing the majority of startups and publicly traded technology firms in the area. Relationships in the software industry are more on a company level as opposed to a relationship between individuals like in Hollywood.

Lawyers like to be informed so that they can anticipate possible problems. A good relationship with a lawyer is one where the lawyer is kept abreast of events. Periodic updates from the executive producer or producer can allow lawyers to head off problems before they occur. Should a problem develop with a client, a lawyer should be brought in if there is concern about wrongdoing or if the problem does not seem resolvable. A good contract anticipates many of the problems and supplies straightforward ways to resolve them. If something unexpected happens, a look back at the contract should provide the actions and responsibilities of both parties. A poor contract is one that does not cover any of the more common contingencies nor specifies a resolution process, such as a termination clause, a buy-out option, an arbitration clause, or other attempts at reducing the cost and time needed to fix a problem. In these cases, a lawyer might be needed to help negotiate a resolution or enter into litigation.

Process

The process that a lawyer uses differs from client to client and task to task. A large part of a lawyer's job is to give **advice** to their client and assess the risks of business, legal, or financial decisions. This advice can concern a new relationship or an existing agreement. For example, a lawyer might advise their client on what can and cannot be done under the terms of the agreement and what course of action is most appropriate, such as in the case of terminating an employee. In other cases, the advice might be more business oriented: for example, on how to structure a deal. Who should own what rights? Should money be guaranteed or contingent upon meeting certain milestones? Should the production fees be considered an advance on royalties or not? Deals can get very complex so it can make sense to have someone on hand who can help advise on negotiating strategy right from the start.

Lawyers are trained to look at things objectively so that they can bring to light issues that others involved might not notice. They are the ones that will bring it to the producer's attention that paying a $200,000 upfront licensing fee on top of a $300,000 production fee will exceed the $400,000 estimated gross revenues by $100,000. It is important, though, for people to balance this advice against their own instincts. Lawyers have a tendency to want to avoid as much risk as possible, but in an industry that requires taking chances, showing too much caution can prevent any project from ever reaching an audience.

Another distinctive process for a lawyer involves drafting many of the **standard agreements** and **forms** that are used in the course of developing a project and running a business. These agreements include nondisclosure agreements, personal service agreements, model releases, and employee contracts. These forms can be used again and again with little modification. If handled correctly, their preparation should be rather straightforward. It is part of a lawyer's responsibility to make sure their clients know they need these documents. Ideally, these should be prepared before any staffing begins. Creating them after the fact can be a prescription for disaster. Work agreements should be specific to a company, region, and industry. While there is boilerplate language for these agreements, a good lawyer will ask questions of the client in order to tailor it to the client's particular needs. They should also advise on where changes can be made on a individual basis without having to review each change.

One of the most important responsibilities for lawyers is in drafting **contracts** ▶ 95. One scenario for creating a contract is where both parties start from a blank sheet of paper and outline the deal. Typically, the two parties will develop a term sheet, which lists out the important terms in

Types of Legal Agreements:

- *Model releases*
- *Permission agreements*
- *Non-disclosure agreements*
- *Personal services agreements*
- *Employment agreements*
- *Production agreements*
- *Distribution agreements*

On What Makes a Good Lawyer

They don't have to know your business—but they have to be interested in your business. They have to be capable of learning some of the things. I don't know if you're ever going to get lawyers who are going to be able to keep up with each thing that happens but they should be curious about it.

If I were a businessperson, I would like them to read the trades that I'm reading and know the business people that I deal with. That is, they should be familiar with the major players in the field.

I also think they should like your product. I know that lawyers may scoff at that, but every client that I have, I like their product or service. I really like what they're doing. And to me, it helps me do the work, because I feel that when I'm in a negotiating thing and we're trying to work something out, I'm sort of driven a teeny bit differently.

—Rich Stim, Attorney

a deal, providing the main structure for the relationship. It is usually handed to a lawyer on one of the sides who then drafts the contract. The contract will go into more depth than the term sheet. Additional clauses usually contain boilerplate language and any differences can usually be negotiated over the course of several drafts. A term sheet may be developed with or without lawyers, although their advice during its drafting can be helpful. Items of importance when starting from scratch include: what the deliverables are, where the rights lie, the milestones for payment, and what happens if either party does not fulfill its commitments.

A second scenario is where one party develops a contract and then hands it to the other side either in writing or over the phone. The other side looks at the offer and either rejects it or offers a counter-proposal. In the case of the latter, the offering party will determine where and how they want to modify it, and the contract goes back and forth until an agreement is reached. It can take one or two passes, or it can take twelve. It is up to the parties involved and their lawyers.

In any contract **negotiation**, a lawyer can provide an assessment of the clauses in the contract, clarifying where needed. Clients should prioritize what issues they have with the contract, and list what changes they would like to see. If the lawyer is handling the negotiations, then the lawyer needs some indication of what the client needs in order to sign the agreement. Regardless of who handles the negotiations, they will reach a point where there comes a time to either sign the deal or walk away. People not used to negotiating contracts are often not thorough enough (and do not look through the contract in detail) or are erratic (and try to renegotiate major points late in the contract). A lawyer may need to overcome these faults in some of their clients.

Tools and Techniques

Lawyers are quickly catching up to other industries in their use of technology. In the past, getting paid by the hour provided little incentive to become more productive. Finishing a task earlier than before simply meant less revenue. Competitive pressures from independent lawyers and from other law firms, however,

have caused many law firms to invest in computers and the use of online and CD-ROM legal databases. Many law firms are installing email primarily for internal use but many other firms—especially those interested in working with interactive media companies—are establishing Internet domains and creating websites on the World Wide Web. **Email** ▶ 84 access is important for lawyers who will interact with technologically savvy clients.

Lawyers need to listen carefully, explain things clearly, and continually educate their clients. A good lawyer will help demystify the law, acting more as a business person looking out for the benefit of their client as opposed to a trial lawyer looking to win a case.

Qualifications

A lawyer is one of the few roles in multimedia that needs to be licensed to practice by a governing body. Although many people are knowledgeable about the law, most people recommend using only qualified legal assistance. Licensed lawyers will treat inquiries much differently than friends and acquaintances.

Additional qualifications will depend on the type of law being practiced. A lawyer working on corporate issues will find little difference between multimedia companies and other kinds of companies. The areas that are most distinctive in multimedia are intellectual property areas, licensing agreements, and production and distribution contracts. These areas share many aspects from either the entertainment or software industries, though in the case of online and interactive TV work, experience in communication law can be important.

A lawyer with a background in one industry can learn the major issues of the others, but a lawyer who is experienced working with all industries will certainly command a higher rate. In terms of licensing and intellectual property, a lawyer should understand these issues as they apply to content and as they apply to technology. Entertainment lawyers and publishing lawyers have an in-depth appreciation for content, whereas technology lawyers understand technology better.

Willaim Schwartz
Attorney, Morrison & Foerster

vivid: Is there such a thing as multimedia law?

No. There is no integrated body called multimedia law. There are lots of different areas of law that are relevant to multimedia. There's conventional intellectual property law as it applies to books, music, and movies, and then there is intellectual property law as it applies to advanced technology, such as software, hardware, and systems. These are not different bodies of intellectual property law but they tend to involve different kinds of lawyers.

For instance, I'm not an entertainment lawyer but I've learned a lot of entertainment law because the technology companies I work with want to acquire rights to do interactive multimedia versions of this or that. Multimedia law is really the overlap of entertainment, intellectual property, high technology, and communications law.

vivid: How do entertainment lawyers and software lawyers mix?

The styles are different. Different language, different expectations, different concerns. A while back, I did an agreement for a client to do a CD-ROM-based version of a well-known book with a world famous author. The author was represented by a literary agent in New York and it was an education for this guy and for me. He didn't understand what different platforms were. It's just not an issue with books. A book is a book. It doesn't have to have interoperability with any other platform. You just pick it up and read it. We wanted them to understand how important it was for us to be able to do development across different platforms and to evolve the non-volatile storage medium in which we intended to distribute the product. Do we get interactive rights or network rights and all those sorts of things—these are just things that in the past didn't occur to an author's representative. Now they do.

vivid: Are there things that high technology lawyers are learning about entertainment?

That's a good question. I've certainly learned a lot. We've all had to learn a lot. For example, under copyright law there are a few different rights that apply to copyrighted work. There's the right to reproduce it, there's the right to distribute it, there's the right to publicly perform it. Those are three different concepts in copyright law.

In the computer field, we didn't really care about some of those things because you just copy and distribute the work. It goes, it runs, and you don't particularly care whether it's displayed at a public demonstration or used privately. You don't broadcast it on television. But in the music world, they care deeply about those distinctions because there's a big difference between playing the composition in your home, playing it publicly, or distributing the composition as music in record form and distributing it as integrated with a film or distributing it as integrated with a CD-ROM title.

In the music world, those are very different concepts and they have different language for them. There's a different sort of royalty structure and different forms of contracts for all these different things. When it comes to the use of their content as opposed to software, they have a much more refined sense of what's going to happen with it. Much more specific, much more focused, and a different structure. In the software world, we have a more one-dimensional view of what use of a product is.

Licensing is another good example. A lot of lawyers will license the use of something and without really parsing what that means. "You can use this any way you want, in any way you want." What does it mean to "use"

"Content" often refers to text, graphics, sound, animation, video, or any combination of these that are present in interactive media products. Lawyers with experience in content issues will be knowledgeable about various ways to reuse, adapt, or create derivative products. Also, they will be knowledgeable in many of the licensing conventions already in place for dealing with content.

Interactive media products also typically have "engines" in the form of software programs that drive the interactions and display the content. A software attorney will understand the type of intellectual property rights and technology as they pertain to engines. These issues include trade secrets, copyrights, and, possibly, patents. Also important are ways the technology can be licensed both in terms of various components and alternative platforms. Indemnification is also an issue that has subtle differences between content and technology.

Clients will be most interested in areas with which they are unfamiliar. "Technology people" may need to understand licensing, publishing, and development agreements as well as copyrights.

A lawyer will likely need to walk these clients through possible negotiating scenarios with licensing sources, publishers, or distributors. They also may have to take more of a lead in negotiations. In terms of copyright, clients will want to understand the risks from a defensive perspective, such as the risk and penalties for using somebody else's material. They will also be interested in how to protect their own materials.

A big area of concern when working for production studios and independent contractors is employment law. Most of these types of clients are unclear on the differences between an employee and contractor and are unfamiliar with the "work-for-hire" doctrine. A lawyer working with these clients often needs to make these issues understood and make sure the contracts provide the necessary assignments and guarantees.

How to Hire

The first step in hiring a lawyer is to decide what type of legal help you need. The type of legal help can include corporate structuring, intellectual property (trademark, trade secrets, copyrights, and patents), contracts, and distribution agree-

William Schwartz, *continued*

something? Does that mean that you can copy it? Does that mean that you can publicly display it? There are some court cases over the word "use." I don't think an entertainment lawyer would ever make that mistake because they know that "use" can mean a million different things and their job is to specify what those things are.

What else do you want to add?

I'd like to remind people, when they think about legal issues, to think about the worst case scenario and the best case scenario and to be sure that someplace in their contract they've addressed them both. When most business people think about a project, it's sort of an 80% rule. They think about 80% of the possibilities but they don't imagine that things could really be a major success or that they

could be an abject failure, especially they don't think about failure.

What their lawyer should be helping them to do is to think about these possibilities because parties doing a contract or planning their product usually have a mindset about what's going to happen and tend not to cover the extremes. That's where they get into trouble. In fact, no one ever looks at a contract most of the time in ongoing business relationships. But when things go really well and there's a movie opportunity that comes out or the whole thing falls apart, these are the possibilities that people don't think about much when they're writing a contract. They don't have it in mind so they don't address it. I would encourage people to think about these things.

Richard Thompson
Attorney, Bloom, Dekom, Hergott & Cook

"Trying to tie a knot between two pieces of rope" is how Los Angeles attorney Richard Thompson describes his job. His current practice is split between interactive multimedia and film/television—two overlapping yet distinctly different worlds.

A graduate of Harvard and Stanford Law School, Richard began his legal career in 1980, in litigation and real estate. "In litigation, by definition everybody is at war. In transactional [contract] law, everybody is attempting to be friends and cooperate. I moved into transactional law because of this."

Multimedia law has a different set of relationships and rules. According to him there's less money in multimedia and it's "a more humane kind of business than film and television; people don't go for the jugular as much." His clients include Philips Interactive Media, Nintendo, Blockbuster, and Spectrum HoloByte, as well as independent producers and developers. His jobs range from work-for-hire agreements to analyzing people's legal rights (what they can and can't do), negotiating business deals, drafting contracts, and acting as an agent. Richard also speaks at industry tradeshows, including Digital Hollywood and Digital World.

Despite the flurry of activity multimedia has spawned, he doesn't think contracts are more complicated now than they were 10 years ago. "There may be two or three more things to think about," he says, *"but whenever a new technology comes along, most of the questions are about interpreting the old contracts." Negotiations haven't gotten much harder, either, although he feels many people have shied away from dealing with multimedia because they're "technophobic." In fact, he sees only half a dozen private practice lawyers in L.A. who have any expertise in this arena.*

Richard's long-term goal is to deal with the real pioneers of the medium, or as he puts it "the Steven Spielbergs of multimedia." He advises aspiring multimedia lawyers to "know how the business works and develop relationships with people in the business—otherwise people won't take you seriously."

ments. Find someone that is an expert in the areas that are either important immediately or over time.

Registering a trademark, for example, is a relatively isolated piece of work. The major steps are a trademark search to make sure no one else is using the mark in a related industry, an application to the U.S. Patent and Trademark Office, and then possibly an appeal if it is denied. Maintaining the trademark might need periodic attention from a lawyer but this work does not necessarily need to be connected to other legal work.

Handling the continual needs of a company, however, is a different story. Each project may have a separate contract needing specific attention. An ongoing relationship with a lawyer pays

significant dividends as both sides learn how to communicate, saving both time and money.

Once you know what expertise you need, the next step is to decide what type of lawyer or law firm to use. Some companies may need a full-time lawyer, possibly working in-house. Other companies or individuals may need work only periodically, such as a few hours a week or month. In these cases, an **independent lawyer** or one working at a law firm will more than likely suffice. Lawyers that work on their own or in a **small law firm** often offer more economical service and faster turnaround. This is because their overhead is usually much lower and they typically perform the work themselves as opposed to passing it to someone else. Also, this type of lawyer is often able to be more flexible on compensation because they have fewer people to answer to.

On the other hand, a **large law firm** can offer a breadth of expertise few individuals or small law firms can match. They can cover corporate law, tax law, securities law, intellectual property law, contracts, and litigation, all under a single roof. They can do large corporate deals, mergers, public offerings—things that would quickly overwhelm a small firm.

Finding a lawyer may mean talking to other people in similar situations. An executive producer or producer should find out who other producers use. A visual designer should ask other designers. Many law firms in industries creating interactive media have established multimedia divisions. You can call these firms and ask to receive materials on the lawyers working in this division as well as a list of their clients.

Looking at the **client list** of a lawyer or firm is a good way to measure their influence as well as identify any potential conflicts of interest. Many law firms represent a variety of clients throughout the infrastructure of an industry. The experience working with each type of company can be invaluable, but make sure that they are not representing many of the companies you are likely to do business with. You want a lawyer and a law firm that is firmly on your side.

Pennsylvania Dutch hex sign for justice

Most **multimedia conferences** have panel discussions on legal issues. These can be good places to go to meet lawyers as well as other people with needs similar to yours. Many multimedia organizations such as the IICS also sponsor periodic meetings on legal issues.

It is best to get the names of lawyers as opposed to law firms. The best relationships are between individuals and not between companies. After identifying several lawyers, call and see if they can do the type of work you need. See if their rates will fit your budget and that they will be able to handle your work within their workload. Qualifying them early can prevent meeting with them only to find they are too expensive or too busy.

If they are unable to represent you for these or other reasons, ask for suggestions of who might. They may recommend someone in their firm or someone they have contact with in the industry. Oftentimes, a more senior lawyer will initiate a relationship but pass the actual work to someone more junior. While a less experienced (and less expensive) lawyer may work out just fine, meet the primary people you will be working with before you enter into a relationship.

A good lawyer should be able to provide clear answers to your questions. If they cannot explain topics clearly enough for you, they are probably not the most suitable choice. Do not be awed by legal knowledge. A good lawyer will make things understandable even to those with little knowledge of the law.

If their experience checks out and you feel comfortable with them, the next step is to negotiate rates, discuss potential conflicts of interest, and detail the terms of the working arrangement. Although hourly rates are the most common pricing method, fixed-price work is becoming more and more popular, particularly with highly definable areas such as work agreements and trademark registration.

Individuals and companies that do not have a lot of money to spend on legal work should address that issue up front. Some lawyers are willing to structure payments to help a company's cash flow. Others are willing to offer discounted rates under the expectation that smaller companies will grow into larger and more profitable companies.

Creating a close working relationship with a lawyer requires attaining a certain level of trust and communication over money issues. Many people request that lawyers submit estimates for how long a task will take and then submit detailed billings. These steps can go a long way to preventing billing surprises.

Rich Stim
Attorney

vivid: How does a multimedia developer or contractor learn about legal issues?

Well, hard knocks is the most common way. It's like the Colonel Tom Parker approach. He did a deal with Elvis and got burned on one section of the contract. He cut that part of the contract out and pasted it on his wall. Each time he got burned, he would cut out the section that screwed him over. And then, that's reportedly how he made his contract; he put all those provisions together.

The trouble with that style of learning is that when you're small, one mistake can wreck your whole business. There are books starting to appear on multimedia law. To the extent that you can sort of get a grip on the rights provisions, you should do that right away. For people assembling works that are pre-existing stuff, you should know the general principles of rights. For your transfer of what you did to somebody else, you should understand that level of rights. Those two things I think you should definitely force yourself to learn. I don't care how creative or whatever type of a genius you are, there's no reason why you can't also be creative and a genius in just accumulating that little bit of licensing knowledge, which will really help you out in structuring your project.

vivid: Do contracts have to be verbose and full of legalese?

Lawyers have a code language. It's just like program code. They cash in on the fact that you may not understand the language. As a general rule, you should never sign anything that you can't understand—all the way through, beginning to end. I try to write my agreements that way, and I see other lawyers are starting to do it too. When you're dealing with a large law firm or if you have venture capitalists backing you who are forcing you to use their lawyers, those lawyers have a CIA-type paranoia. They'll put in all sorts of trap door language and all types of overreaching stuff. Their approach is, "Well, if you don't like it, make me cut it out." Because if I have to cut it out, there's more billable hours for me anyway. Hopefully, you can avoid that type of drafting, or that type of attorney. And hopefully, there'll be some standardization of licensing, forms, etc.

vivid: What else about contracts?

One thing on contracts is that the part that the lawyers always hassle about the most, and the part that the client seems to find the least interest in, are the areas in the back— the **indemnity** ▶ 103, the warranties, the disclaimers, the termination, and the dispute resolution. Those are things I would definitely highlight and tell the client to pay a lot of attention to.

A contract is really three parts. What is it I'm supposed to do; what is it you're supposed to do; and what happens if we don't do it—if one of us doesn't do it. The last part, what happens if one of us doesn't do it, is really what all those things relate to—your warranties, your promises, how your stuff's going to operate, your disclaimers, what it's not going to do, where you're going to sue if you have to sue, and how you're going to resolve it. That stuff can be a nightmare.

My experience in software development, in multimedia, and in publishing, is that there's always a problem somewhere along the contract. If you have some sort of method of working it out, it's going to be relatively simple and painless.

Four Types of Intellectual Property

1 **Trademarks** are names or symbols that mark a product or service so that consumers can identify them and distinguish them from others. Registered trademarks (and servicemarks) have been approved by the U.S. Patent and Trademark Office.

2 A **trade secret** is some piece of information that has value because other businesses do not know it. A trade secret might be sales information, programming code, or a client list, and should be treated as confidential material.

3 **Copyrights ▶** 102 protect original expressions of ideas such as books, movies, music, and art. Copyrights have a long life associated with them (in the case of a work owned by its creator, it is the life of the creator plus 50 years).

4 **Patents** are non-obvious, novel inventions, including machines, drugs, or software. Patent protection lasts for 17 years and applies even if another person developed the same invention independently and had no knowledge of the patent.

The terms of a working arrangement should also specify issues such as how long the lawyer has to respond to an inquiry. Again, some producers are adamant about hearing back from a lawyer within 24 hours. This response may not contain the final answers but it should be a general reaction and include a timetable for delivering the final opinion. Once all the terms have been decided, a written work agreement should be created listing the terms and conditions of the relationship. It is often interesting to note how little attention the lawyer/client agreement is given by both parties.

How to Be Hired

The way to get hired is to first find the people that are in a position to need a lawyer. Executive producers and producers are the primary contacts within production studios, but other companies and individuals will have legal needs. Attorneys should position themselves for certain types of legal work as well as for certain types of clients. That positioning can include speaking at conferences and attending industry events, each time conscious of what kinds of legal issues are important to that audience.

In many cases, people hire lawyers specifically for their grasp of the complex legal issues. Potential clients may not even know what these issues are. One way to approach people is to talk to them about the issues they are currently confronting. Most people will have at any given time specific concerns they are worried about. A producer might be in the midst of hiring contractors, worried about infringing on someone's copyright, or thinking about licensing the electronic rights to a best-selling book. Answering their immediate questions and pointing them in the right direction may mean giving away free advice, but it can also result in a small amount of work that can turn into a longer-term relationship. Beware of underbidding on any initial work, however, or of continually going after small amounts of work. The ultimate goal is to either obtain a large amount of work in a short period of time, or a steady stream of manageable work over time. Continually working on small jobs for a lot of different clients drastically increases the amount of time spent chasing business.

It can also help in meetings with potential clients to ask them what their direction is, or might become. You can then offer some of your insight and then show them how you can help them get where they want to go. Taking this approach helps them visualize what it would be like working with you, thus bringing you one small step closer to a relationship.

Individuals and **small companies** are likely to be price-sensitive. A lawyer may want to consider ways to help fit into their budget prior to the first meeting. For these clients, a lawyer may also have to do a fair bit of education on the type of legal work they can do and why it is necessary. These types of clients may also need more hand-holding. Just listing the options and their risks may not be enough. Also, individuals will only be interested in an impressive list of large clients if the work for these firms translates into a better understanding of issues for individuals. They may think, and rightly so, that large companies will have a priority on your time. Your job is to inform them otherwise and then structure the relationship so this does not happen.

Established multimedia companies are more apt to be interested in a lawyer's or law firm's expertise, experience, client list, and relationships than they are with rates. The type of work that they are interested in is not something where price will be a deciding factor.

Regardless of the size of the potential client or the nature of the work, the bottom line in working with someone comes down to a gut feel for whether or not a relationship can work out. If it is difficult to communicate with a potential client in initial meetings, it will likely prove difficult over the course of the relationship. Choose your clients wisely.

Compensation

Compensation for outside legal work is commonly performed on an hourly basis with rates ranging from $80–$250/hour. Lawyers with specific expertise or significant influence will command higher rates.

Six Tips for Dealing with Attorneys
Provided by Rich Stim, Attorney

1 Learn about Your Attorney
When interviewing an attorney, ask questions about clientele, work performed, rates, and experience. If you speak with a client, ask questions about the attorney's response time, billing practices, and temperment.

2 Get a Written Fee Agreement
The fee agreement is a negotiated arrangement establishing fees and requirements. Read it and understand your rights as a client. If you are suing someone, ask the attorney about a contingency fee agreement.

3 Estimate Fees for Specific Tasks
If you can, agree to fixed costs for certain work rather than hourly billings. If you can't obtain fixed billings, ask your attorney to estimate fees for work.

4 Review Billings Carefully
Billings should be prompt and clear. Do not accept summary billings (e.g., statements such as "litigation work"). Every item should be explained with rate and hourly increment. Late billings are not acceptable, especially in litigation. Also, discourage multiple and "bounced" billings for the same work (e.g., one attorney assigns the work to another, then reviews and sends it back, ad infinitum).

5 Review Your Likelihood of Success
If you're in a dispute, ask for an assessment of your odds and costs (if possible, from more than one attorney). The assessment and underlying reasoning should be in plain English. If a lawyer can't explain your situation clearly to you, they won't be able to explain it clearly to a judge or jury.

6 Look for Ways to Save Costs
If the attorney prepares a document that you will re-use with slight modifications, ask for it in an electronic format (and sign a waiver as to any of your modifications). If you are in a dispute, find out if any forms of alternative dispute resolution (mediation or arbitration) are available. If you're sued, check your insurance policy to determine if you have coverage.

Financial Consultant

What They Do

The financial consultant role is really a collection of roles all having something to do with ensuring the financial well-being of a project or business. This collection of roles includes financial advisor, financial accountant, cost accountant, and book-keeper. A **financial advisor** does business planning and helps raise investment funds. They may play a role similar to an investment banker and, in fact, many times are investment bankers. A **financial accountant** helps set up a financial system and perform or advise on tax preparation. They are usually practicing accountants working independently or for an accounting firm. A **cost accountant** helps maintain the profitability of operating a business. They are typically employees, whereas these other three are more likely to be either consultants or part-time contractors. A **bookkeeper** handles the data entry into the financial accounting system and usually works part-time for individuals and small businesses, but may be a full-time employee within a larger company.

There are two primary areas where financial assistance is necessary. The first is in business planning, and these responsibilities include helping to create the business strategy and raising investment funds. These responsibilites can also extend to deciding on the type of business structure to use and the accounting procedures to put in place. For a production studio or publisher that needs to raise funding, a financial advisor with investment banking exposure is probably the most logical first choice. For an individual or company most concerned about running day-to-day operations, a financial accountant or cost accountant is probably best.

The best advice anybody can give someone going into business for themselves is to find a good financial advisor and lawyer to help structure the business. This advice is important not only for people who wish to grow a business but also for independent contractors who have no plans to hire anyone else. Too many people learn the hard way about tax issues and accounting for overhead. Setting up systems for tracking the profitability of a company is one of the smartest steps an entrepreneur can take.

The second area of involvement is in business operations, the running of day-to-day operations. These responsibilities include managing cash flow (collecting revenues and paying bills in proportions that leave enough cash on hand to run the business), managing payroll, and reporting and paying taxes. Other responsibilities can include helping to prepare budgets and tracking profitability of projects. This area of work focuses on the implementation of the systems put in place during business planning. It has been estimated that half of all businesses that fail do so in the year after record sales. Having good financial procedures in place and following them diligently can help prevent some of the problems associated with rapid growth.

Process

The financial advisor primarily helps in the preparation of a **business plan** and then the presentation of that plan to various investors. Most business entrepreneurs and producers concentrate primarily on the idea, leaving the prospect for revenues in various expressions of hyperbole. For an entrepreneur, they will often describe some "hockey stick" projection—flat growth for the first couple of years and then dramatic growth in the third to fifth year of business. A producer will often be even less disciplined, saying simply, "It will sell a ton," or "It's going to be the next *Myst*."

A publisher or an entertainment company looking for products may not need a detailed revenue plan in order to make a decision on a project. Likewise, a company looking for technology to incorporate into their product offerings may also not need to see a financial picture. But in many cases where investment funds are needed, most professional investors will be less swayed by an idea than by the likelihood of a profitable return on investment. Financial advisors help add realism to the revenue projections and create a strategy to meet those projections.

A good business plan might contain 10 pages of summary, 15 pages of market analysis and strategy, 10 pages on the company and its principals, and 40 pages of financial statements. A financial advisor helps to prepare the 40 pages of financial statements and also to make sure the projections match the information in the other sections. Financial statements typically include pro forma documents in the form of three to five year projected income statements, balance sheets, and cash flow estimates. Details of revenue sources and staffing requirements are also often included.

Once the business plan is created, a financial advisor will often help solicit that plan to **qualified investors**. These investors might include venture capital companies, private investors, entertainment, software, publishing, or communications companies. Part of the value a financial advisor adds is their knowledge of the investment market and connections to various investors. A financial advisor will often contact potential investors, send them the business plan, answer questions, and participate in any presentations to investors. If investors show interest, advisors will often lead or advise in the negotiations.

The role a financial accountant plays in business preparation is slightly different. Their concern is more internal, focusing on the structure of the business to make its operation as smooth as possible. The steps they will take include helping to register a business at the local and possibly state level, setting up the accounting system, and developing procedures and reports for determining the profit or loss of operations. In terms of registering a business, there are several types. These include sole proprietorship, partnership, limited liability company, and two types of corporations, S corporation and C corporation. These business types have different tax and liability

consequences associated with them. Which one is appropriate for a particular company should be determined on a case-by-case basis.

The type of accounting system a financial accountant will help create goes beyond the choice of software package. The first priority is to determine how revenue will be recorded. This can be done on a cash basis or an accrual basis. A **cash basis** records transactions when cash changes hands. For example, revenue is recorded when the check is received. Expenses are incurred when payments are made. A cash basis of accounting can be simple to implement and

is often recommended for individuals and small businesses. An **accrual basis** records transactions when they occur, regardless of when actual payment is made or received. In this case, the dates of invoices or purchase orders are used to determine when a transaction occurs. An invoice might be issued 30 days before receipt of a check from the customer. An accrual basis uses the date of the issuance of the invoice. A cash basis uses the date of receipt of the check. An accrual basis can be more difficult to maintain but it provides more accurate information about the profitability of a company during specific periods of time.

Another part of an accounting system includes determining the chart of accounts to use. The **chart of accounts** is a list of categories for recording revenues, expenses, capital assets, and liabilities. The organization of the chart of accounts can help managers determine which activities cost too much and which ones are not getting enough attention. And since this information is useful for comparing individual company performance with industry competitors, it can be important to have a well-defined chart of accounts.

*Two common types of investing are strategic investing and return on investment (ROI) investing. **Strategic investing** is where funds are provided in order to receive gains in forms other than profit. Access to technology in order to support other for-profit ventures is one of the prime areas for strategic investing. **Return on investment (ROI) investing** is where funds are provided to achieve some form of monetary gains. These gains typically occur when companies go public or are acquired by other companies.*

Cost accountants and bookkeepers play a big role in maintaining the profitability of a company. A cost accountant is typically concerned with **allocating costs and revenues** to discrete areas of a business to determine the relative profitability of these areas. For example, many production studios will have several projects in development. A cost accountant will make sure that all revenues and expenses are attributed to the appropriate projects. They will determine the cost per worker, including their salary, equipment cost, insurance cost, and taxes, and distribute this cost to the projects the worker is assigned to. Overhead costs such as rent and supplies need to be allocated on a per-worker basis or distributed as a percentage across the various projects. This level of detail is important for determining the true costs of projects and, subsequently, their profit margins. This information allows management to choose which projects to do and which ones to leave to the little fishes.

Tools and Techniques

The tools that financial advisors use include spreadsheets and presentation packages for preparing business plans and raising funds, and **software accounting packages** for recording and monitoring the financial transactions of a company. There are many accounting packages on the market and many targeted toward companies of different sizes and types. There are accounting packages for small businesses that are usually under $1000. These have many of the features and reports needed by most businesses but some may be targeted toward companies selling certain products, such as a publisher, as opposed to companies making products or offering a service, such as a production studio.

There are several accounting packages that are more customizable and flexible than off-the-shelf packages. They are intended for larger businesses and can cost anywhere from several thousands of dollars to hundreds of thousands of dollars (after consulting charges are paid to customize the product for a particular company). They are usually built on top of a database and usually feature a client-server architecture allowing simultaneous access by multiple users. Smaller packages may not allow more than one user at a time.

The accounting package will affect the ability to determine the profitability of a business or project. Choose a package that is flexible enough to handle the types of transactions that are expected but with enough structure to provide meaningful reports. Companies will likely need to change accounting systems as they grow. Setting up the right chart of accounts and using them appropriately in the beginning will dramatically help when switching accounting packages later.

How to Hire

Finding a financial advisor is a matter of contacting people in the investment community and asking for recommendations, reading trade magazines for articles written by consultants, and attending conferences and classes on finding financing for multimedia companies. Finding a financial accountant is similar to the process of finding a lawyer. Whether to use an independent consultant or an accounting firm will depend on the price range you are willing to pay and how official you need the financial statements to be. Companies that are looking to go public or be bought by another company should have their books prepared by firms experienced with similar types of companies. An individual or small business might do very well with an independent consultant or a small accounting firm. As with a lawyer, the relationship between consultant and client is as important, if not more, than the prestige of the accountant or accounting firm.

Cost accountants can often be found by placing ads in newspapers or online job directories. While you do not necessarily need someone with multimedia experience, you do want to find someone that has experience with companies performing similar activities to yours. A company that publishes CD-ROM titles has a much different cost allocation than one that creates websites. Find someone that can help formulate a costing system appropriate for your business. Bookkeepers can also be located by placing ads but there are also numerous bookkeepers and bookkeeping companies listed in the Yellow Pages. Also,

Minh-Hang Nguyen
Financial Consultant/Producer

With a background in international finance, Minh-Hang Nguyen, the Financial Controller and Senior Producer at Mindsphere got a taste of high technology ten years ago when she managed the creation of an MIS system for Bank of America that spanned 4 international divisions, 70 countries, and over 1,500 products. "I married my background in international finance to my knowledge of software and systems. As multimedia technology continued to grow, that was a natural way to go." Today, she likens her job of structuring and negotiating deals between Mindsphere and its clients to the role of investment bankers and venture capitalists.

Her experience working on the other side of the client-vendor equation is one that continues to serve her well, now that she represents one of the leading multimedia production agencies in the business. "Because I've been on the client side of the equation I can structure deals in a way that addresses their concerns. I know exactly what their concerns are. My role is to structure deals in such a way that our clients get what they want at a price they can afford." For Minh-Hang, one of the prin-

cipal functions she must fulfill is that of client education. "Some clients don't know what's involved in multimedia production. You've got to educate your clients and bring them along."

The toughest part of Minh-Hang's job comes in finding the delicate balance between client expectations and the Mindsphere production artists' expectations. Not for nothing does she list "Den Mother" on her job description. "The artists we have working with us are the best in their field. You don't want stifle their creativity, yet you have to herd them in the same direction at the same time." Balancing their passion for excellence against the day-to-day realities of deadlines, budgets, and clients' expectations are what can make or break a producer, and Minh-Hang proves that it can be done with warmth and humanity.

---

multimedia organizations such as the IICS may have ads for bookkeepers in newsletters and membership directories.

How to Be Hired

Getting hired in a financial position in a multimedia company, either as a consultant or full-time employee, involves identifying companies that can use your services. In the case of a financial advisor or financial or cost accountant, you want to get in touch with the heads of startups or small companies. You can find these by attending conferences and multimedia organizations. The best organizations, though, are the ones dealing with technical and design issues as opposed to "networking" organizations. Most entrepreneurs are working hard or focusing intently on their ideas, leaving little time for what they often feel is non-productive socializing. Bookkeepers should also attend organization meetings, especially those that have lots of freelancers as members. Speaking at conferences and teaching courses

can be a good source of clients for financial advisors and consultants.

Compensation

Financial advisors are commonly paid by the hour or as a percentage of the investment funds they raise. The hourly rate may be between $75–$200 and the percentage of the investment may range between 5–10%. Financial consultants or accounting firms typically charge anywhere between $50–$150/hour, though partners at accounting firms may charge upwards of $250 or more. Cost accountants will commonly charge between $15–$50/hour. The smaller rate reflects the likelihood of the cost accountant being an employee of a company as opposed to a consultant or independent contractor. Controllers might be paid $40,000–$80,000 and CFOs $50,000–$100,000/year, with CFOs commonly receiving a small percentage of stock in start up companies.

Agent

What They Do

Agents represent individuals, developers, content owners, or corporations, and help them find business, negotiate **contracts** ▶ 95, manage working relationships, and handle financial transactions. An agent facilitates relationships, placing talent/content where needed, and arranging development deals between developers and publishers.

Many of the large entertainment agencies such as International Creative Management (ICM) and Creative Artists Agency (CAA) have created new media groups, and several smaller agencies are working solely in interactive areas. Many people predict a growing presence of agents in many areas of interactive media in part because of the dynamic nature of relationships and transactions involved in creating new media products.

The first part of an agent's job is to know what is marketable. Agents typically represent talent that is "above the line." **Above the line** refers to individuals whose presence or capabilities add a unique contribution and/or create a more marketable product. This type of talent includes, but is not limited to, game designers, scriptwriters, producers, and directors. As for production studios, agencies will represent the ones that most closely fit the types of work they specialize in. For example, an agency in Hollywood would represent companies producing games and CD-ROM titles as opposed to ones producing interactive marketing or sales pieces. Agents represent a number of publishers and content sources as well.

The second part of an agent's job is knowing who is in the marketplace. Agents will know most of the interactive publishers and what they are doing. Their job is to approach them and put together a deal to either place someone on a production team, license a name or set of content, or structure a production agreement between their client and another party.

Representations by agents are almost always **exclusive** ▶ 99 within a certain duration and domain. The duration can be monthly or yearly and the domain can be for certain platforms or a specific set of properties.

A good relationship with an agent will take into account changes in the marketplace and new experiences, skills, and desires of the client. An agent in this regard is as much of an advisor and business manager as they are someone who makes deals.

Process

The process for an agent involves signing an individual or a company to an exclusive contract to represent them. Once the clients are signed, an agent will pitch their client's services or product ideas to appropriate customers. An agent will actively sell properties as well as follow up on leads provided by their clients. In terms of representing individuals or production studios, approaching studios or publishers will vary depending on whether services are being offered or whether original ideas are being pitched. Examples of offering services include a scriptwriter being hired to write a script for an existing set of content or a production studio being contracted to produce a product that has already been conceived. Selling services requires impressive marketing materials that provide undeniable proof of an individual's or company's capabilities.

An agent pitching an original work will also be interested in marketing materials on an individual or company but will require some demonstrable example of the work. The type of materials that are needed include **treatments, scripts** ▶ 186, **letters of intent** for licensing content, and possibly a **prototype**. Individuals or companies with successful projects behind them will need fewer materials.

An agent's job does not end with the signing of a contract. They often serve as a communication point between the two parties in the agreement. Editors in the book trade and producers in the movie industry find it more effective and less stressful to work with the agent to help motivate an author or a scriptwriter. Producers in multimedia are also finding it more palatable to deal with agents on potentially confrontational issues.

Another aspect of an agent's job, especially for talent and content owners, is to receive and ac-

> *You need to make a deal that is good for both sides and not just for the people you're representing. That's where an understanding of both sides comes into play. We know what a good deal is and what a bad deal is. Typically, we're able to structure a deal very efficiently. That's why people do business with us. That's why we're successful and why we stay in business.*
>
> *—Allan Rinkus, Agent, International Computer Group*

count for the money that changes hands. Agents will often manage the contracts, collect fees, and, if necessary, contact publishers and conduct audits. This part of the job has always been a traditional part of an agent's responsibilities, to the point where many agencies have custom database programs to automate these tasks.

Tools and Techniques

A tool common to every agent is a database of contacts with, it is hoped, a large number of these contacts backed by relationships. Other tools are the phone, fax, and email. Face-to-face meetings often happen only at trade shows, on scouting trips, or when the deals are large and complex. One agent views the two Consumer Electronic Shows, the Software Publisher's Association conference, and Intermedia as the primary trade shows for conducting deals. During these conferences, the agent typically schedules back-to-back meetings conducting a majority of their business for the year. Other shows such as MacWorld, Comdex, and Digital World, while interesting, are not as effective from a business standpoint. The timing of shows is important because of the growing trend to produce titles on a seasonal basis. Many publishers will look to finalize many of their titles for the year in early January.

Other tools include a suite of proposals and contracts that can be used for pitching products or developing deals. Once a contract is signed, the particulars in the contract may be entered into a database to keep track of deliverables, payments, royalty reports, and other contractual agreements.

Fax and online newswires and content areas in commercial **online services ▶** 15, 61 are becoming highly valued resources for getting up-to-the-minute information on developments in an industry. Several technically-minded agents are also using the World Wide Web and gophers to research the management structure, financial health, and products of developers and publishers.

Probably the most important technique for an agent is to establish trust with those that they are representing and those they are approaching. In order to get their phone calls returned, agents need to have a solid reputation. Publishers are going to be much more likely to deal with someone they've dealt with successfully in the past than with someone new. Also, they are more

likely to respond when the call is relevant to their current business situation as opposed to a call out of the blue.

Qualifications

An agent has to know the business and development issues in games, CD-ROM title development, and online systems. The needs and business models for each are different, and yet the areas are not large enough to specialize in one of them. Also, the products and markets are quickly becoming integrated across delivery platforms so agents have to be well educated in all of them.

At the same time, agents form an industry all their own. It is not really possible to hang a sign saying you are an agent and hope to be successful. Most agents started out learning from senior people in the business. At large agencies, people usually start at entry-level positions and work their way up to more senior positions.

A knowledge of technology is important only as far as what can or cannot be done. More important are the cultural differences between the **entertainment**, **software**, and **communications industries**. An agent will need an understanding of all three areas in order to be successful. This education not only includes the process, the techniques, and the tools used in building products but also, and probably more importantly, the culture, economics, and trade practices of each industry. Although many publications make fun of the differences between Hollywood and Silicon Valley, these spoofs have many elements of truth to them.

As for specific skills, a **sales and marketing background** is critical to becoming a successful agent. Agents need to be able to identify marketable properties and effectively license or sell them to others. The agent's job includes all the strategies and tactics of a marketing person mixed with those of a salesperson. These include positioning talent, properties, or companies; identifying and qualifying potential relationships; negotiating and closing deals; and managing the ongoing financial aspects of a deal on behalf of the client. Also important is an in-depth knowledge of the companies doing business in interactive media and the type of deals that are being created. Having a great deal of confidence and determination will not hurt either. Hearing "No" is a big part of being an agent.

"The game play in this one is pretty lame."

How to Become an Agent

There are two aspects to how to to become an agent. The first is how to be hired by an **agency** and the second is how to be hired by **clients**. In the first case, the most common path to becoming an agent is to work at an agency in low level positions and work your way up. A knowledge of how multimedia products are put together can help in getting a foot in the door of agencies. The same can be said for knowing the ins and outs of products on the market and why the good ones are good and the bad ones bad. Having an understanding of who the key individuals, developers, and publishers are will also help, as will knowing how to spot up-and-coming talent. Many agents in the music and film industries moved out of grunt work and into representation of clients by finding and signing unknown talent and helping to groom them. The same is likely to be true in entertainment multimedia.

Finding clients includes knowing what the talented roles are and who the people are in those roles. Agents typically only deal with individuals that work freelance, but they may be able to encourage talented employees to leave a company and work on their own for a number of companies. Agents should also know who the best production studios are and what the trends are in terms of content.

Speaking at conferences that draw talented individuals as well as leaders of production studios is a good way to introduce yourself. Many people in the industry are so unsure of the role that agents play, especially in areas such as San Francisco, that any efforts spent educating people on the benefits an agent provides will supply numerous leads. Unfortunately, there will be a lot of effort involved in filtering these leads to find the ones with the most marketable skills.

How to Find an Agent

The first step to finding an agent is to understand what an agent is looking for. They are, above all, looking for marketable properties. These "properties" can be talent, content, or companies. They are not likely to represent a person who just has an idea. They expect people to either have a **proven track record** or a project that is **appropriately packaged**. This includes having a refined story or concept and knowing where all the pieces to a project are and how to get them.

Various industry directories will contain listings of agents. The Software Publishers Association for example has a listing of agencies. Many entertainment guilds will also have listings of agencies. Many traditional entertainment and publishing agencies have new media divisions or have established alliances with interactive agencies. Another way to find agencies is to ask others whom they use or whom they might recommend. Publishers, lawyers, producers, and scriptwriters are the ones that will usually come across agents in the course of their business and should have a name or two to pass along.

Check references, and above all, pay particular attention to the finding someone that you trust and that will have the time and incentive to properly represent you. Most representations have some form of exclusivity to them so make sure the relationship is the right one.

Although agents will typically search out the people they want to represent, that does not mean they will not look at someone who approaches them. It means, however, that you need to have a good idea of what you want an agent to do for you and have marketing materials with you that are in a presentable state. Most agents will have an instinctive feel for what they think is marketable and can reach a decision fairly quickly. The good ones will be up front about their impressions and your chances of success. Instead of becoming defensive in the face of a less than enthusiastic meeting and trying to sell harder, listen to what they have to say and how you can improve your skills or make yourself or your property more salable. Although they may not be in a position to represent you, they can point you in the right direction and give you some invaluable advice for getting to where you want to go.

Compensation

Agents typically receive a percentage of the fee that their client receives. The percentages range from 10% to 15% and count against advances, production fees, licensing fees, and royalties. For month-to-month representation, agents may collect a non-refundable retainer up front. Any fees generated by the agent from a contract during this period will count against the retainer by some percentage typically between 60% and 80%.

Recruiter

What They Do

A **recruiter** primarily represents companies as opposed to an individual and charges a fee for finding individuals to be employed on a project or a company basis by the client companies. Unlike agents, recruiters will often deal with finding and recruiting production talent or talent that is considered "below the line." Recruiters often work for top-level managers looking to hire other managers, such as producers or technology leads or for producers looking to staff a project team or development department. The roles that recruiters are most frequently asked to fill are producer, programmer, and digital artist.

Recruiters often come in soon after a company or division is formed to help staff it. They may also be contracted on an ongoing basis to help fill positions that become available due to a company growing or to people leaving. A recruiter may also be brought in for a specific project or a specific role. Although a recruiter's payment may be tied to the length that a person stays with the client company, there is little interaction between the recruiter and the individuals they recruit once a hiring decision has been made. Although recruiters may serve as sounding boards and advisors for the individuals they recruit, they are representatives of the client companies and so are under no obligation contractually or financially to the individual parties.

Process

The process that a recruiter goes through is relatively straightforward. The rate and duration of success, however, is dependent on a number of issues, including the client company and their location, the project type, the particular roles and pay scale, and the type of work arrangement (such as employee vs. contractor). Market conditions will also be factors, such as the season, for example. The last several years have shown a dramatic rise in title development for the Christmas season. As a result, the summer and fall months are extremely competitive times for hiring programmers and digital artists.

The first step that a recruiter takes is to negotiate their working arrangement with the client company. This agreement commonly takes the form of a percentage of the salary or fees paid to the employee or contractor. The fee may have a vesting period that makes the recruiter more motivated to recruit an appropriate candidate that will stick around for awhile.

Once the terms between recruiter and client company have been resolved, the recruiter typically receives a formal **job description** ▶ 90. A recruiter will need to read between the lines of the job description to understand how the corporate culture fits the particular role. For example, a software company may be looking for someone that fits an engineering-dominated culture as opposed to someone out of the advertising industry. A broadcast company might be looking for a technical person that also has knowledge of their industry. Part of the long-term success of a recruiter lies in understanding these unwritten aspects between the job description and the company culture.

It is important for a recruiter to **rank the client's priorities** in terms of the qualifications they are looking for. This ranking should be done preferably with the one person who makes the final hiring decision. As with any task, working under the direction of more than one person can be difficult, if not impossible. Reducing the number of people who are involved in the decision-making process and getting a clear framework for the work is important.

If these avenues do not prove worthwhile, the recruiter will then become more actively involved and **headhunt**, or in other words, make calls to people happily employed to entice them to change companies. Recruiters will often indirectly approach the subject of working at a company by describing the opportunity and asking if the person knows of anyone who might be appropriate for it. If the person is not interested in it they may provide a list of others. It is through these referrals that a recruiter's list of contacts grows.

The first place a recruiter looks for talent is in their own database. Most recruiters will have advanced systems for tracking the types of people they are hired to look for. In fact, these databases are often the primary assets besides those locked in the recruiter's head. If no suitable candidates turn up, a recruiter will then begin advertising in newspapers, magazines, and online areas. The particular locations, the frequency, and their success rates for advertising positions are kept highly secret by recruiters because they are key assets to their businesses. A recruiter will leave their telephone or fax number or email address and then evaluate each person that responds and refer them on to the client if they are qualified.

Tools and Techniques

The tools and techniques that a recruiter uses are those of a salesperson. They include a database of contacts, a telephone, fax, and email. Other tools include newspapers, magazines, and online areas. The techniques include meetings and telephone calls and the process of identifying, qualifying, and approaching candidates.

Qualifications

The three premier qualifications for a recruiter include **expertise in selling**, an ability to **get along with people**, and an ability to **understand a market**. The selling part is self-explanatory. A recruiter's job is to broker a transaction between their client and an individual. As far as getting along with people, a recruiter will often need to work with both clients and job candidates that are upset. The first group may be impatient because of the lack of talented individuals available at the price offered. The second group may be disappointed because of continual rejection for posted job openings. A good recruiter is able to handle people that are emotional and work around stressful situations.

Understanding a market is especially important where old and new infrastructures are colliding. Understanding a market includes having the knowledge of the roles and tasks on a number of types of multimedia projects. Knowing business models and work arrangements is also important. Finding someone that has the skills but does not fit the business structure will not prove successful in the long term.

Recruiters also tend to have good **investigative skills**. They are able to find out things about businesses and people. They pick up clues from different sources and assemble them into a picture to help them find appropriate individuals. These clues may be emerging roles in an industry or active online places. Or, they may be companies with the potential for high-growth or, on the other hand, companies that are not doing well and thus likely to lay off or lose employees.

How to Hire

At this time, there are only a handful of recruiters that are knowledgeable about multimedia. This will likely change in the next year or two, but for the moment, companies are limited by the number of choices. Individuals tend not to hire a recruiters. Recruiter represent companies, but a person can, as a long-term strategy, contact a recruiter and provide them with appropriate information.

For companies, the first step to finding a recruiter is to recognize that a recruiter's work is highly centered around their location. As a result, a recruiter based in New York will not directly compete with a recruiter in Los Angeles (unless the position is such that a candidate may be encouraged to relocate). A company can ask for referrals from recruiters outside their geographic area.

A recruiter should know the project area that a company is working in. Developing interactive presentations or kiosks is far different from developing programming for interactive TV. The types of **platforms** ▶ 12 and **projects** ▶ 18 matter and so does the corporate structure. A recruiter should listen and ask intelligent questions about the company and the job openings. Finding the right fit for a job and a company is not black magic; it takes strong critical thinking and interviewing skills—skills that are applied to the client company and individuals alike.

A recruiter's client list is important but not necessarily for the names in their traditional sense. Almost every entertainment, publishing, communications, and software company has some new media division or enterprise in the works. A recognized name in one of these industries means very little in multimedia circles unless they have a proven track record of success in new media ventures. Also important is the length of the relationship between recruiters and their clients. A long-term relationship with a small number of successful companies is a very good indicator.

Sean Lord
Recruiter, Interactive Development

vivid: Do you recruit developers, studios, or aggregates of people?

Yes, and that can be a yes in a number of ways. One is a group of people who want to be hired as a team. I've put together people from different companies and molded them as a team for a client company to then give them a block of money. This group eventually formed a company to complete the project. This is all very fluid and is really defining itself at the moment. Personally, I'm as open as possible to make sure that whoever is offering me a check gets what they want.

vivid: What type of people are commonly asked to recruit?

People with a programming background and an artistic ability, not the other way around. The best skill base to have at the moment is not to be an artist that can code but a coder that is an artist.

vivid: Is location important?

Yes it is, and I'll give you an illustration within the Los Angeles basin. L.A. from toe to head is about 100 miles, from Orange County up through to Ventura County and all claim to be within Los Angeles. Individual companies have set up their organizations, for example, in Calabazas and in Laguna Beach, which is this toe to head angle. They've done it principally because the chairmen live locally and so they set up in a location nearest to the chairman. This has proved to be a mistake because when these companies reach their second stage—i.e. when they've had success maybe in the 12th to 15th month onwards, and some people may have left or they need to add people—they've found that their locations aren't working. People are literally too far away to be able to commute. What I believe will happen is that companies will form little groups more and more along the lines, for example, of the San Francisco model, where they are all literally close enough to throw a CD-ROM at. Another approach is for individual companies to set up smaller development groups in key centers—key being where they can get a hold of the staff.

vivid: How does someone get a job with you?

You have to practice at another recruitment agency before you come to me, or you have to have really good sales ability. I mean, you have to be very motivated to do my job. And you've got to be better than me. I don't want to hire people not as good as me.

How to Be Hired

Getting hired as a recruiter is difficult because the role is not a recognized discipline as is programming or design or testing. There are almost no courses to take and no books to read. Becoming a recruiter almost means working as an apprentice and learning the business from the bottom up. There are a number of traditional recruitment firms where someone can learn the recruiting process and sales techniques. Transferring that knowledge to the interactive arena is a bit difficult because of the high knowledge barrier. Since the client companies may not be all that knowledgeable about interactive multimedia, they are likely to rely much more on the recruiter's knowledge than in almost any other circumstance.

Marketing Roles

What They Do

Describing the **marketing roles** in multimedia is a difficult task because many of the companies involved have vastly different structures due to the industries they are modeled after. Marketing in the film and music industry is different than marketing in the book publishing industry. As a result, this section describes marketing activities in general as opposed to a single specific role. It also describes the marketing efforts in multimedia as much for people outside marketing, such as producers and designers, as for those inside it.

In short, marketing people help create or direct the **strategy**, or parts of the strategy, for reaching customers with products or services. Every company in every industry has a need for marketing roles. The most jobs and the most influence in these jobs, however, are with companies that publish products or manage services for distribution. While production studios have a need for marketing people, the number of marketing positions and the ones with the greatest responsibilities are at companies that are closest to consumer audiences.

Within the context of a publisher, marketing people help determine the types of titles to publish, the audiences to target, the budget for title development, and, correspondingly, the number of titles to release within a given year. While these decisions are usually made by top-level management, their decisions are influenced by materials developed by the marketing department. Marketers will then be charged to direct the production of those titles approved for development. Product ideas may be submitted from outside the organization or they may be developed from within. These decisions will need to create balance between the needs and direction of the market and budgetary restrictions.

Marketing managers at publishers are also responsible for establishing and managing the distribution strategy, which is tied directly to the types of titles that are published. The marketing manager will identify the different channels and pricing structures through which to distribute. The channel decisions for mass-market products can include which distributors, which types of retail stores, and which mail-order vendors to work with. Marketing managers also determine how to promote titles, including the release dates, the advertising budget, and the manner of launch.

Process

Within the perspective of the fiscal year, marketers for publishers will determine, based on the budget, the **number of titles** to publish and the development and marketing budgets for each product. At the moment, many publishers are releasing only about half the titles that they say they will. One reason is the difficulty of developing titles and the unexpected delays that result. Another part lies in the difficulty of starting and maintaining distribution channels.

Throughout the year, marketing managers coordinate **internal review meetings** for new products as well as products in development. These meetings may be regularly scheduled, such as on a monthly or bimonthly basis, or as conditions dictate. These meetings typically include executive producers, producers, sales managers, and others who have responsibilities for developing, marketing, or selling products. External meetings with distributors, resellers, and customers, either in formal or informal settings, also figure prominently in a marketer's job, as do regular sales meetings to analyze the sales of current products and present the release plans of future products.

The top-level marketing managers are typically involved in the decision to provide funds to produce a product, often referred to as "green lighting" a project.

The process of determining which products to fund revolves around **spotting trends** in the marketplace and keeping an eye on the **strategies of competitors**. Marketing managers isolate trends primarily by attending conferences, reading trade magazines, and by talking to resellers, distributors, retailers, and, most of all, customers. Product strategies that evolve out of this research usually need the approval of upper management and possibly the board of directors.

Companies are beginning to focus on specific markets and product types. Many entertainment companies, for example, are eschewing **special interest titles**▶ 28 in favor of **game titles**▶ 16 that promote movie characters and storylines. Many large media companies are looking for interactive products that can either be extended or leveraged into television programs, books, or other traditional media forms. They are also looking to create interactive adaptations of existing products. Still, other companies are looking for products that have both CD-ROM and online applications now and possibly interactive TV applications in the future.

Related to determining the types of products to develop is the strategy for developing them. Some companies do not accept outside submissions. They prefer to develop their own products internally. Others do not have production capabilities in house, relying solely on outside developers. Others show a mix of both internal and external titles as well as a mix of internal and external development responsibilities on a single title. The development strategy is dictated by where companies see their leverage. Many consider it in their technology and their development process, whereas others see it in their brand name and their marketing and distribution prowess.

In either situation, it is typically the marketing department's responsibility to establish and coordinate the steps involved in gathering product ideas and deciding which ones to move into production. These steps include coordinating product review meetings, establishing submission requirements, possibly licensing characters or other sources of content, optioning scripts, and funding prototypes. Establishing outside **submission requirements** ▶ 120, 190 typically requires the creation of submission waiver forms and submission instructions. Most publishers wish to see project briefs, company and project team bios, prototypes if available, and production budgets. Many top level marketing people will also deal with agents pitching products or services for their clients. Signing submission waivers and determining intellectual property rights from both publisher and creator perspectives is still touchy and ill-defined. Most publishers will not accept ideas without some form of waiver preserving their rights to develop or publish works that are

similar. These waivers, however, are vastly different from publisher to publisher. Some are four pages in length, while others might be one page. Some are highly restrictive, others less so.

During development, marketers will refine the positioning of the title based on the development and the current market picture. Competing products may appear, product structures may change (the result of the success or failure of a recently released title), or distribution avenues may open or close. Above all, marketers need to be continually aware of these fast-moving changes in the multimedia marketplace and be able to react innovatively, quickly, and decisively.

The money spent on development is quickly being surpassed by the money spent on marketing and distributing titles. For this reason, a marketing manager's tasks are increasingly weighted toward the **product launch** and distribution phases. The marketing budget for games and CD-ROM titles is quickly approaching two to three times the cost of development. In some cases, the ratio is even greater. Acclaim Entertainment, for example, reportedly spent approximately $10 million when it released *Mortal Kombat* in September of 1993. Estimates on the cost of developing the title range between $1 million and $2 million.

As the production nears the end, the pace and the influence of the marketing manager increases dramatically. Depending on internal and external factors, the launch may be rushed or it may be delayed. For example, the simultaneous release

The submissions department in the interactive division at one entertainment company receives approximately 4–5 calls a day from people wanting to submit ideas. They require a signed submission waiver before looking at any materials. Many people do not submit upon receiving the waiver and submission requirements, mainly because they realize they need to present their idea seriously. Every 4–6 weeks the division has a product review meeting where they discuss the top 10–15 title possibilities. They presently publish approximately 10–12 titles a year. So, of the approximately 1,200 inquiries, they consider seriously about 120, and of those, they publish about 10–12.

Marketing within Production Studios

Most production studios and developers will have some form of marketing manager. While at the abstract level, their tasks are the same—to help create and direct the strategy for reaching customers with products or services—the audience and the mindset for a marketer at a studio are much different than they are for a publisher. At a publishing house, the focus is on the marketing efforts between the publisher, the resellers and distributors, and the consumer, whereas at a studio, the focus is primarily on the marketing efforts between the studio and prospective clients. While both types of marketing people need to know the motivations of the other—a studio is lost if they do not keep up with the changes in the marketplace—the marketing manager at a studio will need to think more like an agent in the film or book industry or like an account executive at an advertising agency, focused on creating a one-to-one relationship as opposed to one-to-many.

The role of vice president of marketing may seem a glamorous one—deciding which titles to fund and how to release them—but the job carries with it intense pressure to perform. The heads of entertainment and publishing companies often expect new media divisions to be quickly profitable, and these expectations leave little room for product experimentation or refinement. Successful multimedia publishers such as Brøderbund, LucasArts, and Maxis, however, have spent many years and hundreds of thousands of dollars developing not only technology and processes they can leverage into new products, but also a deep understanding of what appeals to their customers. Companies new to interactive media may not have this luxury.

The ever-increasing budgets for developing and marketing multimedia titles is quickly closing the window of opportunity for small, unaffiliated developers. While it is still possible to create a hit product on a limited budget, the task is becoming as difficult as trying to produce a film on a shoestring budget.

of a movie and a related game might cause the marketing manager to outsource the stamping and packaging to different sources or pay rush charges to move in front of other jobs. Seasonal issues might have an effect, trying to ship in time for the Christmas shopping season, an educational buying cycle, or an introduction at a major trade show.

In creating a **distribution strategy**, a marketing manager also takes into account the specific issues imposed by the product type. The retail outlets for video games are currently quite different than those for special interest CD-ROM titles. The former are sold in many toy and consumer electronic stores while CD-ROM titles are sold in many software, music, and book stores. These outlets also require deals with different distributors, different packaging, and possibly different pricing. Smart publishers decide what titles to produce only after consulting distributors, and have confidence that they can get into the retail channels. Some publishers are producing as many titles as they can in order to increase their chances of getting into the channel, while others are rethinking that "throw it against the wall and see what sticks" attitude and concentrating on a lesser number of higher quality products. Regardless, one title is usually not enough to get into the channel. Several titles are needed.

Tools and Techniques

The tools a marketing person uses are the tools that executive producers, producers, and agents use. They include communication tools (phone, fax, and email), research tools, and budgeting and scheduling tools. A big part of marketing involves knowing product sales figures and receiving customer feedback. The multimedia industry is more like the publishing industry than the film industry in the sense that sales figures are not widely reported as of yet. Therefore, obtaining current information about a company's or competitor's products can be difficult. There are several surveys available featuring sales figures from a small segment of the market. These and other tools and resources help marketers collect, analyze, and present invaluable sales information.

The techniques for marketing and distributing multimedia products to mass-market audiences share techniques from the film, software, and book

publishing industries. The model for games publishing largely resembles the film marketing model. Most games are widely released with large advertising campaigns starting before the launch date and continuing to in-store promotions and product tie-ins. The model for reference and special interest titles is resembling a cross between the software and publishing industries. The advertising budgets are significantly less than what is spent on games, and the emphasis is on creating word-of-mouth in the industry through favorable reviews. Several CD-ROM publishers are also creating and distributing inexpensive CD-ROMs containing demos of their products.

Qualifications

The ability to spot talented individuals, innovative ideas, and salable products is one of the primary qualifications for a marketing manager at a publishing company. Also needed is experience with **existing interactive products**, a good sense of intuition, and the ability to visualize the final form when presented with only a loosely constructed idea. Many marketing managers have experience with other media, such as film or books, prior to moving into interactive media. While this can be valuable in general, experience in marketing outside of interactive areas can sometimes be a disadvantage. In fact, the types of products in interactive media can be so unlike existing products that an unbiased mind might be in a better position to determine the appropriate experiences for interactive venues.

It is important to know both **strategies** and **tactics** for marketing, distributing, and selling products and be willing to pioneer new ones. Changes in the multimedia marketplace are taking place at such a rapid pace—major shifts in direction regularly occur every four to six months—that a marketing person needs to be highly self-motivated and creative. They need to be able to come up with strategies to provide new products and services to customers in ways that might not have been done before. Many people in the game industry credit Id Software with nothing short of brilliance for letting people freely download portions of their *Doom* games on the Internet prior to their release on CD-ROM. This strategy, along with having a highly interactive product as well, has helped make it one of the top-selling products on the market. Others companies such as 7th Level are putting trailers of upcoming products on currently shipping CD-ROMs.

How to Hire

When hiring a marketing person, the first step is to get an understanding of the tasks that person will be expected to perform and the ultimate goals of the position. Someone who is good at the tactical aspects of marketing such as knowing how to launch and promote products may not be the most appropriate candidate for a publishing company looking for someone to help create their strategic direction in interactive media. In this case, an understanding and appreciation for new media products and services is important. While candidates do not need to be experts in the tools, they do need to know what makes interactive products different from traditional ones and how new technologies can be applied or developed to take advantage of these differences.

Many companies look to **recruiters** when hiring high-level marketing people because these positions are specialized enough that the right candidate may be difficult to find. Many companies are reporting that despite large responsibilities and sizable compensation packages, getting people to relocate can be difficult. For other marketing roles, there are many **marketing consultants** working in multimedia that can be brought in part-time if the amount of work does not yet support a full-time position. Good sources for finding these people are conferences and organizational meetings.

When interviewing candidates, you should look for someone who has access to a rich collection of information resources on marketing and sales. The innovations in every area of interactive media include the products and services themselves, the relationships between developers and publishers, the distribution channels, and the launch strategies.

When looking for a marketing manager for a production studio, one of the primary assets is an ability to analyze the environment a company is in and help determine, based on its strengths and weaknesses and its competitors' strengths and weaknesses, the most appropriate marketing strategy. Other things to look for include knowledge of individuals, products, companies, and trends,

and an understanding of the marketing strategies and tactics for high-priced, low volume sales.

How to Be Hired

Many people in marketing positions in multimedia companies have backgrounds in marketing software, books, or movies. And while these backgrounds can be valuable, the marketing and distribution of multimedia products is rapidly changing. As a result, there are lots of opportunities for passionate and hard-working people with general marketing experience. Getting hired in a marketing position at a company either producing or publishing multimedia products, however, involves **targeting** a specific set of marketing tasks. Many people start at entry level marketing positions, assisting in either product submissions, product promotion, or channel distribution. It is not sufficient to simply "try to get a position in a multimedia company." You must focus on specific marketing tasks and how your work will increase a company's market presence, sales, or other types of benefits.

Top-level marketing positions are usually being filled by marketing people with knowledge outside the core areas of the company that is hiring. For example, software publishers are looking to people from the publishing industry. The publishing industry, on the other hand, is looking for people with knowledge of software and technology. This cross-pollination of knowledge and skills will likely continue for the next several years.

Compensation

Marketing positions are typically full-time employment positions. Some promotional tasks can be outsourced to public relations companies or independent contractors, but the majority of marketing positions are salaried. The ranges for top-level managers will likely be between $70,000 and $100,000 a year. Top marketers in the film and music industries tend to receive much more than that at software and publishing companies. Marketers working at these types of companies also tend to have greater decision-making authority on the types of products or artists to support. These industry characteristics typically carry over into the interactive media divisions at many of these companies.

There's a Zen of product development. In an environment that's changing this quickly, there's a limit to the kind of research you can do. I really think the best work emerges when someone really believes in their ideas. The very best ideas come from people who say, "I've got to build this." The very worst ideas also come from people who say, "I've got to build this." You either get a big success or a screaming, screaming failure. Mediocrity comes from people who start buzzing, "Well, what does the market need?" and then try to come up with a product idea.

*—Paul Saffo,
Director,
Institute for the Future*

When you're thinking about consumer products, you have to think like your customers. You have to consider their likes and dislikes. If I'm doing something for kids, I have to hang out with kids. I have to listen to them. That's what a lot of people don't do. They don't listen enough.

*—Janine Firpo,
Former Vice President
of Publishing,
ADAM Software*

Creative Director

Creative directors are not necessarily involved directly with each project. They will often help hire and oversee art directors and interface designers who in turn will have direct responsibilities for creative decisions on projects. The creative director will, however, meet with the project team from time to time to check that the design process is functioning well and that the team has the resources and support they need. The creative director plays a role similar to an executive producer. They try to leverage knowledge, process, and tools across multiple projects as well as act as the final oversight authority for line managers, which in this case are the art directors.

What They Do

Creative directors have two sets of responsibilities. The first is to uphold the quality of every aspect of media production on all projects. They do this by establishing and coordinating a design process within the organization. This task includes making sure that the style, quality, and details of all work are appropriate and consistent. It extends to projects and related materials such as packaging, posters, and promotional materials and even includes corporate aspects such as the corporate identity, marketing materials, and all other collateral. In short, creative directors have the power to set corporate as well as project direction and enforce it where needed. They are concerned with how the company is reflected and represented in all products and media materials.

The second set of responsibilities has to do with the people who work on a project or within a company. A creative director helps hire and train designers and media production people. They also help educate others in the organization on the design process. These responsibilities include describing the direction and vision of the company or any given project and communicating it throughout the company so that everyone understands it. It also means meeting with people periodically in some form of a creative review. A creative director helps create an environment where people feel involved and are continually growing, learning, and being creative. Everyone is creative in some aspect, whether they work with pixels, code, colors, pencils, or numbers. A creative director helps foster that creativity.

Creative directors are responsible for the integrity of all aspects of a project from the moment it starts. A creative director is often heavily involved with the initial brainstorming, storyboarding, and conceptual development, though their job may begin even earlier with the development of a project **proposal** ▶ 120. The proposal needs to reflect accurate estimates of the work required. These estimates are often only realistic if a creative director helps define the task, roles, time estimates, and resources for the design and media production aspects. Producers often do not have the experience nor the training in design disciplines and, thus, have a tendency to cut corners in these areas.

Process

One of the creative director's primary responsibilities is to develop or refine a **design process** and then integrate that process into the current development process of a company. The design process is essentially a series of questions that are answered in a logical order. The answers to the first questions form the basis for the questions that follow and are paramount for determining the direction of a product or service. For example, all technical requirements for a project need to be determined before any media elements or features can be conceived. The reason is because technical limitations can severely constrain what can be done. Creating a set of 3D animations only to find out late in the project they do not perform well on the target **delivery platform** ▶ 12 is not the way to design a product. The goal is to create a cohesive and well-planned product while reducing the amount of unnecessary work. A creative director helps reach this goal by putting in a process that integrates technical concerns, marketing issues, and input from the client and members of the project team at the right places along the way.

The first step in any process will be to establish and articulate the **goals** and **messages** of a product, service, or company. These may already be firmly established, need evolution, or, having never been expressed, need articulation. Design is often thought of as simply the creation of the graphics, sounds, video segments, and animations. True design, however, goes far beyond that, starting with the resolution of many abstract issues. The goals and messages of a product or service will influence whether a product will entertain, inform, educate, or advertise, for example. They will determine the platform or platforms to create the product for, the type of interactions and features that will be incorporated, and the information that will be included and its organization.

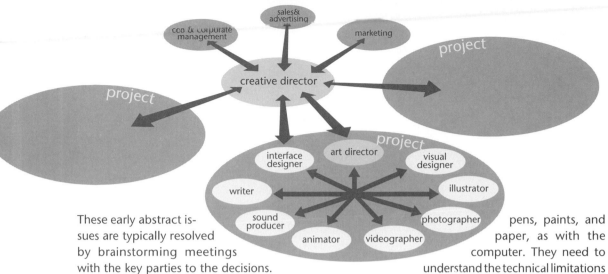

These early abstract issues are typically resolved by brainstorming meetings with the key parties to the decisions. For a product or service, this will mean members of the design team, including the producer, art director, technical lead, interaction or game designer and others involved in conceptual decisions. If clients are involved in the project, they will need to be included in many of these meetings.

The creative director will often participate in these early sessions. Once the direction has been established, the creative director's responsibilities on a project typically diminish to that of **oversight** of the art director and the rest of the design of the project. The steps in this process include the development of scripts and storyboards, the creation of maps or flow charts, the design of the navigation scheme, and the inclusion of creative, productive, or adaptive features. They extend possibly to the development of prototypes and user-testing and lead to the creation of a final design.

Once the design of the product is firmly established and production begins, the design process extends to the creation and integration of the media elements. The script, storyboards, functional specification, and production plan are all used by media production people to determine what needs to be created, where they go, and what they look or sound like. The role of a creative director is to help guide the art director in managing the media designers and in ensuring that the project is not deviating from the original plans.

Tools and Techniques

There are no explicit tools for creative directors to use. Most of what they do is conceptual and personal so they may be as comfortable with pens, paints, and paper, as with the computer. They need to understand the technical limitations of electronic media (both hardware and software) as well as the advances on the horizon. They cannot let their familiarity with the technology constrain their creativity, however. They must look to the constant and universal attributes of communication, entertainment, and information in order to formulate visions of what particular products should do.

Typically, they immerse themselves in products from many different media. Design, illustration, and photography annuals are helpful for evaluating different styles and the popularity of different messages. Annual reels of animation and video are also helpful to stay aware of what is being done in those media. Creative directors find research everywhere—in every advertisement, poster, sign, television show, commercial, movie, and song. Everything that represents what people in a particular market are seeing, hearing, understanding, and experiencing helps build a picture of audience abilities and appropriate communication styles. This research is critical and ongoing. Since it is not always known which products will be active or what markets will be targeted, it is often necessary for creative directors to make a point to immerse themselves in even more materials in the hope that they will be ready for whatever projects appear at any time.

Because creative directors are thinking foremost about communications and entertainment as opposed to the visual and aural representations of these phenomena, they must also have a vision of **interactivity** ▶ 9, 171 and what can be accomplished through interactive media. They must stay current with the state of the art in interactive products as well as push the conceptual boundaries of common perceptions and understandings. They must understand the difference between products and features that merely present rather than truly inform, as well as between those that offer extended, productive, and interesting interactions rather than basic and static ones. They must help find ways of creating adaptive behaviors in products that help them to entertain or communicate well under a variety of circumstances and for a variety of audiences.

Qualifications

Organizational skills are important since creative directors must keep abreast of many different products at once. Continual oversight and articulation of their vision and understandings of

interactivity and communication will help keep projects on track. Great **communication** and **management skills** are imperative. A creative director, no matter how outstanding his or her ideas or vision, will accomplish nothing unless these visions are clearly communicated with the support of everyone in the company and on the project teams.

Communication and management skills are especially important; a good creative director listens to other team members and empowers them with the authority to make decisions. People are more creative, productive, and responsible when they have a voice in the decision-making process, therefore a creative director must be willing to trust others to make decisions.

Creative directors should immerse themselves in the media of their industry and markets. They

Plunkett + Kuhr
Creative Directors

Shocking fluorescent inks, tiny type that crawls across page layouts, jumps the gutter, and refuses to respect the "laws" of traditional magazine design: a pervasive yet fluid use of Photoshop, these are some of the hallmarks of Plunkett + Kuhr's design for Wired magazine. The design team of John Plunkett and Barbara Kuhr have created a Rolling Stone for computer freaks, and its vibrant design is meant to evoke all the manic energy of the information explosion.

At the same time that Wired *has defined and extended the boundaries of what magazines can look like in the information age,* Wired's *on-line spin-off,* HotWired, *has done the same for cyberspace. If* Wired *reports "news from the future," then* HotWired *is the future. With an interaction and graphic design spearheaded by Barbara Kuhr,* HotWired *has set a level of ex-*

pectation for how home pages look and feel on the World Wide Web. Point your browser to http://www.hotwired.com/ and you can put your finger on the pulse of the digital age. HotWired *is a constantly changing online Grand Central Station of news, industry gossip, digital movies, art, music, sound loops and the ranting and ravings of HotWired members.*

How did Plunkett + Kuhr, who are quick to call themselves "general practitioners of design," and whose other clients include The Sundance Film Festival and exhibit design for Carnegie Hall, become the designers to put such a public face on cyberspace? For John, it goes back to mastering the arcane and demanding art of pre-press, knowing what the technology, the press and the printer are capable of, then pushing the capabilities of a six-color press to the limits. "A lot of this you can predict in desktop on your computer, and a lot you can learn through trial and error. Our trial happens once a month and it happens in public."

Barbara had little experience as a designer for online multimedia applications when she was tapped to design the look and feel of HotWired. Working closely with a staff of four engineers, she was able to create a design that, as it evolves, continues to stretch the boundaries of what HTML coding is capable of. "My design is defined by the limits of the technology." Barbara says, as she works on the next groundbreaking version of HotWired.

usually read (or skim, rather) loads of content from many different sources. This is an attempt to constantly stay aware of the changes in a market, industry, or society's vocabulary (whether textual, visual, aural, gestural, etc.). To fall out of step with the way people communicate, what they understand, and what they are seeing and hearing, is to slowly lose their understanding of their audience and their abilities to communicate to this audience.

A creative director must know what **technology** can do and the basic issues affecting it, but a basic proficiency will usually suffice. Creative directors are advocates for the users, trying to push the technology to create better experiences. Creative directors must also be detail-oriented to quickly pick out potential problems. This is where a deep understanding of design, visual media, and aural media becomes essential. Unless creative directors are aware of these details and issues, they will not be able to affect their quality. More than anything else, experience with different media and the ability to work with others and communicate across various media will be necessary. In addition, the ability to react quickly to change and, possibly, adverse conditions, will prove useful.

How to Hire

Creative directors are corporate-level employees and generally work as hired staff. They may be given executive responsibilities (and thus executive-level compensations and benefits) and have a wide variety of powers. Creative directors should have a well-articulated vision of communications and entertainment that is compatible with the direction a company wants to go in. It is sometimes better that creative directors are bit ahead of the company so they can lead it into new directions, but they must not be out of sync with the aspirations and understandings of corporate goals.

Creative directors typically have a **formal education** in design or a related field, such as art. They may come from industries as diverse as film, music, industrial design, publishing, graphic design, or advertising, but they should have a comfortable command of all media forms and their uses and applications. They need to demonstrate understanding of technical issues as they reflect media implementation and presentation

but they do not need to be "technical." They may even prefer to use traditional, physical media to sketch and communicate, but they cannot be adverse to computers or electronic media.

Creative directors can come from many different backgrounds, but they traditionally come from "artistic" backgrounds since these industries traditionally teach the communication of messages and ideas in various sensorial forms. As long as someone understands the forms that affect your business and how to manage others in these processes, they are potentially useful and important to your company.

You may find ideal candidates by using executive search firms or other employment services, but it is often easier to locate them by word of mouth and by networking. Since companies in these industries are constantly changing, there are always good people looking for new opportunities. Sometimes you can find people as companies downsize or restructure.

There are no hard and fast rules or standards with which to measure someone's potential at being a good creative director. In general, however, the ability to **communicate** well, **articulate** their understandings, processes, and visions, and **understand** the appropriateness and peculiarities of communicating in different media are all imperative.

Creative directors should understand how different styles communicate different feelings and how to manipulate or transpose a message into different forms by changing the style, content, or form. Look for those whose work speaks to you in the way you want to speak to your customers and clients. Those who can convincingly and intelligently describe how their processes lead them to successful solutions will give you an idea of how easy it will be for them to help your company. You will need to review a potential creative director's **portfolio ▶ 82** of work, but more important will be the conversation you have with them.

Small companies may find a creative director interested in contracting these responsibilities since there may not be full-time needs. This is certainly possible, but the creative director will need to be kept informed of company policies and direction. This kind of relationship might work best with the creative director on retainer to

The most important training comes form on-the-job experience in many different roles within various industries. Art direction, production, design, writing, and film/video direction are all responsibilities that lead to the development of successful creative direction skills. The best way to learn is under a skilled creative director. Consider working in some capacity for this type of person to learn their approach, understand their vision, and experience their process.

Explaining the Design Process

[As designers] we're extraordinarily bad at telling people how we got there. We work hard for six months on something, then we bring it to our boss and say, "Isn't that clever," and they say, "Yeah," with no sense of appreciation whatsoever. Then you're upset and shocked beyond belief because they don't understand how profound this thing is.

What's happened is you've done 20, 80, who knows how many designs, you've twiddled around, you've user-studied it, you've user-tested it, you've tried this, it didn't work, you've tried that, it didn't work...you're now like a detective, and eventually, you get to the story or you get the key and you open the door. Here's your boss on the other end, going, "And?" That is the most demoralizing, crushing experience of anybody's life.

The reason is that yes, they're not already educated because guess what? They don't do this for a living and you do. Your fault is that you don't say, "First, we tried that track, then we tried this track," the same way that software people do, "This approach won't work. That approach won't work. We tried this approach, and now we're going to modify it with this approach, and that will work." That's the way they think about things. Our job, then, is to explain how we got to where we did.

—S. Joy Mountford, Project Lead, Interval Research

the company. Also possible are periodic creative audits or training sessions for producers.

How to Be Hired

Employment agencies may track openings for these kinds of skills since creative directors operate at a corporate level, but sometimes the best way to find out about these opportunities is simply to **network** in the related industries. Any company that does not seem to have good creative direction (that is, consistent communications, styles, and levels of quality) may be a possibility, but do not assume that these companies will understand or appreciate the needs for these skills either. The best opportunities are often in medium to large companies with established needs and processes that are already creating interactive products or looking to do so. These types of companies include industrial design firms, publishing companies, advertising agencies, and movie, television, and other media studios.

New opportunities open up every time someone leaves a company and every time a new company starts up. One of the best ways to know about these openings is by making contacts in these industries and keeping up with the issues and changes. Consider these openings carefully, however. Those leaving creative directorships may be doing so because management is indecisive, unresponsive, or unappreciative. Likewise, new start-ups may be so concerned with financial backing and product schedules that they may not be concerned with or value creative direction. You must be sensitive to what kind of people are interviewing you and what they might be like to work for. Creative directors work with both project teams and executives and must be comfortable with both.

A **portfolio** of past work is imperative. You must be able to show high-quality examples of related work in multiple media. You will need to be prepared to show work in a variety of formats as well. For example, a particular company may not be prepared to view a Beta videotape. You should prepare presentations of your work at least in print form and possibly video and interactive forms as well. Also, different companies may have different capabilities to preview interactive work. Be prepared to demonstrate your work as many different ways as possible.

More importantly, however, be prepared to discuss the issues surrounding your work at every step. Let those **interviewing** you lead the conversation, but be sure to give them a full understanding of your skills, abilities, and vision. Be clear about your responsibilities on each project and what kinds of responsibilities you envision. Sometimes, interviewers misinterpret creative direction skills and responsibilities and may think that you are claiming credit and experience in media in which you may not have technical skills. For example, seeing high-end television work may lead some interviewers to believe that you have the skills to do the morphing, animation, and special effects seen in the work yourself. They may not even understand how these pieces were produced and directed. You may be required to educate them about the issues and processes of creative direction just to explain your experience and abilities. In this case, they may or may not be able to understand these new definitions.

Since creative directors for interactive media may be employed in several different industries, you may need to stay abreast of changes in many of these to be in the right place at the right time. Industry gatherings like conferences are important networking opportunities. Industry magazines and newsletters can also help you stay informed.

Compensation

Pay rates and compensation vary greatly with the type of company and the amount of responsibility. Smaller companies with fewer products will pay much less than large companies with many products and services. In fact, the bigger and more important the company, the more pressing and important the direction needs and the better the compensation. Typically, compensation is proportionate to the amount of responsibility and the sizes of the budgets. The range can run from $60,000 to $150,000. The industry itself affects salaries. Typically, creative directors in the advertising and entertainment industries are paid more than in the publishing, software, and design industries. You should research sample salaries for the different industries so you know what is fair and/or expected for any particular opportunity you are investigating.

Bill Rollinson
VP Marketing, Internet Software, Inc.

Bill Rollinson insists that he never had a master plan or a "career path" etched in yellow bricks. He began with a few of the key ingredients for successful players in multimedia—fascination with design and the creative process, entrepreneurial instincts, and a lot of energy. He moved to Palo Alto, to found an independent design firm. Timing, luck, and location led him to attract high tech startup companies as clients, and he learned from his surroundings to use computers as design and production tools.

With his creative talents in demand and his track record in place, Bill networked with friends and colleagues to pursue a new, very Silicon Valley goal—participating in the launch of a new business. The startup process and the technologies themselves fascinated him, so he sold the design firm and went to work for a startup software company called Paracomp that went on to became Macromedia.

As Macromedia grew to become one of Silicon Valley's gold standards in multimedia software design, Bill began to feel the familiar urge to be out on his own. "I learned about multimedia tools, and still had the startup bug, so I left Macromedia to start Storybook Software to create multimedia titles for children." This was a personal journey, using the production expe-rience he'd gained with Macromedia development tools and the life experience he'd gained when he became a father. Once again, his venture met with success, and Storybook Software was acquired by software developer T/Maker. The children's CD-ROM Four Footed Friends was completed after the sale, and found a significant audience.

Bill's latest venture, The Internet Shopping Network, is showing all the signs of success that his earlier projects did. Its recent merger with QVC has targeted it as a major player in online merchandising.

Where do online marketing and children's storybooks come together? In interface design ▶ 170, according to Bill. "Whether I'm working on a multimedia children's storybook or an interactive catalog—the design and implementation of the user interface is key. You need to entertain and educate your user. Sure, the design has to be functional, but it also needs to be fun—it should make you smile, and it shouldn't matter if you're 4 or 40, playing a game or buying a shirt online."

Art Director

What They Do

An **art director** is responsible for all artwork created for a project. This artwork may take any form and may be created using a variety of different tools, techniques, and styles. Traditionally, art directors have dealt mostly with visual and graphic artwork. In Interactive media, these responsibilities stretch to include time-based media such as sound, animation, and video. All artwork in a project must be of consistent quality and appear to have a cohesive relationship with every other part. This can only be accomplished if an art director **reviews the creation** of artwork at every step and helps guide the media professionals on the project to adhere to certain design standards.

Art directors often **produce artwork** on a project as well, and they must understand all the design disciplines as well as the tools and techniques used in them. They must be able to communicate with all team members, set and enforce quality and stylistic standards, and organize and track the media elements through the completion of the work. Art directors usually must consult with programmers and project managers over schedules and details of the components. For example, all final artwork needs to conform to standard specifications including file formats and naming conventions, color palettes, sample sizes, and frame rates. These are usually decided early in the project but must be communicated to everyone who produces final artwork.

Art directors typically work under the guidance and direction of a creative director, much like producers who work under an executive producer. The art director/creative director relationship, however, is for design responsibilities. Art directors typically work under producers in terms of a management structure, although in some cases they may work alongside them.

Art directors are common in industries such as publishing, entertainment, and design. Art directors in multimedia often come from these industries after gaining experience with interactive media. Most people have traditional design training and have refined their skills through on-the-job interactions. It is not unknown, however, to find individuals who have learned these skills from experience on projects even though their backgrounds have no traditional design education. Many times, in fact, these art directors have fresh approaches that lead to more innovation since they do not share the same biases that develop with traditional design education. Others, though, may have spotty backgrounds and not understand the depth of the design decisions needed. Art directors need to have a working knowledge of many fields, such as typography, graphic design, color theory, and information design. They also need a cursory knowledge of more specific issues such as maps and cartography, diagrams and charts, illustration, sound design, animation, videography, and video production, as well as understand the technologies used.

Art directors may be staff employees or freelancers. Their jobs are usually full-time on large projects, but may split their time with other responsibilities on smaller ones. They must be detail-oriented and work well with others since they are responsible, in part, for motivating the media production team to produce high-quality artwork within the scheduled deadlines.

Art directors may start at the conceptualization phases, but must definitely be present through **prototyping** and **production**. Their jobs are mostly over during testing but they may need to appear periodically to redo artwork found to be incorrect or defective during testing. Art directors are responsible for overseeing the day-to-day mechanics of producing artwork. They are the first people production personnel turn to when they need answers, decisions, or equipment. Programmers and scripters also look to them when they need artwork for prototypes or versions in production. They work closely with producers, interface designers, content experts, sound producers, animators, and video producers and are responsible for seeing that the design issues of each team member is addressed in regards to intermediary or final artwork.

Process

In the conceptual phase of a project, an art director needs to be sure that **brainstorming** includes innovative styles and design ideas. These clues may be in the form of samples of other artwork in other products or media forms, or simply a list of adjectives derived from the brainstorming session. In any event, it is the art director's responsibility to turn these clues into visual and auditory examples so that they can be evaluated. Art directors must be careful here not to focus the group on a specific style too early but still move this issue towards resolution by the time a project moves into prototyping or production. In some cases, several prototypes may be created simultaneously to evaluate different styles, so the art director may need to identify and direct multiple artists in a variety of styles and media forms at the same time.

Once the goals and messages of a project are defined and agreed upon, the art director and others on the team should be continually looking for materials that convey similar messages and values. Inspiration may come from any-

where. It may come from samples recorded from radio or television, clipped from magazines and design annuals, or grabbed from other interactive titles. Many art directors keep clipping files and shelves of design annuals and directories that allow them to quickly find samples of possible styles. These samples are then shared with the project team to discuss the strengths, weaknesses, and appropriateness of the materials to the project. Annuals and directories with samples also offer the names and contact information for the artists so they can be reached if their styles are appropriate.

At the beginning stages, artwork may be rough and delivered in non-electronic forms. Traditional media such as paper, paint, and markers are often quicker for creating initial artwork, storyboards, and sketches. These media forms are perfectly acceptable, depending on the client's expectations, and often save time and money.

Art directors will need to be familiar with the limitations of both development and **delivery platforms** ▶ 12. Development platforms tend to be more powerful computers with faster proces-

Brooks Cole
Creative Director, Designer, and President, Mindsphere

Brooks Cole, Creative Director, Designer and President of Mindsphere, one of the hottest multimedia production companies in Sausalito, California, counts among his most important job skills the ability to "learn new techniques by using the latest technologies, then teach them to gifted people who share a similar vision."

Brooks began his career in communications while he was still a marketing and design student at the University of Denver. During that time he had "a virtual conversion experience which convinced me that immersive media can trigger a process leading to self realization." Brooks's long range goal is the "transformation of human consciousness by ultimately enabling individuals to visualize and interact freely with their imagination in responsive, immersive environments." In a word: epiphany.

Meanwhile, he's been specializing in combining the disciplines of advertising, graphic design, animation, and interactive multimedia.

Mindsphere's current focus is to utilize new technology as a means to empower its clients' ability to visualize and market their innovations. Brooks has staked out growth industries such as biotechnology, computers, electronics, and communications as target areas for Mindsphere's expertise and tool set. His work for clients includes animations for Colossal Pictures, an interactive sales kit for Brøderbund, the design of an online prototype for 20th Century Fox, and an interface for Silicon Graphics' interactive television test bed in Orlando, Florida.

Brooks provides some from-the-trenches advice for those contemplating a career in multimedia. "Learn voraciously," he says. "Remember to have a life. Use the ultimate virtual reality available—your own mind."

sors, better and larger monitors, and more capabilities than those used by members of the audience. Art directors are responsible for all artwork looking and performing acceptably on the target delivery machines. At some point, this initial artwork will need to be recreated using digital tools to verify that the styles will work with the size, resolution, and color capabilities of the target delivery equipment.

Art directors usually lead the visual and audio development and meet often with media production teams in critique sessions. A **critique session**, or "crit," is where work is evaluated by everyone in the group without reservations and with the intent to make each person's work better. Team members without traditional design backgrounds may not understand how a crit works and may be hurt or offended by the comments and issues raised. Art directors must guide the crits to stay focused and constructive. After a few critiques, most team members will become comfortable with them, but it can be a long and painful process for those who have never had the experience of their work being challenged or improved upon by others.

Tools and Techniques

As mentioned previously, all media are applicable for the creation of artwork. Some styles, especially, can only be created with more traditional media like paints, sculpture, or paper. They then must be digitized with cameras and scanners or by using some other conversion method. Other styles are easier to create directly with digital tools and are somewhat easier to prepare for final use.

At some point, every screen element will pass through an image manipulation application. The most common one used in the interactive media industry, as well as the design, entertainment, and publishing industries, is Adobe Photoshop. There are certainly other imaging manipulation applications that work in similar manners but art directors and designers all need to understand how they work and what they are capable of.

Art directors will need to be familiar with the technologies that affect the artwork. These include the processing speeds, color capabilities, screen size and resolutions, and display performance of computers, televisions, or other electronic devices. They may also need to know the sound or video constraints. Art directors are responsible for knowing that some forms and styles of artwork or media, no matter how appropriate or wonderful, will not perform well in certain situations or environments. For example, video for personal computers is still fairly primitive and suffers severe performance problems. Horizontal panning of vertical lines often shows the artifacts of these performance problems (like tearing) more easily and should be avoided if at all possible. Likewise, type is often difficult to read on most screens since the resolution is so coarse. The text, typography, and layout in a project need to reflect these technical constraints.

Because **creative and adaptive features** ▶ 169 are being increasingly added to interactive media, art directors may need to choose styles or direct artwork that performs well in a variety of circumstances and with little control over how it is used. For example, some programs allow users to combine their own materials with those that are built into the products. In these cases, it may be important to generate artwork that will complement users' materials, regardless of what they look like.

Qualifications

Aside from a great knowledge of artistic issues such as typography, color theory, and graphic design, you will need to understand the **technological issues** that affect each one. You must be able to interpret how the project will appear in final form on the final delivery medium and plan for the technological issues that will affect its quality. You must also understand the process for creating all artwork and what types of people and resources are needed in order to meet the schedule and budget. You will not necessarily understand the mechanics of every action in the creation of the artwork, but you will need to appreciate the limitations and possibilities of the medium, technology, and process.

Art directors must be able to **work with others** extremely well, sometimes coaxing from them more work than they think they can produce or in styles which they have had little previous experience working in. On the other hand, they must run interference for their people and get new resources or time when this is necessary. An art director needs to be tough but fair to the people that report to them and to the people they report to.

The performance for art directors is measured by results. These results mostly hinge on meeting time and budget expectations because aesthetic goals are more ambiguous and difficult to describe. Many times producers and clients are unable to appreciate many of the aspects of quality design. This means that they may not understand why it took so long to produce artwork because they are inexperienced in the nuances of type kerning or color palette optimization. A good art director is able to educate others on design issues and be able to persuade producers to devote sufficient time and resources to design activities. They will also be able to design an integral part of the development process.

How to Hire

Art directors can be found through **professional design organizations** and from **media-specific placement agencies**. Of course, word of mouth is most helpful, especially if others you know have personally worked with someone. Art directors are not usually represented by agents, nor do employment agencies track jobs for these types of responsibilities.

Many art directors prefer to work free-lance on specific projects and for the duration of that project (giving them the freedom to pursue other projects or interests once it is completed), while others are in search of full-time employment. Because these responsibilities are so immediate and tangible as opposed to those of creative directors, they are more respected and planned for with projects. Producers, however, may not plan for a realistic amount of time for the iterative process of design. Often, project managers are unaware of how much time is necessary to develop the creative direction for artwork before production can begin. This is true even for a prototype. An art director will often need to review budgets and schedules before they become set to put the design task in more realistic terms.

Since art directors need a good working knowledge of most design aspects, they usually have **portfolios** or **samples** of their work. These materials, along with an **interview**, are the most important things with which you can evaluate someone's experience and abilities. The materials help you judge their design competency. The interview will help you judge their management abilities. It is the only way to get a sense of how they deal with others and what their understanding of key issues in interactive multimedia is.

Many of the responsibilities art directors share are not necessarily evident in the finished process because many of them are managerial ones. Still, if you see a project that seems complete and holistic—in which all of the all of the artwork and media seems appropriate and fit together—it is a testimony to good art direction. The people credited for art direction, project management, or creative direction all share credit for this accomplishment and may all be good candidates for hiring.

How to Be Hired

Most art directors start as designers and production people in one discipline and then develop skills in other media forms. All the while they gain experience tracking media elements and working with and managing others. They typically assume more management responsibilities and then move into the art director role.

As with other roles, networking is the most important form of finding work. The key to networking is to interact directly with those who can hire you or refer you to these people. **Executive producers**, **producers**, and **creative directors** are the most common roles that have hiring authority or influence for art directors. The difficulty is that these people can be anywhere. Try attending industry gatherings such as conferences and seminars. This strategy can be especially useful if you attend the kind of conference or seminar that business and project management people are likely to be attending. Likely courses for this include business development, financing, project management, and legal courses and seminars.

*An art director may want to hire a **content manager** ▶ 189 to assist in tracking the acquisition, preparation, and integration of media elements. The content manager may use a database or a spreadsheet to track these items and coordinate their status with the media production people and the programming team.*

167

Most developers understand the artistic tasks an art director performs but may not realize the management tasks that are a significant part of the role. In these types of cases, you may be able to turn a simple production assignment as an artist into a chance to become an art director. Beware of assuming the extra work and responsibilities, especially if extra compensation and support are not offered. Also beware of working on any project that does not have an art director as an explicit part of the project team. This may indicate a producer that has little understanding of the design tasks involved in creating a successful product.

When you do make contact, try to relate your skills and experiences in conversation and set up another time to get together to discuss possible projects in more depth. If you can set up an interview, bring along a portfolio or samples of your work. Be sure to check ahead of time what file formats and equipment is available to be sure that you will be able to show your work. In showing your portfolio of work, emphasize not only the styles and media you are comfortable in but also the variety. It is important that potential producers know that you are capable of working in whatever style is appropriate, regardless of the work you have to show at the time.

Also, be sure to describe your ability to organize your work and that of others. An art director's managerial skills are just as important, if not more so, as their artistic background. Showing complete work from a broad product range can help convey the sensitivity needed to keep artwork consistent and of high-quality. This may not be apparent in just one piece. And do not be afraid to offer ideas about the project. There is a chance the producer may use them whether they hire you or not, but ideas are actually worth very little (compared to their execution). If you appear to have lots of ideas, you will be much more valuable in their eyes than if you hold back and appear to have few ideas and little interest.

Compensation

The compensation for art directors is typically pretty low in comparison to programmers and producers. The salaries and rates commonly follow those found in related industries and available in most industry guides. The way to increase the compensation level is to become well-versed in all forms of media and in how they accentuate or relate to interactivity. The art directors that are in the most demand have skills that go beyond graphical design or screen layout. They extend into the creation of interesting **experiences**. Additional compensation such as royalties or profit-sharing are unlikely unless you help develop the concept for the project, service, or business. Free-lance art directors should be concerned about getting compensated for assigning any copyrights to their work and should also receive explicit demonstration rights.

An art director should be as concerned about the structure of the position as they are about the compensation. Working for a producer that has a heavy hand or mercurial instincts toward design will almost certainly lead to dissatisfaction. Structure the **work agreement** ▶ 95 to clearly define the responsibilities and authority of the position.

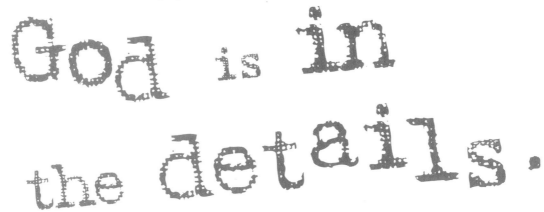

Claire Barry
Senior New Media Designer, Clement Mok designs

"My love for pixels originated in Legos," says Claire Barry. "I love taking discrete bits of information and building things out of them." A senior member of the new media creative team at Clement Mok designs, she gets to exercise this passion on a regular basis.

Claire has built many information-rich digital products in the past decade. She designed navigation and visual elements for CMd and Rocket Science's Web sites; art directed and designed a kiosk for the launch of Herman Miller's Aeron Chair (which included a 1,600 frame stereo navigable movie); and worked on an interactive biology textbook, interactive movies on demand, online shopping services, corporate training kiosks and a major interactive music CD-ROM.

Her love of computers began at the Academy of Art in San Francisco, where she earned a BFA in Graphic Design. She was a designer for a packaging firm, and later joined SuperMac Technology to both write the specification and design the interface for PixelPaint Professional. Claire worked with SuperMac's Digital Video group to create sales communication tools for VideoSpigot and DigitalFilm, including VideoSpigot Interactive, the first CD-ROM with QuickTime movies.

Claire has witnessed firsthand how multimedia has changed the role of art director: "At the top level, you have to be much more audience-aware, since it's two-way communication. You have to encourage your audience to participate. Logistically, it requires a much broader skill set. The discipline and tactical skills for logo design are more contained than developing metaphors for an online service." Project teams are changing, too, with the addition of specialists in audio, video, and other areas. However, she points out that designer's skills are broadening as well, just as they did when computers first gave designers the ability to work with type and edit photographs. She applauds this trend, noting that "the most successful studios have people with broad general interests."

She stresses the need for solid foundational skills in all designers: "Develop good graphic design skills and sensitivity to aesthetics," she advises. "Then learn the cognitive components of interactive design; issues relating to user interactivity, user response, and navigational systems." Hands-on production experience is critical, particularly the ability to make things quickly. "We're not always building final products. The shelf life of a website can be six months or less."

Interface Designer

What They Do

Interface design is one of the newest careers in multimedia. Unfortunately, the term interface design suffers from a great deal of misunderstanding. Most people think of it as the design of icons, backgrounds, and other onscreen elements. While this may be part of the job, it is only the most visible and certainly just the beginning. An interface designer is responsible for the entire interface of a product. This includes not only what users see when using the product, but what they hear, touch, and feel.

Interface designers are responsible for the cognitive model users develop when working with a product. This model refers to the way users think about it, and about its organizations, its workings, and its capabilities. Part of the problem with some of the current multimedia titles on the market is that they do not develop strong cognitive models. *Myst*, on the other hand, is so successful in part because it develops a rich sense of place and, just like a great movie, does not interrupt that experience at inopportune times or

in inappropriate ways. Its structure is so captivating and yet still understandable and consistent. Interface designers do more than make products "easy to use." They make them clear, rich, and meaningful. In fact, another term for this role might be experience designer because they are designing what the user is experiencing.

Interface design encompasses the disciplines of information design, interaction design, and sensorial design. **Information design** ▶ 9 is about the organization and presentation of the information or entertainment. **Interaction design** at the top level is concerned with creating the time-based experience the user will encounter and, at the tactical level, with designing the specific manipulations the user will perform in the interface to move through the product. **Sensorial design** embodies all the media forms that can be used to communicate with a person. It includes writing, graphic or visual design, sound design, and video design. A skilled Interface designer will have a background in all of these areas.

Many interface designers are employed full time typically within hardware manufacturers, software manufacturers, industrial design firms, and multimedia studios. These designers tend to work on interfaces for larger, more complex products and on both soft and hard interfaces. In addition, they may be involved with core research as opposed to developing products intended for sale. Freelance designers and consultants tend to work more on smaller products such as individual multimedia titles, kiosks, and marketing pieces. This type of work mostly involves designing soft interfaces and tends to have less complexity and fewer opportunities for huge leaps in innovation.

Interface designers are an integral part of a development team and often are responsible for coordinating and driving the creative development ahead. They are typically hired and managed by the **producer**, although the **creative director** and/or **art director** may also have hiring and managing authority. The issue of who is auteur, or even whether there is one, in the creation of

The Spectrum of Interactivity

The overriding force that is currently driving much of the innovation in multimedia is the exploration into the meaning of interactivity. Interactivity is a relatively new phenomenon within the context of technological devices and informational products. The nature of what interaction is—and what it can be—is redefined continuously by new products, new research, and new ideas.

Interactivity can be looked at as a spectrum that extends from passive to interactive. **Passive experiences** are typically characterized by low user feedback, low user control, and simple navigation. Characteristics that separate **interactive experiences** from passive ones are just the opposite—high user feedback, high user control, rich and informative displays, and sophisticated navigation. (Sophisticated does not necessarily mean complex. A flight simulator with a joystick has sophisticated navigation that almost everyone can understand.)

All products and experiences fall somewhere on this spectrum. There is no value judgment on which end is better or worse. Some products and experiences should be more passive than active. The important point is for designers to place the products and experiences they are creating along the spectrum at their most appropriate point.

Other aspects of interactivity include **creative** or **productive features.** Creative features give audiences a way of participating by producing something themselves. A children's storybook, for example, might allow a child to paint or rearrange elements in the interface. A music title might let the user modify the music or assist it in creating new compositions. An interactive documentary might allow the viewer to structure their own narrative with the material. Humans are extremely creative organisms and enjoy making things for themselves, but too few products currently allow us to do much in these terms. Creativity doesn't have to be merely entertaining—it is also produc-

tive. A business plan builder, for example, might have features that make it easier for a person to create a business plan with their own information. Essentially, software has allowed people to be creative for years, but there are few products that alllow people to create things or use their own content.

Adaptive features are those that cause the product to change in response to users' profiles, actions, or other behavior. Incorporating these fea-

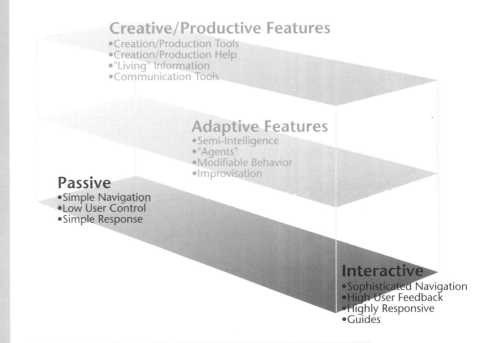

Creative/Productive Features
- Creation/Production Tools
- Creation/Production Help
- "Living" Information
- Communication Tools

Adaptive Features
- Semi-Intelligence
- "Agents"
- Modifiable Behavior
- Improvisation

Passive
- Simple Navigation
- Low User Control
- Simple Response

Interactive
- Sophisticated Navigation
- High User Feedback
- Highly Responsive
- Guides

tures can allow a product to respond individually to users of different sophistication, who speak different languages, who have different interests, or who have used the product for different periods of time. These kinds of features do not need to be "intelligent" although they may give that impression. For example, an adaptive encyclopedia might notice that the user is looking through flowers and offer to help filter just for flowers. It might notice that someone is only responding to expert-level information and begin to only provide that level of content or assistance. These features are usually more expensive and difficult to add to a product, but interactive products that have some measure of adaptability are likely to provide more meaningful experiences.

multimedia is largely unresolved but the interface designer figures prominently in any discussion on the matter.

Interface designers should be highly involved at the outset of a project and continue an active role until the start of production. In the conceptualization of the project, they are responsible for helping to define and express the project **goals** and **messages**. They also must be aware of the profiles of target users, the characteristics of target machines, and the nature of the information in the product. In products created for clients, interface designers help to get clients to communicate their thoughts about the product and their expectations. Many clients will have pre-conceived notions and so it can be important either to follow these notions or educate the client on alternative directions.

Interface designers will often be involved in the creative direction of any prototypes. A prototype is a small working version of the product used for evolving the design. (Prototypes are also created to help sell the project to investors and publishers.) The most critical part of prototyping is user testing. This is where the product assumptions made by the development team are tested against typical people who are likely to use the product when completed. It is important that this testing is accurate and realistic. Influencing these users, even unknowingly, will produce false results and lead to an incorrect understanding of the product's potential success with users. Many companies perform final user testing after production has been completed. While this testing offers them the ability to refine products, it should not replace user testing during the initial design.

Once the design has been completed, the interface designer's responsibilities drop off sharply. The end of design might include a finished and signed-off prototype or it might mean a completed set of documents and plans outlining the content and structure of the product. Interface designers are still needed through production and possibly testing but most of the decisions concerning the interface should have already been made by the time production begins. Addressing the design of the interface anytime after this point will cause delays, budget overruns, schedule slips, and possibly risk the success of the product. Unfortunately, these types of situations still happen quite often. The work during production consists of coordinating with the media production and programming staffs and clarifying the finer points of the design.

Process

Interface designers move a development team through a series of steps that eventually lead to a clear definition of a product. The decisions and assumptions at each step along the way affect every decision that occurs later in the process. An interface designer, along with possibly the creative director, assembles the appropriate people and helps lead the meetings. They will commonly produce periodic reports of the progress so that everyone on the team is operating under the same assumptions. These descriptions are critical to the timely development of a successful interface. They also allow everyone on the team, including clients and new members, to understand why the interface has been developed in a particular way.

The first milestone for an interface designer is the creation of a **product specification**. This is similar to a treatment in the sense that it describes the direction of the product but it goes deeper to include items such as the delivery platform, audience, and available content. It is developed through the use of brainstorming sessions among producers, scriptwriters, programmers, content experts, marketing people, and possibly clients, visual designers, animators, and sound designers. The goal of these initial meetings is to provide a general framework with which to proceed. This framework is provided by first thinking up possibilities without any limitations attached, and then gradually matching these possibilities to the constraints imposed by technical, marketing, or client concerns. The rest of the conceptualization phase is to refine the concept within this framework.

This abstract description may contain several possibilities for the structure and format of the product. These may be tested with small simulations or a large prototype may be built to help refine the most likely possibility. Many companies omit creating any prototypes, which is fine for products that are in a series or are well understood. Most designers, though, stress the need to develop and test one or more prototypes. The prototypes serve to test abstract items such

Information design is a discipline, an approach, and a process to good communication. It is really pervasive. It's about organizing your ideas and the data that you're trying to communicate, paying attention to the messages and goals of your communication, and then finding really appropriate ways to present them so that they are clear, accessible, and easily understood. Interaction design is more about the audience's experience, whether it's a performance, an electronic product, or even a book. Interaction design is really about the experience that you're creating and how you're communicating those messages through what you're allowing the audience to do.

*—Nathan Shedroff, Creative Director, **vivid** studios*

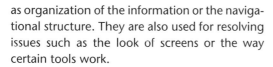

Nathan Shedroff
Creative Director, vivid studios

Nathan Shedroff graduated from the Art Center in Pasadena in 1989 with a degree in transportation design. During his years of study, however, he came across Richard Saul Wurman's work in the field of information architecture. While still at school, he approached Richard Saul Wurman for an entry-level position at his company The Understanding Business. He cleared his 30-day trial internship after the first week and soon rose to designer and then to senior designer, helping to design many products for the Pacific Bell Smart Yellow Pages and the book Information Anxiety.

In 1990, Nathan co-founded vivid studios with the idea of producing both print and electronic works centered around information architecture principles. "I want to see better products out there," he explains. "This is one way to affect a lot of projects." Over the past five years, Nathan has led creative teams in developing new interaction paradigms for digital reference tools, online worlds, and productivity software working with clients such as Hands On Technology, Softbank, ETAK, The WELL, Delphi, Apple Computer, Paramount New Media, and TED conferences. He is a co-

author of Understanding Computers, and has participated in publishing over twenty other print and electronic titles including Information Anxiety, Danny Goodman's Macintosh Handbook, Multimedia Demystified, and Voices of the 30s.

His rigorous design training plus years of hard work in print and electronic media has provided him with skills, knowledge, and experience that few can match. And in a fitting tribute to his efforts, in February of 1995, Nathan took the stage along with Jonas Salk, Nicholas Negroponte, and Penn & Teller as one of the featured presenters at the Richard Saul Wurman's TED Conference.

Nathan advocates exposing yourself to a wide range of ideas and activities. "The things that are most imporant are not expressly taught anywhere," he says, "so you never know what experiences are going to matter."

---

as organization of the information or the navigational structure. They are also used for resolving issues such as the look of screens or the way certain tools work.

At the end of the prototyping stage, the interface designer, with the help of the programming staff, will prepare a detailed **functional specification** 130, 251, 258. This document, along with possibly a script or content list, will describe the product to the production team and be used throughout the production phase. The functional specification needs to describe every intended action and interaction in the product and every imaginable result. For example, what happens when a user clicks on a tool? When should the cursor change and what should it change to? What happens after they stop drawing? Does the tool remain active or does it revert back to an

arrow cursor? If the product is capable of performing differently based on certain criteria, these adaptive qualities must be outlined and described so that programmers can implement them. The more complete the specification, the more smoothly development will proceed.

Tools and Techniques

There are few specific tools used by interface designers. Some are more comfortable sketching and working with paper prototypes early, while others jump immediately to the computer to design or program variations. The form and process of development will often be determined by the product itself, as well as the needs of the development team and schedule.

Interface designers typically work with a variety of media to develop and communicate their

*Information designers are **editors** but in a greater sense. They provide the filtering mechanism that turns raw content into something more meaningful, but they go beyond editors both in their understanding of the different ways of organizing information and in their uses of multiple media forms.*

173

Traditionally, interface design has been software or screen-design oriented. It's more dynamic today where you have to think about the process which a person will experience in working with an application or a title, or even a hardware device. My background is theater and I've produced and directed quite a lot of it. So I talk a lot about the time-based experience, about what happens over time as somebody uses a product, a computer, a PDA, or whatever it is. That time frame can be one session or you can stretch that to weeks or years, but it's important to understand that people's expectations change over time. Most software applications, especially productivity tools, don't take that into account. They design one screen at a time.

—Scott Maddux,
Hardware/Software
Interface Designer,
Hasbro

ideas. These can include paper media (such as paper, markers, pens, and acetate), electronic media (such as computers, screens, painting and drawing software, animation and modeling software, scanners, and video equipment), and performance media (such as role playing, improvisation, scripts, acting). Some interface designers even prepare their own rough prototypes if they are familiar with **authoring tools** ▶ 253 or programming tools. While these skills are not always necessary, they can allow a designer to create small, quick examples much faster and easier than trying to oversee and direct someone else. However, for more complex and novel prototypes or for ones taking longer than a day or two to complete, skilled programmers should be brought in.

Brainstorming is a critical technique used by interface designers because they are often asked to rethink basic assumptions about the interface and to produce original and unique interactions. This task, however, requires that they be able to think originally and transfer different kinds of experiences into potential computer interactions. In other words, they need to be able to "think outside the box" and be willing to suspend their disbelief and criticism of new possibilities.

Another related technique is to visualize themselves in the user's situation. This technique seems like a basic one but it can be very difficult to do. For example, many interface designers are expert users with fine mouse control and good eyesight. As a result, some may have a tendency to put in too many features or design controls or labels that are too small for others. A good interface designer will look at their designs from other vantage points and edit them accordingly.

Qualifications

The specific issues involved with the interface are numerous. They include areas such as the use of colors, icons, characters, and **points of view** ▶ 32, 55, 176, 192. It extends to the structure and presentation of information, navigation, and the use of metaphors, cognitive models, guides, and agents. Also included are interactivity levels and features and age, gender, and culture issues. Learning these issues does not happen overnight. They are complex, abstract, and serious enough

that it may take several years of specific and applied study just to become acquainted with them. The field is also rapidly growing and changing. Staying abreast of developments takes a large commitment as well.

Interface designers should **understand the technology** involved with a particular product, at least to the extent that it affects the interface. They will need to not only understand the concerns of other members of the team but also the limitations of the technology as well. Interface designers are expected to push or work around these limitations as much as possible.

Above all, they should be able to **work closely with others** in a team setting. They will need to communicate effectively both verbally and visually and may need to help others communicate their ideas and concerns as well. They need to be able to incorporate input from clients, potential users, producers, technical leads, art directors and others, but also be strong enough not to let the design be compromised by input from too many sources.

If you separate the specific disciplines, the qualifications for an information designer are slightly different than those of an interaction designer. Ideally, you want to be well versed in all, but certain projects may have greater need than others. For example, a children's storybook may not have a need for an expert in structuring information because the information is primarily a single story, although the product may have simple branching capabilities or side stories. Most scriptwriters take on the task of creating the story or stories. An interaction designer, however, will still be needed to provide assistance in creating the structure as well as defining the way to navigate and use any additional features and tools. A reference product, on the other hand will have a huge need for an information designer.

How to Hire

Interface designers may work as freelancers or full-time. Different designers are interested in different arrangements and different kinds of work. It is up to the employer to understand how much use they have for an interface designer, for how long, and how much work needs to be covered. Employers may find the perfect designer for their company only to discover that a particular designer is only interested in working as a contractor or consultant. Other times the opposite may be true. Employers may need to be flexible in how they hire these people since the right mix of their skills and interests is more difficult to find than most other roles.

It is not easy to hire interface designers, mostly because it is not easy to find them. There are almost no programs that currently offer degrees in interface design (this field is barely fifteen years old) although many colleges and university programs do offer a few courses on the subject. Many interface designers come from visual design backgrounds. They attended art or design schools, worked in commercial and graphic design fields, and then gradually gained experience with computer and multimedia screen design. Others come from a cognitive psychology background, studying how people think and perceive. They gained experience in human factors or industrial design departments mostly in the computer, aircraft, and automobile industries. Still others have experience in scriptwriting, information design, or programming, learning more about specific interface issues and gaining more experience solving interface problems as they work on projects.

Professional organizations like the Association of Computing Machinery Special Interest Group in Computer-Human Interaction (ACM SIGCHI) can provide leads, although some of these groups tend to approach the subject from an academic angle. Also, the interface community is especially open and it is common for interface designers to refer others for work when they are not available. The community is still small and so finding one interface designer will typically lead you to others.

Because this field is so new, there is no consistency of philosophy or experience across which candidates can be judged. There are also no standards of study or abilities yet. Some of the best interface designers do not even have a typical professional background in any field related to computers. They may come from an art or design background or a psychology background. In fact, many of the best interactive experiences are designed by interface designers with performance backgrounds.

A resume containing a mix of **unusual work experiences** as well as **personal experiences** can be a good indication of someone qualified for the role. Practice and study in a variety of areas often lead to good interface design skills. A resume, however, will only provide a glimpse. But an interview with a prospective candidate is the best way to discover his or her philosophy and

Twenty-five Cent Training

For a really good example of multimedia interfaces that work well—it's such a cliché, I hate to bring it up—but visit your local video arcade. Interface designers could do a lot worse. I've actually known designers who were given a roll of quarters by their boss and told to go down to the arcade game and study how these things worked. You could do a lot worse than that as far as learning how to design a craft because video games have to be instantly approachable. There are little instruction cards that come along with most of them, but if you ever see anyone sit there and read them, you know the game has failed. But using about two controls, a joy-stick, and a button or two, they're basically able to convey this incredibly rich world of interaction. Where the interface is so much fun to use that people, you could argue, play the game for the sake of using the interface.

You can take the same kind of guidelines and apply them to simple CD-ROM-type navigation tasks. Where, with a couple of controls and some very simple rules about how you navigate, you go from one thing to the next. When you're designing multimedia, the rule should be that it's at least as easy to use as the local video game. I think that's a very achievable goal because you're working in essentially the same medium.

—Peter Bickford, Interface Designer, Apple Computer

photo by Caroline Joe

Abbe Don
Interactive Multimedia Artist

Abbe Don is one of the few interaction designers who has managed to extend the possibilities of human-computer interaction beyond button clicking and a hardwired Pavlovian style "click/response" interactivity. Abbe's designs for Apple Computer's The Guides Project, *Sunburst Communications'* Voices of the 30s *and her own independent projects emphasize the "human" half of the human-computer equation, enabling the end user to participate as contributor and collaborator.*

Her 1991 Share With Me A Story, *installed at the Judah Magnes Museum in Berkeley, California, encouraged people to bring photographs from their family history to the exhibit, scan them, type captions, then add a soundtrack narrating the history of that photo. The result was a computer-based oral and visual history of each contributor's family photographs; one part meditation on family, one part homage to the Kodak snapshot, and one part ground-breaking use of computers to build a living, breathing interactive community. Visitors at the exhibit who arrived sans family album were inspired to scan the pictures from their driver's license, and family photos*

Abbe Don's
Interactive Heuristics

1 Use **personal stories** and **idiosyncratic structures** to organize information and users' experience. People naturally weave stories together in a multi-linear or poly-linear manner but in school they learn to organize things linearly in a very top down fashion. Once you have the linear flow, free things up.

2 Use characters to represent multiple **points of view**. The most effective use of characters in the interface is to use them to represent information from multiple points of view, especially in domains such as history, news, or storytelling. In addition, characters can be used to help users find information from a particular point of view rather than requiring users to struggle with a more traditional query interface.

3 Work with people who can engage in simultaneous **top-down** and **bottom-up design**. In other words, balance a "user centered" perspective based on user scenarios and the ideal world with a functionality and system perspective based on the limitations of hardware, software, or bandwidth.

4 Provide **experiences** in which the user co-creates and transforms the content, not just branches through "shovelware," consuming randomly accessible data.

5 Use **improvisation** and **performance** in the early brainstorming phases or at any point when the design, production, or programming teams are stuck. Take improv and performance courses to keep you on your feet and avoid getting stuck with the same old techniques and same old approaches to problems.

6 Keep your sense of **humor**, **passion**, and **patience**, especially when collaborating with others.

© 1995 Abbe Don

How to Be Hired

If you are an experienced interface designer and are looking for work, the best place to start is with other professionals and industry contacts you know. Most people in these industries see and hear of opportunities constantly. If you are just starting out and have little or no experience, check with large computer manufacturers, software publishers, and some multimedia publishers first. Not only do many of these companies have established interface design groups but they also have **internship** ▶ 91 programs. Some companies, especially those from the en-

attitudes about interface design. It is often possible to hire people for interface consulting and then look to hire them to a longer term contract or as an employee if they work out well.

from their wallets, to tell their own, often fascinating stories. Of course, everyone could simply view the montage of photographs and listen to the spoken stories of their co-contributors. Abbe counts as one of her proudest moments the day she overheard a group of four elderly women exclaim, "Oh, I didn't know I could use a computer for something like this!"

Abbe's formative experiences in the field of interaction design and human-computer interactivity are pulled from a diverse range of sources. Inspirations include reading Hopscotch, *by Julio Cortazor, which introduced her in 1981 to the concept of interactive fiction; to working in 1985 with Richard Saul Wurman at Access Press, where she learned first-hand the concepts of information design; to her 1988 internship at the Human Interface Group at Apple Computer. However, her interactive breakthrough came as a graduate student in the Interactive Telecommunications Program at NYU where she created the first version of* We Make Memories, *an interactive narrative that simulated the storytelling style of her great-grandmother.*

Abbe continues to return to Share With Me A Story, *this time using the co-creative model in the design of her new website. Users of the Internet will soon be able to log on, send a scanned photo and attach their own individual stories.*

tertainment industry, may use other titles such as game designer instead of interface designer.

If you have an education from a school that teaches interface design in some capacity then you might highlight this on your resume and in any accompanying cover letters. Otherwise, you should highlight the projects you have worked on, any applicable personal experiences such as theater, counseling, or teaching, and your ideas and philosophies.

Producers, creative directors, and art directors will be most interested in seeing samples of your work. **Finished products** are the most desirable, but even school or personal projects can be valuable to show. Also, electronic versions of the work will have the most impact. It is important that you walk people through what your respon-

sibilities were on each project and why you took the steps you did. Taking this approach will give you an opportunity to highlight all the things you thought about in designing the project. If you give them a demonstration of the features and expect them to "get it," you are likely to be disappointed.

Remember that when you are being interviewed by a prospective employer, you are also interviewing them, their company, and their products. You should be looking for work that is challenging, interesting, and will offer you growth. You also want to consider the chances of a project making it to market. Many companies have teams that generate a variety of product designs, but only a few are developed fully. Another thing to consider is their appreciation for interface design. You may have to educate others or continually have to defend your ideas. Also, many companies have a tendency to leave little room for adequate design. This is especially true with startup companies or those rushing to get their products to market. While these opportunities may give you a lot of experience, they may not be as fulfilling as you might like.

Compensation

Compensation in new fields almost always varies greatly. Interface design is no exception. There are few standard prices for interface designers, either for contracting or full-time employment. The range of salaries can be anywhere from $40,000 to $120,000. This, of course, depends on experience, responsibilities, and skills. For contracting, hourly rates can be anywhere between $50/hr to $200/hr based on the same criteria and also by the length of work. (Short-term jobs typically pay more.)

Prices for work in the entertainment, computer hardware, and software publishing industries will lean toward the higher end of the spectrum, while traditional book publishers will be at the lower end. The type of project will also influence compensation levels. Research and title development will not pay as much as development of interfaces for new products, industrial products, business products, or operating systems. In general, the more complicated and expensive the product, the higher the compensation will be for the development of its interface.

Salaries and prices are so unpredictable in part because the value of a great interface is difficult to calculate. Unlike testing, where a bug in a program can cause a noticeable drop in sales, a product with a poor interface simply never sells, leaving it hard to tell whether it was because of the interface, content, audience, or marketing.

177

Game Designer

What They Do

A **game designer** is a special form of interface designer. It has been placed on its own for a couple of reasons. The first is that it encompasses some distinct responsibilities, namely to design games that have a high entertainment value to them. The second is because it is becoming a recognized role within a number of different companies.

A game designer designs interactive games. These games can either be developed for cartridges, CD-ROMs, or online worlds. They can be traditional games such as chess or checkers or they can be innovative games such as LucasArts' *Full Throttle*, Brøderbund's *Myst*, or Maxis' *SimCity*, combining narrative elements with game play to form a truly unique entertainment form. **Game play ▶ 22** is a term that has received more and more attention in the past year or so to refer to those elements which makes a game appealing. It is hard to define, just as what constitutes a game is hard to define. If you ask game players about games, they will tell you things like, "That one is lame but this one's great." If you ask them why, you get the answer, "I don't know. Because that one's boring and this one is fun." While they often cannot describe what good game play is, they know it when they see it.

Skilled game designers, though, are able to point to various characteristics in each that make them appealing. They are knowledgeable about the different types and genres of games and know how to turn them into entertaining experiences. Trip Hawkins, founder of Electronic Arts and 3DO, once said that a good game should be simple, hot, and deep. Experienced game designers know the tricks to make this happen.

The opportunities for game designers are growing rapidly because games have been one of several bona fide successes in interactive media. Many of the top ten titles in sales listings for CD-ROMs are games and more and more companies are investing large sums in developing and marketing interactive games.

Game designers start at the beginning and are typically active and vital members of the project team until the products ship. Many make analogies between a game designer on a game and a director on a movie. They both tend to "own" the artistic vision and work closely with a producer to put the resources together to realize that vision.

Process

A game designer may develop an idea and pitch it to internal or external sources. Or, they may be brought in to take a concept and infuse it with elements of game play. In the first case, they may be heavily involved in creating a **treatment ▶ 186**, which is a one to ten page brief on the idea, and then present it to others to get their approval to move forward. These "pitch meetings" typically take place in front of marketing representatives, producers, and possibly an executive producer. When pitching a game to outside publishers, game developers just starting out often need to produce prototypes to help others visualize the game. Game developers with one or more games under their belts are often able to work with just a treatment and, possibly, a script.

A **script ▶ 184** for a game is similar to a script for a movie. It describes the sequence of events that take place within the game. Unlike a movie script, however, game scripts typically do not have a beginning, a middle, and an end. They do not start on page 1 and progress to page 120 in a linear sequence of scenes that all depend on the previous scene or scenes. Game scripts do not have a suggested length or structure. While they tend to use the same typographical style and layout of movie scripts, their non-linear nature tends to make them longer than scripts and jump to pages further back in the script or to sections that appeared earlier. There are few rules or even guidelines.

A game designer might develop the script on their own but it is more common in the industry for a game developer and scriptwriter to co-develop it. In fact, many scriptwriters with film backgrounds are moving into the game industry

Electronic game design offers a wealth of career opportunities for people with imagination. Many of the games that our books—both the strategy guides and the novels—are based on are science fiction, fantasy, and horror, which is simply another market for that kind of material. But the kinds of things that games can be—from Tetris *to* Myst *to* Ecco*—are limited only by the ability of human minds to conceive of new permutations and new ways to entertain and intrigue our fellow humans.*

—Roger Stewart,
Publisher,
Prima Publishing

Brian Moriarty
Game Designer

Brian "Professor" Moriarty built his first computer in the fifth grade. This early experience with digital electronics led him to pursue a degree in English literature at Southeastern Massachusetts University. He found his way back to technology, however; after college he was technical editor of a computer game magazine, and eventually wrote and designed his own games. Brian authored three of the original Infocom interactive fiction titles: Wishbringer *(1985),* Trinity *(1986), and* Beyond Zork *(1987). His first graphic adventure,* Loom, *was published in 1990 by Lucasfilm Games.* Loadstar: The Legend of Tully Bodine, *an action game designed in collaboration with Ron Cobb, was published last year by Rocket Science.*

"Lots of game testers become designers," Brian explains, as well as writers and designers from other disciplines. There's no standardized path to becoming a game designer in the U.S., unlike in Japan where one can earn a degree in computer game engineering.

Brian is quick to point out the difference between game design and presentation; in his eyes, presentation (everything from high-end graphics and sound to elaborate packaging) is breaking new ground, but game

design is, by and large "the same old same old. Interactivity is going retrograde, because it's better [financially] to spend the money on presentation." CD-ROMs with live-action video, often touted as the next generation of interactive entertainment, are really just *"pretty ordinary games being tacked onto movies,"* he feels.

However, many of these games have done quite well in spite of limited interactivity. *"The puzzles in* Myst *are standard, yet it succeeds because of nice presentation,"* he explains. Myst *hit the market as CD-ROM drives were peaking, and was "the best looking box on the shelves."* Although this point-and-click explorer story follows in the footsteps of earlier games like The Manhole *and* Cosmic Osmo, it is viewed as a breakthrough product and has sold phenomenally well. Brian predicts consumers will see a crop of Myst-clones before the end of 1995.

Brian intends to push design boundaries in his latest position, as co-founder and head of game design for a mysterious Silicon Valley startup so new it doesn't even have a name. The four-person company is developing multi player online games. "We'll stay small for awhile," he says, *"but eventually plan to conquer the universe."*

> You're a bit of a movie scriptwriter and a director in that you define the action. But you have to define it with lots of options, and there's a player instead of a viewer.
>
> —Chris Shen,
> Game Designer, Sega

and having a great deal of success. It is not unusual to see scriptwriters occasionally play the role of game designer and vice versa.

Along with the script comes either **flow charts** or **game maps** ▶ 186. These documents provide some graphical description of the structure and connections for all the decision points within a game. One simple gaming structure is to create

a single pathway that players are supposed to proceed down and if they chose different paths along the way they either lose points or they lose the game. More complex structures take the form of interconnected places with more freedom of movement and variability. These structures are commonly represented with maps that indicate the connections between each place and the obstacles that are unique to each one.

Once the structure is completed and the game receives the green light and moves into production, the game designer watches over the media production staff and the programming staff to make sure all the elements are in their right forms. As soon as the structure begins to take form, the game design helps to refine the pacing and the game play to make sure that it creates the appropriate experience. This refinement typically takes place throughout the production of the game. Good game designers, though, are able to make this process a converging one and resist the temptation to either continually take different directions or tinker with it so that it loses all its shape and substance.

Tools and Techniques

A game designer doesn't use too many tools. They try to give structure and communicate their ideas and so anything that helps them do that is a big help. Word processors are important and illustration or charting programs can help in building flow charts for game maps. Some designers might use simple authoring tools like *HyperCard* or *SuperCard* to develop quick prototypes that show some of the navigation or gaming structure. Primarily, though, a game designer relies on others to take the game concept and make it a reality through their talents and tools. A game designer relies on interface designers, visual designers, sound producers, animators, video producers, and programmers to do this.

The techniques a game designer uses are coming up with lots of ideas and putting them in a form that communicates them to others. This process includes creating a setting with **goals**, **obstacles**,

and **challenges** ▶ 22. Some games might introduce characters and other **narrative** ▶ 26 elements to establish this setting. But even with these elements, the technique mentioned by most game designers is the relying a lot on interaction throughout the development process. Since there are so few games to point to as models, and even these are quickly outdated, it is difficult to know when your ideas are the right ones until they take a form where they can be tested.

Qualifications

The best game designers are deeply interested in the subject and make games a big part of their lives. Much like movie directors who grow up with a passion for film and video, game designers grow up with a passion for games. They have clear memories of playing their first computer games and get excited when talking about ones that changed their lives. Look for excitement and then look for knowledge of what makes different games fun. Being able to work with others and direct them is also important, but without the other two, the best production in the world will end up flat.

How to Hire

Since the tasks a game designer performs are relatively discrete ones—namely create a game that provides hours of fun—it is easier to distinguish what a game designer adds to a product than it is for other roles in multimedia. As a result, the first place to look when hiring a game designer is in the credits of games that you enjoy and that are similar to the one you want to develop. Some game designers/scriptwriters are represented by entertainment agents, so this can be an option. Game designers in game companies might be willing to change jobs if the benefits and responsibilities are greater than their current ones. If you cannot find game designers with established credits, the next step is to find someone who knows games and has a deep passion for them.

Controllers

Game designers have to understand remote controls. They have to know what a remote control is capable of. Right now, you have video games that operate with your simplest off-the-shelf remote or one that ships in the box with a typical Sega or Nintendo machine. But then, you have after-market remote manufacturers and software developers that design for the added features in these remotes. There's a real interdependency between the hardware and software.

—Scott Maddux, Hardware/Software Interface Designer, Hasbro

Chris Shen
Game Designer, Sega

Chris Shen once played Space Invaders for five hours non-stop. "Mom went shopping and when she came back I was still playing. She was kind of worried. She didn't even know that it was still the same game; the score was something like 27 million." Little did she suspect that he'd continue to be so engrossed with games once he grew up.

But games are an important part of Chris' life. As a game designer for Sega, he gets in his daily fix, "I play at least an hour or two hours a day, usually after work, and at lunch if it's really bad." Chris discovered game design after receiving a degree in product design at Stanford, working first on board games and eventually finding his way to Sega, where he's worked on CD-ROMs like Jurassic Park.

He describes his role as that of a "player's advocate: I have to imagine what they would expect and what they would be able to figure out, and then communicate that to the people making the game." Sega's project teams typically have 10–15 people, and it's Chris's job to explain his ideas to all of them. "A lot of my job is spent answering questions," he says, stressing the importance of good communication skills for designers.

He also spends a lot of time keeping up with new developments, in hardware, software, and pop culture. "In the game industry we talk about cycles of games; when a new machine or technology emerges, there's a definite pattern you follow. It's really rare to see a new game that doesn't fit into a previous trend."

"Games are coming closer to modeling reality," he says, mentioning that Sim City is hard to describe but "completely engrossing to play." Chris speculates that peripherals will be the next big thing: "We're still using keyboards and mice, but in the next 10–15 years we'll see peripherals that mirror reality. When you throw your arm in the air, the person on-screen will throw his arm in the air."

"Board games offer social interaction," he continues, "which is harder to get in computer games right now. With new peripherals, maybe that won't be the case any more." How else does he think games may change in the future? "Well, if Sonic's still around, I bet he won't do a lot of the things he does now. Maybe you'll be Sonic yourself, running down the track instead of watching him, non-interactively. Things may work in all three dimensions very spatially rather than just a two-dimensional scrolling game."

How to Be Hired

The best way to be hired as a game designer is to have previous game credits and approach game companies for a full-time or freelance position. Since this role is one of the more recognized and established roles in the industry, getting a job as one has a similar structure and process to it as does getting a job as a director or actor in Hollywood. You need to build up a name and then approach the executive producers and produces with the authority to hire and green light projects.

Barring any official experience, budding game designers can get into the business in two ways. They can design, pitch, and build their own games. Or, they can work at various positions

vivid: How do you create an interesting game?

You do play balancing, and you've got to watch it as it's built. No one's going to say whether it's right or wrong—other than you, really. Along the way, am I going to worry about graphics and glitches? No. I'll point them out and forget about them. They'll get fixed somehow or another—but until you build it, you're not sure whether or not it will work.

Maybe somewhere out there is a complete design genius who can envision it right off and know it's going to work. But most people here have an idea and think it might work. Then you build it. You do lots of iterations and you see what it looks like. Maybe it's not exactly what you expected or you discover something you hadn't even thought of. You just cycle it, over and over again. You try it, you test it, you learn something, you go back, and you fix things—or you start over. It's never going to look exactly like your first idea. It's never going to feel the way that you imagined it 100%.

Chris Shen, *continued*

vivid: How do you fit into the process?

The thing that you end up doing as a game designer is have either answers or explanations. A lot of your job is spent answering questions because when you first come out with a game idea, the people building it have no clue until you tell them something, until you describe it. Until you explain everything, it's a mystery. Those seven or ten or fifteen people—these are the programmers, artists, and musicians—who spend a lot of their time helping the designer flesh out the design. For me, that's probably where at least half the design happens.

I've got a real rough idea that's maybe two pages or ten pages but if you were to describe it in text and pictures, the whole design would probably be 200–300 pages, easy. By them asking questions, you may run across things that you never would have thought of until they asked it.

vivid: What kind of advice would you give to somebody wanting to get into game design? What kind of experiences would you suggest they get? What kind of education do they need, what sort of passions do they need in this field?

If I look at any of the game designers I've met, none of them have gotten there by the same path. Maybe that's true of most people, whatever they are in life. But what you have to do is find something that you have real genuine passion for. Decide for yourself where your passions lie. If they're in art, then you can develop a good designer resume just from having a strong art background. Maybe that'll be your strength in communicating ideas.

But the bottom line is, can you come up with something that excites people and makes them want to play with it and have fun? Can you communicate that to people that are going to actually build it? Can you go from the theoretical and descriptive side to the concrete

implementation of it? Those are kind of the two basic tools you need, whether or not you communicate visually or with code, or by using a program to do it in animation, it doesn't matter as long as it's effective.

I guess as far as an education goes—as long as you aren't held back by the technology side of things—as long as you can at least grasp the basics—I don't think that you need to be a programmer to be a designer. But you probably need to be able to listen to programmers since they're going to really affect how you design.

It's hard for me to say because it's almost as if it just seems natural to me. Maybe that's unreasonable, that you just do what you love, you do what comes naturally. Maybe that's not the right answer for somebody who isn't sure. That there's no formula is the only thing I can say. No one way.

vivid: Do all of your friends think that you have the coolest job imaginable? You get to sit around all day, play with games, and kick around ideas.

Yeah, they do. But you do have to kind of qualify things for people that think that your job is a complete walk in the park. It's fun to play games, but when you have to play the same one that's broken over and over again until it's fixed—it's not all that fun.

vivid: What's your favorite thing about your job? What's your least favorite?

My favorite thing about my job is seeing someone play a product that you've built. When you're done and you see them doing all the things that you hoped they would, and having those experiences, that's probably the most satisfying thing. The least satisfying has got to be when you pitch a project and it doesn't work. People kind of look at you and say, "Eeuuuuhhhh." That definitely happens.

within game companies and then gradually move into the game designer role. Working in the **testing** ▶ 269 or development at these companies is one way to gain experience and knowledge about games, although game designers seem to have a variety of backgrounds and experiences.

The executive producers and producers hiring game designers are going to be interested in two things. They will either want to see good ideas, represented in the form of treatments, scripts, or gaming maps, or, they will want to see someone who knows the gaming industry, including what genres are popular and why. They will also want to see someone who knows how to create products that game players like.

Compensation

Some game designers are full-time employees of game companies and receive salaries and possibly equity in the company, while others are freelance contractors who receive weekly, monthly, or one-time payments and possibly a small royalty. Even though the role is recognized as valuable, the game industry is so new that few people are seen as being above the line, with the possible exception of the designers of *Myst*, *Doom*, and a few other games. As a result, it is difficult to command more than production rates. One of the ways to receive better compensation is to develop ideas and retain some form of ownership to them. These ideas first have to be represented in some form that makes them valuable such as a treatment, script, or prototype and then they have to be shopped to people who can fund and distribute the game. This process can be simple or hard depending on the idea, its representation, and the efforts in pitching it.

Scriptwriter

*A copywriter writes text that appears on screen. A scriptwriter develops a script that describes the structure, setting, and media elements within a product. In **virtual communities** ▶ 28 and **digital periodicals** ▶ 32, writers and editors provide original viewpoints and help make sense of the vast amounts of information and events taking place in the real world and in cyberspace.*

What They Do

An **interactive scriptwriter** is part traditional writer (in the sense of a film scriptwriter, novelist, or storybook writer) and part interactive designer. The difference between traditional writing and interactive writing lies in the inclusion of various forms of interactivity within a work. This interactivity might be a non-linear story structure with branching storylines or adding creative or productive capabilities similar to those found in traditional software applications. A producer often looks to a scriptwriter to develop the entire structure of a work or teams a scriptwriter with a game designer or interface designer to co-develop the structure.

An interactive scriptwriter is a visual thinker with the ability to put these thoughts onto paper clearly enough so that others, with a variety of backgrounds, can understand. Few people have interactive scriptwriting experience. While there are many that understand writing for traditional media—who understand characters, stories, conflicts, and dialogue—there are few that understand interactivity and how it can be applied to traditional narratives. Bridging this gap between writing and interactivity is one of the purposes of a scriptwriter.

More producers are beginning to recognize the need to include writers early on a project to help form it into shape. In the past, more than a few relied on programmers or animators to perform the tasks a writer might perform. But even the producers who recognize the need for scriptwriters are often unsure of the process a scriptwriter uses and the materials they develop in the course of their work. As a result, scriptwriters that have one or more interactive scriptwriting credits and can show samples of their work and demonstrate the process are in great demand. In a few years, the relatively easy entry into this field is likely to change as more people develop skills as interactive scriptwriters and as the discipline becomes more understood and refined.

The most common way scriptwriters work is to be given a body of material, and, either working alone or with a designer, give structure to the material. Creating this structure has a process that eventually leads up to the development of a script. This script is then used by the others on the project team to create the product. A second and less common form of scriptwriting is to create an original script and then to offer it to companies looking to produce original works. This approach can be frustrating since many companies are only looking to adapt existing materials into new media.

The type of work spans the project spectrum. One area of heavy activity is **games** ▶ 22. Many film scriptwriters are being hired to create the settings and characters around which the game play revolves. Other areas for scriptwriters include **children's projects** ▶ 20 such as storybooks and learning products. Companies creating reference and other special interest titles also need writers. In some cases, writers may be needed to create the onscreen text that is often a part of these titles and, in other cases, they may act more as information and interaction designers providing structure to the body of existing material and adding interactive elements. **Marketing and sales projects** ▶ 46 are also areas of opportunities for intrepid scriptwriters. Many companies are creating interactive advertisements, direct sales pieces, and catalogs for diskettes, CD-ROMs, and online places, and need copywriters and scriptwriters.

A scriptwriter commonly works from the very start of a project until it goes into production, and sometimes while it is in production. The script (and a functional specification) forms a blueprint for the creation of a project. It, along with storyboards created from the script, is used by visual designers, sound and video producers, animators, programmers, and testers. Without a script, a project can only move forward at risk of chaos.

A scriptwriter is a solitary person for much of the time. They may work closely with a producer or a creative director as they develop a script, but the majority is spent working alone, describing what happens where and when. Once the script is completed, a scriptwriter has little additional responsibility other than to work with a development team to help maintain the integrity of the script as it progresses from storyboards into production. Sometimes the scriptwriter will be called in to rewrite a section or piece if a problem is encountered during production.

If a scriptwriter wants to be part of the project after the storyboards are approved, then they would need to take on a role other than scriptwriter after the script is complete such as interaction designer or co-producer. As scriptwriter Deborah Todd says, "You have to write so that everybody understands what you visualize and then trust that people are going to do their job. At some point, you have to let go. The problem that people beginning in this field have is that they fall in love with their work and they don't let anybody near it." An interactive scriptwriter, especially a beginning one, needs to be able to let go.

Process

An interactive scriptwriter produces a script that describes everything that happens within an interactive project. The process to create this script typically follows a very structured approach. The first step is to develop a **high concept** or **premise**. The high concept is a very brief description of the project designed to give listeners an immediate grasp of the project. Those who have seen the movie, *The Player,* may recall the satire on high concepts in the movie industry. Movies are often described by making similarities to successful movies in the past. In multimedia, more and more references are being made to

Not all writers need to be a part of a project team to get a job in the industry or have an influence on it. Traditional print newspapers, magazines, and newsletters have a large need for people to write about interactive subjects. Multimedia is a technology touching on almost every industry. As a result, the publications serving these industries will need people knowledgeable in the people, technology, and products surrounding interactive media.

Also, many writers are writing for online publications or their work is being published by their publishers in online venues. While the structure for compensation for this writing is all over the board, many writers' organizations are trying to reach agreements with publishers and online services to create standard forms of payment for online publishing. These may be either flat fees or tied to frequency of access by online readers.

Deborah Todd
Interactive Scriptwriter

Deborah Todd has leveraged a career writing in Hollywood for Saturday morning cartoons such as The Pink Panther *for MGM/United Artists into the new domain of interactive scriptwriter on CD-ROM children's books such as ZoomBooks'* Professor Iris' Fun Field Trips.

Deborah feels that her background writing for cartoons has helped her master the minutiae of writing interactive scripts. "In writing for cartoons," she says, "everything must be spelled out precisely. The animators can only illustrate what you put into your scripts. In writing for interactive multimedia, every detail, every transition, mouse click, and art effect has to be scripted before a programmer can begin writing code."

With several CD-ROMs to her credit, Deborah now spends much of her time flying to Hollywood to pitch deals. She is nothing if not prolific, and her energy is indefatigable. "You may pitch six different ideas in a story meeting, and all of them can be shot down. But that doesn't mean they aren't good ideas. Someone could have had the same good idea and pitched it a week earlier."

For writers looking to join a multimedia production team, Deborah suggests they first write for the experience, then the credit, and finally the money. "The first interactive multimedia job I took I did for practically no money," she says, with some regret. "But I wanted the credit." And she's been able to parlay that into a new career.

*Projects that rely more on communication aspects between others have less need for scriptwriters than ones with pre-existing content. As a result, online communities have more of a need for **editors** and **moderators** than for scriptwriters.*

products that are similar to successful multimedia products. A term like "*Myst*-like" for example is becoming more and more popular. Comparisons to Living Books titles abound as well. Unfortunately (or fortunately depending on your perspective), there is not a wide variety to make comparisons to so those pitching a concept may not have examples to refer to (or if they do, it may be to a product that was not a commercial success). A high concept in multimedia should ideally give some indication of the interactivity as well as the content because the interactivity is what is going to set it apart from the same concept in other media forms.

Some successful pitches have been made with just a high concept, allowing producers to secure funds for the development of the scripts, signing of key talent, and building a prototype. Pitching a product in this manner may work for people with successful track records or those adept at presenting and selling ideas and bringing people into their confidence.

A scriptwriter takes a concept or premise and develops it into a **treatment**. The treatment should be long enough to convey the experience and structure of the title but not so long that it discourages people from reading. Treatments are typically anywhere from one page to 10 pages in length. A treatment should explain the goals of the project, the setting, the story, the arrangement of information, characters, and features, and a description of the interaction. For a game, the game play should be described; for a children's product, the creative activities or types of hotspots should be described.

The next requirement is an outline and most likely a **flow chart** or **game map** ▶ 179. These materials describe what actions occur and how users move from one place to the next. They should provide a complete picture of the structure of the product and how the nodes, sequences, or scenes connect. A game might have a map of the gaming region. A website might have a flow chart in the form of a hierarchical tree or interconnected web.

The development of a **script** follows the creation of the outline. The structure and form of interactive scripts are not yet set. Many follow the format

of film scripts—developed when the common writing tool was the typewriter—and attempt to include interactive notations. For some titles, specifically those that have a main story spine containing small interactive loops off of this spine, this format can work well. More complicated structures, however, can be hard to represent in a linear format. As a result, flow charts and maps are useful for not only writing a script but also conveying the connections between the discrete places in the script.

In the film industry, scripts have a relatively rigid size and structure. A common rule of thumb is that each page represents one minute, so that a 2-hour film should have about a 120-page script. Many genres get even more specific. For example, a comedy should be about an hour and a half in length and dramas about two hours (unless you are Kevin Costner in which case it can be three hours). Interactive titles, to date, have no such rules. Very few have innate knowledge about how long or deep a title should be.

The script for *Professor Iris's Fun Field* was 54 single-spaced pages, which in the double-spaced film script format would make it the size of a feature film. Indications of scripts for interactive movies point to a length about three times that of a feature film. As genres begin to form and as project types become more defined, guidelines are sure to arise as to the structures, length, and content of interactive products, as well as for the format of interactive scripts. These formats may resemble film scripts for some project types and storybook structures for others.

Tools and Techniques

The most common, and many times only tool, for a scriptwriter is a word processor. There are some products specifically for writing interactive scripts but they are too new to judge their effectiveness. Many writers may use reference sources, and more and more scriptwriters are taking advantage of information in CD-ROM and online databases.

As far as technique, the best one is to follow an expansion process, moving from concept to outline to flow chart to script. While doing this, a scriptwriter needs to keep in mind the purpose of the project as well as the level and types of

Things an interactive scriptwriter needs to know:

* *subject matter*
* *audience*
* *process (premise, outline, flow chart/ map, script)*

It's more of a guideline than a rule.

interactivity. Once the structure is defined, the details can be added within a cohesive framework. Also, many writers recommend making as much forward progress as possible before stopping to edit or refine work. Their thinking is that once you stop, you risk losing the threads of the story as changes in the material introduce numerous permutations in the remainder of the story.

Perspective ▶ 26 is a mechanism that can be played with within an interactive title in a number of ways. The first is the dimension of the point of view, meaning first or third person interactions. Games typically contain first person interactions within the game play, while many storybook-like titles are third person. For example, *Doom* is a first person experience. The user is the main protagonist and the action and view reflects the set-up that you are there. Other games, like *Critical Path* or *Daedaleus Encounter*, may feature a twist on this idea and portray the game player as a supporting character whose actions influence those of the main character. In these situations and in many of the setups, there are third person perspectives built in as animated characters or real actors deliver and perform scripted dialogue and actions. The storybook, *Just Grandma and Me*, on the other hand, is strictly a third person experience, where the actions of the main characters and the supporting characters are viewed by the viewer.

Another use of perspective is to represent **viewpoints** through different characters. For example, a restaurant guide might use real or simulated critics to provide different evaluations of the food, service, or ambiance. Seeing an event from one person's eyes is often quite different than from another person's eyes. Modeling these viewpoints in a new media title brings interactivity in the form of seeing how each one views an event.

Finding and developing innovative game, story, and information structures is one of the keys to making new media projects different from other media sources. An **innovative structure** is what makes a CD-ROM title on food a different experience than a cookbook or cooking show on television. Without something different, that takes advantage of what a computer and a modem can

possibly do; new media titles will never satisfy users as older more established forms of media do.

Including **creative features** ▶ 165 in a title is one way to increase the level of interactivity of a title and differentiate it from other media forms. Combining content with capabilities for users to add materials, restructure content, or create things with it poses many challenges, but enthusiastic rewards. An example is the home improvement title *How to Build a Deck* from Books That Work. It makes use of what a computer can do easily to provide a product that adapts to a user's particular circumstances. The same material in a book would leave much of the mathematics up to the reader, limiting its usefulness.

Another dimension that can be added to products and to online places is the element of **interaction with others**. These interactions can be as simple as creating a conference area within a commercial online service or a USENET group on the Internet. Providing a place for people to communicate with others about a subject matter can be another way to market a product and generate revenue. More sophisticated interactions can include more multi-user domains (MUDs) where the interactions are enhanced by users participating not only in the story but in the creation of the story, sets, costumes, and genres. Even more exotic capabilities include interactions built directly into the product such as allowing multiple players to interact simultaneously. *Doom*, for instance, lets players on a network play within the same world and time-frame. They can team up against the monsters or battle amongst themselves.

Qualifications

A scriptwriter has to write well enough so that people that are not writers can understand the story, the setting, and the actions. For example, you have to show how a title starts, what goes on, and how it ends. For characters, you have to show what they say, what they do, and how they do it. If a sequence is supposed to be dark and gloomy, then the description needs to communicate this so the visual designers can create correspondingly dark and gloomy screens.

Introducing drama into an interactive product is an area that is not well understood at the moment. Many game designers are working hard trying to find the right combination of game play and narrative while many interactive fiction writers are trying to deconstruct storylines and then let the user reconstruct them as they interact with the product. Still other multimedia developers feel the creation of dramatic storylines comes primarily from the players and that the "author's" job is simply to provide the structure, the tools, and the environment in which this creation takes place.

Scriptwriters don't need to know how a computer works or how to program code but they do need to know what a computer can and cannot do. Even while knowing the limits, however, they should continually dare to stretch them, otherwise few others will. Programmers may rebel, producers may scowl, but industries will not progress until the technologies are pushed by innovative, compelling ideas.

Also, knowing how to **construct a story** is as essential in interactive writing as it is in traditional writing. Regardless of whether that story is a non-fictional work like a travel diary or a fictional work like a mystery crime game, there must be some sort of beginning, middle, and end. There must be a means of building tension, capturing attention,

Various organizations representing writers are actively pursuing agreements with movie studios, producers, television networks, magazines, book publishers, and other media representatives and companies to structure agreements that cover the use of writers' works in interactive areas. These agreements might include royalties for work appearing on CD-ROMs or in video games or flat fees or per-access payments for online use.

and then moving, or letting the user move to one or more resolutions or a final goal. The characters or the content must be presented in consistent and appropriate manners and the settings must give the viewer a sense of place. Information designers and game designers can help, but it's really in the hands of the writer to do this.

Good **organization skills** are important so that a writer doesn't lose track of story threads or characters. The branching nature of interactive structures makes keeping track of possibilities much more difficult than a book or a film. Loose ends can possibly be caught and fixed during production but it's less expensive and time-consuming to do so at the script stage.

Tim Oren
Vice President, Future Technology, CompuServe

vivid: Is the role of the writer to create the characters and points of view that people can use to access the information or the story?

I don't think we're necessarily trying to guide people into information. It could be more like exposing elements of the story as time goes on. We haven't got the whole truth on this, just a handle on one of the places to start and that is accenting the character. There are forms out there that accent the character but have less strong models of a dramatic flow. Most of them are pretty old, although some of them have gotten recreated—things like Saga and Myth, which use the same character repeatedly.

George Lucas, for instance, is very explicit in his sourcing of that type of material. On a more mundane level, look at things like soap operas. Basically, you take a bunch of characters and throw them into situations day after day after day. If you look at the structure of any particular episode, it's really primitive. It's basically just cut to fit in the commercials, but what seems to keep people coming back is their attachment to the particular characters, their lives and times, combining their stories and their families. That's the interesting piece.

vivid: One of the holdovers in this new medium is characters and that's a very ancient idea.

The survivals of oral storytelling into the current culture are some of the interesting places to look—things like improv. Not everybody can do that, but some of the notions about how you interact if you're portraying a character are some of the interesting things to point at. We're not going to know this for 30 years.

vivid: How is interactive multimedia affecting storytelling?

It's letting you explore that middle space between the authorial voice and a bunch of people just sitting around talking—an interesting combination of representation, technical skills, and storytelling. There's this really unprobed space in the middle, which on alternate days you can think of as this huge opportunity, and then the other days despair of ever finding something compelling in there. That's the new thing, the fact that you've potentially put a live processor in there that to some extent can enact the intent of artists without the artist being present. That's the biggest difference.

How to Hire

Scriptwriting credits are one of the more valuable credits in a "title," partly due to the appreciation shown scriptwriting in the film and TV industry. As a result, one of the ways to find out who the best interactive scriptwriters are is to look at the **credits** of the top titles. Although an interactve scriptwriting credit is not always listed at this point in multimedia, this situation will likely change. As the role becomes more defined and practiced, it will become more prominent.

Another way to find an interactive scriptwriter is to ask **other scriptwriters**. Scriptwriting tends to have a close-knit community and so scriptwriters are often supportive of others in the field. If one scriptwriter is not appropriate, either because schedules or styles do not match, it is likely they will know others that may work out.

A third way is to enlist the help of agents representing multimedia talent. The advantage of an **agent** is that they may represent a number of interactive scriptwriters which may save time. One phone call can replace a half dozen or more. Some producers may be reluctant to go to agents, but if a scriptwriter is already represented by an agent, the agent will eventually be involved with the negotiations regardless of who is contacted first.

Consider looking at **professional writers groups** for scriptwriters when searching for writers skilled in a particular genre. A good writer in a certain subject matter can be paired with a game designer or an interface designer to collaborate on the develop of the structure and form of a title. There are general writers' groups and specific ones such as the Mystery Writers of America and the Western Historical Society.

Ideally, an interactive scriptwriter should have one or more credits and have working samples of their work. When looking at interactive products, try to get an idea of who the scriptwriter worked with and what they specifically did on the product. Since most interactive projects are highly collaborative efforts and because the creative roles can vary from project to project, a final work may not give a clear indication of a single individual's contribution.

Outside of a working product, producers should look for vivid writing, the ability to tell a story, an understanding of story structures and/or information structures, and good organization skills. Graphic writing is needed because a script needs to communicate clearly to people in a number of disciplines. Scenes or worlds that are poorly described are likely to be interpreted differently by others on the project team. Understanding of the current structures of products is similar to understanding the common structures of films. Without that understanding in the film business, few fledging scriptwriters can hope to sell a script. Without an understanding of story or information structures in interactive products, interactive scriptwriters have the same problem.

How to Be Hired

There are two common types of arrangements for interactive scriptwriters to work on new media products. The first is a situation where a studio is trying to adapt some type of content, such as a story from a movie or storybook or a set of photographs or scans of artwork. These materials will need structure, organization, and possibly annotation in order to create viable new media products. Producers are beginning to recognize that they need a writer or set of writers to create a form and a structure to these types of existing materials. Getting this type of work is one of the best ways to break into interactive writing.

The second type of arrangement for interactive scriptwriters is to create original works. This can be done either by being commissioned by a studio for an original script—though this is likely only for scriptwriters with a proven track record— or by creating a treatment and a script and shopping it to prospective buyers, preferably with the help of an agent.

Since producers are only now beginning to see the value of having scriptwriters on a project team, it is even more foreign for them to option original works. Although the future looks good for interactive scriptwriters for both **CD-ROM** ▶ 59 development and **interactive TV** ▶ 65 productions, the opportunities for soliciting original work and the support structure for moving these into production is not as advanced as in the film

Incorporating features for users to be creative or productive or communicate with others touch on areas of interaction design and moderating. These overlaps indicate the dramatic changes in tasks and job descriptions that are occurring as traditional roles move into interactive environments.

There are definitely polar ways of looking at agents between Hollywood and Silicon Valley. In Silicon Valley, when I put people in touch with my agent, they say, "Agent? You have an agent? Why do I have to talk to an agent? Can't we just work this out ourselves?" In Hollywood, when I mention I have an agent they say, "Oh, that's great. What's their number? I'll talk to them." I think the impression in Silicon Valley will change but, even so, having an agent has definitely made my life easier.

—Deborah Todd, Interactive Scriptwriter

189

Writing is easy just stare at a blank page until droplets of blood begin to form on your forehead. —anonymous

industry. As a result, the hardest part of creating original works is shopping them around and getting someone to pay money for them. This path is only recommended for experienced scriptwriters who have built a name in the industry or accumulated a list of impressive credits.

Finding work is a matter of first identifying the type of writing that you are good at and that you want to do. Having the knowledge and a passion for a subject, an audience, and a type of project is almost essential to becoming successful in any field but even more so in scriptwriting. A writer often starts with a blank page or screen and something has to be formed out of that nothingness. Passion and a knowledge of a subject area are two of the best things to start with.

Next comes finding the multimedia companies that are producing projects in your areas of interest. Listings of companies are available in multimedia directories. Looking at reviews in magazines and at product listings in catalogs is another way of finding companies. Asking friends and acquaintances in the industry is a third. When looking to work on other people's materials, look for companies that are developing products with intensive writing needs such as companies creating games with complex characters and settings or ones creating lots of advertisements and marketing pieces.

Find out who the **producers** are and who does the hiring. Or for original works, find out whether they accept original scripts and who manages submissions. Some companies may be looking for writers to keep on staff, while others may be looking for them only on a project-by-project basis. A personal relationship with a producer or acquisitions manager within a studio is one of the more valuable things for a scriptwriter to have.

For original works, you probably want to send a treatment. You can try to set up a meeting to pitch the concept, but this approach is more accepted in the film industry than in the publishing or software industries. A **credit list** ▶ 182 is important and for work in "work for hire" situations, writing samples are almost a requirement.

A credit list should ideally contain one or more interactive credits, though at this point non-interactive credits can be just as impressive provided you position them correctly. Work on film and TV scripts, newspaper writing, and promotional writing are all assets that can lead to writing positions on interactive projects.

Samples do not need to be long or numerous. Quality, not quantity is extremely important. A single short work or two is almost guaranteed to be reviewed sooner than a folder of six or eight different types of work. The person looking at the samples is looking for how well you can write, not necessarily how prolific or expansive you are. You can show these capabilities later.

Getting a producer to be familiar with your work and having them find it favorable is a big milestone. Even if they do not have a present need for writers, stay in touch with them and let them know what other projects you are working on. As you become more experienced and as they begin to notice, your availability and their needs may coincide.

More and more established interactive scriptwriters are being represented by agents. Most speak highly of the advantages an agent affords. The scriptwriters get to concentrate on writing while the agent helps to line up work. In order to represent a scriptwriter, agents are going to be interested in many of the same things that producers are but will be particularly interested in seeing previous interactive credits.

An agent can be invaluable for shopping original works. They are likely to know who is looking for what kinds of work and will be able to get the material to the right people. Both of these tasks are difficult to do. The first because the market for original works has not matured. The second because of copyright fears on the part of both parties. Most publishers have **submission agreements** ▶ 120, 155. Some are one page in length while others are upwards of four pages. Some are more fair than others from the perspective of those submitting materials. An agent can help in getting around unfair agreements.

The best position to have is to be asked by a producer to submit an original work, in which case you or your agent can negotiate around "standard" agreements. If you are not in this type

Dana Atchley
Interactive Writer and Performer

vivid: What do you do? What do you call your-self?

I'm a storyteller and a content person. There's going to be room for me no matter what happens. That's the excitement for me. In the race to push pixels faster, there hasn't been enough attention paid to why you're pushing and what you're going to achieve with it. Oftentimes, you'll see really remarkable examples of what people can do with the technology but they don't stick with you. You just sort of say, "Gee, that was fabulous. Look how many layers they did and how fast all that stuff happened." But it's instantly forgettable. I want stuff that isn't instantly forgettable. I want people to remember what they see, not because it's a technological wonder, but because it was a good story.

vivid: If all this technology weren't available, would you still be a storyteller?

Oh yeah. It's a habit. I never really understood that's what I did until two years ago, when somebody was doing a piece on storytelling and I realized, "Well, I guess that's what I do." In fact, when I began serious work on the show, Joe Lambert said to me, "Your problem is not with images and music. You need to work on your stories. Why don't you get rid of the images and music, and just write?" We did that for six months and the writing got very big, fat, and full because I was having to carry the burden of the narrative without the images and music. I was required to write more. Once we added the music and images back in, then I could strip and clean out a whole lot. But what writing them out tended to do was to define what these stories were about, why I was telling that story, and what significance it might have later in the show.

One paradigm we need to break is that you can create an interactive TV application and walk away from it—a paradigm that comes out of the television and film industry, that you work for six months, edit for three or four weeks, 24 hours a day, and then you walk away.

If you come from the computer world, you may think of this as a shrink-wrapped world. I create software, test it, shrink-wrap it, ship it out, and then wait for the next rev. In the interactive world, you update every day. That's something that people don't understand. They don't understand it from the television world and they don't understand it from the software world.

—Vincent Grosso, Interactive TV Project Director, AT&T

---

of situation, then it is unlikely that you will be able to negotiate changes in the submission agreement. And if you try, it may decrease your chances of having your materials considered because a producer may not want to devote the time and expense necessary to rework the agreement.

When presenting to people, you can successively disclose the materials, first providing a treatment and then potentially a script, provided they are interested. You want to protect your materials, but at the same time, you need to realize that publishers need to see a fair representation of your work in order to adequately consider it. Also, they receive hundreds of submissions containing many similar ideas and are not likely to put up with unreasonable demands.

Compensation

Compensation for writers is all over the board. In some cases, companies are offering fixed prices for work on a script and, in other cases, writers are salaried employees or paid by the hour. Writers that are creating copy for digital magazines or advertising pieces are likely to be paid on par with journalists or advertising copywriters. Scriptwriters working on games will likely be paid in ways similar to scriptwriters in the film industry.

The most important part of getting compensated for writing is not necessarily the amount or the manner of payment, it is in the definition of the deliverables. A common mistake is not to clearly define what constitutes a finished work. As a result, writers often have to write beyond what they anticipated which can eat into their profit margin. Try to define the length, the format, and the content in the work agreement so that expectations on both sides are clearly understood.

Also, for beginning scriptwriters, the amount of payment may not be as important as a scriptwriting credit. Taking on low-paying work in order to get credits and then increasing your pay rate is not a bad strategy at all. You are not likely to receive any **royalties** ▶ *97* in many work-for-hire situations but with an impressive credit list or an original work, there is a possibility for royalties in the 0.5–1.5% range.

Editor/Moderator

A form of editor/moderator is someone that is hired by a company to scan newsgroups in search of references to particular products. These people will log the reference and respond to it if it is a question or if it unfairly maligns the product.

Point of view ▶ 32, 55, 176 is the ultimate context tool. You need some way of coming to the right conclusion without having to look at everything. Point of view is the quintessential human way to do that. It's what news reporters and news anchors deliver. It's what columnists in magazines deliver.

Rush Limbaugh has a particular point of view and you're going to see the world through his filter. William Buckley has another point of view, as does George Will. Their most valuable asset is the point of view they bring to their work, which will make them in demand in cyberspace. Publishers and news stations are going to discover that their scarcest resources walk home every day.

—Paul Saffo,
Director,
Institute for the Future

What They Do

Editors and **moderators** are people that filter information or moderate discussions. In interactive media, most people in these roles work primarily in **online environments** ▶ 15, 28, 61. The difference between the two is subtle. A moderator's work is typically confined to moderating a group or a discussion area. They read through postings to mailing lists, newsgroups, and decide which ones to publish. They act as a sort of referee, keeping the discussion pertinent to the topic and, often, members away from each other's throats. They set the tone of their groups and define what is and is not appropriate behavior. David Barr, moderator of the USENET newsgroup comp.unix.wizards, invests about half an hour per week on it, while Howard Rheingold has built an entire career around moderating groups. Networks of contacts, fans, and friends act as information sources and armchair critics for his work.

Editors are involved more with a topic as opposed to a place. They essentially provide a point of view on certain subjects and may originate information or simply filter existing information. John Gehl and Suzanne Douglas are editors of two newswires, *Edupage* and *Innovation*. Several times a week, they send out email messages containing summaries of top news stories relating to high technology. Edupage is a free service and started a couple of years ago with 300 email addresses. The list now contains over 35,000 unique addresses and it is estimated that between 300,000 and 500,000 people receive it through various gateways.

Editors and moderators continually monitor a topic or a place. The work may be a few hours a week or several hours a day. They may have regular times to moderate discussions or have to meet a schedule for regular postings.

Process/Tools

The process is vastly different for starting a publication or a group than it is for moderating or maintaining it. In the case of starting a **newsgroup**, **bulletin board service (BBS)**, or **MUD** ▶ 30, it typically means coordinating with system operators and senior moderators to start a new place. Once established, the job consists of following the procedures established by the host service or the members of the group.

Starting a mailing list typically means using an automated **list server** ▶ 29 that allows people to subscribe and unsubscribe from the list automatically. Maintaining a mailing list by hand is, thus, unnecessary. Creating a website requires locating a server to host the website, designing and creating the webpages, and possibly building or licensing extended interactive components such as forms, discussion areas, or transaction processing systems.

Qualifications

The primary qualifications needed for editors or moderators are **net skills** as well as **great writing** and **editorial skills** to keep a publication or conference active. If readership or membership drops, then it may be almost an immediate indication that the editor is not doing their job. Current moderators suggest reading any groups extensively for many months in order to get a sense of what people are saying and thinking. Misunderstandings can be serious, especially for an editor or moderator.

How to Hire

It is fairly easy to hire people to edit online materials or moderate discussion groups. The most common way is to draw from the group's readership and membership. In fact, most conferences start through petitions from regular members of another conference. Look for those who post often, are active, or who have consistently insightful things to share. These may be candidates to fill openings for editors or moderator positions.

We turn down editorial people if
--Will Kreth, Section Editor,

How to Be Hired

To be hired as an editor, try offering your services to various online services, existing newsgroups, or mailing lists. Another way is to look for postings online for positions in these areas. It is important to start out small and learn the net culture before proceeding. A third way to get into this area is to start your own mailing list, website, newsgroup, MUD, or other type of publication or place. The opportunities are almost limitless right now but the window may be closing fast as more and more online sources appear.

Compensation

At the moment, compensation is pretty low—especially for moderators. Many people do it for free. This is because few people currently value such services in terms of money. This will change. Also, there are people in line to take moderators' places. Besides, it typically does not take much time. However, some services do offer additional free connect time or other perks to moderators.

The pay is also low for editors—especially for those managing mailing lists. Although a few people are charging for their postings, the current environment does not support for-profit ventures. This is likely to change over time, both as electronic payment systems appear and as acceptance of nominal subscriptions increases.

People working at online magazines typically receive salaries, although these are comparable to print publications (which tend to be low). There are opportunities for individuals to develop a following and then either charge for access or sell advertising in some form or another.

Will Kreth
Section Editor and Contributor, *HotWired*

Will Kreth has spent more time online than most people. In April 1992, Will became the first employee at Wired *magazine. Today, he is both the Section Director of* HotWired's *PIAZZA section and a contributing writer to* HotWired, Wired *magazine's Internet-based cyberstation on the World Wide Web. Prior to helping start* Wired, *he worked for PF Magic, Apple Computer's Discovery Studio and the Apple Multimedia Lab.*

For the last two years, Will has hosted the Wired *conference on The WELL. He is also involved with the marketing, research, and development of* HotWired, *which in its first three months registered nearly 100,000 members.*

Will frequently speaks at industry conferences on such topics as the future of independent video multicasting via the Internet, potential roles of independent musicians and recording labels in using the Internet, online advertising, and authorship and copyright in electronic publishing.

In his eyes, the best aspect of communicating online is that it gives people the ability to leave appearances behind and communicate a bit closer to a pure "intellect-to-intellect" level. The flip side is that it also allows people to hide behind facades, avoiding those issues that are best dealt with f2f (face-to-face).

"The most exciting thing for me is the melting of time and distance," he says of his online existence, "when I can have friends and work collaborators send me email from Manila, Hamburg, Tokyo, Sydney, New York… You don't need to look much further to see McLuhan's 'Global Village' has arrived in the hands of millions of people. 'Empowerment' is so damn cliché now, but it seems apropos for what the net has done."

Will's advice for netizens everywhere? "Be fair. Fight for your opinions. Keep an open mind. Build your friendships by being a good friend." And, most important, "Have fun."

they don't have net experience.
HotWired

Tim Oren
Vice President, Future Technology, CompuServe

vivid: One of the things that's intriguing about digital communication is its permanence, but one thing against online communities, though, is the fact that it's so transient. If you're not tuning in one day, you're missing a chat and there's no way to recreate that history. There's this whole anxiety of what you're missing. Where's the balance between the two?

I don't think it ever completely goes away. There's always the anxiety of, "Boy, I felt rotten last night and I didn't go to that party. I heard it was great."

vivid: But you may have had only one or two parties you could have gone to, rather than 10,000 chat group discussions.

There are some limits in saying that in the current medium. A lot of people talk about great discussions online but if you actually capture the stuff and try and read it later on, it really isn't all that good. In most cases, it's a mess.

One of the worst experiments we ever tried in writing an article for one of our projects was to have people sit around and talk and then take the transcript and edit it down. Boy, was that a train wreck. You use the medium differently depending on whether you're talking in the moment or talking for the record. There are some limits in it no matter what you do. There are some possible technical ones. If the voice-recognition stuff ever really gets off the ground, saying, "Listen to me and transcribe," there will still need to be some human agency taking that transcription and turning it into something that's a worthwhile record.

Normally, people only go back on records of this sort if they're trying to summarize an interview or review the legislative intent in the event of a court case. There's a heck of a lot more videotape shot on cameras than ever gets viewed because it's a terrible summary medium. Anything that has a real-time axis has this problem and it's not going to go away.

vivid: So we're always going to have editors. We're always going to have people that are filtering data.

The way things are going, editors are going to be in GREAT shape. What you've got is an explosion of information that's going to bring people into more potential contact with other people and information than the technology can cope with. You're going to need a lot of people in the middle. It's going to be a huge opportunity to find the sweet spots in this connectivity.

If I were an editor or a reporter, I would rejoice. If I were a publisher whose business franchise rested on my control of the channels for that type of information, I would do some serious thinking. If I'm right about where all of this goes, in 20 years you'll have the equivalent of the Esther Dysons of the world, or let's say the John Markoff type, potentially being able to set up a roadside stand. (I hate these metaphors.) At that point, do they still need *The New York Times*? Do they still need *Forbes*? If they've got a medium that can aggregate an audience in a customized fashion for them, it's going to get real interesting. The stuff that has the highest value, back to the salience argument, is the stuff that will move that way first.

Content Expert

What They Do

A **content expert** is anyone that has the authority to provide some measure of authenticity or accuracy to the information in an interactive project. Content experts have long been a recognized part of multimedia projects but their role has recently become better understood.

A content expert might provide authenticity to a game by providing details of how animals might behave or what a period of time might look like. All titles have **authenticity** and **accuracy** concerns, but nonfiction titles focus on them to a greater extent than fiction titles. Many of the publishers and developers of encyclopedias and medical titles, for example, are investing significant sums to verify the information they provide in their titles.

A content expert's role can range from strictly advisory to direct involvement. Content experts, for example, may actually provide writing or source materials such as photos, audio samples, or video sequences. One extreme form of participation is appearing in audio or video segments offering information, insight, or advice. More and more special interest titles are using documentary techniques and including noted experts as narrators, storytellers, or guides.

A content expert may be an expert in a subject matter such as whales, political issues, or Roman archeology, or they may have worked on a variety of projects in an area and have a wealth of ideas and approaches for everything. An expert in science fiction, for example, might be able to offer advice on everything from the look of spaceships and their propulsion systems to the forms and visual systems of alien life forms. An expert in dialogue might be consulted not only to help write the script, but to help train voice talent. In fact, content experts hired for projects may not even be experts in the subject matter. They may be experts in an audience such as children or business professionals, or a market such as government or education, or even a language such as French or German. Multiple experts may be appropriate, each for a different purpose, depending on the project.

Content experts may also take the form of expert researchers who, while lacking specific knowledge in a subject, are adept at researching details, exerpts, and other materials for authenticity and accuracy. For example, the film industry often uses research companies to verify the accuracy of scripts and make sure there are no liability issues in the form of inappropriate use of names.

Process

The process a content expert goes through will vary according to the phase of the project. The first phase a content expert is often needed at is at the beginning, helping to form an innovative

Content Managers and Content Licensers

*Two other forms of content roles include **content managers** and **content licensers**. A content manager is a form of production assistant and they are important in any project where there are a lot of media elements to acquire, prep, and integrate. A reference title, website, or interactive press kit, for example, might have many text, graphic, sound, animation, or video elements to track. A content manager typically works with clients and other content sources to coordinate the transfer of the source materials, and work with members of the project team to track their progress through development. The internal tools a content manager uses include spreadsheets and database programs.*

*A content licenser plays a role similar to an agent or attorney, though they do not need to have a legal background or license. Content licensers are experts at finding and acquiring the rights to copyrighted materials and negotiating with the copyright holder on licensing terms and fees, if any. Many producers turn to content licensers when they begin having to pay to use certain properties. A content manager is often sufficient for obtaining materials from a client or people willing to sign over rights free of charge, but a content licenser can be handy when the task of getting rights becomes more complicated. An **agent** ▶ 148 or **lawyer** ▶ 134 may be used for situations where the rights form the basis for a product and/or are extremely difficult or expensive to get.*

Content licensers may gain experience working as a content manager on one or more projects and then strike out on their own when they've got enough experience or contacts.

and original concept. In this stage, a content expert may work with a producer, scriptwriter, game designer, or interaction designer to create a setting for a game or the general tone and content for a special interest title. Another example might be the case of an expert in personal finance helping to define an online service for purchasing mutual funds. The expert might not only help define what information is important, but also help develop productive and adaptive features that allow users to make decisions relevant to their own financial situation.

The second place within the development process for a content expert is for **approval of the scripts and storyboards**. Once these materials have been created, but before the project moves into full production, a content expert can help spot errors before work extends beyond paper.

Re-recording a sequence of voice-overs because a date is wrong is guaranteed to be more expensive and time-consuming than amending the script before recording anything. Refining the appearance of dinosaurs in storyboards is far less expensive than in minutes of fully rendered animation.

The third place is during **production**, to oversee the creation of illustrations, animations, sounds, set designs, or costumes for video sequences. A content expert might work with visual designers to refine the look, or animators to refine the movement of characters or objects. This type of talent may not be needed until a script has been approved and the project fully funded.

The fourth place is during **testing** for verification of all content. Here, the content expert is hired to

A content expert with a speaking or acting part not only has responsibilities in the content expert role but also those of voice artist or actor. The producer should make sure the content expert knows the process and techniques for these roles as well.

Pat Hanlon
Content Expert

One of the true pioneers of interactive educational multimedia, Pat Hanlon has been working in the field since 1985, shortly after the dawn of the Macintosh. As a high school English teacher at San Francisco's Lowell High, Pat attended an afternoon workshop with developers from Apple's Educational Division. Her life would never be the same, and neither would HyperCard, a fledgling programming tool for the rest us that was still in its infancy back in Cupertino. Following that workshop, Pat realized that "the range of compelling materials I could use in my high school English classes -songs, interviews, essays, speeches, photographs, films and texts-could quite possibly be organized and controlled by a computer." The result, which was years in the making, was first called Grapevine, and it was a computer-based, multimedia exploration of John Steinbeck's The Grapes of Wrath *and the depression-era setting in which the book takes place.*

A deal was struck with Apple. Pat and Robert Campbell, the school librarian, would receive a complement of equipment and software and a modicum of instruction from the folks at Apple. In return, Pat, Robert and their project would serve as guinea pigs for the development of HyperCard. As the team at Lowell

High put HyperCard through its paces, Apple would learn what real people needed from computers. In the process, HyperCard would undergo some serious revisions to accommodate Pat's real-world needs. According to Pat, "The idea of putting these materials into a computer and creating 'a library in a box' was compelling and provided a clear vision for the Grapevine Project." Today, the finished product is called Voices of the 30s, *published by Sunburst Communications, and serves as a first rate example of educational multimedia.*

verify the accuracy of a script or soon-to-be-completed product, the process is one of going through the script or product and preparing a list of inaccuracies. In this case, the content expert might work under the **producer** ▶ 125 or **scriptwriter** ▶ 184. For content testing, the content expert might work under the direction of the **test manager** ▶ 264, and will likely be provided with forms and directions for logging errors. The difficulty in this work often reflects the amount of information and the variety of media that need verification. Enough time should be budgeted for making several passes through the material.

Tools and Techniques

The tools and techniques are those of a researcher. The tools are knowledge and experience with a particular subject, as well as a good understanding of how to find needed information.

There are no explicit tools to use, but anything may prove useful as a research tool. Traditional tools such as libraries, encyclopedias, and other collections of sources may be just as valuable as word processors, spreadsheets, and databases. Content researchers should probably be familiar with using online tools like ftp, gopher, and WAIS sites to search on the Internet. The wealth of information available via the Internet is growing rapidly and this source should not be overlooked.

Content experts must be both resourceful and detail-oriented. Sloppy research or fact-checking can cause legal liabilities. Persistence and accuracy with regard to details is a valuable technique for avoiding future problems.

Qualifications

The primary qualification for the content expert is to be **knowledgeable** in an area critical to the success of a title. In some cases, though, expertise may not be sufficient. Some form of a license or accreditation may also be necessary. For example, a content expert for a tax preparation product probably needs to be a Certified Public Accountant (CPA). A legal expert should have a law degree and have passed the bar; a medical expert should have a medical degree and be licensed to practice.

Not all experts, however, need bona fide credentials, especially in fictional works. For example, Tom Clancy worked in the insurance industry at the time he wrote the techno-thriller *The Hunt for Red October*. Without formal access to confidential materials, Clancy was able to develop his knowledge of submarine warfare by talking to military personnel and reading off-the-shelf resources.

Many times a content expert will need to transfer their knowledge to others on the team. Or they may need to write, speak, or appear on camera. The ability to **teach others** and to communicate effectively is often a crucial skill needed by a content expert. If a designer can get a clear picture at the outset of what they need to produce, they will respond faster and make fewer mistakes than if they were to produce something and then be told later that it is not correct. A great content expert will also be able to transfer some of their passion for the subject to the members on the project team.

A content expert brought on in an advisory role in the beginning of a project does not necessarily need to be organized. They usually respond to the prompting of the design team with information off the top of their head or accessible at some later date. As the project moves to a script and into production, and as content experts assume more responsibility for ensuring accuracy, organization skills become paramount. A content expert will need quick **access to research sources** and have a methodology in place to make sure that no items are missed. Once a title moves into its digital representation, the process of verifying content can become more difficult as the structure and navigation may obscure areas of content.

Knowledge or familiarity with any form of multimedia or technology is typically not a requirement. Some cases, such as content testing a beta version, may require a computer and a rudimentary knowledge of operating CD-ROMs or navigating online services or World Wide Web sites. A content expert's primary asset is their knowledge of a subject or their skills at research. Others on the team will provide the knowledge of the technology.

Consider capturing interviews or brainstorming sessions with content experts on audio or videotape. These recordings can be used to check notes, verify design ideas, or train new talent for the project. It may or may not be worthwhile to capture these sessions at the highest possible level of quality, since it will probably not be adequate for use as audio or video in a project.

*Content experts want to be careful about the guarantees they provide for their services. They should pay particular attention to the **indemnification** ▶ 103 clause in contracts they sign.*

How to Hire

The producer is the most likely person to hire a content expert. While finding people capable of being experts may not be that difficult, coming up with a **job description** ▶ 90 is often the hardest part. While it might be tempting to hire a content expert for the duration of a project, it is often not necessary, provided the producer brings them in at appropriate spots and gives the entire project team clear instructions of their tasks and responsibilities.

A clear job description of the work entailed will also help determine the form and amount of compensation. Consulting may not be a content expert's primary form of income so they may not have a formal pay structure. A fixed price for providing or verifying materials is one way to structure a relationship. Hourly pay is another. A job description and list of deliverables will be important for coming up with a fixed price. They will also be useful for preparing a time estimate for their services.

Content experts can be found in several ways. One way is to use **professional content research firms**. Several firms cater to the film industry and are beginning to offer their services to multimedia developers. These can provide complete coverage as well as formal levels of accuracy. Their prices are likely to be higher than an independent expert on the subject because their overhead is higher due to carrying professional liability insurance.

People that make a business being experts may have **agents** representing them. These experts are likely to be seen on TV and quoted in magazines and newspapers. It may be difficult to find out who represents them and how to get ahold of them. Calls to talent agencies in Los Angeles and New York may provide some leads or other suitable experts.

Another way to find them is by looking for content expert **credits** or their equivalent in a variety of **publications**. Movies will often list technical advisers, and books will often contain a list of acknowledgments. Editors or presidents of magazines, organizations, research centers, and conferences on a particular subject are also good sources of leads. There seems to be a magazine on almost every subject imaginable now, so a call to the editor of an appropriate one might provide a list of possible experts. The same is true for conference directors.

Professional organizations are a good source to find experts in tax, law, medicine, or other professional fields. Consider officers or committee members. Many times writers can make excellent content experts. Some genres of books, such as mysteries and westerns, have organizations specifically targeted to writers of this genre.

Once there is a list of prospects, the producer can approach each one and gauge their level of expertise. If they've done work that is similar, ask them what they charge. If they've never done this type of work, ask them what they think is reasonable.

How to Be Hired

A content expert interested in working on interactive products needs to clearly indicate their level of expertise. A content expert should have a **credit list** ▶ 82 as well as a list of organization memberships and awards relevant to a particular area of expertise. Education or experience as a content advisor in films, TV programs, or multimedia products should also be listed. Source materials in the content expert's possession might also be of value.

Once your qualifications are in order, you should let others know you are available for advising on projects. These people should be in both your area of expertise as well as in multimedia companies developing or producing titles on the same or similar subjects. It may take a long time to receive an offer, but continued exposure will help bring your name to mind when a need arises.

Another way to become involved in new media products is to **pitch ideas** to publishers or studios. This approach needs to be handled with care for fear of being seen as a competitor as opposed to a consultant. In Hollywood, the producer is typically the person who has the rights to an idea, so at some point in the process of pitching ideas the content expert may find themselves playing a role similar to that of a producer.

Stage presence may be a requirement if a producer is looking for someone to appear in the title either in voice, image, or both. If this type of work is appealing, list experiences that indicate some ability in these regards. Consider putting together a sample demo tape or reel or record any appearances on radio or TV programs.

Compensation

The compensation structure will depend on the level of involvement in a title and the amount of original material provided. Compensation for advice or verification will likely be on either an hourly or fixed-price basis. For professional verification, such as in the case of a financial consultant, lawyer, or accountant, the rates will likely be standard hourly rates for those services. Writing or other media provided by a content expert, as well as audio or video appearances, might warrant **royalties** ▶ 97 alongside licensing fees, depending on the importance of the material to the success of the title and the negotiating skills of the content expert or their agent. The more the material forms the basis for a product or service, the more that royalties are applicable.

Angelina Bruno
President, Multimedia Licensing Consultants

vivid: What are the disasters in licensing content?

These are the disasters that could happen. You included someone's content in your product and it is not portrayed in a light they are happy with. Nowhere in the contract did they say they needed to check it but they're very upset. They're basically saying I want it out and you've already pressed the CDs and they're out.

vivid: How do you get around that?

I've never had that happen but I would say you would try to make an agreement to remove it in a future version. You would spend time walking through it with them. I've been amazed by the power of persuasion.

vivid: What's disaster two?

You licensed it from somebody who had no right to say it was theirs. They're not the real copyright owner and you've got to go somewhere else and now they say no. That's a problem that money fixes. Money fixes a lot of problems.

vivid: Has that ever happened to you?

Not yet. Disaster number three is that there is something that, for whatever reason, fell through the cracks. You're demonstrating it, it's out in the public and the person who you licensed other stuff from comes to see it and says, "You have something of mine in there that you never talked to me about." And you go, "Oops." I had that happen. They were angry. We tried really hard but things happened. We paid them for it. I think that's pretty much it.

vivid: How do you deal with finding out who owns the copyright to what?

You go to one of these clearance people—either attorneys or clearance agencies—and you get them to take care of it. You'll go nuts trying to do it on your own. You need to deal with someone who is getting clearance rights on a daily basis. They you simply have to okay the clearance agreements.

We had a paleontologist named Robert Bakker who we called up for advice about how dinosaurs would behave in certain situations. He came over to spend a few days with us. He'd say that if you put a person in this situation, the dinosaur would react this way. Because he was so much fun, we suggested to him that he be a part of the game. So he came in and we videotaped him doing little scenarios about what an animal might do if it were in this situation or that situation. He gives clues to the game and information about dinosaurs.

—Clifford Lau, Animator, Sega, talking about the creation of the Jurassic Park CD-ROM

Visual Designer

Becoming an expert in visual design means more than just having an ability to draw, paint, or move pixels around. It means learning anything and everything about disciplines that have been practiced for many years or even centuries. It means knowing design in the abstract as well as in correlation to human physiology and perception. It also means practicing. Visual design, like writing, is not something that can be done well when doing it only part time.

What They Do

The area of visual design is really a combination of many different visual areas. It includes graphic design, calligraphy, illustration, and photography, as well as image scanning and manipulation. **Visual designers** may be proficient in one of these areas or in many of them. However, each of the disciplines mentioned is a rich world of visual communication, and to expect a visual designer to be a master of all things visual is not realistic. All visual designers, however, are similar in the respect that they create appropriate visual materials for a multimedia product. Visual designers may work full-time or contract to companies for specific projects or jobs. They usually work under art directors but may be hired by creative directors or producers.

Visual designers may come from different backgrounds, but most commonly, they have had formal training in their craft from an art or design school. Some develop their skills on their own—especially in the case of photography and illustration—but the best and most versatile have at least studied the fundamentals of visual communication on the side. These include the disciplines mentioned above, plus color theory, composition, and iconography.

Graphic Designer

Graphic designers create original artwork either using traitional tools or electronic ones. Everything that can be done in print can be created on the computer. In fact, most of the digitial tools for graphic designers are very sophisticated and fluid to use. Most graphic designers are capable of working in a variety of styles, although many are only interested in pursuing a particular personal direction. Each style communicates in a different way and speaks of a different set of feelings and intentions. Staff graphic designers will be required to fulfill more

Tools photographers use include the traditional such as cameras, lights, filters, and props, as well as the electronic such as digital cameras, Adobe Photoshop, Kai's Power Tools, and HSC LivePicture.

varied design needs, while contractors and freelancers may be able to choose only work that fits their objectives.

Graphic designers need to know many issues about the creation and use of artwork, whether they learned these in school, from books, or from co-workers. Most graphic designers stay closely in tune with developments in their industry. They subscribe to a variety of design magazines to see new things, such as *Communications Arts*, *How*, and *I.D.* Most also keep files of interesting visual materials collected from magazines, books, invitations, and other sources. These may be used as inspiration and influence or to help clients describe their preferences in direction. Many clients do not have visual design experience and therefore do not have a vocabulary with which to discuss the visual design of their materials. Adjectives can be a good stand-in when this occurs, but visual "scrap"—collected materials of a variety of styles and content—can serve this purpose even better.

Graphic designers will often be called upon to produce charts, diagrams, and maps. These are particularly tricky for electronic products since the screen resolution is often so low. Clear and legible charts and diagrams are not as easy to create as they may appear and should be given ample time and thought. Several issues in their creation can affect their accuracy, but these are often overlooked or unaddressed by inexperienced designers. They include scale, area, mass, color, and quantity. Books like *The Visual Display of Quantitative Information* and *Information Anxiety* discuss these issues with examples. Maps are also not as easy to create as they may appear. **Cartography**—the study and creation of maps—is a sophisticated discipline and is often practiced by specialists who study mapmaking over years. Graphic designers can create simple maps without formal training but they will likely need to know about issues such as projection, levels of detail, and attribute labeling for more complex maps.

Typography refers to the art of communicating with type and creating typefaces. Although type is easy to work with on computers, many people do not approach it with the sophisticated care that it often demands. Graphic designers need to be trained in the use of typographic characteristics in order to use it professionally. Kerning (the space between specific sets of letters and numbers) and leading (the space between lines of type) are but two issues that, in practice, are rarely addressed with the care that a skilled, professional typographer or designer would take. While typographic attributes typically will not change the meaning of a message, these can substantially affect the legibility and expression of that message.

A last area of graphic design is the creation of **symbols** or **icons**. These graphics are designed to communicate a message visually (not verbally) and stand for a concept, product, company, or process. In effect, they function very much as words do, often taking the place of words. They can be depicted in a variety of styles and techniques. Some symbols are meant to stand for more universal concepts and things, such as elevators, restrooms, telephones, and restaurants, while others are more specific and may be trademarked, such as corporate logos, logotypes, and product icons. Often, symbols or icons are used to communicate to those who speak other languages, as in international airports, although this use is particularly sensitive to cultural differences and can be confusing if these differences are not addressed. Many designers are not comfortable designing icons or symbols, while others specialize in it. It is rare to find a designer who can design icons, symbols, use typography well, design charts, graphs, diagrams, and maps, and compose as well. Clients and companies may need to seek specialized help or hire a few designers to cover all of their needs.

Graphic designers will usually work closely with other project members as part of a team. They will certainly work closely with other content creators, photographers, and image manipulators. There are lots of opportunities for both freelance and full-time work—especially in areas with ties to the book publishing and advertising industries.

Lisa Lopuck
Visual Designer

Lisa Lopuck's life changed the moment she saw Robert Abel's Guernica *in 1989. "For me, that was it. Multimedia was a wide open medium, perfectly ripe for young designers to come in and forge the way." And that is exactly what this art director and designer has done for clients ranging from George Lucas to Kaleida Labs; from The Voyager Company to Synapse Technology's standard setting* Columbus: Encounter, Discovery and Beyond. *For her, the transition from a background in traditional media was a part of an exciting adventure. "I took it upon myself to seek out more examples of multimedia, talk to everyone involved, and finally, start my first project."*

In addition to writing a book on multimedia graphic design which is due to be published by Peachpit Press, Lisa is currently a faculty member of the San Francisco State Multimedia Studies Program. Her class, "Graphic Design: The Transition into Multimedia" is specifically targeted to traditional graphic designers interested in leveraging their skills into the arena of new media. In the course of two all-day sessions, Lisa introduces her students to the production methods, technical considerations, and design issues that pertain to multimedia. These include the concept and planning of the interactive architecture of a new media title as well as storyboarding techniques and graphic technical requirements.

Lisa advises anyone who wants to make the transition to a career in multimedia to "first educate yourself on the medium and the projects out there, and then find a situation where you can learn hands-on." Unless you have the luxury of working on a student project, that means interning or volunteering with a production company until you build some marketable skills. "If you want to get into multimedia," Lisa continues, "focus on one thing and do it well."

Calligrapher

Calligraphy and typography differ in the way type is used. Both are concerned with the arrangement of letters and numbers to communicate mood and message, but calligraphers are skilled at creating new and unique letterforms, usually with traditional media like paints and charcoal. Most have little or no experience with computer tools and prefer traditional tools. Calligraphers specialize in hand-drawn letterforms and traditional writing styles, although often elaborate, but some contemporary calligraphers are pushing the field into new territory, adopting current tools and reacting to modern (or postmodern) influences. Calligraphy is usually scanned into a computer from some physical medium and may not be as flexible as other forms of visual communication. The lack of calligraphy present in electronic media makes it a good area for expression, innovation, and participation in the near future. Calligraphers may want to learn electronic tools—especially if they plan to innovate the field in this area—but in most cases, they will not be required to. Most calligraphers will probably continue to use traditional, physical media and will be hired as freelancers for particular projects.

Illustrator

Illustration is the depiction of just about any subject in artistic form through drawing, painting, airbrushing, sketching, graffiti, and any other possible visual medium humans have developed. Illustration comes in even more varieties than styles of graphic design. It can be realistic, even photo-realistic, or abstract. It can be traditional, modern, contemporary, or futuristic.

Almost all illustrators are able to communicate effectively in a few media and styles, but most are not likely to be able to do so in all media or all styles. Some illustration styles are more complex than others and require more skills and time to develop. Many illustrators are self-trained, though an equal number are professionally trained. Illustrators should be chosen by demonstrated proficiency in the styles desired. They should also be able to generate ideas rapidly for compositions, layouts, and subject matter, and make recommendations on how their style can be used effectively with regard to screen resolution and, possibly, animation.

Illustrators will typically work alone except for project meetings with the team. Most of their work, whether using traditional or electronic media will require concentration and solitary action. Occasionally, they will get together with others such as the art director or creative director to check progress or consult on how the illustrations are being used.

Photographer

Photographers often specialize in certain kinds of photography such as food, portraits, landscapes, animals, products, or still lifes. They may have a range of styles they are comfortable working in, but they will probably prefer some over others. Photographers must understand a variety of issues pertaining to pictures and their intended uses. For example, the style and use in the product may call for different compositions, lighting, filters, or effects. These need to be determined well in advance of the actual photography and will need to be confirmed by the creative director and art director. Since the final work will most likely be shown on a screen of some kind, the resolution and color quality of the presentation device will also be important to the photographer.

Photographs in either slide, negative, or print format will need to be scanned into a computer for use. If this is not done by the photographer, then the photographer will need to be aware of the process and how it will affect the final work. Some photographers are using **digital cameras**, though these are suitable primarily for work that has limited color or grayscale range such as shooting low resolution photographs for websites.

Many people specialize in digitizing and manipulating photographic materials. Most everything that can be imagined visually can now be done on computers with the right tools and artist. However, computerized tools can never compensate enough for a poorly taken picture. It is still important to control all of the elements well and take the best photograph possible to begin with. Also, there are still a few things that can only be done accurately with a camera, including the use of specialized filters and film (such as infrared).

Graphic designers use traditional tools such as pencils, pens, paper, sketchpads, and copiers, as well as electronic ones such as Adobe Photoshop, Adobe Illustrator, *and* Macromedia FreeHand.

Traditional tools for illustrators range from pens, paints, and paper, to spray cans and airbrushes. Common electronic tools include scanners, digitizing pads, Fractal Design Painter, Adobe Photoshop, Adobe Illustrator, *and* Macromedia FreeHand.

Photographers employed full-time will need to function well in a wide variety of styles, whereas contractors and freelancers may be able to stick to a few chosen styles since they will find work from a variety of sources and in a variety of media.

Photographers will often travel to locations to shoot pictures. They are the only visual designers that travel regularly in their work and typically travel with assistants to help them with equipment (much like roadies do for concerts). The travel may or may not be glamorous and will always be serious work.

Image Manipulator

Image manipulators are those who scan and prepare photographs for the screen. They are also artists who use the same photographic electronic tools to create original illustrations and designs using multiple media. These artists are able to work in many different styles and quickly create multiple variations of their work. This is partly due to the tools, but mostly due to an interest in varied styles. Also, those with these skills often gain them without formal training and may not have an overriding artistic direction in their work. They may be more open to changes in work style and material and less set in particular visual stylistic directions.

Visual designers are present mostly in the design and production phases. They are critical in these stages to communicating the ideas and messages, the interface and interaction, and the overall mood of the product in visual terms. It is helpful to have a visual designer present during all brainstorming to keep a visual record, through sketches, of the ideas discussed and the decisions made. Visual designers will also be able to offer valuable opinions and ideas that can help shape the product at these early stages. They perform the bulk of the work in production, along with sound producers, programmers, animators, and video producers.

Process

Visual designers are typically responsible for producing sketches and artwork throughout the project's development, but especially during and after brainstorming and ideation, during design and prototyping, and during production. In ad-

dition, they will be consulted or responsible for the creation of visual standards and specification documents. These standards are described thoroughly so that all production team members will be able to produce work in tandem that is visually consistent.

During **design** and **prototyping**, visual designers commonly generate many original, interesting, and appropriate designs that explore different aspects of the product's content. It is common to work both vertically (from the uppermost and first interactions down to the bottommost interactions) as well as horizontally (across the range of interactions at any given level) through a product simultaneously. Each direction offers different challenges and this is an effective way to test ideas against the full extent of the product. Deliverables in the beginning may be rough sketches or collages of found artwork, colors, and materials proposed for the interactions. As the product ideas become more stable and clear, these sketches will get tighter and more detailed. At some point, the ideas will need to be developed on the screen and represented in their final medium to be sure that the ideas are feasible and realistic. Some designers will be most comfortable starting with the screen—even for sketching—while others will prefer to work first with traditional media. A mix is usually best and there is no one correct way to work.

Visual designers are integral members of the development team at all times. They may work alone to complete artwork but will be involved with project team meetings and work together with other team members closely. Freelance photographers, cartographers, calligraphers, and illustrators may work less with the project team during production if the visual standards are clearly described and the art director has organized the project artwork well. In these cases, production artists and designers may be able to work at home or remotely and turn in their work either in person, via delivery, or via electronic connection. Many illustrators and photographers work for companies all over the nation or world even though they rarely leave their homes. There is nothing better than face-to-face meetings, but new technologies and services have made these

*The work of photographers and illustrators is often the subject of CD-ROMs or online places. In this case, the photographer or illustrator is functioning also as a **content expert** ▶ 195 and must take on these responsibilities in addition to those of their profession.*

Animation ▶ 210, 214 is an art unto itself. Not everything is meant for movement, and illustrators do not always have experience animating their illustrations. It is possible, though, that an illustrator and animator might work together to make a moving sequence, each contributing specialized expertise to create the finished product.

If you currently lack traditional design process experience or skills, you can learn by either taking courses at local colleges or reading books and practicing. Even experienced designers must constantly expand their skills and keep them in tune. The best way to keep your skills honed is to constantly give yourself challenging projects of your own. These projects not only allow you to continually grow your skills and experience, they also demonstrate skills you may not ordinarily have a chance to show. Personal projects are just as relevant to show to prospective employers as professional experiences are as long as they are up to the same standards of quality.

kinds of working relationships possible. This type of remote work can only happen during the production phase when the standards are clearly defined. The prototyping phase is much too participatory and interactive to produce work remotely since the most important work will be the sharing of ideas.

Visual designers work much the same whether the project is a CD-ROM, an online place, a kiosk, or an electronic marketing demo. The constraints of each project type and medium make a difference in the quality of the presentation and performance of the materials, but the visual style should not be affected much. In some cases however, compression algorithms may make certain color palettes or style perform better than others. This may also affect the quality of photography and illustration. In general, visual designers should understand what the constraints are for different types of projects and must immediately identify the constraints, limitations, and desires of the clients involved. Visual designers must perform a balancing act between the client's identity and desires, their personal vision, the constraints of the project and technology, and the subject matter itself.

Tools and Techniques

Visual designers work in a **variety of media** and with a **variety of tools**. Some prefer traditional tools, some electronic tools, and still others a combination of the two. Regardless, every designer will need to understand how their work will be affected when transferred to digital media. Photographs and illustrations will be more coarse, text will be less legible, and colors may shift.

Most designers work with more powerful computers. The processing demands inherent in graphics work requires faster and more powerful processors and larger hard drives. Visual files take considerably more space than text files. Audio and video consume even more. Visual designers often use cartridge drives, digital audio tapes (DAT), and recordable CD-ROMs for archiving and production. Floating point co-processors or processors with these built-in are almost mandatory in machines used by digital designers.

Fast, sophisticated equipment is helpful but is no substitute for getting inside the mind of clients or art directors. Designers work closely with other team members and with clients to produce appropriate artwork. This requires them to listen well to client comments and intentions and find ways of communicating ideas to them. Sketching is often a practical method since it is so fast, but some clients may not be able to visualize or understand concepts unless they are almost fully rendered. Others, in contrast, may read too much into final-looking artwork and not be able to separate the concepts from the implementation. In this case, colors, typeface, form, style, and wording may distract a client from the real issues and ideas at hand.

One way of eliciting client and team ideas concerning stylistic issues is to have them collect things that they like or that represent the styles they are interested in pursuing. These can be clippings from magazines, packaging, and books—even television. These will help everyone understand more clearly what is intended and appropriate and what to design away from. Another technique is to use adjectives. Clients may be able to describe the appearance of a product using words. These, however, may mean different things to them than they do to you. It is important to find adjectives that can be understood clearly by all.

A technique often learned the hard way is to get a clear picture of the work required very early in the process. It is imperative to have a clear understanding between you and the influencing parties before any work gets too far along. It can be devastating both emotionally and economically to find out that all the final work on a project must be recreated from scratch because the style is not the one desired or because compression algorithms, color palettes, or processor speeds specific to the project render the artwork unusable.

Qualifications

All digital artists and visual designers must know how to use the **proper tools** and what effects specific technology will have on their artwork. This understanding often comes with experience. But while technical skills will get you steady

Maurice Tani
Graphic Designer

Maurice Tani's decision to change careers hit him like a ton of bricks. Actually, the object that pinned the erstwhile art handler to the floor in 1989 was a ton-and-a-half of etched glass. During his hospital stay it became painfully clear that Maurice would not be returning to his old job. With insurance and worker's compensation paying for retraining, Maurice began taking classes in desktop publishing, gravitating to courses in Photoshop, Illustrator, and Director.

For Maurice, the new digital tools simply provided an extension of interests he had begun developing since college. "When the new wave music scene broke in 1979," he says, "I got into creating punk rock posters using Letraset and Xerox machines. That really was art of the streets. It's funny, and I hate to admit it, but in my college art and photography courses, I didn't enjoy the art process. I didn't really enjoy the darkroom. The oils and chalks weren't really speaking to me. But the poster graphics, that I liked. Something about the process of manipulation, of paste-up and photocopying, just clicked for me."

Maurice began freelancing almost immediately after graduating, with referrals coming via word of mouth, and also through the school, who would get calls from corporate clients asking, "Who do you have who will work cheap?" The answer was Maurice, who had sufficiently mastered the techniques of Photoshop and Director to deliver interactive presentations for Northern Telecom, Accugraph, and for a law firm litigating the performance of two competing pieces of high tech medical equipment.

At the same time, Maurice found himself in demand as a Photoshop tutor for small groups of students. As much as he has learned in formal course work, he believes the best way for people to learn the techniques of graphic design for interactive multimedia is to "create their own personal project they can sink their teeth into." According to Maurice, "That kind of learning is much more effective than going to classes or taking a tutorial. Anyone can follow directions, but the directions are meaningless unless the result has some value to you."

In addition to freelancing for clients such as Hyundai Design Center in Los Angeles and Symantec, these days Maurice is busy designing graphics for the World Wide Web. Anyone with a web browser can view his contribution to websites for Sony Electronic Publishing (http://www.sony.com/SEPC), Borland (http://www.borland.com), and 3Com (http://www.3com.com).

work, the most challenging and rewarding work goes to those who have highly developed **design skills**. Someone that is able to work through many solutions in a systematic way and arrive at the most appropriate visual representation will be far more valuable in many cases than someone who knows the tools but tends to work in only one style.

Graphical designers need to be **dependable**. Good art directors and producers will provide explicit instructions on your deliverables and their deadlines. You will be expected to meet these deadlines with artwork that is in an appropriate state for the phase of the project. Some artists and designers do not place a high value on these parts of the job. Art directors and producers, however, do and are not likely to rehire undependable designers, no matter how good their work is.

How to Hire

A variety of people may be involved in hiring a designer, but the most appropriate would be the creative director, art directors, and producers. Creative directors are most appropriate for evaluating prospective designers for corporate-level, full-time jobs since these affect all communications and many projects, while art directors may be more important for hiring freelancers for part-time and more limited or quick work.

Many designers specialize in certain styles and it may be difficult for them to work contrary to those interests. In this case, it is best to find someone who is comfortable and capable of working within the styles that are appropriate for a particular project. When hiring a designer, look for examples of work that interest you and that relate to your projects. If possible, let a designer know before meeting him or her what kinds of work you are interested in. This will allow them the chance to assemble an appropriate portfolio.

Just seeing someone's work that looks great does not ensure that you and they will be able to work well together. Some designers are used to (and expect) a great deal of control over the project and may not enjoy the process of working closely with others. Others may have rigid ways of approaching and solving problems and may not be interested in developing ideas along other lines. Still others may not be used to the large number of pieces in some interactive projects and therefore not be able to pace themselves appropriately. As a result they may spend a lot of time on few pieces, putting them hopelessly behind on creating the others. A portfolio and conversation is the best way to get to know someone's work, interests, and capabilities. One without the other is a handicap for both the designer looking for work and the manager looking for help.

You can find designers through many **professional design organizations**, but the best way is to consult **other people in multimedia** for recommendations. You can also find capable designers through **art and design schools**, but recognize that these students may not have much professional experience. They might serve

Nancy Pinney
Visual Designer

For much of her professional life, Nancy Pinney was an artist in search of the right medium. Her peripatetic career has taken her on a journey from the crazed clients of advertising in Los Angeles to creating funky art furniture to the disembodied realm of cyberspace, where the computer artist, illustrator, and interactive designer has worked on numerous CD titles and some of the hottest sites on the World Wide Web, including Sony Interactive and Rocket Science.

Nancy's life changed drastically when Eastman Kodak opened its educational facility for graphic imaging professionals a block from her house in Camden, Maine. Called the Center for Creative Imaging, the school was a seedbed of new technology and a magnet for the most talented innovators in the industry who were employed there as teachers of short, intensive hands-on courses. Although Nancy had never touched a computer in her life, she applied for, and won, a position as an assistant. Within three months, she was teaching classes.

When Eastman Kodak shuttered the school, Nancy went West, where the industry was taking off. Three weeks after her arrival, she found herself working on Peter Gabriel's Secret World. Nancy describes her work on that project as, "My breakthrough experience. At the time I didn't really have a grasp on the concept of 'multimedia.' I was a Photoshop *guru. My job was to create screens whose interface was the screen itself. It took me a while to grasp the structure and organization that followed. Interface design has now become an integrated part of my design process."*

Nancy has some straightforward advice for graphic artists making the transition from traditional media to the interactive arena. "I would suggest building a very strong visual portfolio and then beating on as many doors as you can. Once you get your foot caught, you'll never be able to pull it out."

well as interns but few students still in school have the skills yet needed to produce professional work. They may have tremendous ideas but without the experience that comes with solving professional problems, meeting deadlines and budgets, and cooperating with others. Most students will need to learn a lot about their responsibilities. Also, many may not have experience with electronic media and may need to learn what effects interactivity and computer technology have on their work.

Many designers prefer to work as freelancers or contractors, whether hourly, daily, or by project, and on their own premises. Others prefer full-time jobs and the security that comes with them. There is almost as much variety in working arrangements as there is in visual styles. Be clear on what kinds of arrangements you are looking for and what type of work you envision needing. If you find someone who fits your needs well, be prepared to be as flexible as you can to meet their needs too.

Some visual designers use "reps," short for representatives, who basically perform the same function as agents. Reps may sell and manage the project or may merely connect a client and an artist. They usually take a percentage of the project fee, typically around 10%. Reps are common for illustrators and photographers but few graphic designers use them. A few visual designers have agents as opposed to reps, but these designers are usually extremely well known in their fields. These designers include internationally known photographers, illustrators, and graphic designers, who often charge very high fees and are extremely selective about the work they take on.

How to Be Hired

As with other disciplines, networking is the best way to make contacts that can generate new work. These leads may not pay off for a while and so they should be approached as much for professional and personal development as for work. Deal only with those people who you feel comfortable with and enjoy. There is enough work to go around that there should be no need to put up with potential employers you are not comfortable with or do not find completely trustworthy.

Copyright Issues

*The issues of **copyright ownership** ▶ 102 is particularly important to visual designers. The creator of a work is the copyright holder unless the creator is an employee or the work fits under the **"work-for-hire" doctrine** ▶ 102, 136 for contractors and is specifically called out in the contract. Most photographers and illustrators retain the rights to all work but typically assign rights to an illustration or photograph for specific, limited uses (such as one use, certain media, or certain forms). To use the work for any other purposes requires additional licensing (and compensation). Graphic designers may transfer all the rights to the final work to the client but retain the rights not only to the materials used to create the final work (including sketches and electronic files), but also any alternatives that were not used. These traditions are unchanged in interactive media, although granting limited use rights may take a different form due to the nature of the media. If clients want full, unlimited rights, or all of the materials and alternatives created in the process, visual designers should charge them more for these rights and materials. Some visual designers charge three to five times their price for final artwork or unlimited use.*

"Reps" may be a good idea if you do not yet have a clientele list or a recognized name. Reps are agents for specific artists and designers and negotiate deals with clients as well as find work for those they represent. Reps make it their business to stay in touch, network, and make sure that deadlines are being met. They can be valuable assets not just for work but also for professional development.

A resume is a necessary start at representing yourself and your talent, but a portfolio will be even more important. In most artistic and visual disciplines, your portfolio will speak louder for you than anything else. It will still be necessary to explain and demonstrate your skills well—especially those of managing your time, meeting deadlines, and working with others—but if you do not have the design skills a client is looking for, the rest is not going to be valuable to them.

Your **portfolio** ▶ 82 should be up to date at all times, which includes good representations of your latest work. Your portfolio should be bigger than necessary and you should always have stand-by work available so that you can configure a portfolio on a moment's notice with the type of work that a prospective client is interested in. You

Corrine Okada
Illustrator

San Francisco-based Corrine Okada is an illustrator and graphic designer equally at home in the world of digital and traditional media. When Summagraphic, manufacturer of pen-based drawing tablets, wanted an artist to demonstrate their new drawing tablet designed for the natural media software emulation of Fractal Design Painter at Seybold's recent San Francisco exposition, they turned to Corrine. With her background as a digital art instructor at the Center for Electronic Art and Foothill College, her stints as guest lecturer at the Product Design Department at Stanford University and the Academy of Art in San Francisco, and her experience as a private tutor of Painter, Photoshop, and Illustrator, Corrine would prove unflappable on the exhibition floor.

Corrine tells her students trying to break into the industry that one of the best ways to get started is work as a demonstration artist at a trade show. "The best thing I ever did was demo software at a trade show. That connected me to hundreds of potential clients. And I got to network with other tablet artists."

As a teacher and tutor, Corrine has her finger on the pulse of what students and employers are looking for. "In every job interview the conversation revolves entirely around software. Which I think is shortsighted. It doesn't matter to me if someone doesn't have great computer skills as long as they have solid drawing and design skills. It is more important to master the essentials of design instead of the software. I see a lot of people with self-taught software skills that may have ten freelance jobs on their resume, but have never had a steady job. That's a common trend in this industry."

must be perceptive enough to know when to show more variety than they ask for, and when to show only what they ask for. Some employers are not interested in seeing work other than the type they are specifically looking for—even if it demonstrates wider skills, broader interests, or more depth. Others, however, do appreciate seeing well-rounded work and the ability to be flexible. Be ready to respond in whatever direction is appropriate.

If you have any samples to leave behind, such as printed screens or a demo disk, this is a big help to employers. When they meet you or first hear from you, they may not have any need for your services so they may not take the time to return your calls or set a meeting time. However, if you have sent them something they can refer to, then they can browse your work without having to contact you. Samples do not need to be elaborate. A simple slideshow of work or small, quality images may be enough to remember you and keep them interested.

David Wasserman
Photographer

David Wasserman has looked at life through a camera lens for years, but wasn't always a professional photographer. He started out as a systems ecologist, studying animal behavior and biophysics, and photographic data was an important part of his research. As he explains, "Somewhere along the way, photography overtook biology," and for nearly a decade now he has supported himself as a photographer.

"From the outset, my style was unusual," says David, who specializes in portraiture. He attributes Photoshop to raising the demand for conceptual work, "due to the ease with which the visually impossible can be created." These days, David relies on Photoshop, Kai's Power Tools, and similar tools to allow these impossibilities, from simple retouches to bending the laws of the physical world.

"These digital tools not only allow for greater ease but substantially broaden the aesthetic possibilities open to me," he says. "The borders between photography, painting, and graphics aren't very clear in my more recent work."

One of his latest projects is the Photo CD Terra Incognita, *the first in a series of discs produced for Texture Farm, a company co-founded by David and his partner Fred Smith. David created and manipulated natural abstract photographs for this collection of 100 images that can be used in print and digital mediums.*

David now routinely solicits multimedia developers as well as editors, designers, and ad agencies for work. He has readily embraced the new technology, however he has seen other photographers who are "terrified," primarily because the amount of assignments has dropped. Although he thinks some of their concerns are well founded—for example, the federal government has been very slow to address copyright issues and theft issues associated with digital photography—"in the long run, this is going to generate a lot of work for all of us."

Also, make sure you take the time to look at the work of others that you are dependent on or are dependent on you. These include art directors, photographers, animators, videographers, and technical leads. Little is more frustrating than working with people that are not fully qualified or that lack appreciation for good design.

Compensation

Salaries and rates for visual designers vary greatly in multimedia and there are few measures for compensation. The most common measures are the ones from traditional design industries such as desktop publishing and advertising. These, however, do not adequately reflect someone who understands interaction and can fulfill a variety of roles with rare or unusual skills. Competition in active areas such as San Francisco may drive rates down as long as there is enough of a supply of knowledgeable, experienced designers for the demand. Otherwise, the rates may be much higher which is currently the status in New York City and Los Angeles. While there are many visual designers in both of these locations, there is a shortage of those with experience in interactive and electronic media.

2D Animator

What They Do

2D animators take a sequence of static images and display them in rapid succession on the computer screen to create the illusion of motion. The mind sees individual images but processes them as a continuous sequence of events—hence, motion. The threshold for seamless animation is generally much higher in film than is possible in most general purpose computer platforms. These computers cannot display as many frames per second (fps) as might be needed and so computer animators are continually fighting the fps battle in an effort to fool the eye. Good animations, especially character animations, take a great deal of time to create. Consequently, animation is one of the most expensive means of communicating information in interactive multimedia.

2D and 3D animation are similar in the sense that they are both time-based sequences of visual images but the tools and the skills can be vastly different. 2D animators do not have to concern themselves as much with issues such as lighting and perspective, although some 2D animators may simulate 3D animations through the use of shadows and other visual plays. 3D spinning logos, for example, may be simply a sequence of images that are sequenced together in a form similar to a flip book of images. A true 3D animation would start with a wireframe model and then use shaders and other techniques to provide truer perspective and shading.

Process

The process of creating 2D animations typically begins the old fashioned way, with the 2D animator creating a variety of quick pencil sketches. For character-based work, these sketches are often detailed series of cartoons that cover pages in an attempt to capture nuances of character and emotion.

Once the sketches are approved, the animator will usually progress to creating **storyboards**. They may work from a script created by a scriptwriter or go over each scene directly with the art director. Storyboards specify where the animations fall in the flow of the screen-by-screen progression through the project, and they also indicate the user interaction, such as a button click, or a mouse movement, that invokes the animation. **Key frames**, showing the most important elements of the animation and indicating direction, lighting, and visual climaxes, are illustrated as well. **Transitions** from one key frame to the next are usually spelled out in a sentence or two of copy.

Detailed storyboards are crucial; they provide a quick, inexpensive guarantee that the 2D animator understands the design goals of the project and is on track. Revisions at the storyboard stage can be made quickly and inexpensively. Changing final art, or worse, rewriting lines of code as the project moves further along in the production process, can be extremely time consuming.

After the storyboards are finalized, the 2D animator can then move on to the process of bringing their vision to the small screen. Some of the original sketches may be scanned in and cleaned up using an image editing program such as *Adobe Photoshop*, or new artwork may be created using one of the popular drawing tools such as *Macromedia Freehand* or *Adobe Illustrator*. If the animation consists of a simple movement across the screen, the animator identifies a start and stop point, then specifies the duration of the animated sequence. Most animation software applications automatically divide the duration by a frame per second to create a seamless animation.

For more interesting animations, the process is more time consuming and requires creating **intermediate frames**. Intermediate frames created are assembled in the editing component of an animation tool. Each individual frame must now be copied and pasted into the animation software. The background must be cleaned up and the frame saved. This process is repeated successively as an object is moved over a screen. Finally, when all frames are assembled, the animator can run the animation, judging whether it runs too fast or too slow. Timing can be changed by resetting the animation speed. Creating many small movements as opposed to a few large ones means the animation will appear smooth when it plays back.

For very complex animations, in which many objects move over the screen simultaneously, animators create animations in **layers**. A background is created and saved in its own layer, then separate layers are created for each moving object. Again, the moving object must be cut, moved slightly, and pasted into the background. But with the background saved as a separate layer, there are no "holes" left when an object is moved. And with the creation of a number of layers, multiple objects, each in its own layer, can be animated across the screen.

Tools and Techniques

For creating preliminary sketches and individual components, a 2D animator will use many of the same tools as a **visual designer** ▶ 200. They may use traditional media tools such as paper and pen or electronic tools such as illustration or scanning and image manipulation tools. For the actual animations, a 2D animator will often use a tool such as *Macromedia Director* to insert the components and arrange them on or offscreen in a time-based sequence.

As for techniques, it is crucial that the media production team create and adhere to a naming convention for all digital files. Coordinating all the artwork can quickly become a major issue, especially when you consider that multiple forms of the same object are often needed. Many times

Frequently, animators will create the illusion of movement and expression with animations that take place on tiny pieces of screen real estate. Examine a cartoon character animation, for example, that runs on a desktop computer. Instead of animating an expression of an entire face, a good 2D animator will move only the eyebrows, or only the mouth. It is one of the ways 2D animators have become experts at working with the inherent limitations of the computer.

Art Reviews

One of the many formal meetings that take place during the design and production phase is the art review. This is essentially a slide show that takes place on the computer as the animators, visual designers, scriptwriters, and programmers review the work created thus far in the project. Art reviews are first conducted with the art director and then possibly with the producer, client, or publisher. Key screens are reviewed, colors are approved, and the placement of art is examined on a screen-by-screen basis. Art reviews have several functions. First and most obvious, has the animator executed the creative vision of the scriptwriter and the visual designers? Has the artist followed the storyboards in the script? Are the pacing and transitions appropriate? If there is copy onscreen, is the copy spelled correctly? These seem like minor points, but if unchecked they can be expensive and embarrassing headaches to fix downstream in the production process.

Another important, and often surprisingly unspoken purpose of the art review is to make certain the client is pleased. In addition to the internal dynamics of the art production process, the production team must also consider the outside world inhabited by the client. These considerations range from the minuscule, such as, "Is the logo rendered accurately? Is it the right color?" to larger concerns such as, "Are production processes depicted in the right order?" If an animation depicts the building of a high tech piece of equipment, for example, do the component elements appear on screen in the right sequence? If animations are married to an audio or voice-over track, do the visual and aural elements synchronize? If clients are unaware of the capabilities of multimedia, they may have unrealistically high or low expectations about the deliverables and their concerns will most often be raised here. If clients are not invited to address those concerns early in the production process, they may never get onboard with the production team. The consequences can be disastrous.

Assuming that all goes well in the art review meeting, the animator returns to the drawing board to make changes. These revisions are reviewed by the designer and, quite possibly, the client in another smaller, less formal meeting. Once approved, the art is handed off to the programmer for integration with other media in the project. For the 2D animator, it is now on to the next project, or the next job (at least, until the next round of changes comes in.)

the individual components are rearranged or modified with new components inserted or existing ones removed. Considering that some operating systems only support file names of eight characters or less, creating a workable and meaningful naming convention can become something of an art in itself. Without a proper naming convention, the resulting confusion can cause lots of wasted effort and many long and heated discussions.

Qualifications

First and foremost, the 2D animator must be extremely **familiar with the tools** of the trade. This expertise with the technical capabilities of the software and hardware must be backed by thorough knowledge of the production process and the capabilities of the target machine where the animations will eventually be viewed. A good 2D animator understands the limitations of the medium, especially the trade-off between image size, frame rate, and the computational horsepower required to create the illusion of movement onscreen.

Animations place tremendous demands on a computer's resources. A good rule of thumb here is that the larger the image size, the longer it will take the CPU to process and display it; consequently, the frame rate will be lower and the animation appear jerky and awkward. Because a computer must "remember" the animation and store that image in memory while also remembering the image "behind" the moving object, animations tend to be small and discrete. If animated objects are too large, the result is an animation that crawls across the screen at an agonizingly slow rate while the computer grinds away, loading images while it paints and repaints the screen.

Good **communication skills** are also important, since much of the production process requires the ability to communicate successfully with teammates. Not only must 2D animators quickly understand the design objectives, they must then demonstrate their understanding in art review meetings and by creating sketches and storyboards.

2D animators must also have a **passion** for the work. Their ideas must be clearly communicated during review meetings, and they must be able to work long hours in isolation and without much

Kathleen Egge
2D Artist

When asked about how she made the transition into multimedia, Kathleen Egge says, "Actually multimedia came to me. I was offered the chance to do some design work for a ZD Labs kiosk." Kathleen began moonlighting on the kiosk while holding down her steady job. "I found myself staying until 2 or 3 in the morning because I was having so much fun." Three nights later, Kathleen quit her day job and never looked back.

In addition to her recent freelance projects for Clement Mok designs, SuperMac/EMachines, and Walker Interactive, Kathleen considers her recent 60-second computer animation project for Colossal Pictures and their client, Nickelodeon, one of her most rewarding. "I was surrounded by highly energetic, creative people that were just buzzing with ideas," she says. "We had a lot of freedom for creativity."

Kathleen is quick to stress the spiritual side of the creative endeavor. To her, animation is not just about pushing pixels around on the screen.

In addition to having to consider the design of animations from start to finish, build to powerful climaxes, create the transitions and make certain that they flow well, Kathleen believes, "In order to work and be really creative there has to be harmony within and on the team. In animation, I have to be in touch with the creative person inside of me."

Kathleen's practical advice comes straight from her own experience trying to learn new tools and new technologies. "When I got in, the first thing I did was buy a computer. It was expensive but I considered it an investment. I got a hold of some tools. I learned the tools, went through tutorials, learned from friends, and explored a lot. I've even hired private tutors to teach me specific things.

supervision. Cutting and pasting frames requires precision and a certain tolerance, if not enjoyment, for the highly detailed nature of the work.

How to Hire

After getting an idea for the type of animation needed, ask each member of the team to recommend people they have worked with. They will be able to provide you with the names of people who have a track record and know the ropes.

Professional associations of illustrators, animators, and graphic artists are an excellent source of talented individuals. If you live in a city with a chapter of the International Interactive Communications Society (IICS) or an animation software or authoring tool users group, simply attend a meeting and make a job announcement during a break. Often, these organizations will be happy to let you post your job listing on their jobs hotline or bulletin board system as well.

An often overlooked talent pool is the computer education and computer graphics departments of colleges and universities. There are many raw but talented people sitting in a classroom somewhere, mastering the software tools they'll need to take us in new directions.

One thing to keep in mind is how well this person will fit in with the rest of the production team. In addition to relying on your instincts, check references to determine if this individual is a team player. Producing interactive multimedia demands long hours and close quarters. As teams struggle to meet their deadlines (and it is always a struggle), 60 and 70-hour weeks are not uncommon. You want someone who cares passionately about their work in order to defend its merits, but you also want someone who will appreciate the collaborative nature of multimedia development.

How to Be Hired

First, build a **portfolio** of your work that can accompany your resume. If possible, provide examples of your work on a videotape, diskette,

Syquest cartridge, or recordable CD-ROM. While a traditional portfolio might get you a job in a traditional agency, if you are looking for work in multimedia it makes sense to show your work in a format appropriate to the medium.

Increasingly, artists are developing **interactive portfolios** using *Director* or *HyperCard*. These portfolios often divide the work into several categories, allowing potential employers to look at illustration work, advertising work, interactive credits, and personal work. Complete with menus and sometimes even a soundtrack, these interactive portfolios not only show off the artists' work effectively, they also provide a compelling demonstration that the artist is willing to go the extra mile and get involved in multimedia. If you decide to go this route, remember to keep the interaction scheme simple. You want your potential employer to be able to quickly and easily view your work, and not get lost in a complex menu structure. And your presentation must be flawless. Any bugs or typos in your interactive portfolio will not be looked on kindly.

If you do not have any professional credits, it is perfectly acceptable to show work you have created on your own. The main point is to demonstrate expertise with the tools as well as an appreciation for the goals and constraints of each project. You want to make it simple for a prospective employer to make the leap from you and your work to whatever project they may have a need for, whether that need is now or in the future.

Compensation

The compensation for a 2D animator is not as great as that of a 3D animator. Hourly rates will vary from $25/hr to $75/hr depending on the skill of the animator and the complexity of the animation. As with other media production professions, the issue of who owns the **copyright ▶ 102** to the artwork is very important. Many independent contractors assign the rights to the final animations to the client but retain rights to intermediary work and to pieces not used. Animators that create original characters, however, often license the work for specific use but retain the rights to the characters.

Since computers do not care how old someone is, how they dress, or what kind of social skills they can muster, it is important that prospective employers learn to look past the surface affectations of an individual to examine their work and their personality. The 19-year-old with a ring in her nose who just skateboarded into the job interview might be just the person needed. They may not be great with clients, but it is the quality of work they create onscreen that counts.

3D Animator

What They Do

3D animators are the hired guns of multimedia, with the skills, the hot boxes, and the software that can turn a running man into a blob of molten metal in *Terminator II*, or make dinosaurs come to life in *Jurassic Park*. For these skills they can command rates over $100 an hour.

3D animators are in hot demand for work not only in multimedia but also for film, TV, and advertising work. It is a hard profession to learn but it can be highly lucrative.

In the last several years, 3D animators have made enormous contributions to the use of computer graphics in the entertainment medium. In the process, they are radically changing the economics of entertainment productions. From the megabucks "render farms" of Industrial Light and Magic's high octane SGI machines to the 3D animators of *Babylon 5*, working out of their garages on Amiga computers equipped with NewTech's Video Toasters, the paradigm of special effects production is changing. The extremely expensive hand work of traditional animation and special effects houses are going the way of the horse and buggy, if not the dinosaur. As the work of Industrial Light and Magic so emphatically underscores, why build a model of a dinosaur on a Hollywood back lot when a 3D animator can create one on the desktop that will be less expensive, more realistic, and more extensible than a series of "real" models.

From an economic standpoint alone—with computer generated models costing one-half to one-tenth the cost of traditional model making, painting, and photography—3D computer generated art is becoming increasingly popular with many film production studios. There are no union rates to pay and no actors' equity reports to file. The quirky, post-modern characters with an attitude in *Reboot* do not ask for raises or demand a larger trailer. One of the notorious stories that circulated in Hollywood at the time of the filming of *Jurassic Park* concerned a studio executive who asked when the special effects department would be able to create lifelike computer-generated actors to accompany the dinosaurs.

Process

3D animators will often inherit the interactive multimedia project as it moves into the production process. Working from a script and storyboard that provides screen-by-screen depictions of the project, they will create their own **storyboards** that render in even finer detail a breakdown of the 3D animation. These depict the motion of objects across the screen, illustrating key frames with a thumbnail sketch. Each key frame will indicate direction of motion, "camera" angles, as well as light sources and shadows. Transitions between key frames are described by a few brief lines of copy which accompany each storyboard. Upon the review of the storyboards, the 3D animator will begin to create wireframe models and render them, saving their work in a file that will be handed off to the programmer for integration into the final project.

Once the 3D storyboards are reviewed and approved, the 3D animator must construct the illusion of 3-dimensional spaces, then move 3-dimensional objects within that space. The process begins with a technique called **modeling**, in which the 3D animator builds a wireframe model of their images. Wireframes are essentially the engineering skeletons of objects. In the same way that a human skeleton communicates basic information about the human form, these wireframes communicate just the basics about the 3D object to come. While sketchy, these transitional illustrations have the benefit of being easy and quick for the computer to calculate. Each time the 3D animator changes the perspective, adjusts the camera angle, or manipulates the shadows cast by the object, the computer can quickly calculate the changes and display the revised wireframe. In this way the elementary shapes of 3D objects can be quickly rotated in space and viewed from different angles.

Once the wireframe objects are modeled, the 3D animator then dresses their framework with a skin in a process called **rendering**, which mathematically calculates the surface textures and

Clifford Lau
Animator, Sega

When you create an animation in the traditional way, you have to have a bunch of senior artists doing the key frames, and then a bunch of other people—in-betweeners, colorists, etc. But with software, once you build a model, you can just animate it, key frame it, squish and stretch it, change the camera angle, or redo the animation.

These tools are really great for production because if you have to change something really quickly, you can do it. Essentially what we're doing is making sprites that work in games. We pull them down to the color resolution that we have and the general resolution that the game can take, but we're creating 24-bit maps of these animations to begin with. Then we isolate them, chromakey out the background, and pull those

sprites in. We do cycles of running and jumping, biting, or whatever. These are brought into the game environment and then the programmer takes those animations and says, "Okay, this is the bite behavior at this point in the game. If you do certain things, the thing'll come out and bite you, or run away from you, or whatever."

The software really allows us to say, "This animation works, but if we could only do it this way...." If we had to go back to the traditional method, it would be a huge hassle to get the key framer back, to do another set of key frames, and have the in-betweeners rework from that. It's a very arduous process, whereas now, we could go to the machine and say, "Let's make him run this way and change the camera angle to this." We can do that within a day. That would take a month otherwise.

qualities of a wireframe outline. This creates the visual cues that fool the viewer's eyes into believing in the illusion of three dimensions on a two dimensional screen.

There are several levels of rendering, using various software algorithms that provide a spectrum of sophistication and quality. Hidden-line rendering, as the name implies, hides the interior lines of the wireframe and draws only the outside edges. Quick shading renders objects with a solid color to define the surface and indicate the effect of light sources on an entire surface. Gourad shading hides the hidden lines of a wireframe and fills the space between with averages of color and illumination to provide greater realism. Phong shading calculates the color for each pixel in a 3D model to create an even higher level of rendering fidelity. Ray tracing, the next step up the quality ladder, calculates the values, intensities and directions of rays of light bouncing off 3D objects to create a near-photorealistic effect.

Calculating the mathematical equations that define color, surface texture, gradations of light, reflections, and shadows can take hours. Depending on the needs for lifelike animation embodied in projects like the water sprite of *The Abyss* and the dinosaurs of *Jurassic Park*, the creation of the wireframe can be incredibly complex and take hours. Consequently, one of the

things a 3D animator (and a 3D animator's client) must do is wait.

The illusion of motion is created in a painstaking process in which the 3D animator identifies key frames which specify the beginning and ending points of the animation as well as critical points along the way. In an automated process known as **in-betweening**, the computer will automatically generate the interim frames required to provide the appearance of a smoothly moving object on the screen. Before the animator proceeds to a final rendering sequence, it is usually a good idea to review the sequence of the entire animation in wireframe. A few key frames can be identified and rendered in high resolution in order to provide production managers and clients with an interim animation review. These snapshots may be the last chance to make adjustments or revisions before the time consuming task of final rendering begins.

There are several distinct styles of animation, including the frame-based flip-book style of animation, in which rapidly changing scenes convey the illusion of motion. A second style of animation uses layers or channels to keep moving objects separate from their background. Other animation techniques include fly-throughs, which allow simulated movement through a 3D environment, an extension of which are the virtual

A number of operating system companies and other people in major positions to influence technical developments are taking steps to standardize 3D libraries. This effort, in combination with faster computer chips and affordable 3D accelerator cards, promises to make 3D animation a more integral part of most software and multimedia products.

reality applications which let a user "walk through" an architect's vision of a building before it is completed. **Fly-through** animation techniques enable the animator to select a view of an animated environment, identify key frames and process the changes between the frames. The effect is similar to flying through or over a cityscape in a flight simulation program. And of course, there's morphing, a technique which allows one shape or figure to automatically blend into another over time, and threatens to become the visual cliché of the nineties.

Gray Holland, 3D Modeler and Animator, Alchemy

vivid: What distinction do you draw between modeling and animation? Is animation just a model put in motion?

No, no, no, no, no. There are a lot of dynamic elements to it, obviously. There are things that I notice now when I'm watching movies that I didn't notice before. Like if the camera is swooping around the object instead of the object spinning around the camera, or spinning upon its own axis, or the difference between panning and rotation.

A lot of these tools actually have linear depictions of that movement that you can edit. You can see discontinuities or glitches. You might want something to come up and crash and then bounce back, and stop immediately and come back. In the tools that Alias provides, you can go in and break lines and play with them in the same way you would in Illustrator. Only here, you're playing with the line that depicts the rotation, the scale, or even the evolution of a shader, changing one color to the other, or becoming transparent. But it's interesting how the metaphor of the line holds throughout the program; it's something that we all can understand. A pure 2D line has a lot of power.

vivid: What kind of advice would you give to someone who designs right now but who wants to break out of the beaten down path? What should they learn? What kind of tools should they be using?

From what I see (and this is somewhat incestuous and prejudiced), the best people in the multimedia industry are almost all design-centered people. At some of the industrial design schools there's a tremendous amount of care and sensitivity taught, the dedication to doing it right, and doing it with all the best tools. For example, all of my printing is done on Iris prints. I work with the best software on Silicon Graphics, and the best that I can find on the Macintosh. You've got to keep working on the edge because this stuff runs out of date every six months. You've got to be smart about it to keep grabbing and using these new tools, but not forgetting the old tools.

Still, you need to crawl before you can walk, and you've got to walk before you can run. I think you need to be able to draw before you can start playing around with a Mac. You've got to know what a good line is. I think you've got to know how to do 2D design on the computer before you can do 3D design. You don't have to follow that process but I think you have to understand the whole spectrum. You should know how to work with clay. That's one of the most valuable things.

I knew how to model things in the real world first. Even if you study people like Picasso, his earlier work was concerned with depicting reality. He learned how to first do reality before he started messing with it. He could capture the back of a woman with one line because he had drawn the human body so many times. He's just distilled it to the essence of that line. That's really what I love about Picasso, more than his work itself; seeing his progression and what he could do at the end of his life was phenomenal. Three lines capture a centaur. Just phenomenal.

The artisan, or the craftsmanship of the artist is still fundamental to becoming an artist. It's Alias this week and it might be something else next week. I want to know what the new tools are because they're always going to be empowering. I'll be able to reach that much further, out beyond my limbs. That's really what the computer allows you to do, to go beyond what you can do with a pencil and paper.

Tools and Techniques

With the high price of **3D animation software packages** such as *ElectricImage*, *Wavefront*, or *Alias*, comes high power. Describing movement uses the component of an animation software package called an animation engine or animator. Using an animation engine, a 3D animator can create a sphere at the beginning of an animation, for example, drag it across the screen with the mouse, and record its path of travel. The animation engine can then compute all the permutations—including changes in lighting, shadows, and surface texture.

If the design goal for the animation demands that a sphere transform into a pancake by the end of the animation, 3D software packages provide tools to make this effect a reality. The animation engine enables the 3D animator to assign values for its frictional coefficient, its mass, elasticity, and the frictional coefficient of the objects the sphere is bouncing into, then set a force vector. The animation engine does the rest, animating the simulation "automatically." The practical application of a simulation like this might be to create the realism required in a flight simulator, in which a plane successfully lands on a carrier flight deck, or pancakes in a fiery crash.

Along with high price and high power comes a radically steep learning curve. Think of the time it takes to learn 2D software packages like *Photoshop* or *Illustrator*, and add a third dimension. Suddenly, your level of difficulty explodes. With the addition of a third dimension, the level of complexity can increase a hundredfold. Add movement and animation, effects like panning, rotating, and spinning, and the learning curve gets steeper. The mastery of these effects is one of the reasons 3D animators are in such demand and earn so much money.

When the 3D animator's work is finally rendered, it is saved in a low resolution format and handed off to a programmer for integration into the interactive program. Final animation sequences are usually compressed and saved as QuickTime movies or as Windows AVI files. This optimizes storage requirements and enhances playback performance on target machines.

Qualifications

In addition to a thorough mastery of the development tools, the 3D animator must be a master of **visual communication**. Beyond technical issues of timing, frame rate, synchronizing animations to music or vocals, and the creation of a believable 3-dimensional space, animations can convey nuances of emotion and personality, and help define an environment. How these skills are deployed, and what style of animation best evokes an audience response are issues that are independent of hardware and software platforms. These tools of the trade include color theory, life drawing, composition, and solid drawing skills. Using the fastest rendering program running on the fastest RISC chip made will not get the animator very far if they do not posses these basic skills.

Not only must the animator be able to plan animations with coherent beginnings, middles, and ends, punctuated by powerful compelling visual climaxes along the way, but a good animator must be able to understand and create storyboards, rapidly sketch out ideas, and work closely with the art directors, visual designers, and programmers on the project team.

And in addition to having a good eye and artistic judgment, the 3D animator must be able to **learn voraciously**, simply to stay abreast of the software and hardware changes that continue to revolutionize the field with each new product update. Just as a carpenter who goes to work on a house will show up at the job site with more than one tool in his tool box, the 3D animator will have a variety of tools at their disposal. What's more, the 3D animator has to be willing to drop their favorite tool the moment another one is released that promises an advance in speed or ease of use. In 3D animation, where time *really* is money, any new piece of software or hardware that promises to speed the production process will get a long, hard look from the early adopters. As PCs begin to reach toward truly high-end applications, last year's workstation may become this year's white elephant.

This means the 3D animator must be willing to spend significant amounts of time and money researching the latest software and hardware

*In some interactive products, such as a CD-ROM title, it is often possible to include an animated sequence within the credit screen. Any animator who wishes to do this should include a provision for it in their **work agreement** ▶ 95.*

releases. Additionally, the 3D animator must be willing to make a significant investment in training on the target platform and software.

How to Hire

Ask to view a 3D animator's **demo reel** ▶ 83 of the projects they have worked on, or to see samples of their work. If you need third-party recommendations of 3D animators, check with the animation software companies themselves. They will often be the best source of recommendations, since they will know intimately who the best practitioners of their software are. Some of the top animators also serve as beta testers for their favorite vendors, working for weeks at a time wringing out the bugs of the newest release. But be prepared to pay dearly for their services.

How to Be Hired

Because these skills are so specialized, and consequently so expensive, the production companies

How to Get Started

As 3D software becomes more powerful and easy to use, the work is becoming increasingly sophisticated. The countless animated toasters, dancing gas pumps, and flying Listerine bottles that populate television commercials can attest to that. Unfortunately, with the "out-the-door" price for a fully equipped Silicon Graphics machine loaded with Alias, SoftImage, or Renderman software approaching the low six figures, potential 3D animators face a tough choice. Either take out a large bank loan, apprentice with someone who can provide time on the machine, or wait for the day when new computer chips can provide the processing horsepower required to create these compelling animations at an affordable price.

Meanwhile, large, well-funded corporate graphics studios, design and engineering divisions of Fortune 500 companies, and the computer graphics departments of colleges and universities remain the places where a young animator can learn the skills on these high-end machines.

Some of the more popular animation software companies offer their own, in-house training programs. There may be no better way of getting up to speed on these types of complex software programs than enrolling in an intensive, hands-on training session. You will be able to learn from the masters, and the advice you will get will come straight from those who help develop the software.

that can afford them tend to be working on big budget productions such as commercials, television shows, films, and well-funded multimedia games or special interest titles. Finding work will combine a certain amount of detective work, talent, and luck. First you have to find the companies that are currently using 3D animation in their work. Preferably the work they are doing should fall within your interest and skill level.

One of the best sources of production company names and addresses—and potentially, jobs—are the talent directories targeted to film companies and advertising agencies. Here you'll find a list of production companies broken out by area of expertise and by region, all of whom offer their services to the agencies they hope will hire them. It is a simple matter to flip these source books into your own job hunting resource of potential employers.

When it comes to job hunting, persistence pays off. You have got to get in the door to show your **portfolio** ▶ 82, and, unfortunately, the people you need to reach are usually too busy to look at every portfolio. Ask if there is a particular day of the week they have open to see new people and their work. You might try making your appointment very early, or very late in the day, before the crush of work is overwhelming, or after the last FedEx shipment is rushed out the door. This is one area where networking can pay huge dividends, since a personal introduction or recommendation will almost always open the door to an interview.

If you are just getting started you may have to work at a lower rate, to make it worth while for a production company to try an untested commodity. However, once you have a professional credit on your resume, it becomes easier to convince a potential employer you have the skills they are looking for.

Compensation

3D animators are compensated as well as almost anybody on the production team. The demand for good animators comes from film studios creating motion pictures, advertisers creating animated commercials, and multimedia devel-

Cody Harrington
3D Animator

"My love of expressive media tools has been an obsession since childhood," says Cody Harrington, recalling his first Brownie camera and drum set. Today he expresses himself with many different tools. In addition to his talents as an animator, he is a filmmaker, videographer, illustrator, photographer, and musician. *"Had the media culture been developed at the time, the film degree I received in 1978 from the University of Houston would've read 'MediaMaster of Arts.' Unfortunately the entertainment industrial-complex of the day forced multi-talented people into singular career paths. They wanted 'focused,' well-disciplined graduates, not scattered techno-junkies. Wired magazine would've been outlawed in Texas back then."*

But Cody never let himself be pigeonholed into doing just one thing. In 1979, he began as a freelance motion picture technician on feature films and television commercials, eventually working with director James Cameron on The Abyss *(as part of the underwater FX unit). This sparked his interest in 3D digital animation. Cody's next stop was Apple Computer, where he produced interactive multimedia prototypes and broadcast graphics. Since then he has mastered many tools for 2D and 3D animation, image compositing, and interactive scripting, and rekindled his musical talents with digital recording.*

Juggling is one of Cody's strongest talents; because he is constantly shifting not only projects but disciplines as well, he's learned to shift gears smoothly and rapidly. For example, there's the time he was creating animations for a CD-ROM project in San Francisco: "Every three days I'd set up a serious four-day 3D render, hop on a plane to LA to record with my band, and fly back to SF in time to comp the rendered animation into the project interface. At one time I had a 30-day render going in SF, while I was in LA working on other projects."

The key ability Cody identifies for artists is to be "close to your imagination. You can always become proficient with the tools, but if you don't know how to tap into your imagination, you won't have anything to work with." One way Cody manages this is by turning to his dreams for inspiration, "It's like a steady stream of consciousness, almost as if I never really go to sleep."

opers creating games or CD-ROMs. Hourly rates can vary from $50/hr to $100/hr for less sophisticated animations created on Macintosh computers and PCs using inexpensive 3D modeling or animation programs. Rates for complex animations requiring high-end computers and animation tools range between $100/hr to $200/hr.

As important as compensation is, **credit** ▶ 105 is equally as important. It is such a new field and with new tools offering new capabilities, you may create innovative techniques or develop a highly recognizable style. As a result, you want to receive prominent credit wherever possible.

Linda Jacobson
President and Co-founder, Virtual Reality Education Foundation, Inc. (VeRGe)

Linda Jacobson has always been an explorer. As a journalist, speaker, author, and consultant, she has focused on providing reports from the front lines of high technology, enriching the information with ideas about how we might get the most out of each generation of creation, from high-tech music to the forefront of virtual reality.

After earning a degree in journalism, Linda went into technical writing. She moved to San Francisco from New York and started working with dozens of publications, including Computer Life, Verbum, Keyboard, A.I. Expert, New Media, MacWEEK, *and* Whole Earth Review. *She also lent a hand in the original launches of* Wired *and* Computer Life *magazines.*

Her interests in virtual reality grew with the seeds of the field itself. She has served as Virtual Worlds Editor for Wired, *helped document ubiquitous computing inventions at Xerox PARC, and written the seminal field reference for PC-based VR:* Garage Virtual Reality, *published by SAMS.* Garage VR *begins with a look at the tradition of boot-strap innovation, from Samuel Morse and Thomas Edison through Tom Zimmerman and Jaron Lanier, pioneers of virtual reality. Her first book,* Cyberarts: Exploring Art and Technology, *profiled the use of digital technologies in creating art of all kinds.*

Linda believes that virtual reality and multimedia are two sides of the same coin—both powerful tools across infinite numbers of applications and fields. "Virtual reality is essentially a human-computer interface, and as such it's employed as a problem-solving tool in various professions—engineering, manufacturing, medicine, therapy. It needs to be used more in education, in schools." As a part of the philosophy of bringing the two fields together, she performs as the voice of a cartoon character with the multimedia musical ensemble D'Cückoo, showcasing VR technology, multimedia performance art, and world music.

Linda feels that one key to virtual reality lies in its strength as a medium for communications and building art—"When VR tools get into the hands of people who understand the ways and means that humans communicate and create art, then we'll see VR start reaching its potential as a medium whereby people can experience things and co-create with each other." This is another reason that she believes that VR and multimedia developers would do well to join forces. As she notes, "I see virtual reality and multimedia as symbiotic, because a virtual world is built from multimedia data. Multimedia developers and virtual world builders have much to offer each other, and through collaborations would have much to offer everyone else." The key never lies in the tools or the media—it's the explorer who uses them.

Sound Producer

What They Do

Sound producers are a critical part of almost every multimedia team producing for CD-ROMs or other delivery formats that can deliver sound in real time. They are especially prominent in the **game industry** ▶ 58. Recognition of the need for high-quality sound has greatly increased in publishing and development, as well as in the marketplace. More and more experienced sound professionals are being hired to add scores and sounds to new products as well as to older ones being released on new platforms.

A sound producer is part manager, part creative artist, and part programmer. Their responsibilities often include designing and producing all sounds within a product, including musical scores, vocals, voice-overs, sound effects, and ambient and/or navigational sounds. Each type has its own particular process as well as its own production and technical concerns. For example, creating a musical score might mean writing music, possibly composing lyrics, recording musicians and vocalists, and then digitizing, editing, and integrating the sound into the product. Creating sound effects might mean sampling them from a library of stock effects or venturing out into the world with a DAT recorder and a resourceful imagination.

A sound producer is often hired and managed by the **art director**, though they may work closely with the **producer** on budgeting and scheduling issues. Sound producers often find, hire, and direct composers, musicians, and voice talent. They may also use a sound engineer during recording sessions in order to let them concentrate on directing musicians and voice professionals. They make use of a sound editor to edit, compress, and integrate the sound components. In other instances, sound producers may perform the roles of composer and sound editor themselves. Performing multiple roles may be a reflection of a sound producer having multiple talents or a reflection of a limited budget.

Sound producers are commonly brought in once the concept has been clearly defined and after

storyboards have been created. They will often stick with a project throughout testing to help make performance refinements. Their peak work period, however, is often soon after they are brought on board. 12- to 18-hour days, 6 to 7 days a week are not unusual for many sound producers.

For products that are heavily animated, sound producers are often especially busy. Many of these animations such as the introductory sequence and the closing sequence (or sequences) often need sounds created before the animators can create their final renderings. Animated characters with dialogue or sequences synchronized to music are examples of other areas where sounds must be furnished before animations can be created. Less dependent work such as transitions, action sequences, ambient music, and sound effects can be created and integrated later in the production stage, but the number and length of these pieces usually makes this integration difficult.

In a few cases, work may begin before the concept is refined for the expressed purpose of testing new technologies and approaches. Just as a technical lead or animator might test ideas as they are being conceived, a sound producer will often do the same, making sure that music seek times will be reasonable or that a certain style or level of fidelity is possible.

Process

Most sound producers work under the direction of an art director, creating sounds that correspond to the art director's view of the title. The first step is to get a clear idea of the **scope of the work** required. This is reflected in a sound production list which includes the types of sound, the quantities of each and their style, the length, and the technical requirements. Getting to this level of detail requires review of scripts and storyboards and talking to animators and programmers. It also may mean testing to see what is technically possible given space and performance constraints.

The growing number of games and CD-ROM products and their increasingly sophisticated aural interfaces offer opportunities for sound producers. Also, increasing bandwidths for online services are creating opportunities for online audio landscapes. For example, communal places where people go to interact with each other may have visual and aural cues that indicate the level of activity, much like the sounds from a party, restaurant, or nightclub indicates their levels and types of activities.

My goal is never to have anybody waiting on me. There may be periods of 20-hour days followed by slack periods where I'll get another job while the animators are catching up.

—Dezsö Molnár, Composer, Musician, and Sound Producer

On fixed-price work, where the sound components are not defined, a sound producer may want to split the bid into two components—one for defining the work and one for producing the work once the scope is known.

The sound producer next works with the art director and producer to **schedule** the production. Many of the sound components will be needed by other team members before they can do their work. These should be produced first, followed by those without critical dependencies.

Musical Scores

A **score** is a main musical piece. It may have variations, but the main theme will always represent a product, passage, mood, or event. Sound producers may or may not compose the score for a product themselves. Many do, but they will often hire composers whose style matches that of the product. The composer may be someone that has been contracted in advance, such as a well-known recording artist, or someone that joins the team later. In this case, the sound producer directs the composer and helps manage the production.

Many movies and television programs already license popular music because it is recognizable, and it is often cheaper than creating original scores, since it already exists. This trend is likely to grow in multimedia over the next several years, though for now it is often easier and less expensive in multimedia to create original scores.

How much music is needed for interactive products can be difficult to determine. The amount of **game play ▶ 22, 178** for some games might total over 20 hours. The viewing time for an interactive coffee table book might be upwards of six hours. Producing and delivering that amount of music is not economically possible. For this reason, and because it is difficult to synchronize interactive events, most musical scores in new media products are looped to replay continuously.

A sound producer works with the composer to design and compose manageable pieces. The sound producer might also have to help a composer come to terms with the non-linear structures of many projects. The components in most traditional scores can be arranged chronologi-cally as they might appear in a finished piece, but game or interactive story structures require more modular and sophisticated arrangements. Some engineers are developing interactive music engines to create quality scores on the fly that map appropriately to action and interaction.

Sound Effects

Sound effects are short sounds that help build a realistic understanding of particular actions. These actions might be events occurring in a game or events taking place in the interface after being initiated by users. (The latter are usually termed interface sounds.) Sound effects are different from the other sounds found in multimedia projects because of their small duration and their specific connection to events. As a result, many sound engineers specialize in sound effects.

As with the composer, a sound producer directs the sound effects engineer, and together, they finalize the production list, technical requirements, budget, and schedule. The sheer number of effects needed for some projects and the wide range in costs of acquisition—licensed from a sound stock library versus original recordings—can put budgets and milestones at risk if they are not carefully managed.

Voice-overs and Vocals

A sound producer finds and directs voice talent when creating **voice-overs**. They start from scripts created by scriptwriters and then choose vocal artists based on the narration needs. In some cases, voice artists are hired at the beginning of a project, if they are celebrities. In other cases, the sound producer locates the voice artists as needed. Experienced sound producers recommend using professionals instead of succumbing to the temptation to use "friends." Voice is the trickiest aspect of a sound track to get right and a professional will save time, money, and frustration in the end.

When a voice artist is in a distant location, especially in the case of a celebrity, sound producers often rent a studio "on location," sometimes with a sound engineer in tow to make things run more smoothly. Most large cities have sound studios, and they are easy to find by looking in various audio and video directories, source books, and phone directories. Sometimes a high quality DAT

There are a couple of reasons that I work with many composers. There are a lot of cool projects out there that I think I'm not the right composer for, but I still enjoy finding the right composer and pointing them in the right direction. Because I'm a musician myself and a bit of a technogeek, I feel that there are musicians out there who know me and trust me to adapt their work sensitively.

—Thomas Dolby,
Composer, Musician,
and Sound Producer

The great thing about games, like movies, is that you have a fairly captive audience and they're generally going to center themselves on the screen and between the speakers for the duration. When you have them in that position, you can do all kinds of stuff. You can move things with CueSound, you can use Dolby surround technology, you can use THX, as well as positioning characters and events offscreen. It can help to think of things in a cinematic fashion.

—Spencer Nilsen,
Director/Executive
Producer,
Sega Music Group

223

recorder, a good microphone, a quiet room, and good sound editing software can replace the need for a sound studio.

One of the more challenging tasks in directing voice-over talent for interactive projects is in getting sequences that are appropriate to the structure of the product. This means first understanding the structure and then being able to direct the voice artists in adapting their intonation and delivery to support that structure. Many times, the sound producer will sit down beforehand with the talent and explain the product. It is also important to keep everybody in character. A sound producer cannot expect voice artists to know their roles.

Transitions

Transitional sounds are important for covering the change from one scene or place to another. Sound transitions can help blend the sounds in one space with the sounds in another. They can also help blend to places that are visually distinct even when neither has any sound associated with it. But performance limitations in multimedia, such as seek and retrieval times for CD-ROMs and download times for online services create severe design constraints to producing fluid experiences. As a consequence, transitions are usually small, easily accessible, and take little processing power to play. Cartridge games, for example, often use FM synthesis in an internal chip in the game machine for these sounds, using several tones that modulate with each other to create different sounds.

Editing, Compression, and Integration

Once the individual components are created, a sound producer oversees final editing of the pieces and the compression process. Most sound editing is performed on sound editing tools on the computer. In some cases, the editing may include cleaning up the sounds or changing levels to improve the balance. In other cases, the editing may intentionally distort the sounds to produce a desired effect.

The compression process can be straightforward, as in many slower-paced CD-ROMs, or it can be technically challenging as in the case of many cartridge games or fast action CD-ROM games. The difficulty will depend on the sound specifications of the project. The sound can be created as

Red Book audio, which is CD quality audio, or it can be of a lesser quality. Sampling rates can be 44K, 22K, 11K or less, and sample size can be 8 or 16 bits. When the sound is reduced either in sampling rate or sample size, any imperfections will be amplified. As a result, recordings have to be clean, otherwise you will end up with lots of hiss and other unwanted noise.

Tools and Techniques

The tools a sound producer uses include sound design and processing tools as well as management tools. These sound production tools are described in detail in the **sound engineer and editor** ▶ 237 role and the management tools are described in the **producer** ▶ 125 role.

The most important technique is to get a clear idea of the **style** of the music the art director wants. Experienced sound producers will have the art director describe the sounds in descriptive words: "Is this dark and gloomy or is it happy? Should it sound like the 1920s, the 1950s or somewhere in the future?" They will ask for references to movies, bands, or vocalists. They will play records and sing songs—all in an effort to keep from spending time going in the wrong direction. Sound producers must also understand the art director's experience of sound production. Some art directors can hear rough takes and use them to visualize the final sound. Others will not, and might need more finished work to make decisions.

It is also important for a sound producer to be **organized**. A sound producer should know the number, length, style, and technical format of all the music and sounds before composing, recording, or sampling begins. They should also record or sample the pieces as near to the right length as possible to reduce editing time. Being organized for recording sessions is also critical unless time and money are not issues. The cost of the studio plus the cost of musicians, voice talent, and engineers means a sound producer has to direct the set-up, the recording, and the take efficiently to limit the number of people standing around doing nothing. Good sound producers use people's time effectively and keep distractions to a minimum.

When directing experienced voice-over talent, one sound producer suggests letting them take

*The film business uses the term **foley artists** to describe sound effects specialists.*

In the Sonic CD, it's back-to-back Red Book audio. There is very little seek time. We were able to keep the pieces of music short enough that the laser would do mirror or laser-only seeks as opposed to carriage seeks. We could keep the transition time musically down to well under a second and under half a second in most cases— maybe ten frames— and then off you went on a new Red Book track.

—Spencer Nilsen, Director/Executive Producer, Sega Music Group

the first cut. They may have a deeper insight on what they can bring to the recording and may not need, nor appreciate, heavy-handed direction. If the approach isn't right, the sound producer can then step in to coach. In some cases, producers can make use of words and segments and paste them together as opposed to waiting for a perfect, complete take.

Qualifications

Most professional multimedia sound producers are **musically trained**. Although they may not have a formal music education background, they do have a well developed sense of music and a vast knowledge of styles and their emotional connotations. They should play instruments or be able to convey precise instructions to instrumentalists in familiar, understandable terms.

Knowledge is not enough, however. A sound producer has to be able to **communicate well**. They will need to draw information out of people as in the case of an art director and the type of style envisioned. They will also need to direct other composers, musicians, vocalists, and voice talent. A good sound producer asks a lot of questions in the first case and is a demanding but instructive coach in the second case.

A sound producer should **understand how interactive products work** and where the connecting points are. In a linear product, one segment will flow into another and so on. In a non-linear product, one segment could conceivably flow into any number of segments. Although separate transitions can be used to cover each distinct break, the one-to-many as opposed to one-to-one structure can pose creative and technical challenges. Knowing what these challenges are is important to doing quality work.

Related to a rich knowledge of musical styles and talent is an **adaptive** and **inventive** mindframe. Because of the tight schedules and the large number of musical scores and sounds often found in game and narrative titles, sound producers and special effects people must be able to improvise. Also, the amount of sound needed and the short period of time available to create it often means that a sound producer must be able to produce needed materials quickly.

Dezsö Molnár
Composer, Musician, and Sound Producer

When people say that Dezsö Molnár is a rocket scientist, they not just saying he's smart. He really is a rocket scientist. Dezsö began his career in aeronautics by volunteering as an 18-year-old for a private rocket startup called Truax Engineering. Their mission: to design a new space shuttle to replace the old, outmoded, and dangerous design following the Challenger disaster. By the time Dezsö was 23, Truax was getting funding from the Navy. With military money coming in, he says, "Things got increasingly secretive. When they threatened to move the company to San Diego, I said, 'You know what? I really want to be a rock musician.' So I walked. I had my mid-life crisis at age 23."

He started a rock band and has been actively pursuing that for several years. Last year, he took on the job of creating the soundtrack for the Sega game Zero Tolerance *by Accolade, which has already "gone gold." Since then, Dezsö has been able to follow his passion for creating music and high tech engineering design almost exclusively. The other multimedia soundtracks he has helped compose and produce include the games* Cover Up *for ASCII Entertainment Software,* Thumbelina, *and the* Emperor's New Clothes *developed by Technopop for Trimark Interactive.*

The erstwhile rocket scientist can also be found on the road with a $5 million virtual reality project complete with a semi-tractor trailer, an inflatable 60-person theater, and a couple of Lawnmower Man-*style spinning gyroscope machines which visitors can strap themselves into. The exhibit, which Dezsö did preliminary engineering work on, had been traveling around the country for some time when he received an unexpected call. "It was 6:30 in the morning and they said, 'Catch the next plane to New Orleans.'" So far, Dezsö says, "we've done shows in New Orleans, filmed a commercial for MCI starring Calvin DeForrest (that's Larry Bud Melman to you Letterman fans), and now we're in Charleston, South Carolina, where the rig was built for some tune-ups."*

When he's not creating multimedia soundtracks or working on virtual reality equipment, Dezsö returns to his first love. As one of the Survival Research Laboratories' engineers, he gets to tinker with rocket powered cars and will produce the soundtrack for SRL's most recent videotape, entitled Calculated Countdown to Imminent Doom.

Thomas Dolby
Sound Producer

"If I was 16 now, and a real rebel," Thomas Dolby says, *"I don't think I would buy an electric guitar or a drum kit. I would buy a handicam and a desktop editing system."* More than a decade ago, Thomas Dolby's loopy surrealism in She Blinded Me With Science *set a new level of expectation for what a music video could be. Now that rebellion has become an institutionalized part of the rock and roll in-*dustry, Thomas is looking for new territories in which to make his iconoclastic mark.

In the early '90s this trend setting artist and producer moved into multimedia, creating his own interactive company, Headspace, which has created the film score for three IWERKS amusement rides, scored the interactive CD-ROM game Double Switch for Sega, and installed a virtual performance of Mozart's Quartet No. 21 in D Major in New York City's Guggenheim Museum SoHo annex. There, listeners can become participants by donning a VR head mounted display, which allows them to interact with the musicians and even trigger events.

His most recent work, sponsored by Interval Research, is the design and construction of an easy to use, computer-based music making software program. Announced at a press conference in the UK attended by such visionary synthesists of music and technology as Peter Gabriel and Brian Eno, the software allows a user to sit down at the computer, grab the mouse and begin making music with each and every mouse movement. "This is an exciting time for me," Thomas says. "My role has always been to try to take the bull by the horns and try to do something really radical with the new technology, to try and rethink things."

---

vivid: How is music changing in new media products?

What they've done traditionally is that somebody's brother-in-law has an eight-track recording studio, and so he sends them over some MIDI music on a DAT, and their engineers kind of shoot that into the game. Some of the larger houses have two or three of their own music people, but it would be quite a big step for them to actually go to a Hollywood composer and get a traditional film score from them.

There are other problems. Say you're a game developer and you ask John Williams if he'll score a game for you and he agrees. He says, "Well, how much music is involved?" And you say, "Well, it's a branching storyline, but we'd like you to take care of all the different branches." He says, "If I laid them end-to-end, how much music would it be?" They do some sampling and say, "Five and three-quarter hours." Now, even if John Williams had the time and the budget to write and record five and three-quarter hours of music to cope with all of the different permutations of the game, you wouldn't have the RAM to store it within the game, even with compression. So that's obviously not going to work.

What they tend to do, then, is work with cheesy sets and have fairly awkward transition sequences. If you graduate from scene one to scene two, there's a little hiccup, and then suddenly, your music is in a new key. It's very irritating and people end up turning it off.

But there's a more fundamental problem with scoring. In a linear experience like a movie, the filmmaker has already set a kind of a contour and a dynamic to the

Thomas Dolby, *continued*

emotional and the dramatic tension and release of the piece. As a composer, I try to match that, enhance it, and underpin it with the moods of the music. But the whole essence of interactive entertainment is that now the audience is making up the movie as it goes along. In that kind of a situation, how can I, as a composer, possibly enhance their experience? I don't know what their experience is going to be but I do know that the experience of a 14-year-old arcade game fan is going to be different from that of your great aunt. He might go around karate-chopping things. She might just browse. There's no way that the same piece of music is going to be appropriate for both moods.

vivid: So how do you account for that then? Do you plot out all the possible scenarios?

I've been taking various approaches to this problem for different projects, and it's starting to become refined into a software program called AVRe (pronounced "aviary"). It stands for Audio Virtual Reality Engine, and I've been building it over the last year, getting input from the different composers I work with so that it becomes a more malleable tool.

You know how in *Peter and the Wolf* every character has its own instrument and melody? Well that's a technique that film composers have always used. There's a love theme, a theme for the bad guy, and so on. In some instances—let's say that when the bad guy is sneaking up on your lovers—the composer may try to interweave the bad guy theme with the love theme. What AVRe does in an object-oriented fashion is assign instruments, sounds, melodies, code sequences, and rhythms to every space, object, and character within a game, and then interlock them in a musically pleasing manner. It's built so that you avoid any conflicts musically.

vivid: Musically, meaning mathematically? Are there rules that you can set in this instance?

Music is mathematical but it's also intuition. It is possible to set rules and constraints. Every action within a game can modulate how those sounds and pieces of music interact in a way that is appropriate for what's going on.

In other words, this is a program that knows who you are, where you've been, what you're doing, how you're playing the game, how much danger you're in, and how close you are to achieving your goals. All the information that's important to the game designer has a direct impact on the score that is generated, and as a consequence, I feel that it is possible to enhance different peoples' experiences—or the same player's experience on subsequent days—by creating a score that is appropriate from within the actions of the game.

The neat thing about this is that it's a very economical way to work because instead of dealing with huge chunks of audio to cover all of your permutations, the chunks of audio are actually very, very small—but they're triggered in different ways by what happens within the game. So that's AVRe.

vivid: Do you employ the same approaches to designing music for a space in which a variety of interactions take place simultaneously?

In music, context is everything. If I play you Brahm's *Lullaby* on a musical box, you'll think, "Oh, what a beautiful baby," but if I bring in an ominous drone on the basses in the wrong key, you're going to think this baby grew up to be an ax murderer. That's purely a question of context. Brahm's *Lullaby* hasn't changed, it's just been thrown in a different light. So by juxtaposing different musical elements, I can change the context.

It certainly helps if they [sound producers] can deal with [technical] things on their own without having to depend on each other's technical expertise, but it's not a prerequisite.

—Thomas Dolby,
Composer, Musician,
and Sound Producer

Technical expertise may or may not be a requirement, depending on the platform and type of project. Some projects such as game cartridges have enormous technical constraints. Knowing how sound is reproduced—even down to the chip level—is often a must in these situations. In other cases, such as a CD-ROM, the programming team is likely to be able to handle many of the technical issues or bottlenecks. Most sound producers in multimedia, though, do tend to have a lot of experience (some say too much) with computers and digital sound technologies. This knowledge helps them combine roles and accomplish tasks without involving any of people on the programming team.

How to Hire

Finding people interested in producing audio on a project is not difficult. Selecting one that is qualified, though, is. Many people in multimedia—programmers especially—have a background or big interest in music. This affinity for music, however, does not necessarily make them good sound producers or musicians. It takes knowledge of **different styles**, of the **tools and techniques**, and of the **process for creating and integrating sounds** into an interactive product to produce well.

At the moment, there are few training resources for sound producers or directories listing them. A producer typically has to call other producers, look at **credits** on shipping products, and have knowledge of the sound producers in an area and in an industry. One of the first steps is to decide whether the sound producer needs to be a permanent hire or can be a freelancer. Both models are found with interactive media, though much of the work is performed by freelancers. Also, knowing the type of project or projects will help determine if a sound producer needs to be able to produce a number of different styles or if a particular style will suffice.

Along with knowing the hiring structure, it's also important to know the **budget** and the **timeframe** and have a reasonable idea that these are not going to change. Because of their hectic and compressed work schedules, it is difficult for sound producers to juggle two projects at a time.

As a result, this makes fitting into a sound producer's schedule almost as difficult as finding them.

Hiring sound producers with several titles in their portfolio is one of the best safeguards. It's not necessary for the prior sounds to be similar to what is needed, however. In fact, a portfolio showing a wide variety of styles might be preferable over one that shows a lot of similarity. Not having a sound production credit for a multimedia project should not disqualify a candidate, but it does mean they should be able to demonstrate an extensive knowledge of the different aspects of the job. It also means that a prospective producer should be willing to complete the job at all costs.

How to Be Hired

The art director and the producer are the people most likely to make the hiring decision. Most of the effort in getting a job should be directed at getting in front of these two people. Rather than sending an unsolicited **demo tape** ▶ 83, it is important to qualify the project itself, to see if they have a need for sound producers and what their urgency is. Demonstrable work, either in a CD-ROM product or on a demo tape or audio CD, is a must. Try to arrange a face-to-face meeting so that you can explain the pieces and put them into perspective in terms of the product and the technology. The soundtrack for a cartridge game, for example, is going to sound much different than the soundtrack for a CD-ROM. Sending a demo tape without covering the specific constraints could quickly put you out of consideration.

Beyond the portfolio, a sound producer should be able to **speak eloquently** on the process of creating sounds for interactive multimedia projects. The art director and producer will be looking for someone that can "own" the sound, or in other words, someone that will take full responsibility for all aspects of sound in the product. They will want someone who can find and hire the appropriate artists and manage all the hardware and software needs for the music end. They will also be looking for someone that they can work with and that can work with others on the team, especially the animators and programmers.

Spencer Nilsen
Director/Executive Producer, Sega Music Group

From a life-long love affair with music, Spencer Nilsen's career diverged, briefly, to a teen-age infatuation with motorcycles. After falling one too many times, Spencer picked himself up and sat himself down at the piano keyboard. The decision to swap one kind of Yamaha for another led Spencer to a solo piano recital at Carnegie Hall, work as a concert promoter with the likes of U2, The Police, the Who and others, and, since 1993, to Sega Games of America, where he is senior music director.

Spencer's foray into the world of digital gaming music came about fortuitously. "Sega called out of the blue and asked if I was interested in meeting with them." His role as a music designer begins with the fleshed out storyboard or a video which depicts movement or characters. Meeting with a producer, he runs through a "spotting session" highlighting key moments and defining mood and emotion. If this sounds like a traditional Hollywood approach to scoring films, there's a reason for that. Says Spencer, "I'm trying to bring the film approach into gaming and game music because I really feel it will enhance the whole experience."

Depending on the type of game produced, Spencer's objective will be to either populate the game with interesting sonic effects, called "stings" in industry parlance, as in Joe Montana Football, *where bursts of music or sound effects such as crowd cheers highlight part of the game. The other end of the musical spectrum can be heard in* Echo the Dolphin, *where Spencer's role was to compose music that forms an integral part of the gaming experience. Here traditional themes and musical motifs are created in order to submerse the player in the world of the game.*

"I got into this industry, quite frankly, because I saw an opportunity to have no boundaries," he says. In the last year, Spencer, an admitted workaholic, has completed six scores for Sega, a total of more than 500 minutes of his original music. Project credits include the Batman Returns *CD,* Echo the Dolphin *CD,* Sonic the Hedgehog *CD,* Jurassic Park *CD, and* Joe Montana Football *CD.*

When Spencer looks over the horizon, he sees an industry in transition, fracturing into specific professional disciplines much like the film industry, with its guild-like structure of specialists. His advice to people getting into the field is to first and foremost "concentrate on the music." Then, "if gaming is what you love, hang out and get to know everything there is about it. You will then eventually end up there. You know, it's a progression."

Compensation

Sound producers can be paid through salaries, hourly rates, and fixed-price work. Salaries for experienced sound producers might start at $50,000 and increase up to $80,000. Hourly rates can be $40/hr to $100/hr. As important as the compensation is, **copyright ownership ▶ 102** can be equally as important. In many cases, it will be difficult to own the copyright to a work unless that work has been created previously and licensed to the company using it. There is often a trade-off between getting a paycheck and maintaining the copyright ownership. There are cases where a sound producer or composer receives royalties, but these are rare, and even then the range is a fraction of a percent to one percent.

Owning the derivative rights, or receiving royalties on derivative works, is increasingly becoming more of an issue in multimedia sound production, especially as multimedia soundtracks find their way into audio CD channels. Sound producers should try to include language in their work agreements that takes derivative rights into account.

Voice Artist/Vocalist

It's like radio because what you're doing is visualizing your character and bringing them to life. I tell my students that you can't just focus on your voice, you have to focus on your character. You have to make your character come alive.

—Lucille Bliss, Voice-over Artist

What They Do

A voice-over is an offscreen oral delivery of scripted material. Voice-overs are used for many project types, especially those that address the audience or user personally. They are used for narration in special interest titles, dialogue in children's storybooks, games, and instructions for training pieces and help systems. Many CD-ROM titles—especially those influenced by the film and TV industry—make extensive use of voice-overs to help achieve the appropriate dramatic effect.

A **voice artist** can be valued for having a non-characteristic voice or a signature voice. A **non-characteristic voice** is one that does not stick out. Though pleasant and appealing, it is intentionally not memorable. A **signature voice** is one that is distinctive and memorable—the audience associates it almost immediately with the product or situation where they heard it.

There is a wide variety in the type of work that voice artists do, mainly because interactive media projects are combining aspects from animated cartoons and films, documentaries, television commercials, instructional videos, theater, and many others. In addition, the increasing practice of including multiple languages in products and simultaneously releasing products around the world means there will be more need for voice artists capable of speaking foreign languages during the initial production of a product.

While there is great need for voice artists, the job picture isn't well defined. Artists range from **unionized professionals** ▶ 52 with experience in radio, TV, and film, to **aspiring actors and vocalists** looking to break into this growing industry at an early stage. To compound this, the companies creating products range from those familiar with professional TV and film production styles who are paying union rates and using union talent, to companies unaccustomed to hiring voice professionals and therefore unfamiliar with the conventions and compensation practices.

The need is not as great for singers as for general voice artists, but there is some work in multimedia. Only a fraction of voice artists can sing well, which can present a problem for sound producers who need vocalists.

Sound producers find, hire, and direct voice-over talent and vocalists. They may look for a single voice for a large amount of work, or a number of voices for shorter parts. Voice artists and vocalists typically work for several hours or a single day, although in some rare instances the work might span several days. If the scripts are rewritten, the client changes their mind, or the sound producer is not skilled enough, a voice artist may be called back into the studio to re-record sections.

Process

The voice recording process commonly involves getting a script, arriving at a studio or other recording location, meeting with the sound producer to understand the part, and then performing several takes. The process is really no different than traditional sound recording. Though the script may be difficult to follow because of its non-linear structure, the speaking parts will still be in discrete segments. The sound producer can help describe how to understand where each piece connects to the others. This direction can be helpful for understanding the inflections to impart in the material.

Tools and Techniques

Most sound recordings are completed in a professional studio with sound-proofing and high-quality recording equipment. This equipment usually includes **digital audio tape (DAT)** recorders and professional **microphones**. Several sound producers use portable DAT recorders to record small voice parts outside of the studio.

The techniques voice artists use in interactive platforms are the same ones found in traditional voice work. Different styles, such as character voices, may be required to imitate celebrities or narrate commercials. A voice professional also has to be able to make subtle changes in inflection at the word level.

Lucille Bliss
Voice-over Artist

Lucille Bliss has lived a thousand lives, each of them with a different voice. A renowned voice-over artist, she has put words in the mouth of many characters in radio, television, film, and more recently, interactive CD-ROMs.

Her most recent interactive works include The Learning Company's Reader Rabbit's Ready for Letter, *Computer Curriculum Corporation's* Don't Throw It Away—Recycle, *children's stories* The Mouse *and* The Tortoise and the Hare, *and a promotional for the game* Speed Racer.

Creating works that entertain and educate younger audiences is nothing new to Lucille: she did a series of audio cassettes that taught children speech skills, and provided the voice of Smurfette in the animated TV series The Smurfs *and Bamm-Bamm in* The Flintstones.

What was different for Lucille was getting used to the stop-and-go style that interactive titles demand. "Everything in radio was done live," she recalls, "and for audio tapes I'd stop only when something needed to be edited." With CD-ROMs, however, "you can't read straight through. You have to stop and repeat words, especially for young children, and allow

pauses for them to respond," as well as read multiple scripts for products with many user options. She adds that for CD-ROMs she has to stick to the script exactly because often there's a book that accompanies the disc: "Your delivery must be exact, with no interjections, no changes. And you go a bit slower, especially for children."

To prepare for readings, she watches the graphics on screen to get a feel for her character. "Acting, of course, is very essential," says Lucille, who trained as a professional actress for radio. "You need an acting background to understand the character, to get that into your voice." She suggests that people interested in doing voice-overs keep a cassette recorder at home and talk along with television shows, such as cartoons. "You need to hear yourself," then play back the tape and "compare yourself to the pros."

Qualifications

Experience is one of the primary components sound producers look for in voice talent. Although a good voice is important, that quality alone does not satisfy the requirements needed for professional voice-overs. Sound producers do not want to train voice artists and vocalists. They want them to be able to take directions quickly and be comfortable in a studio environment. They also want them to be able to tap into emotions in the company of others. Ideally, artists should have some character in their personality as well as in their voice. In addition to these elements, voice talent should be easy to work with and highly versatile.

How to Hire

Always look for **professional voice artists** and vocalists and always pay for the work. Using friends or people on the production team is no longer the option it might have been in the early days of multimedia. Non-union productions certainly have more flexibility in rates and forms of

payment than union productions, and many producers recommend paying by the job as opposed to the hour. Voice professionals that agree to this structure, however, should get a clear definition of the work making sure there are limits that protect themselves.

Listening to **demo tapes** received from individuals, agents, and sound studios can be a good way of finding voice professionals for some jobs, but finding talent for more dramatic characters may take some time. A sound producer may want to contact voice trainers and actors who have experience with people or situations that might meet the needs of the project.

Sound producers need to choose voices suitable for the majority of the audience, however the final decision is a highly subjective one.

Finding voice artists capable of speaking or singing in foreign languages poses some unique problems. It pays to work with someone that is familiar not only with the language but the

A fair amount of voice-over people are familiar with multimedia and if not, they're catching on very quickly. Sometimes I use demo tapes but usually not. I like to hear someone's voice and put them where I want to put them. For example, say I need a toad. Most voice-over tapes don't have toads on them, so what I'll do is go to a voice teacher and ask them if one of their students would make a really good toad. Usually, they'll just light up and say, "Oh, I know exactly the one you want. Talk to so-and-so." That's it. I'm done. I've got a toad.

—Dezsö Molnár, Composer, Musician, and Sound Producer

Bill Rollinson
Producer of *Four Footed Friends*

vivid: Where in the process did you start thinking about making Four Footed Friends *international?*

I was influenced mainly by my work at Macromedia. One of the jobs I had while I was there was **localizing** the products in different languages for shipment around the world. We did Japanese versions, German versions, and French versions. Unfortunately I had to deal with it "after the fact," so when we were designing our product, we decided to build in that capability in right away. One thing that differentiates interactive media from other mediums is that you can have all these different languages in there.

vivid: Did you find that to be a real selling advantage?

It's definitely a selling advantage. It broadened our market and it got people's attention. If all of a sudden you're going along in English and you can switch it to Japanese or French or German on the fly, it catches people's attention. They see value in that.

vivid: Was that ability to switch an after-thought?

No. It was designed to switch up front and it evolved as we learned more. When we went into the studio, we recorded all the voice-over for all four languages. The sound files were converted to QuickTime movies that could just be substituted in and out in the product, depending on which language was chosen in the interface.

vivid: How did you decide what voices to use? Whether they were male/female, young/old?

It was hard. We tried to use a variety of different voices. With the first title, we chose to use an Australian narrator to give it more of an international feel, plus it was an older book so it kind of lent itself to the material. The woman who did it didn't have a very strong Australian accent. It sounded British to someone who wasn't trained. It's sold in Australia and they love it because no one had really done products for them.

It was okay in the British market, although you need to be careful because a lot of times when you're doing things internationally, you run into a lot of cultural things—especially with different French dialects—Canadian French versus Parisian French versus southern French. Which do you choose? It's very subjective. We tried to get a balance. We weren't trying to teach a specific dialect or a specific way to speak, we were just trying to expose kids to different cultures and different ways of saying the same thing.

vivid: How did you choose?

We tried to have variety within the product. You can never be right all the time. We just tried to give it the right balance.

culture as well. Where possible, hire talent that has grown up or had significant experience in the countries the products will be distributed in. Otherwise, while the grammar might be correct, the diction or accent may not be.

How to Be Hired

Demo tapes are critical, but almost every sound producer has a stack of them on their shelves or in a box. Therefore, a voice professional needs to make sure the tapes are delivered to the right people and under the right context. Having a conversation prior to sending them can be important. Sending unsolicited tapes without any previous notice is usually not successful. An interactive CD-ROM is an interesting approach, overcoming many of the problems with cassette tapes and their lack of random access. Few people, though, have created these and many of the people in the hiring process (such as agents) may not have ready access to CD-ROM-capable computers.

Since sound producers are often the decision-makers for voice talent, keep in touch with them, periodically calling or sending revised list of credits. Personal relationships are important. A sound producer wants to know that someone they work with is interested in the work and will not let them down.

Sometimes a sound producer may not be aware of the range of work that someone can do. The demo tape may not communicate this adequately. Voice artists should continually develop their range of work and actively promote these abilities. Flexibility in scheduling and in recording locations can be important for many sound producers. The sheer number and complexity of voices can make the work two to three times that of a feature film. Remember, with many interactive structures, characters can have more than one reaction at each instance. Unlike film, where standard lengths dictate and constrain the amount of voice-over in any one film, there are few parameters to go by in multimedia productions to determine how much is enough.

Compensation

Compensation ranges from hourly rates at union scale or less to five figure payments for celebrity voices. This range is so varied because there are many industries involved, including entertainment, advertising, and software, only some of which are familiar with using voice professionals. More and more publishers are using celebrities for games, children's products, and special interest titles and this trend is likely to continue. There have been several cases where actors from television programs and movies have received upwards of $80,000 for appearing in CD-ROMs. There have also been cases where non-union beginning artists have accepted nominal fees in order to participate in creating high profile productions.

Maya Daniels
Voice-over Artist

Maya Daniels first made the leap from written to spoken word nearly a decade ago, when she was an advertising copywriter and account executive at a radio station with no female disc jockeys—she voiced ads requesting a female announcer. She didn't do any other voice-overs for the next six years, until a producer she knew approached her. But even after that job, she still hadn't considered a professional career in voice, until she heard about a series of voice classes. So she quit her 9–5 job, and while taking the classes, realized how demanding the profession was—and how much she liked it. Maya made contacts and started working, and has been doing voice-overs seriously ever since.

In three years, she's provided voices for a variety of interactive projects, from business software to children's titles like Thumbelina *and* The Emperor's New Clothes.

Maya also worked on the Sega Genesis title Zero Tolerance, *which she laughingly describes as "a real shoot-em-up game. I'm the voice of calm amidst the storm." To prepare for her role (which included informing players about weapons status and other vital stats), she envisioned herself as the computer on Star Trek.*

Interactive projects are quite different from the commercials she used to do. For one thing, they are much longer, frequently having thousands of lines. Whereas laying down the voiceover for a commercial can be done in an hour or two, interactive projects can last several days. Many of these works are created in a non-linear fashion as well. Maya cautions that "you have to be an expert at cold reads, because often you're working frame-by-frame. You have to be able to create a character on the spot."

Also required are a great imagination and an innate sense of timing to get the script down. "You have to be fast, and able to take direction," says Maya.

Maya has little difficulty finding jobs; in fact, the jobs usually find her. Although agents are starting to cast for CD-ROM work, she advises other voice-over artists to go directly to the production companies. "I've never been on a cattle call for an interactive job," she says. She also recommends "The Reel Directory" as a good resource.

Composer/Musician/ Sound Effects Specialist

What They Do

Composers, **musicians**, and **sound effects specialists** write, design, create (or sample) music scores, background sounds, and sound effects for interactive projects. These sounds are commonly edited and processed by sound producers or editors and then integrated into interactive products by programmers.

The opportunities for creating sounds and music for multimedia products are growing rapidly because many producers and designers are recognizing the value that great sound brings to a project. Also, the technical constraints that often made sound sound like it came from an ice cream truck are quickly lifting so that fuller sound capabilities are possible.

Composers, musicians, and sound effects specialists are hired by sound producers. They enter a project, most commonly, after the storyboards have been created. Experienced composers and sound effects specialists are often given lots of leeway to create appropriate sounds. The reason producers hire sound professionals in the first place is because their style matches what the sound producer is looking for. At the same time, though, this leeway does not mean complete carte blanche to create any sound whatsoever. It

Having any kind of paying job where you're making music is kind of an anomaly. It's no different in multimedia.

—Brian Coburn, Composer, Musician, and Sound Effects Specialist, Sega

needs to fit what the art director or sound producer are looking for.

The list of sounds that are needed is developed from the script and the storyboards. At times, sounds may be needed prior to the start of production on a section. Sound work in multimedia often means lots of work under very tight deadlines. At other times, the sounds can be created at any time prior to the media integration that takes place near the end of production.

Process

The process for **sampling**, **recording**, and **creating** sounds for multimedia borrows significantly from the film approach to sound. Most projects will have a fairly captive players or viewers that center themselves in front of the speakers for the duration of the experience. The same opportunities to play around with the sound in film productions present themselves in multimedia projects. Sound can be modified, enhanced, and distorted to clarify recordings and create special effects such as reverberation to simulate sound coming from a large stadium.

Musical scores form a large percentage of the sounds needed in games and CD-ROM titles. These scores are used for introductory and closing sequences as well as playing or viewing sequences. The latter sequences are usually looped, meaning they are choreographed to play continuously, starting over immediately after reaching the end. The reason is because a user can be in a certain sequence indefinitely. In a special interest title on the history of the Russia, for example, a viewer could move forward or pause or move back or explore other areas at a pacing that is unpredictable and likely not repeatable. In an online world, one user might linger in a room and lurk while another "teleports" to another part of the world. Designing music that will support all these random experiences is difficult given the current technology.

Sound

*Sound is divided into music, noise, and sound. People think of it all as the same, yet there are very different messages from sound, from continuous feedback, from anticipatory feedback, and from discrete events as opposed to continuous events. Music is usually viewed as more of a continuous event. What Thomas Dolby has developed is much more indicative of this, primarily because things aren't linear anymore. They're **non-linear experiences** that need to be broken into and out of, gradually and without abrupt scene cuts. With video, you use the metaphor of a cut but that's not what sound does. Sound goes away and comes back. It doesn't cut off in an instant. It's ambient, it fades in and out. Sound is so incredibly powerful but it's just very difficult to do it right. We really don't know what we're doing and so we don't do it. Boinks and beeps—how profound.*

—Joy Mountford, Project Lead, Interval Research

A composer writes lyrics and composes the music. They may also direct the recording of the musicians and/or vocalists. (Sound producers may also do this.) A composer will often record **rough examples** of the music, all the while trying to avoid having to hire musicians for this step. The composer will show these roughs to the sound producer and/or art director to see if it is in the right direction. If not, more roughs will be created until the right approach is determined. Once the roughs are approved, the sound studio is scheduled, musicians are hired, and a recording session takes place. Different parts may be recorded separately and then blended in by the sound producer or engineer. There may be numerous takes and the sound producer and composer often need an instinctive feel for which pieces are good enough to use. This process of recording numerous takes is quickly fading as the tools allow for real-time compositing of discrete elements.

A sound effect is a specific sound that is a direct result of an action. This action can be controlled by the user, like opening a door, for example, or as a result of other objects such as a dinosaur or an alien entering the stage. The software industry has a history of using sound effects, also termed interface sounds, to refer to a sound that is cued to an interface control or action. More and more products including CD-ROMs and online places are using interface sounds to either reinforce an experience or to provide an audio cue to the initiation of an action by a user.

Sound effects can be obtained by composing and recording them originally or by getting them from stock sound effect libraries. There are a number of audio CDs and CD-ROMs that contain sounds ranging from gunfire to car engines to train whistles and many are royalty free. Sound effects people usually start with the sound libraries. Only if none of these sounds work will they then go out and create sounds on their own, recording them with a DAT recorder. The decision about where to get the sounds from is usually based on whatever is the timeliest, least expensive, and gets the artist what they need.

Tools and Techniques

The tools for a composer and musician are the same tools for creating music for any other situation. Many composers create music with **digital tools** but just as many create with **traditional instruments**. Sound effects specialists use a combination of sampled sounds from stock libraries and originally recorded sounds using DAT recorders and high-quality microphones.

Important techniques include getting a clear idea of the scope of the work. This includes the amount and length of sound elements, the technical specifications, and the styles or styles needed. Many sound professionals create rough cuts and refine those until the style is approved and then go into full production.

Qualifications

Although sound professionals do not need to understand technology beyond the digital tools to create or manipulate the sounds, they do need to understand the limitations and the types of formats. For example, at the cartridge level, there is a very limited sound palette. It allows only six to eight MIDI instruments at a time. Any musical composition needs to reflect that simplicity and so a composer needs to concentrate on the melody, the harmony, and the rhythm, and not overcompose.

Composers and musicians should be able to take direction from others. The sound producer or the art director will have a better picture of how the sound will work within a project and may need to direct the compositions towards the right emotions. One sound producer says that any composer or musician that claims they are an artist loses points with him quickly. On the other hand, composers and musicians should be bold enough to take chances and go outside normal boundaries.

Two of the primary qualifications for a sound effects professional are to be adaptive and inventive. They should be adept at identifying, creating, and manipulating sounds in either the real world or in sound editing tools. The scope of the work usually means they have to be organized and able to handle multiple tasks at once. They also need to be fast.

I'm responsible for the sound effects if I'm producing the overall soundtrack of the game. That doesn't mean that I necessarily produce all the sound effects with my own hands. I do as much of that as I can. If it's an integral part of the score, a lot of times we'll integrate certain effects into the score itself. In that case, it's under my wing, but we have a number of people here at Sega, and within the industry, who have a lot better knowledge of that than I do. There are sampling wizards who can have something sampled and tweaked in a matter of minutes. It's great because that combination of a producer with a musical background and someone with a sound effects background gets you the best of all those worlds.

—Spencer Nilsen, Director/Executive Producer, Sega Music Group

How to Hire

The most important decision in hiring a composer is whether or not the style matches what is needed for the project. The sound producer and art director typically make the decision based on this factor. Price, how easy a person is to work with, and promptness are other factors.

Where you look for a composer or a group of musicians is dependent in a large part on the budget of the title. More and more film composers are being commissioned for CD-ROM games but only because the budgets can support the cost of this talent. Corporate projects or special interest titles are not likely to have the budgets for this route. Since there is not a huge dependency in knowing technology, a sound producer can look for composers or musicians from traditional outlets. All should have experience being in recording sessions and know the preparation steps. A **credit list** ▶ 82, a **demo tape**, and an **interview** are probably the most important things to consider when evaluating a candidate. Some composers or musicians may offer to create a sample after hearing a description of the title and the sound desired.

Sound effects specialists are often a breed apart from composers and musicians. Their process for obtaining or creating sound effects can be as important as their portfolio because their portfolio may not represent what they are capable of. Also, the budgets and time frames will dictate to a large extent what is possible. Sound effects people, like composers and musicians, do not need to be savvy in multimedia but they should know digital sound tools. Creating sound effects is a highly specialized skill, and so finding someone can be difficult. Searching in film and video venues is probably the best place as well as looking for people with experience in interface design.

How to Be Hired

Getting a job creating sounds for a multimedia project relies largely on getting in front of the sound producer. Some companies have full-time sound producers while others hire independent sound producers as needed. Knowing which production studios do a lot of sound production is one of the first steps to take. Some companies have in-house facilities and staff for generating many of the sounds needed for their products. LucasArts and Sega, for example, have full-time staffs devoted to creating the sound for their products.

Since the type of sound work is dependent on the type of title being created at any moment and since the duration of sound work is typically a fraction of the total development time, companies do not always have a need for composers, musicians, or sound effects artists. As a result, you should build relationships with sound producers and let them know you are not only musically talented but are a professional and will be able to get them what they need. Keep sound producers up to date with new credit lists and possibly demo tapes, but make sure they are presented appropriately.

Compensation

Composers and sound effects specialists can either receive a salary if they are a full-time employee or they can be paid by each sound element or by the job. Salaries will typically range between $30,000 and $50,000. Fixed-price payments seem to vary widely. They can range from a couple hundred dollars to several thousand dollars per piece. Complete scores might range between $5,000 to $20,000. Musicians are usually paid by the hour, though popular musicians or bands may receive large fixed payments. The hourly rates will be similar to traditional recording rates.

At the moment, many are creating scores and sound effects in part because of the new creative expressions allowed by new media. Traditional music and sound effects avenues have become crowded. Interactive media offers the opportunity to create a lot of material in a short amount of time. As with a sound producer, it is important to look at the **copyright issues** ▶ 96 involved in your work and try to preserve as many rights as possible within the given work structure. **Royalties** ▶ 91 are probably unlikely except for noted composers and musicians. Compensation for derivative rights, however, may be more likely.

Sound Engineer/Sound Editor

What They Do

A **sound engineer** handles the sound equipment before, during, and after recording sessions. Their responsibilities include setting up equipment, performing sound checks, recording music or voice parts, and then mixing them together. A sound producer may perform these tasks, but a good sound engineer is often recommended—especially for large groups of musicians, expensive voice actors, or complex recordings.

A **sound editor** edits sound files for length, tone, and effect and then converts the resulting sound files to the format needed. They will digitize any analog sounds and then use digital sound tools to blend and manipulate all the sounds in preparation for inclusion in an interactive project. This may include elimination of noise, changes in timing or pitch, and editing of breaths or "ums" in voice parts. They work under the direction of sound and video producers and are present from the start of sound production through integration and sometimes into testing. The work can be tedious at times but ultimately rewarding because of the impact the sound has on the final product.

Tools and Techniques

The tools a sound engineer uses include DAT recorders, mixers, and microphones. Keyboards, MIDI controllers, and a sound engine may also play prominent roles. For large and complex jobs, a digital or analog multitrack recorder with good noise reduction is essential.

The types of tools a sound editor uses include a reasonably fast computer, a large hard drive, an analog-digital sound converter board, and a digital sound editing tool. MIDI software is also a possibility as well as compression software. The sound compression for CD-ROM titles and inclusion in online areas for downloading is relatively straightforward. The compression for games cartridges, however, can be a complex process requiring a lot of time, special knowledge, and possibly specialized hardware.

Qualifications

A sound engineer needs to be experienced with most sound recording equipment and music instruments. They need to understand the language of music, composition, and recording, and be willing and available to work on short notice and in remote locations.

A sound editor needs to know the digital tools and should have a traditional background in sound production and editing. Although they often work under the direction of a sound or video producer, they will often be relied on to make design decisions. Good sound editors need to be quick, organized, and have an ear for quality.

How to Hire/How to Be Hired

The responsibilities of a sound engineer in multimedia are no different than in any other sound-related profession. The way to find them is to call **recording studios** and talk to other sound producers, composers, and musicians. Look for someone with a good reputation for understanding sound equipment and handling recording sessions. In terms of finding work, the best way to get into multimedia is to build relationships with multimedia sound producers. Sound producers will be interested in a sound engineer who is dependable, professional, and available on short notice.

Many sound producers or programmers often perform the role of sound editor. For large jobs, it makes sense to find someone specifically for editing and preparing all the sound in the project. The process for finding a sound editor or getting hired as a sound editor is the same as it is for a sound engineer. Sound studios and others in the sound business are good sources of leads for both qualified people and job opportunities.

Compensation

The compensation for sound engineers is typically the standard rate for traditional sound engineering work. The rates for sound editors can vary between a production assistant's rate and the low end of a sound producer's rate.

In many productions today, the sound producer often performs the roles of composer and sound editor. As productions get bigger and sound tools more sophisticated, these roles will likely be performed by separate individuals.

Video Producer

What They Do

The technology for producing and playing video on the computer has made great strides in the last three to four years but anyone that hopes to see acceptable full-screen full-motion video on consumer hardware at consumer prices is going to be sadly disappointed. Video can add a tremendous amount to multimedia products, especially for demonstrating a technique or showing a person talking, but not in the same manner as other video sources like television.

Some games are using video in special circumstances. Sometimes it is used for setting the game scenario. For example, the user might come upon a video screen in some command center or room and see some grainy broken video of someone explaining what happened to the ship or the city and what needs to be done. Both *Myst* and *Iron Helix* use this technique. In other cases, "blue screen" technology is used to superimpose live action sequences within animated worlds. Mechadeus has mastered this technique in their games *Critical Path* and *Daedalus Encounter*.

Special interest titles also use video to explain techniques or show narrated sequences. Voyager's First Person series and Against All Odds' *A Passage to Vietnam* use blue screen technology to allow narrators to walk around the screen and point out items in the interface.

But by far, the most common use of video in multimedia projects is in **corporate training products** ▶ 44. These are either run from multimedia networks or produced on CD-ROM. As the technology improves, more and more video on computers will appear in consumer products in innovative and highly amusing or educational ways.

Video producers manage the entire process of scripting, shooting, and acquiring original video assets and then edit them for use in interactive products. Sometimes they merely edit existing video. Depending on the amount of video and its use in the product, the video producer can be the principal producer or designer or they can be a line producer much like the sound producer and report to the art director and producer.

The video producer is a role that is **part managerial** and **part creative**. The management aspects arise because of the need for planning, budgeting, scheduling, and coordinating the resources needed for shooting and editing video. If the video producer is not experienced in managing the process, many weeks and thousands of dollars can be wasted. The creative aspects come in to play because the video producer often has a primary role in assembling the work. Many video producers in multimedia also play the role of director on video shoots as well as the role of video editor. If there is a separate video editor, which happens often, then the video producer works alongside the editor to help make the editing decisions.

Video producers can be involved from the start or they can be brought in after the storyboards have been created. Most producers and art directors, however, recommend bringing in experienced video producers early enough so that expectations are not created that cannot be met.

Process

The process of producing video for interactive projects follows the same process for traditional video projects, which is **pre-production**, **production**, and **post-production**. The first two are almost identical in both worlds. For creating original video assets, the pre-production starts with a set of goals, moves to a script, and then into storyboards. Videographers (or cinematographers) and actors are hired, locations are scouted or studios rented. The support crew is much the same and includes lighting and sound people, gaffers, grips, and prop and makeup people. The production phase is also same.

Frank Scales
Video Producer

Frank Scales's video career began at Rochester Institute of Technology and has taken him across the country and around the globe. He has developed audio and video elements for the CD-ROM From Alice to Ocean, *produced programs for an interactive tourism network in Australia, and last year worked on an edutainment CD-ROM.*

Frank calls the transition to desktop video a natural progression; not a revolution, but an evolution. According to him, "film is still king" in terms of quality, but videotape is faster, cheaper, and a better communications medium. "It's easier to manipulate, and easier to show. But not everybody knows how to use the tools yet. We're not even in adolescence when it comes to non-linear editing. Everybody in L.A. is rushing to learn about digital video."

However, the industry is growing rapidly, especially with equipment prices dropping (a basic online editing system can be purchased for $50,000, significantly less than the multi-million dollar price tags similar systems carried a few years ago). Interfaces are becoming more accessible to less technical people, which will open the doors even wider and encourage more exploration.

The new tools and technologies offer producers many new creative options, from spectacular visual effects to more efficient work methods. The team dynamic is extending "beyond telecommuting. We're overcoming the limitations of physical presence and scheduling, and being given the luxury of working in our own creative spaces." Frank, who works out of his home, is a strong advocate of working in your own environment, where you feel most comfortable and can work whenever and however you like, "My best work is done between midnight and 4 AM," he says, happy that he's no longer constrained to a daytime schedule.

Frank also stresses the need for self-discipline in order to do this. Part of this discipline includes a willingness to take in as much information as you realistically can. "Right now it's all changing so quickly that it's difficult to keep up," he says. He also prefers a hands-on approach to learning. "Most of the technical information I learned in college is out of date. Schooling is not a top priority—the best reason to go is to get access to the equipment, but if you can buy the equipment instead, then do it," he advises. "A hungry technical appetite is crucial."

Once the video has been shot, then the editing begins. In cases where the video is used for explanatory purposes and the scripts are well-developed, the editing can be straightforward. In other cases, where different shots are assembled into one piece, the process to get to a finished piece can be an energy-draining experience. In cases of talking heads, a sound producer commonly looks through the existing video on tape and makes a log of useful pieces. This log is then turned into an **edit decision list (EDL)** that determines which sequences to digitize for further work. There are more and more tools that help automate the process of logging and digitizing, and if there is a lot of raw material available, this process can be one of the most time-consuming parts of the job.

Digitization of video simply means that the tape machine is connected to a special computer video board that samples the video at a specific frame rate, with a certain sample size and then compresses and stores the video clip, typically to very large hard drives. Editing tools use a variety of **compression/decompression algorithms (codecs).** Some use standards like MPEG,

MPEG-2, AVI, or QuickTime, while others might be proprietary. Different codecs perform differently—some are better at graphics, some at video, some at sound.

Compression and decompression during editing can be handled with hardware or software compressors, although the hardware compressors are generally faster. The process is **symmetric**, meaning that it takes the same time to compress as it does to decompress. With some compressors, the time to compress video takes disproportionately longer than it does to decompress. This type of compression is **asymmetric**. Most video producers and editors will have one compensation rate for when they are at the computer, actively working, and another lower rate for when the computer is simply compressing video on its own.

Tools and Techniques

Video producers use a variety of both computer and non-computer tools. For creating video (shooting it), there are a variety of **cameras** that may have acceptable quality. The lowest-quality cameras are probably Hi-8 video cameras which are affordable and offer better-than-television resolution. Professional cameras, like the Betacam, offer much better resolution that is "broadcast quality," meaning that it is suitable for professionally broadcast television programming. It is a good idea to capture video at the highest resolution possible and affordable. This allows you to use it in ways that you may not have foreseen, or in opportunities that may not have been identified. For example, a popular game may be optioned for a television pilot or an interactive TV program. If all of the video was shot with Hi-8, then it will most likely need to be reshot with better equipment. If, however, the video is already of higher quality, it might save some time and money.

A **tripod** is a necessity for most video shoots. Except for the purposely shaky style of some "personal"-looking advertisements and music videos, even movements that seem imperceptible at the time of recording will be very noticeable upon playback in a studio. There are some cameras that are specially built to counterbalance movement, such as the Steadicam and Steadicam Jr., but these tend to be expensive

either to buy or rent. There are a few high-end editing systems that help smooth out movement in video, but these are also expensive and hard to find.

Aside from the camera, it is necessary to use **lights** that are color-corrected and do not cast color in either the beam or in the shadows (unless this is the desired effect). Even outdoors, lights are often required in order to control the direction and detail that records in the camera. There is no substitute for great lighting and it is very difficult to correct in post-production.

Because video production and editing is so processor-intensive, it is mandatory to get the fastest, most capable computer you can. Any money you might save on buying or renting lesser equipment will be lost quickly waiting for the computer to process, edit, and compress.

It is also necessary to have at least one (if not more) video tape player/recorders for making back-ups, dupes, and sample reels. Every time a copy is made (called a generation), the quality of the copy is less than the original. Most video producers make copies right from the first (the master) and limit how many copies they make from the master to preserve its quality. It is acceptable to use copies that are several generations old if it is merely for review, or creating EDLs, but the final video that will be digitized and edited should come directly from the masters.

Sound is most often overlooked and disregarded when shooting video. Invest in quality **microphones** that are separate from the camera. Use lavaliere microphones or boom microphones when necessary. Beware of background noise and guard against any disruptions during shooting. Recording sound well seems obvious but it is too commonly ignored with the result of poor, inadequate quality.

There are several software tools that can help create log files and EDLs. There is also software available to automatically process many clips at once in order to save time and tedium. Since each platform and software package has its own set of tools, you should research the particular tools that meet your needs and requirements. Many special effect software tools also exist that can help composite or create innovative stylistic treat-

The hardest thing to do is get that first cut of a video or first draft of a script because it's a work in progress. You have to allow the raw creativity to flow without filtering it through the critical or editorial part of your mind. That will come later, but at the beginning you have to put that part of your brain to sleep.

*—Paul Gilbert,
Video Producer and
Interactive Scriptwriter*

ments of video. Even image-editing tools like Photoshop can be used for processing video.

Because digital video takes so much time to digitize and space to store, many experienced video producers and editors digitize only what they need. They are good at scanning video quickly and narrowing down the pieces they need and then only bringing those sequences plus a few seconds before and after into the computer.

A technique that has become popular in many CD-ROM products is to shoot video in front of a **blue screen**, remove the blue background, and replace it with some other picture. It is a relatively easy trick to do, but cannot be done haphazardly. When done well, the video image can be integrated seamlessly into the scene.

Qualifications

If you've developed your eye, your instincts, and you know the **digital tools**, you should be able to work on multimedia projects quickly and easily. Working with video on the computer is not so different from traditional video production as long as you understand the constraints with the current technology and the subtle techniques to get the best quality and performance for the desktop.

Composition skills are a must for someone that is shooting any original footage. These skills include knowing the proper lighting techniques, guarding against reflections, and working within the dynamic range of video. Video producers should also know traditional video and film production techniques. They should have a deep understanding of and know how to make innovative uses of perspective, shot, depth, transitions, and camera movements.

Video producers should constantly be updating their skills and knowledge of the tools. Video technology changes radically every two years and in minor ways every four months. These changes can mean improvements in playback quality and performance or in improved productivity in editing performance. New stylistic techniques are constantly being invented that add to the visual language. Leading video producers help to innovate these techniques but they also know to abandon them when they have turned into clichés. Most producers and art directors will

sigh with relief when they come upon a video person who is competent, who they can get along with, and who knows the technology and the trends. An additional plus is someone who continually makes themselves available for work on little notice. For producers or art directors, this is a dream come true.

How to Hire

The producer or art director will typically hire the video producer. The first thing they need to do before they start looking is to determine what their needs are. If they need to script and shoot original footage, their needs will be far greater and more diverse than if they need someone to simply edit video from existing tape and prepare it for a multimedia project.

In the first case, the producer or art director will want to look for someone who has managed video shoots, including hiring actors, finding locations, and renting cameras. The tasks may be undefined and may need a video producer who can define them and then create a budget and a schedule. A **demo reel** ▶ 83 is one of the more important pieces of material in order to judge traditional composition and editing skills. Without a demo reel or samples of actual products to look at, it will be almost impossible to judge a candidate's suitability.

In the second case, you may need someone that is an expert in editing video. You should look for a demo reel in digital form, so you can evaluate the finished product in terms of digital playback performance. You will want to weigh the technical sophistication of the editing and the playback more than the composition. Ask questions about the process they went through to create the work. Note any glitches in the video, or breaks in the synchronization, and take note of the color quality. An experienced editor will be able to discuss every aspect of the quality and give you alternatives as well as boundaries for achieving the quality you desire.

Finding video producers often requires inquiries in the video world and talking to tool sellers and user groups for digital video products. Many of the professionals in the video industry are already conversant with digital tools and multimedia requirements. Colleges with film departments might also be good sources.

I think that a lot of the people who are going to show us the way are still in school. If I was 16 now and a real rebel, I don't think I would buy an electric guitar or a drum kit. I think I would buy a handicam and a desktop editing system because, in rock music, there are very few sacred cows left to shoot down. In film and TV, it's so much more conservative, so much more staid, so many more standards. That, to a rebellious 16-year-old, is a very enticing prospect.

—Thomas Dolby, Composer, Musician, and Sound Producer

Sheryl Hampton
Video Producer

Co-founder of RPM productions, a multimedia production partnership that combines full-service multimedia product design with production services, Sheryl Hampton is one of the premier practitioners of the black art of QuickTime video. While most of us look at the quirky, jerky QuickTime movies the size of an Elvis commemorative postage stamp, and think, "Awesome, video on the desktop!" Sheryl has quietly become an expert on creating digital video that doesn't shake, skip, drop frames or jump out of synch with a voice track. It is the kind of work that gets noticed, too, by such high profile clients as Levi's jeans.

*Equally at home using Newtech's Video Toaster, Radius' Video Vision, or Video Spigot, Sheryl is also a consummate pro when it comes to figuring out her clients' needs and spec'ing the work to be done. "Say we have a video that needs no edit-*ing whatsoever and it's a 60-second commercial that's going to end up on a CD-ROM. First of all we find out the specs for the CD-ROM. Is it double or single speed? Does the client want more frames per second or would they prefer a larger image size? There's going to be a trade-off between the two. If the work requires straight video compression, what are the output options? That will determine the way the video is processed and compressed." RPM provides answers to these questions and more.*

Sheryl offers some cogent advice for multimedia wanna-bes. "If a person really wants to get into multimedia production, be prepared to take on a non-paying or low paying internship ▶ 91 to learn the ropes, because most of the multimedia development companies that are around don't have the money to spend on training people or on getting people over the learning curve. They need people who can bring in money immediately."

How to Be Hired

Getting hired as a video producer means either having the management and creative skills needed to coordinate a large video production or having the technical and creative capabilities necessary to make video look good on the computer. People with experience in traditional video can get into multimedia by concentrating on the pre-production and production areas for multimedia projects and bringing in qualified digital video editors for the post-production work. People with knowledge of interactive post-production work can go to traditional sources and look for work in their budding interactive divisions.

Compensation

Video producers are usually paid salaries, in the case of employees, or hourly, weekly, or monthly rates, in the case of freelance work. The hourly rates are typically for straight video editing work and can range from $50–$150/hr for operating time and $40–$60/hr for processing time. Most producers will try to negotiate weekly or monthly rates for extended work. In some cases, video editing is priced by the minute of video. The range here is between $50 and $100 per minute of video.

Videographer

What They Do

While anyone can use a camcorder to shoot video, a professional **videographer** knows how to create appropriate, compelling, and high-quality video that uses interactive technology to greatest advantage. Video is probably the most complex, time-consuming, and resource-consuming media to create. While animation may be more expensive per minute, video productions can require many people and tremendous time.

Video can be as simple as a location shot without audio, actors, or special effects, or as sophisticated as the most elaborate scenes in feature films. Videographers are responsible for making the most of the location, lighting, actors, props, and scenes since all of these culminate in the image recorded through the camera's lens. The audience never sees (and will never appreciate) the work done in pre-production to set up a video shoot. What matters is only the images recorded, digitized, edited, and delivered.

Because people are so familiar with television and movies, their expectations of video are high—in terms of visual appeal, quality, and meaning. Coupled with interactivity, video takes on new meaning. Very often, the conventions that form the basis of "standard" video techniques will not be adequate. For example, long shots of people talking on camera ("talking heads") are usually boring and uneventful interludes between action in most interactive media titles.

Videographers will be expected to innovate the artform in order to create evocative, interesting techniques that make the most of both the video medium and interactivity.

Depending on the budget and the quality demanded, a stripped-down video shoot will require a videographer and a **sound engineer** ▶ 231 at the minimum. If the budget can accommodate it, a lighting technician will complete the crew. However, out of practicality and professional necessity, most videographers have learned the rudiments of lighting a scene effectively.

Frequently the videographer will also double as the video art director, responsible for the smooth running of the production while on the set. A complex video shoot may require a complement of stage hands, grips, props wranglers, electricians, sound technicians, and multiple camera people.

Process

Because the current video technology for in interactive multimedia produces less-than-faithful quality, drops frames, and "tears" when the processing power is not available, it is helpful for the videographer (and the producer, too) to pre-visualize the results of their camerawork on the desktop. This may mean that extensive test shots are produced, digitized, and compressed to determine the best shooting style for the product.

This planning takes place at the very beginning when a shoot list is assembled. Some subjects simply make for better video than others, due to the way digital video is compressed. Since video records such high amounts of visual information, the storage capacity of digital media and the transfer rates of that information—especially from CD-ROMs—become significant issues that bear directly on the creative vision of the production team.

Decisions regarding the kinds of scenes to be shot and the techniques to use need to be made early to find the appropriate balance between **quality** and **performance**. Crowd scenes, for example, will not compress well, and consequently will not play back well on the desktop. Understanding what works well in desktop video is an important first step in planning a video shoot.

Tools and Techniques

To achieve high quality video on the desktop, it is crucial to start with the highest quality source video available, since with each step in the digital production process the original video signal will increasingly degrade. For most professional productions, this means shooting with a Betacam

A computer displays video on the screen differently than a TV does. Unlike TV, computers do not interleave the video signal, which gives computers better control and quality, but because the processors and throughput are not usually adequate, the video can often be choppy. In particular, strong vertical lines do not pan well, since the frame rate is not high enough to show seamless motion. There are other peculiarities in the present state of computerized video performance, making scenes with lots of detail such as crowds or forests difficult to handle.

camera, which costs in the neighborhood of $30,000. Another, less expensive option is to use a Hi-8 camcorder. Although the Hi-8 will not provide nearly the same source quality as Betacam, its better-than-TV resolution will provide a passable level of quality when digitized and compressed.

A separate high-quality **microphone** and a **tripod** are requirements for most video shoots. The most common problems when shooting video are that the sound is not good enough and that there is too much camera movement.

Qualifications

A videographer for interactive projects needs to have **traditional filmmaking skills** as well as an appreciation for the current state of **digital video technology**. Depending on the platform and the delivery media, the videographer, in conjunction with the video producer, will be faced with numerous decisions on what the lighting, background, and camera movements should be. In time, the technology will catch up with the artistic vision, lessening this need. The videographer should know what the technical specifications for the video will be. These include the frame rate, frame size, duration, color palette, and any special effects.

How to Hire

The producer or video producer typically hires the videographer. The best sources, besides other producers in multimedia, are film and video organizations and schools. Be sure that the videographers have experience shooting digital video at or near the specifications you will need for your project. Ideally, they should also have experience with video editing but this is not essential. A demo reel, preferably in digital form, as well as an interview, is a must to learn about their approach to filming, their style, and how well they work with others.

How to Be Hired

Multimedia production studios, advertising agencies, traditional audio/video production firms, and video editing services are all likely places for videographers to market their services. In addition, large corporations are increasingly turning to their in-house media departments to master this new technology and communicate to their staff through **training applications** ▶ 44, their customers through **interactive marketing pieces** ▶ 46, and to their shareholders via interactive annual reports. Familiarity with and mastery of digital production tools will become a requirement as job seekers try to differentiate their skills and move into this new field. You should have a credit list, a demo reel of your production credits (usually on VHS tape), and examples of your work in digital form, either on a Syquest cartridge or CD-ROM.

Digital Video Editing and Compression

Editing video is a time-consuming task, beginning by **logging** hours and sometimes days of recorded video footage, noting key scenes, and, if the video is time-stamped, their corresponding SMPTE frame numbers. (The Society for Motion Picture and Television Engineer has created a standard time code which stamps each frame of video with the hour, minute, second and frame number.) By referring to the SMPTE numbers, precise synchronization of video and audio can be achieved. Once the video is logged, the "in" and "out" SMPTE frame numbers can be keyboarded into a software package that will automatically begin the process of digitizing the selected footage.

It is crucial for the digital video editor to have an understanding of the relationship between compression ratios, transfer time, and playback quality. Additionally, the digital video editor must be aware of the various hardware and software solutions available in the marketplace. QuickTime, from Apple, provides a multi-platform multimedia movie format along with a suite of media compressors and decompressors. Compression ratios range from 5:1 to 8:1 and do not require any special hardware. By contrast, MPEG (Motion Picture Experts Group) compression delivers compression ratios ranging from 50:1 to 200:1. However, MPEG compression requires special hardware to enable playback, and these can cost from $500 to $1,000. For a broad consumer application, a CD-ROM using QuickTime video might make good sense. However, for a kiosk for public display—which can be stocked with its own hardware—an MPEG board might deliver superior results.

Depending on the amount of video and the speed of the processor, **digitizing** can take a long time. But once the video is in digital format, it is edited using an online, nonlinear software editing application such as Adobe Premiere. These software packages allow many video clips to be arranged and sequenced together. Because the clips are digitized, the physical limitations of video tape are overcome. Clips can be moved in sequence, changed, and manipulated using a variety of built-in transitions and special effects. Since each transition has its own performance needs, a good video editor will keep in mind the impact of a given transition on the playback performance of the video. Edits which use less data-intensive transitions will allow the computer to process frames quickly and enhance the quality of the desktop movie.

With 180 seconds of video playing in a 160x120 pixel window at 22 kHz sound, creating a 16MB file, the need for video **compression** quickly becomes apparent. Desktop video editors understand the trade-offs between compression and quality, the various forms of lossless and lossy compression, and the necessity of selecting a transfer rate appropriate to the playback medium.

With the huge amounts of storage offered by CD-ROMs and the impressive performance gains using digital equipment, there has been an explosive interest in creating video on the desktop. Breakthrough technologies like QuickTime and Microsoft's AVI formats have only fueled the interest in digital video. While the cost of entry is dropping, the financial barriers remain high. Fast, powerful computers equipped with editing software and professional quality video digitizing boards capable of capturing full frame (640x480 pixels) video at 30 frames per second can cost $10,000 or more. Those willing to spend the money and commit the time to learn the software will find ready-made careers either forming their own digital editing studios or working in a post-production house, where the rates for creating a digital video range from $50 to $100 per digitized minute of video.

Performer/Actor

What They Do/Process

Performers and actors interested in pursuing a career in interactive multimedia have several options open to them. **Performers** who write their own material view multimedia as another color in their palette of creative expression. From Laurie Anderson to Mark Petrakis, aka "Spoonman," they are adapting digital tools to meet their individual need for creative endeavor. These artists often write and perform in their own material, interacting with the computer via infra-red and hand-held pointers, headsets, body microphones, and more. They are essentially incorporating digital technologies into their work and making it subservient to their expressive needs.

In addition to possessing a basic familiarity with the technology, performers will often work with a technical guru who can advise them of the capabilities available to them, and keep the machines running smoothly during rehearsals and performances. One key ingredient for any performer who hopes to interact with complex computer equipment in front of a live audience is the ability to improvise at a moment's notice. Those who live by interactive multimedia die by the system crash. When the familiar bomb icon appears, as it surely will, performers onstage must be ready with a fallback plan, entertaining the audience while techies madly scurry around checking cables, rebooting, and reconfiguring system files.

The qualifications for an interactive performer or actor are the same as in traditional performing arts. You need acting ability, courage, and perseverance.

Actors, on the other hand, are handed a script and storyboard as the project enters into the early phases of the production process. Rehearsals not only cover characterization, motivations, and line readings, but in many cases, how to perform in a blue screen environment. These are most often shot out of sequence, to accomodate production schedules, location availability, and the budget.

Many **interactive scripts** ▶ 186 call for shooting several different scenarios based on the same story point. For example, an interactive movie may have several options for the player to select, with each option providing a different sequence of events. An actor may not need to know the complete structure of an interactive project, but some knowledge beforehand of the product can make it easier to stay in characer.

Production companies often work in cramped studios where most of the action is filmed against a blue screen background. Actors must be adept at performing in a vacuum, without the benefit of traditional props, scenery, or sometimes, other actors all of which will be digitally composited later. Following the shooting of all live video scenes, the actor may be called back to the recording studio to record additional dialog or voice-over parts.

How to Hire

Increasingly, production companies are realizing the value of hiring **traditionally trained actors** to perform in interactive multimedia productions. While the technology may be new, the abilities to convincingly portray emotion, motivation, and intent , as well as to develop a character still hold true. Gone are the days when the vice president of marketing could don a wig and expect to effectively play a part in front of a Hi-8 camcorder. Casting **agents** ▶ 148 working with a producer can speed the process of finding the right talent. If time and budget allow, a desktop screen test may enable the producer to make an informed decision that takes into account the quality of desktop video and its impact on the performer's role.

Dana Atchley
Multimedia Performer

"In the race to push pixels faster," says multimedia performer and storyteller Dana Atchley, "there hasn't been enough attention paid to why you're pushing and what you're going to achieve with it." Dana is bucking that trend through his art—interactive multimedia storytelling before live audiences.

"My grandfather got a 16mm camera in 1928 and in his lifetime, he took maybe four hours worth of film," says Dana. "Nowadays, people have already shot four or five hours of tape by the eighth month of pregnancy. What do you do with all this stuff?" Assembling "that stuff" into a meaningful form is Dana's passion. His concept of the "electronic family album"—a digital version of the leather-bound books of snapshots every family owns—is the center-piece of his **performances ▶ 39**. He has built a digital collection of still and moving images, personal stories, and favorite songs, all accessible via an inviting interface that lets users follow particular timelines or threads. Dana shares his album with audiences in his San Francisco studio, at industry conferences, and social gatherings around the world. He wears a wireless headset and waves an infrared mouse at a screen behind his stage, on which his album is projected. Audiences are led down the different roads of his life, and given a very personal glimpse into one man's psyche. Despite the racks of Macintoshes lining the walls and cables littering floor and ceiling, his shows create a very intimate, human ambiance.

Technology has played an integral role in Dana's performances since the early '70s, when he began using film and video to enhance his live performances and document his travels. "There's an excitement around this technology that reminds me of the way we felt in the '60s," says this ex-hippie who once roamed the U.S. performing under the name "Ace Space, the Colorado Cowboy." "We're going to change the world. It's tempered by the reality of the '80s, and the giant digital cluster of bucks that are going on in megamergers and all that stuff, at which you just shake your head." However, he's not worried about being drowned out in the corporate shuffle: "I'm a storyteller and a content person. There's going to be room for me no matter what happens."

How to Be Hired

For actors interested in appearing in interactive multimedia productions, the job pathways are similar to traditional acting careers. Traditional **unions and guilds ▶ 52** such as the Screen Actors Guild (SAG) may provide recommendations to producers and notify their membership of audition opportunities. Additionally, in areas where regional theaters are particularly strong, newsletters may list multimedia acting opportunities.

Compensation

Compensation for acting should follow standard union rates for a lot of projects but in some cases, publishers and studios may not be knowledgeable about working with actor's guilds and may pay less than union scale. Be sure to negotiate a contract specifying your time commitment and hold them to it in the event the shoot takes less time than anticipated.

Lighting, Set Design, Costumes, and Props

What They Do/Process

An adjunct of traditional film and video production, lighting and set design, costume shop, and prop production skills are, nonetheless, still in demand in multimedia productions. **Lighting designers** must have an appreciation of the impact of their designs as they appear in digital form. Lighting schemes that work for video and film applications may have to be revised to accommodate the particular idiosyncrasies of desktop video, compression algorithms and transfer rates. Understanding the implications of these factors on the video, knowing in advance what works, and even desktop screen tests will help the lighting designer achieve the best results.

Set designers must have the ability to visualize how their designs will be viewed on the desktop. Interesting sets, chock-a-block with lavish attention to physical details will have to be foregone in favor of simple, bold sets that provide a meaningful visual context and can be compressed easily and look good on the desktop.

Costume designers and **property managers** are charged with providing actors with the costumes and props that contribute telling details to character and scene, thus creating an aura of believability around the actor's performance. Period costumes and props may have to be researched carefully to establish historical accuracy. Additionally, costume designers and props people need to know which costumes photograph well. When video is combined with computer digitization and fussy costumes, glittering jewelry, diagonal stripes of contrasting color, or finely detailed suits in patterns like glen plaid, the images literally tear or jump around on screen, distracting the viewer from the action.

Lighting and set designers, costumers, and prop wranglers go to work early in the production process, assisting in the planning of the video or film shoot. Working from storyboards that sketch out the fundamental details of each scene, they may meet with the producer or art director to learn the context of the video shoot and understand its objectives. Lighting designers may provide a list of required equipment to the producer. Set designers will come up with pencil sketches and models of their designs which may then have to be constructed by a carpentry crew. Costume designers illustrate their designs (usually with traditional media), and provide fabric samples when appropriate. Prop managers begin tracking down the required props, scouring thrift shops or rental agencies, and if necessary, fabricating the required props in model shops.

How to Hire

Ask to see examples of work in interactive media. If that isn't possible, track record of traditional stage, video, and film work will give you an idea of the individual's ability. Check references and query other members of the past production teams regarding skill levels and the ability to work

Eric Blum
Gaffer

For nearly 15 years, Eric Blum has been lighting commercials, music videos, feature films and industrial films. In recent years, he's added a new platform to his repertoire—computer screens. Eric lit scenes for the interactive teen drama Kids at Risk, released on CD-ROM and videodisc by the Computer Curriculum Company (a joint venture between Simon & Schuster and Paramount that develops new media for educational curricula). He also worked on an interactive guide to San Francisco for kids, which he describes as "wacky, flashy, jittery, MTV imagery—stuff that technically would have been a mistake" but was cool for this audience.

Kids at Risk is a movie with multiple outcomes. Users determine the course of characters' actions, then learn the ramifications of their choices. "I'm used to shooting linear movies" says Eric. "It was interesting getting into non-linear narrative." Although the shooting techniques don't differ much, it is tougher to keep a consistent look across all scenes. The disc was all shot on location, rather than in a studio (unlike interactive games, which use lots of blue screen). Eric has worked on games as well, but says that "putting real people in games is like using motion picture techniques from 1912. That's going to change a lot in the next few years, but right now we're in the stone age."

Technology has changed considerably since 1981, when Eric received his MFA in Cinema Production from USC. Many projects are now shot onto videotape. However, video can't match the quality of film, and digitized video loses even more detail. "Most things don't look natural" on desktop video, says Eric.

One of the biggest limitations of multimedia is that digital compression makes certain techniques unusable. For example, Eric couldn't use smoke, a favorite element in night-time street scenes, because of the jumps between frames. Smoke wafting in front of a black area would end up looking like a patch of gray on a monitor.

CD-ROM budgets are generally small, thus crews tend to be smaller and less rigidly structured. "People help other departments more than they would on a larger project," he notes.

as a member of a team when deadlines are tight. Resourcefulness and perseverance may be more important than experience.

How to Be Hired
If you don't have interactive credits under your belt, traditional credits combined with an understanding of digital media may suffice to get you in the door.

Compensation
As with other video roles, **union scale** ▶ 52 will prevail in many cases. A fair number of CD-ROM productions, however, are still low-budget affairs, so be prepared for lower rates and more responsibilities than might be expected in a traditional film or video shoot.

Technical Lead

What They Do

The **technical lead** or the **lead programmer** on a project is one of the cornerstones of the project. Without a capable technical lead, good interactive projects cannot be built. In the early days of multimedia, most projects were created by technical people primarily to satisfy technical challenges. These days, project teams have creative specialists like writers, interface designers, art directors, visual designers, sound producers, and animators who give form to the experience. The technology people simply help realize this collaborative vision.

The technical lead is usually hired by the president or executive producer for full-time positions and by a producer for project-based work. For a full-time position, the technical lead may be called the chief technology officer (CTO) or the vice president of technology. In this capacity, their primary responsibilities are to help craft and implement the technology strategy for a business or division. Within the scope of a particular project, a technical lead helps define the structure and interactions of a product and advises on the technical implications of certain decisions. They will help design the product and hire and manage programmers.

Technical leads need to understand both **management principles** and **technology** (current and future). Choosing the wrong tools on which to build a product or series of products can jeopardize the viability of a company as easily as poor development practices. In some companies and projects, the technical lead often has the unenviable role of doing hands-on work while at the same time managing the work of others. The size of some multimedia teams may not be large enough to support a full-time technical manager, so the technical lead often programs as well. These two tasks take different mindsets. Management requires awareness of others and a willingness to accept reality. Programming requires focus and a belief in the unattainable. Some people can move between these states effortlessly, but it is hard even for experts.

Technical leads fit in at the point when a product begins to become more than just an idea. A good mix in conceiving a product is to separate the creative and technical responsibilities but have them both heavily involved to help challenge and constrain each other. In some cases, the technical lead tempers the design ambitions of the scriptwriter or designer. In other cases, the creative people can help push the technical people to do things that they had not thought of. This collaboration can help solve problems quickly and innovatively. For example, the bookworms in the children's storybook *Four Footed Friends* originally inched their way across the screen, but children found this sequence boring, and so developers were called in to speed it up. When a scriptwriter on the project happened to make the suggestion to do something common in traditional cartooning—make the bookworm disappear in a "poof" to reappear in another "poof"—the problem was solved.

The technical lead stays with the project through production and testing. The technical lead is important at the beginning of any project to help establish platform, technology, and market specifications. During the conceptual phase of development, it is critical to decide target markets, target **platforms** ▶ 12, proposed technologies to use, and possible development tools to use. These decisions will profoundly affect the course of the project and should be made with considerable research, thought, and input from everyone on the team.

Process

The process for the technical lead is similar through each project type. The scope of it will vary depending on how much innovation is required. Products that are low on the **interactivity scale** ▶ 171, that do not provide a lot of options for the user and do not have a lot of custom code often need only a fraction of the time and resources that highly interactive ones need. Products that are part of a series and use the same engine also need less time and fewer resources.

Computers are young enough as a medium that practically anyone can work hard at it and produce stuff that's at the leading edge. It's kind of difficult for people to start businesses in garages unlike a few years ago, but the fact remains that it's still a very young, fresh medium and you don't have to go to school for ten years to understand how to build computer-based products.

—Frank Boosman, General Manager, Virtus Corporation

Larry Doyle
Programmer

"Basically, it's man against machine," says Larry Doyle, when asked about the role of a computer programmer in interactive multimedia. Larry's career path has taken him on an interesting trajectory, arcing from lead guitarist and songwriter for Love Club, the Goth rock band, to lead programmer on some of the most challenging multimedia CD-ROM applications currently in development. Instead of picking up a Fender Stratocaster, these days Larry is scoring in Macromedia Director.

For Larry, this work is all of a piece, as he's been able to leverage his musical ability into multimedia applications that combine interfaces for musical instruments with interactive video. If you were in the audience at the finale of Peter Gabriel's 1993 WOMAD festival, you may have been digging in the dirt to Larry's work. He helped create the video wall of images controlled by an electronic drum kit played by Peter Gabriel outside the Future Zone tent.

Currently a consultant at Marcromedia, Larry travels around the country, putting out other people's fires and teaching them the finer points of object-oriented programming. One of the things that excites him about programming interactive multimedia is the opportunity to take the creative vision of a production team and make the computer manifest that vision. "This is where the rubber meets the pavement."

Qualities that make for a good programmer, are, according to Larry, the ability to look at concepts and figure out ways to execute them using the capabilities of the underlying code and limitations of the target machine. As Larry says, only half jokingly, "Like good sex and great guitar playing, programming takes relaxed concentration. You can't force yourself to be a programmer. Programming can be grim at times, it takes a lot of patience. One of the big plusses of multimedia programming is you have something wonderful when you are done. You have language, sound, visuals, animation and interactivity. And that's positive feedback. I find that to be a real reward."

Managing a development team is not something that can be done easily by non-technical people. Part of the reason is that the job almost requires having been in a programmer's shoes to know what to expect. The other part of the reason is that programmers tend to be less tolerant of people that do not have a firm understanding and appreciation for programming.

In the design phase, the technical team works with others to sketch out the product. In addition to providing feedback on what the development time and costs would be, a technical lead or programmer may create small working segments within an authoring tool to simulate certain effects. They may also expand or advise on the ideas developed by scriptwriters, game designers, or interface designers. Once the general structure and interactions of the product are determined, it then lies in the hands of the technical lead to design the product in terms of the software components. What the product looks like externally to viewers or players and what it looks like on the inside are often completely different. The technical lead coordinates the process of arriving at that abstraction between the interface and the internal workings.

Hand in hand with the design goes the functional specification. A **functional specification** ▶ 130, 173, 258 is a document that describes the interactions of the product from both a user's and programmer's perspective. A script describes a product by deconstructing it into linear segments, while a technical specification describes a product by deconstructing it into events invoked by either the user or the program itself. It de-

Leo Hourvitz
Director of Multimedia Tools, Pixar

Leo Hourvitz has a way of getting in early. The second software engineer hired by Steve Jobs at the fledgling NeXT Computer, Leo became, a few years later, the first hire at Pixar's Multimedia Development Department, where his official title is Director of Multimedia Tools. Leo received an MS from M.I.T.'s Architecture Machine Group, the predecessor of the Media Lab, worked for the Macintosh software group, then went to NeXT where he says, "I got kicked into management because I didn't protest hard enough."

Leo's transition to interactive multimedia came when he realized the workstation world already had the interactive graphics capabilities he wanted to help create. "What I really liked working on was interactive computer graphics, so I started looking for an opportunity in multimedia." A mutual friend arranged an interview at Brøderbund, and soon Leo was manager of system software. At Brøderbund he directed a 12-person group who "did the tools, toolkits, porting libraries, new technology as well as on-going development for Living Books. Anything that wasn't a title with a ship date."

At Pixar, Leo is currently directing the start up of a CD-ROM development group. With Pixar dedicated to becoming the first fully digital

studio—their full-length computer-animated feature film Toy Story is due to be released by Disney—CD-ROM has become one of the mediums on which Pixar is focusing.

In his role at Pixar, Leo is intimately involved in the creation of multimedia titles. "Interactive titles are a gas!" he exclaims. "You do something to the computer and the computer reacts. And what's even more fun is you do something and a character that has a bit of life on its own reacts to it. That's the part that keeps me jazzed." It doesn't hurt either, that Leo has the good fortune to be working with people he eagerly credits as "far and away the finest 3D animators in the industry."

Leo is quick to deglamorize the world of multimedia. "You're not going to get that banking software salary," he cautions. "And," he notes, "programming is a smaller part of the project than it is in application software. Multimedia projects are not mostly programming. Most of the effort will go into art and sound and that's a new experience for most programmers. They are going to have to learn how to talk to artists in their terminology. For example, to a filmmaker a 'locked camera' means that the camera doesn't zoom, dolly, pan or truck. Programmers would describe the same thing as 'the background doesn't change.' When your project team is trying to describe what happens on the computer screen, it becomes a relevant issue. So you've got to learn a whole new vocabulary."

scribes how each event or interaction—each button selection, each move—connects to the next event. Programmers use the functional specification to build the product. Marketers use it to determine product features, strengths, and weaknesses. Test managers use it to build the test plan and then to make sure the product does what it is supposed to. Without a specification, the quality assurance group has little way of knowing when a product is complete.

In conjunction with these development tasks comes management tasks. A **budget** and **schedule** ▶ 126 for the programming portion of the project needs to be developed. These two parts of the job are why it is important to have a technical person involved at the beginning. Not only can the technical lead provide the information on what can and cannot be done, they also provide an estimate on the fly of what it will take to develop what is being conceived. As the design becomes more solid, the technical lead can refine these estimates to create a detailed list of tasks and milestones. With this information, the technical lead determines the types and number of programmers needed.

A technical lead also hires and directs the different types of programmers needed for a project. Projects can vary at the software level in any number of ways, including **operating systems** (such as OS/2, Macintosh, Windows, and UNIX), **authoring tools** (such as *Macromedia Director* and *Apple Media Tool*), **computer languages** (such as C, C++, PostScript, and assembler), **software components** (such as databases, communication protocols, and printing facilities), and **platforms** (such as Macintosh computers, PCs, and game machines). In addition, the personalities needed within a single project can also vary. There may be a need for someone who prototypes quickly, another who designs and defines the application programming interfaces (APIs) between each internal and external software component, another adept at getting rid of bugs and making code, and still another to create tools for the others to use. An analogy to this can be found in baseball. There are starting pitchers, mid-relievers, and late relievers, and each is valuable in their own way. A technical lead finds, trains, and manages the programming team.

In projects with a large number of programmers, one of the biggest headaches can be managing all the changes that are occurring across numerous files. Multiple programmers often need to work on the same files at the same time for different purposes. A big part of the technical lead's job is to establish procedures so programmers do not erase or overwrite the changes of others. Procedures such as code check-outs, code resolutions, and builds help formalize and make the development process run more smoothly. Code check-out means that programmers register which files they are currently working on and then check them in when they are finished. Code resolution means that differences in files modified simultaneously get merged into a single file. A **build** ▶ 259 is a version of the product that has been merged and compiled. It may or may not go to the testing group. Builds are used as milestones to help target development as well as also establish a unified code base from which to continue development.

Tools and Techniques

A technical lead uses budgeting and scheduling tools for planning and managing the programming resources. Their most important tools, however, are the tools they use in developing the product. These tools include authoring tools, software components, and coding tools. An **authoring tool** ▶ 259 is a software program that lets programmers, animators, and designers create interactive products. Essentially, they provide the engines which drive the navigation and viewing of content. Many authoring tools, however, only provide a certain level of functionality. Programmers often either need to enhance their capabilities with component or custom code or create an entirely separate engine. In these cases, technical leads will look to license existing software components such as animation and simulation **engines**; communication, transaction, and printing routines; and encryption or compression schemes.

In cases where these components are either unavailable or not suited for the requirements of the project, a technical lead may need to manage the design and development of software code to perform the necessary functions. The most common tool used in this process is a **compiler**. A programmer typically writes in a high level language and then compiles it, which means that the high level source code is turned into something a computer can understand. During this process, the code is also linked, which means that all the data and code references in the different sections get resolved into their true locations. In large projects, the management of separate pieces of code is a job in itself.

An important technique for managing people, especially programmers, is to double or triple their time estimates until you have worked with them long enough to know how realistic these estimates are. Also, take into account that tasks that would take you a certain amount of time are going to take them much longer. One of the most difficult tasks in programming is to meet deadlines. A technical lead should be involved in creating schedules that are realistic.

One of the ways to help meet the forecasted dates is to divide up the work into small, easily achievable steps and monitor the progress towards them every one or two days. Some programmers have a tendency to "worm hole," in other words, spend a lot of time on unimportant details. Keeping tight reins on their activities will prevent reaching a deadline late in the process to find that only 10% of the code has been developed. As for assigning different roles and sections to the programmers, it can be a good strategy to put several programmers together and then let them work out these issues for themselves.

Qualifications

A technical lead should have direct experience with a **project type** and **set of tools**. Most technical leads rise to this position only after serving as programmers on several projects over the course of several years. During that time, programmers learn the tools, the process, the product architecture, and the management techniques needed to manage a team. Producers that hire technical leads just because they seem to know a lot about technology are setting themselves up for disappointment. There are so many areas within software development and so much to learn that few can move from one area such as database programming to multimedia authoring and make qualified decisions.

Another important requirement for a technical lead is to understand current technologies and be adept at reading **future trends**. A technical lead does not have to be an expert at using these tools, but they do have to know what they can and cannot do. They also need to know if and how it can be augmented to add additional functionality. For example, many authoring tools support external code modules. A technical lead needs to know how these work and what the limitations are. Another piece that is crucial is to know how long a task will take. This time is highly dependent on the tools that are being used. Again, a technical lead does not need hands-on experience with a tool to get this information. They can learn about tools by watching others use them, but ultimately, they do need to understand the tools themselves.

More than a few CD-ROM publishers are successful because years ago they created their own authoring tools and playback technologies. The challenge in creating proprietary tools is to know when to stick with them and when to switch to third-party tools. Though it can be easy to make this decision in hindsight, it is difficult to do it at the time it needs to be made. Businesses that stick with proprietary tools too long can end up at a serious disadvantage as the cost of maintaining the tools and keeping up with the latest technology becomes exorbitant. On the other hand, businesses that adopt third-party tools that are not completely finished or well supported can risk the success of their project, and then quite possibly, their entire business. A good manager tries not to become attached to any particular tool, often hedging bets by using a small team to explore new tools and technologies.

A good technical lead will need to find and **manage other developers**. They need to know when to motivate and how to motivate, how to pad time estimates for each team member, and how to get two or more developers to work together effectively. Other qualifications are the ability to complete a project and the ability to make it a high quality one. Not being able to complete a project can occur when the technical lead simply loses interest and moves on to something else. Many developers like challenges, they like problems to solve. Once they solve these problems to their satisfaction, they like to move on to other problems. This type of person should not necessarily be avoided—in fact, they are excellent people to have around—they just should not be made the technical lead of development. Also, some candidates may not have the process in place to make a high quality product. While the producer can offset this tendency by monitoring the level of quality themselves or by giving the test manager the authority to drive the completion of the product, it is often easier to have a technical lead that is equally concerned about quality and performance.

How to Hire

While producers and art directors can come from a variety of backgrounds and industries, technical leads tend to either come from software or multimedia. The best people are in great demand and can essentially write their own tickets. Before you starting looking, you need to know where they will fit into the management structure of the project or business and what you are willing to offer. In some cases—especially with programming tasks that take more than one person, a well-qualified but high-priced consultant can be paid hourly rates throughout the project to advise the programmers and audit their progress. In other cases, someone might be needed to help formulate and direct the technical strategy of the business.

When searching for someone to work on a game or special interest title, look at the **credits** for many of the more complex titles. They do not have to be popular or well-designed, they just need to run well. Although many of the technical people listed will be full-time employees and often have many incentives to stay with the developer or publisher, others may be working on a project basis or be interested in entertaining other offers. People at **companies creating multimedia tools** are other resources to look into. They may be qualified and interested in the position or they may be able to point you to others. **Developer training and support groups** can be particularly helpful in providing leads. **Developer conferences** and other technology-oriented events are also good places to look, but understand that most of the attendees are more suitable for programming roles as opposed to management ones.

The best candidates have several years of experience working with a particular set of tools but also know the trends affecting the tools and the related project types and industries. You want an expert in the technology who knows the hidden tricks such as undocumented bugs and the ways to get around them, but you also want someone who can see where technology trends are going. You want to avoid betting your company on outdated or overpriced technology.

Seeing a body of completed software and multimedia products is important. You should go through the products on your own as well as have the candidates walk you through. Focus less on the creative aspects and more on the technical ones. Get an idea of the budget and schedule and the problems they ran into. The answers to the latter may give you a good idea of their planning and management skills.

How to Be Hired

A developer who has managed the technical development of high-quality software or interactive media project has a set of skills that are transferable and in high demand. Since the prospects are so good, it really only takes positioning yourself appropriately and then identifying good prospects. There are lots of companies to consider with each having their advantages. Large entertainment companies, television and cable broadcasters, book publishers, and advertising agencies are likely to have a large need for someone to help guide their technical strategy. At the same time, they may not have appreciation for technology as many of the multimedia publishers that formed around the technology. Smaller studios and game developers are good possibilities. One of their advantages, depending on how you look at it, is their eagerness to pursue new technologies and their tendency to have an extremely lean management structure.

Executive producers and **producers** are the most appropriate people to contact. The executive producer will typically be looking for a person to manage all technical operations on a company-wide basis. A producer is likely to be concerned only about a particular project or set of projects. Previously completed projects, good references, and a good interview are going to be the primary assets in getting a job. Have demo materials available and be sure there is proper equipment available to run them. Consider bringing a laptop computer as a backup. When showing products you have worked on to a potential employer, refrain from giving them the typical insider's product demo. People too close to a project have a tendency to spend too long on a demo and go into too much detail. Concentrate less on showing how cool the product is and more on some of the technical and management challenges that you faced in putting the product together. Show several that were created under

Most projects involving software development are late. CD-ROM projects commonly ship four to five months from their initial targeted dates. (Large software applications or operation systems often slip by a year or more.) There is pressure, though, from circles outside the traditional software circles to change this tendency. Entertainment and game companies, in particular, are investing in large marketing campaigns for new games releases. Unpredictable development schedules puts these campaigns in serious jeopardy.

255

different circumstances and technologies. Leave them excited about your work, not worn out and weary.

The references and the interview should highlight your technical competency as well as your management skills. Also, you want to come across as being easy to work with and dependable. Creating multimedia products is seen more and more as a creative enterprise and not a technical feat. You want to be seen as someone who can help realize the creative vision and not someone who will hijack the production and take it to your own ends.

Compensation

Compensation for a technical lead is probably one of the highest of all the roles outside of top level management. An experienced technical lead can command a high salary or hourly rate in almost any organization developing interactive products. The salary range will vary between

*3D is going to play a more important role in the **interface**▶ 170, especially with navigating through large quantities of information. Something we haven't taken advantage of is the Z axis. We go up, down, left, or right, we have scroll bars for that. But we haven't started to dive in and out of information yet. That will come.*

—Scott Maddux, Hardware/Software Interface Designer, Hasbro

Aric Wilmunder
Manager, Software Tools and Technology, LucasArts

Cross-platform development is one of the big issues that's facing those of us in development. There are so many different platforms out there right now, and there are so many that are on their way. Trying to design systems that allow you to take data from one platform, use it, and manipulate it on a variety of other platforms becomes more and more critical.

My goal with our story engine—and that is to give the artists, the designers, and the musicians the ability to build entertainment products without having to concern themselves greatly with the platform that's sitting underneath it this week—because last week it was Atari, Commodore 64, and Apple IIs and this week it's IBM and Macs and next week it's Power PC, the Pentium, and the new consoles.

A director shouldn't be worrying about what size theater you're watching his movie in. He should be worrying about making the best movie he possibly can. Musicians shouldn't be worrying about what size sub-woofer you've got in your theater. They should be worrying about creating the best orchestral score for a movie. That's the direction that I'm really trying to push technology into.

One of my current joys is getting data that runs on PCs and then being able to turn that directly around and run it on Macs or on Segas or platform XYZ. Without that, you're going to be getting products with the same names that have vastly different gaming experiences—all depending on the platform that you're on.

Our story engine has run on either twelve or thirteen different platforms so it is possible. The downside is that there tends to be a compromise, whether it's performance or not taking advantage of a capability of a particular platform. What I like doing, though, is letting a design team focus on building a great product. You might have one designer working a year and a half, plus three scripters, plus three or more artists, plus three musicians. What you're looking at in the long run is ten or more person-years focused into building a great product. If you can then take that great product and move it swiftly and cleanly across platforms, you're able to maximize the effort of the initial design team. But you have to try to do it without compromising the game's integrity.

J.A. Nelson
Technical Lead, Seismic Entertainment

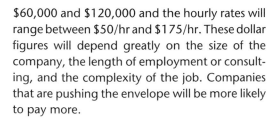

Seven-day weeks and 16-hour days are part of the job description for J.A. Nelson. "This is my land. I love it!" he says of his current immersive schedule as lead programmer and technical lead at Seismic Entertainment. In addition to his role as lead programmer, his responsibilities include making sure there are no technical problems with the media, the software, or the design. Specifically, that means he must make sure that creative visions are technically possible and offer alternative solutions to potential wormholes that threaten to throw projects off track and over budget.

That doesn't mean J.A. walks around saying no to ideas. Instead, he acts as a facilitator and programmer, working to come up with new solutions to implement the designer's vision. In that capacity, J.A. acts as a creative team member finding solutions that can lead the design in new directions.

One of J.A.'s most important roles concerns creating the architecture of the underlying project code. As J.A. describes it, "The architecture defines how the code is to be organized. And that's important for code reusability, functionality, being able to make design changes instantaneously or very quickly, efficiency, speed, and the general well-being of your programmers. And cost. If you do the brainpower before hand and then lay down your code, you can keep costs down. You do

all your thinking first, design it all, find your problems, create the technology, do tests, then hand it off to the team and, in theory, it all works."

That sort of down-to-earth, no-nonsense approach to what can be a rather arcane process is one of the reasons J.A. is in such demand as a technical lead and lead programmer. "The fun part of this job is getting the chance to lay down some great architecture and excellent code," according to J.A., who thinks of code on three levels: "First pass is 'Get it working.' Second pass is 'Clean, professional code.' And then, if the time and budget permits, there's 'artwork.' And the difference between clean, professional code and artwork is apparent only to another programmer or a designer if they ever need to reuse the code. The end user will never know the difference."

"My true love is writing code," he continues. "At Drew Pictures [whose game Iron Helix *broke new ground in the interactive gaming world] I sat in the basement for 16 hours a day writing code with headphones on. That's one of my true joys."*

$60,000 and $120,000 and the hourly rates will range between $50/hr and $175/hr. These dollar figures will depend greatly on the size of the company, the length of employment or consulting, and the complexity of the job. Companies that are pushing the envelope will be more likely to pay more.

Stock options ▶ 93 or **royalties** ▶ 91 are also distinct possibilities in many situations. Many experienced technical people have worked at previous jobs where they have received one form

or the other. Having this type of precedent will help greatly when negotiating with potential employers or clients. Otherwise, do some research among acquaintances in similar positions and do not hesitate to consider multiple offers and weigh them accordingly. Other things to consider when making a decision, though, are the **viability of the project and the company** ▶ 92. Life can be too short to invest a year or more on a project that never ships or reaches its full potential.

Programmer

What They Do

Programmers create the underlying software that runs a multimedia program and responds to the user's actions. In the ideal situation, the programming team will build the product from a detailed plan. In a less than ideal situation, the programming team will make it up as they go along.

There are several levels to the programming role. The first is the **lead** or **senior programmer**. This person typically takes the project from beginning to end and lays down all of the code or is ultimately responsible for it. They work with the technical lead closely and, in some situations, are the same person. The next two levels are **programmer** and **junior programmer**, with the latter signifying someone who is relatively recently out of school and new to application development. All three roles write and debug modules of code or possibly create tools for other programmers on the team to use.

Another form of programmer is a **scripter**. A scripter usually works in scripting languages, often within an authoring tool, and primarily creates simple navigation schemes and integrates media from the media production staff. A scripter might work in tools such as *Macromedia Director, HyperCard,* or *Apple Media Tool* and create titles, kiosks, and presentations. Scripters may also work in languages such as PERL or Hypertext Markup Language (HTML), both of which are extremely popular in **World Wide Web** ▶ 16, 61 development. Although technically programmers and scripters are the same, programmers tend to have formal programming background while scripters may only have knowledge of a certain language or process.

A final programming role is that of **system administrator**. Although the image is that of managing hardware assets and cabling, a large part of their job is to configure, archive, and back-up systems and protect machines against viruses and monitor security. All of these tasks require some level of sophistication in understanding and possibly programming software.

A single programmer may be brought into the conceptual stage of development in order to help provide guidance and feedback on various ideas for the project. Programmers here need to be careful not to turn down ideas right away as being unfeasible. They should give the ideas time to sink in to see if there are alternatives that will work. Programmers are used in the design stage to build simple tests to validate design techniques and help create prototypes. These prototype can be used for selling ideas to publishers or investors or for refining the product design. All programmers are busy in production and most continue through testing until the product finally ships. Some stay on afterwards to fix bugs or create new versions.

Process

The first major milestone after a prototype is the **functional specification** ▶ 130, 173, 251. One or more programmers will often help the interface designer and technical lead create this document with the interface designer. The document should provide all the details needed to create the project. It should be complete enough so that it could be handed to a set of programmers unfamiliar with earlier discussions such that they could build the product without further assistance. Building a multimedia product without functional specifications is a lot like building a house without a blueprint.

Within the framework of the specification should lie an architectural design as well as an interface plan. These two supply all the information needed to create the various modules. The modules are discrete units, typically separated by logical function. For example, there will be a set of modules for printing or for running the simulation engine in a game. **Object-oriented languages** let programmers encapsulate both data and functions on that data into one complete entity. This structure helps isolate code so that changes in one area has less likelihood of affecting other areas. An example is chess. Each piece has a set of data (its location) and a set of operations on that

Don Brenner
Programmer

When Don Brenner is not trekking through the Himalayas, getting locked up by Chinese border guards while attempting to sneak into Tibet, or volunteering in a Guatemalan orphanage, he can be found very late at night with a quart bottle of Cobra at his side, cranking out some of the coolest Lingo code being written today.

Don shows up for work late in the afternoon. So late, in fact, that most people are heading for home while he's just sitting down to the computer. However, once there Don is a magician, performing feats of code in a single night that would take other less skilled programmers days to accomplish. A recent all-nighter found him creating video sprites in the 64,000 layers of QuickTime, enabling a program to display many QuickTime movies simultaneously. Imagine a QuickTime video in which a TV is playing its own video in the background. Now imagine "grabbing" the TV and moving it within the larger QuickTime movie while its video continues to play and you begin to get the picture. Currently, Don is writing X-commands to enable Director to handle this capability.

Don's career as a programmer began at the age of 13, when he began writing video games in assembly language. Bored with that, his interest turned to anthropology and eventually education. The new learning theories he encountered led him back to programming. While his most recent credit includes the work he did as a programmer on The Daedelus Encounter *for Machadeus, Don is undergoing something of a career change himself. Increasingly, he finds his interests lie in the field of educational design. "My main goal is to find new ways of representing information to make learning interesting" he says. "I think my technical background will be a big factor in design since I know what works and what doesn't in multimedia, and I can create designs that take advantage of the computer's underlying C code."*

data (the way it can move). Adding another piece with a different type of movement does not affect the other pieces. Developing projects in object-oriented languages such as C++ and Objective-C has significant advantages and savings over doing it in traditional languages such as C and Pascal.

As programmers create these modules, they will test them, possibly under the guidance of testers. At various points in the development process, they will create builds. **Builds** ▶ 253 are versions of the product that meet certain guidelines. They are a way to formally measure progress. Throughout development, programmers are commonly integrating media components supplied by visual designers, sound producers or editors, animators, and video producers.

At some point in the process, an **alpha version** ▶ 265 will be created. This version signifies the beginning of the testing phase. The next major milestone is **beta testing** ▶ 266 which is followed by **golden master** ▶ 266, which is the version that is suitable for shipping. Throughout testing, programmers will respond to bug reports and try to find and eliminate the problems, hopefully without introducing other ones in the process.

Tools and Techniques

The primary tools a programmer uses are authoring tools, compilers, and debuggers. An **authoring tool** ▶ 253 is usually an interpretive programming environment meaning that the programmer can develop a program and run it without having to take any intermediate steps.

The instructions that the programmer programs gets interpreted as the code is processed. Most traditional languages such as C and C++ need to be compiled and linked before running. The compiling turns the source code into machine readable code. This step can take time, especially with large and complex programs. Programmers may use both authoring tools and **compilers** if they are integrating into the authoring tool modules written in a traditional language.

For compiled programs, **debuggers** are almost essential for finding and resolving bugs. A debugger matches the compiled code against the source code and allows programmers to view the contents of memory. Programmers can usually set breakpoints at certain locations to stop a program to look at the variables and to step through specific lines in the code.

Other important tools in a programmer's arsenal are **references** on languages and tools. Most programmers will have dog-eared books on programming topics within easy rich. Resources from developer support groups for computer platforms, authoring tools, or programming environments are also popular. Many groups provide phone and email support and also publish frequently asked questions on CD-ROM and in online formats.

One of the best techniques for a programmer is to work within a detailed functional specification and to let others on the project perform their jobs. Programmers have a tendency to want to create or change design elements or mess with the sound. You should avoid doing this because it wastes time that could be spent developing the underlying software. Make your concerns on these matters known but leave the final decisions to the people who have the responsibility for them.

Another technique is to develop the sections assigned in broad brush strokes and then refine each section after a rough working version has been built. A common mistake is to spend a long time on one particular area redesigning it and reworking it until it is perfect only to find that little time is left for the remaining sections. Setting small milestones every few days and aggressively

trying to meet them will help keep projects focused.

Qualifications
The best programmers have a lot of experience, but this experience can be defined many ways. One of the more important experiences is to have **created and shipped a product**. Only those who have been through the process can begin to appreciate all the things done in the beginning and along the way to keep a project focused and on target. Another form of experience is practice writing code. There is almost no substitute for learning about data structures, algorithms, and bug tracking. A novelist or writer can only get better by writing. (It was once said that Jack Kerouac wrote one million words before he was 21.) The same is true for programming. No other form of training provides the same ways to think about problems as writing lots of code does.

Good programmers also tend to have the ability to **focus** on one area for long lengths of time. The nature of programming means that they need to weave together many threads. Not connecting the parts in the right way results in bugs. These can show up right away or years later. Related to a high concentration level is **determination**. Programmers need to create things that work. The discipline is less subjective than in other disciplines. Either it works or it doesn't. Partial credit is rarely given. Determination, coupled with knowledge, is often the only way to get there.

Scripters need to be diligent and proficient. Their tasks are similar to page layout. They often need to keep track of many elements but usually at only a surface level. They have less need to understand structures and traditional programming techniques unless they want to move into positions of more responsibility.

How to Hire
The first thing that needs to happen when hiring a programmer is to get an idea of the type of programmer you need. On the surface level, this includes whether they should be full-time or freelance and in what language and/or authoring tool they should specialize. More detailed ques-

tions to answer include whether they should be fast at prototyping, good at design, or skilled at finishing. Should they be good at taking over someone else's code and making it work, or do they need to start from scratch? Answering these questions will help you narrow your search dramatically.

Advertising positions or using recruiters are common ways to find programmers. Other good ways are attending conferences and user group meetings. Instructors at local universities or multimedia education programs will often recommend several of their best students. Make an effort to look at working versions of what they've done. If possible take a look at code samples and have others on the programming team interview the candidates too.

When you find someone that seems to fit, make sure you train them and then watch them closely in the beginning. There is little middle ground in programming. Either you have the skills and can fit into an environment or you don't. In many situations, a manager may need to make this call soon after hiring.

How to Be Hired

Almost every company creating products has an immediate need for qualified programmers, so good programmers should not have difficulty finding work in interactive media. The project should appeal to you, especially since you might be working on it for five months to a year. The company should value programmers and have a good structure in place for managing projects. Working on projects that are notoriously late is not all that fun, nor is working for companies that treat programmers as widgets to move around in the process.

Related to knowing your interests is knowing what tools and programming areas you consider yourself an expert in. Someone who knows all the tricks about a language or programming tool tends to be much more valuable than someone

who learns fast but has only a general knowledge of programming. **Technical leads** and **producers** are the most likely people to hire programmers. Good managers will look for experts and so you should identify companies that need people with your specialty and present a good case for your skills.

Resumes ▶ 81 can be important, but **credit lists** ▶ 82 are gaining more and more acceptance and viability. Technical leads and producers will be looking for evidence that you can complete projects. A resume tends not to emphasize that but a credit list does. In order to have a credit list, though, you need to have credits. If you do not, you might want to consider working on small short-term projects to build that list while looking for more substantial and rewarding projects. You can also start at a lower rate but set up an aggressive review schedule that increases your salary or rate should you meet certain performance standards. If you perform contract work, be sure to factor in your equipment and overhead costs. Also take into account the time not spent working and make sure your rate reflects that down time.

Compensation

The compensation range for a programmer varies greatly across project types, industries, and possibly even seasons. Experts at programming *Macromedia Director* are finding themselves in huge demand from game and CD-ROM companies. The recent rushes to get titles out in time for the Christmas season resulted in numerous calls during the summer and fall months. Traditional C and C++ programmers are in demand at online services and other developers doing a lot of custom development. The salaries for programmers will range from $35,000/yr for people straight out of school with computer programming backgrounds to $70,000/yr for senior programmers. Free-lance contractors can receive anywhere from $50/hr to $100/hr. The scripter role is likely to be an entry-level position, as is the system administrator role in many instances. The salaries and rates will reflect this.

People coming out of school typically have the excellent programming experience and fundamentals but do not have the experience working on shipping projects. They can make excellent additions to almost any programming team but they need to be managed well and teamed with programmers who have developed products before.

System administrators need some level of experience but they also need to be just as quick in finding solutions to things they are unfamiliar with. Someone who can find the answer quickly is just as good as someone who knows it off the top of their head.

photo by Rosalie Blakey

Patrick Milligan
Programmer

Patrick Milligan makes dreams come true. When one of his clients calls with a vision that needs to be realized, Patrick provides the programming and scripting expertise that brings the vision to life on the small screen. Patrick considers himself a "details kind of guy, and a finisher." He draws a parallel to carpentry: Some workers are framers, who excel at building a foundation quickly. Others are called in toward the end of the project, to work on the finishing touches. "If I were a carpenter," Patrick says, "I would be into building cabinets."

Some of the multimedia "cabinets" Patrick has worked on putting the final high finish on, include Jazz, A Multimedia History, *and projects for EBook, Gray Matter Design, and Haukom Associates. He also teaches a programming course at San Francisco State University's Department of Multimedia Studies. The class presents an overview of the most popular authoring tools on the market, including* HyperCard, SuperCard, PLUS, Director, Asymetrix Toolbook, Authorware, *and* Grasp.

Lately, the favorite authoring tool in Patrick's tool chest is Macromedia Director *because it "lets you express a broad range of different interactivities and different styles of interaction. But with that power comes the price and responsibility of attacking the learning curve, and understanding how to use the tool. Not everyone is going to be able to do that. That's where guys like me come in."*

vivid: What roles can programmers play?

Part of what they do is understand what's possible and how to get there. Sometimes, the artistic vision gets out of synch with what you can realize today with the technology. As an example, I was working with an architect that had unrealistic expectations about how you could do walkthroughs of a virtual space under construction. There was no way with the current technology to get to where his vision was, to what he wanted to present to his clients. So you need an understanding on how far you can push the technology, and you get this by keeping current with what's happening, what things are feasible, what's available, and at what price point. You need to make use of the newer capabilities as they come out.

But some people get burned out by being too much of an early adopter. It's very, very expensive to get on some of these band wagons. If you jump too early on some of these leading technologies, you may not have enough cash to see you through. If you jump on too late, you're going to be behind. There's a delicate balance on picking up on and applying the technology at the right point in time.

vivid: Today, programmers are almost essential to any multimedia project. Is that going to change as the tools get better? Will there still be a need for programmers?

Many years ago they said, "Well, you know, programmers as a species are limited because, eventually, computers will program themselves and we won't need humans in the loop." I think we're quite aways away from that in terms of software development. I also think that we will never completely remove the need for someone to program in multimedia.

I do think, though, that we will open the door to a lot more people to be able to approach that. Tools like *HyperCard* opened up the door to a lot of people who might not have otherwise programmed their computer. It kind of seduced them in to say, "Oh, this is easy." Then, of course, when they discovered when they got really into it, it's like, "Well, this is really programming." But the fact is, they kind of got snookered in, to giving it a try. You get seduced by a simple button script that says, "Go to the next card." Before you know it, the things you really want to do really do require understanding how to program. But, I think we will see the tools get better to the point where you won't need as much in the way of programming.

We'll have designers of information containers and the people that will actually fill the information in won't need to know programming to do that. It's like templates for *PageMaker*. We'll be able to hand out a programmer-created template for a multimedia title that requires assembly but doesn't require a broad set of tools to screw it together. Programmers will be focusing more on these building these meta-tools to facilitate the production.

vivid: What do you suggest to someone that wants to get involved in this new media as a developer? What should they learn? What courses should they take?

Well, having a good sound grounding in the basics of computer science certainly doesn't hurt. Understanding data structures and a variety of programming languages and so forth is helpful. So is understanding the kinds of things that a computer can do and that you can apply to different problem domains. So I certainly wouldn't discourage people from getting a grounding in the basics of computer science as it exists today, but my personal preference would be to steer people toward higher level languages that would give them a lot of

leverage. I personally am not a fan of C. I think it's an arcane, cryptic language. It's very popular and, in the right hands, it can do wonderful things. But I'm more of a Small Talk and higher level object-oriented programming kind of person.

In fact, object-oriented programming is something they should get a foundation on because I think that will be the way of the future. They haven't quite figured out how to make object-oriented programming work in the sense that integrated circuits work for hardware design. But, you want to be able to encapsulate functionality so a module you've written once plugs and plays with the thing you're working on at a later point. Or, if it doesn't, you can do a few tweaks without going under the hood. Traditional code—like C or Pascal—sort of sets like concrete. It's very difficult to mutate it once you've written it. Whereas some of the softer languages are more like jello or modeling clay. It's that kind of domain that I find more interesting.

vivid: What other points would you want to get across?

If the issue is, "What's the role of software development in future multimedia?" I would say that as the tools get easier and easier to use, programming efforts will be pushed in the direction of providing much more interesting interaction and environments than we have today. The bottom line, from my point of view, is that this is fairly embryonic. We're still at the stage in multimedia development that the movie industry was at when it still took someone with a chemist's and mechanical engineering background to run and operate the camera and keep it functioning to make movies. We haven't got our D.W. Griffiths yet. But when they come, I for one will be ready for them, and glad to continue in the role of making it possible for them to express their vision.

Test Manager

What They Do

The **test manager** role in multimedia is a direct descendant of the software test manager role. Although most other media industries have some form of quality assurance, they put nowhere near the emphasis and resources on it as the software industry does. Just as a chief financial officer's primary responsibility is toward the shareholders, the test manager's primary responsibility is to users, clients, and customers. This responsibility means that if a product does not work properly, the blame ultimately lies with the test manager. To be fair, management must first recognize that a high level of quality is important and devote sufficient resources to achieving it. The test manager, however, is concerned as much with process as with results. They often put in place processes within the entire company to ensure that all aspects of a company's operations—not just products—are as efficient and error-free as possible.

The recognition that **quality assurance** is important in multimedia is growing quickly, thanks in part to several widely publicized instances of flawed products. This recognition means more opportunities for people who can create and manage testing organizations. Where these organizations reside within a company varies. Some companies have centralized testing departments that all products pass through before release. Test managers in these companies may report to the head of operations or quality assurance. Others include testing as part of product development, in which case testing managers may report to producers or executive producers.

Regardless of the structure, the test organization plays a crucial role in developing an understanding among all groups involved in the project, including marketing, development, and customer support, on what constitutes a finished product. A test manager's signature is often needed before a product can be released. Also, the test manager often has the primary authority over a product from the time it enters formal testing until the time it is released. This means that the test manager will direct the actions of testers and developers alike. In some companies, test managers may be responsible for implementing version control and backup procedures and checking for viruses within the product and possibly within the company. Assisting **customer support** ▶ 274 operations may also be a part of the job.

The test manager role is usually a full-time position that extends across several projects. Within a single project, the heaviest area of activity on a project for test managers is from the point when the product enters formal testing until just after the first customer shipment. They are involved before testing begins even to the point of product design. Here they can advise on the risk of making certain decisions and their implications on testing. Including a feature such as printing might seem simple to a designer or programmer, but when considered in terms of quality, the risk of introducing bugs or increasing the cost of testing and support might outweigh the benefits.

Where a test manager begins and how much involvement they have before testing begins will depend on the commitment to quality that senior management has made as well as the complexity of the project. The complexity in turn is influenced by the **size**, the amount of **custom software** developed, and the level of **interactivity** ▶ 171. On large projects, they will be deeply involved in creating test plans and setting up large beta testing programs. On smaller projects such as kiosks or marketing presentations, they may oversee the activities of a tester.

Process

A test manager should be brought in early in product planning. Here they will help determine whether the product can be tested within a certain budget or schedule. It might be possible to put together a CD-ROM in two months but it is likely to take another month to make sure it will

The budget for testing in software development is approximately 40% of the total budget. The current average budget for testing in multimedia is about 5%. These figures and the noted problems with more than a few multimedia titles surely point toward an increase in the importance of testing, the number of opportunities, and the dollar percentages invested in quality assurance.

Acquiring the knowledge of the testing process and obtaining testing equipment are significant investments for many developers. These high costs increase the likelihood of seeing more independent testing labs offering multimedia testing services.

AnnD Canavan
Vice President of Production, vivid studios

For several years, AnnD Canavan has watched her career progress from quality assurance (QA) into project management, and she wouldn't have it any other way. She feels that QA is the perfect background for project management. "Because QA has to adopt the user's mindset," she explains, "we're very clear about meeting client expectations up front." Project managers, she reasons, have the same goal; however, unlike QA, they have the luxury of setting those expectations from the start rather than just checking that they've been met after the project is finished. In her manager's hat, AnnD can now assure that quality is built into each project, as well as establish communication standards to keep the entire team in synch.

She developed her talents for managing teams at Lotus Development in Cambridge, where she was a QA Manager for Lotus 1-2-3 and Marketing Support Coordinator for Lotus Notes. At Lotus, she supervised engineers, established standards, tools, and test scripts, and developed and managed the automation laboratory. Her education was in the humanities (AnnD received a BA in Sociology/Psychology from Stonehill College and pursued graduate studies in telecommunications at the University of New Hampshire), however she believes that students in any field can excel in QA, as long as they are focused on the two keys to successful teamwork—details and communication.

vivid has seen significant benefits from implementing the tenets of her "QA mindset." This means understanding that any team effort can be taken in a sense as a production line, where every step along the way needs to be of the highest quality. Every team member knows their role and can be trusted to reach for the extra something that sets their products apart. AnnD's record with vivid shows 100% on-time deliveries to clients, as promised, at or above client standards. This represents not just effective QA, but coordinated teamwork from start to finish.

A Libra who always has her scales handy, AnnD is adept at balancing the demands of her calling; as she puts it, "People in QA have to be idealists, to strive for ever-elusive perfection. Yet they also have to be realists, because there's never enough time, and you can never prove a project is defect-free. After all," she says knowingly, "it's much easier to prove the presence of a bug than its absence."

work on all the machines it is supposed to. Not having an experienced test manager provide that information at the beginning can create expectations that cannot be met.

Throughout the design, a test manager will prepare a **test plan**. The test plan is the most important document a test manager will create. It explains the scope of testing involved and should be created at the same time the functional specification and production plans are created. A good test plan provides a testing budget and a schedule, staffing requirements, hardware and software needs, and environmental issues or dependencies. It also provides a description of the bug report form and the bug tracking database. It defines the metrics that answers the question, "When is testing finished?"

During production, the test manager helps the producer determine the true progress of the project. The first major milestone for a test manager is alpha testing. An **alpha version** ▶ 259 of a project is the first version that provides a certain level of usability and can be put through tests by the testing organization. The tests performed in this stage are based on the level of functionality present in the first alpha build. Ideally the testing organization uses the detailed development schedule to determine a modular testing approach.

The next major milestone is beta testing. A **beta version** ▶ 259 is a version that is "feature complete," or in other words, where the code base has been completely written and the content is fully integrated. A beta version might be compared to the first draft of a book or the rough cut of a movie. It will contain many bugs and discrepancies but the process to move it to completion is a matter of refinement as opposed to creation. Within the beta cycle, there are going to be many versions as bugs are fixed and the code frozen to allow consistent testing procedures.

Somewhere between alpha and beta there is a meeting between all groups involved in the project to "freeze" the content and the features. The decisions in this meeting solidify what stays in the product and what does not. Preferably, content and features should be taken out and not added or enhanced.

During the testing process, the testers will create bug reports in response to problems and enter them into the bug database. Test managers and testers will create bug lists to review the status of testing and help isolate problem areas. They may schedule bug triage meetings to determine which bugs to fix first, which ones to fix next, and which ones not to fix. This process continues until a golden master version is reached. The **golden master** ▶ 259 is the version that is handed to the disc manufacturer or client or released to the public. The time between golden master and the first customer shipment is the most nerve-racking period for a test manager because of the anticipation for a sudden rash of customer complaints.

Tools and Techniques

The management tools that a test manager uses are no different from the management tools that a producer uses. These include tools to prepare budgets and schedules as well as tools to com-

municate with testers, producers, developers, and upper management. Status reports to and from all these parties are important because a test manager has to know when testing will be completed and the product or service is ready for shipping. Many packaging, marketing, and distribution plans hinge on meeting or knowing the specific dates for completing a product. A two-month slip in testing is far more critical than a two-month slip early in production because marketing dollars are more likely to be committed at later dates in the schedule.

Specific testing tools and techniques include test scripts, bug reports, bug databases, and test automation tools. A test script is a document based on a functional specification that lists a specific sequence of steps for testers to follow. These steps confirm that the proper events occur in response to each specific action. Test scripts allow the testing organization to repeatedly and independently cover many scenarios for using the product. They can be given to different testers with few additional instructions, and help in verifying acceptable behavior for different machines, platforms, or versions. A large part of testing is assuring predictability. Running detailed tests described in test scripts is one of the best ways to do this. The goal of each test script is to prove the software works as specified, including error conditions.

Bug reports are forms used by internal and external testers to describe a problem that occurs during testing as well as after a product ships. It's important that these forms ask for as much descriptive information about the problem as possible. A lot of time can be spent searching for a problem in a different part of a program or on a different machine. A **bug database** is simply a database of the bug reports. It lets each person on the testing team, as well as the technical lead, producer, and others, check the status of testing. A well-designed database also provides different views of the information in it to highlight potential problem areas.

There are many tools available to automate a variety of testing activities. These tools help to reduce costs and increase testing efficiency. Some of these tools are for white-box testing; others are for black-box testing. **White-box testing** is testing that relies on knowledge of the internal workings. An example of a white-box tool is a code-coverage tool. This tool records the areas in the code that have been visited as testers use the product, providing an internal mechanism for spotting significant areas that have not been tested.

Black-box testing makes no assumptions about the internal workings of a product. An example of a black-box testing tool is a keystroke capture tool. This type of tool captures input commands from the keyboard, mouse, or other input peripheral and saves them, allowing testers to replay the commands for later tests on different versions or on different machines. Quite simply, it reduces the number of people that are needed to sit at machines and type in basic sequences and allows for the desired repeatability attribute important in testing.

Qualifications

The most important qualifications for a test manager are to know the **testing process** and to have good **management skills**. Although interactive media products are relatively new, there are proven methods for testing software that directly apply to them. A good test manager knows the essential steps, tools, and techniques involved in testing. They should also be experienced at implementing them within an organization that contains a set of highly diverse people.

The management skills include planning, leadership, and problem identification skills. The planning skills allow a test manager to forecast the resources and time needed to adequately test a product and to put the metrics in place so all players know the status at any given point in the testing cycle. The leadership skills are important in hiring, training, and motivating a large group of often inexperienced testers. Good testers typically have personality traits and skills far different from that of designers and programmers. A qualified test manager will be able to quickly identify people suited for testing.

Having the problem-identification skills simply means being able to quickly answer the questions, "Do we have a problem?" And if so, "How big is it?" Test managers that ignore, or are unable to see, patterns indicating poor quality are not likely to last long. As for other traits, a test manager should be organized, methodical, and detail-oriented. Design skills and creative brilliance are not needed for testing. An eye for quality is.

How to Hire

Before hiring a test manager, it is important to understand where the test manager will fit into the **management structure** ▶ 92. In other words, who will a test manager report to? Will there be a separate quality assurance department or will it be a part of development? If testing is only needed for a single project, how and when do you bring the test manager in? In the case of a publisher working with outside developers, a test manager may be hired not to implement testing procedures but to independently validate that products received from developers are fit for release.

Test managers at other multimedia companies make good prospects, as do those in traditional software companies. Prospects from software companies may not have experience with multimedia platforms or products, but working with a knowledgeable producer from the beginning, they can pick up this experience without adversely affecting the production and testing schedules.

Look for someone with an eye for quality, and a commitment to represent the user. Someone with a software programming background may not make the best choice because they may have a cavalier attitude toward users. A test manager also needs to be decisive and strong in the face of adversity. Since they are commonly the ones that make a final decision on when to ship, they need to be strong enough to say, "No, it's not ready."

How to Be Hired

The first step to being hired as a test manager is to find out who is responsible for issues of quality within a company. Smaller companies may not recognize quality assurance as a separate area that is outside project management or development. Larger companies may have separate departments. The structure and the level of recognition of quality assurance in a business will strongly influence the type of approach you should take.

If you're looking to make the move from a test manager of a software company to a multimedia production studio or publisher, for example, and there is little structure or emphasis on testing, then a **sales pitch** on the importance of quality assurance might be the best strategy. There are a number of stories of poorly tested products that damaged company reputations and incurred significant costs. Recent stories include the flaws in Intel's Pentium computer chip, Intuit's tax preparation programs, and Disney's release of *The Lion King* CD-ROM. All cases caused uproars among users and damaging headlines.

Also, try pointing to the increasing **cost of customer support** for multimedia products. Although customer support calls are often the price of publishing or producing any multimedia product, adequate testing can greatly reduce the cost and associated bad feelings that often come with a user having to contact customer support.

More established companies are going to look for specific experience with multimedia products as well as formal training and knowledge of the testing process. If you do not have multimedia experience, you may want to apprentice as an associate producer in order to develop knowledge of all the steps and issues in developing multimedia products.

Compensation

The compensation for a test manager in multimedia will strongly follow the compensation for test managers in the software industry. Many companies view the role as a middle management role as opposed to a vice president or director level and so they will pay accordingly. The salary range appears to vary between $40,000 and $80,000 a year.

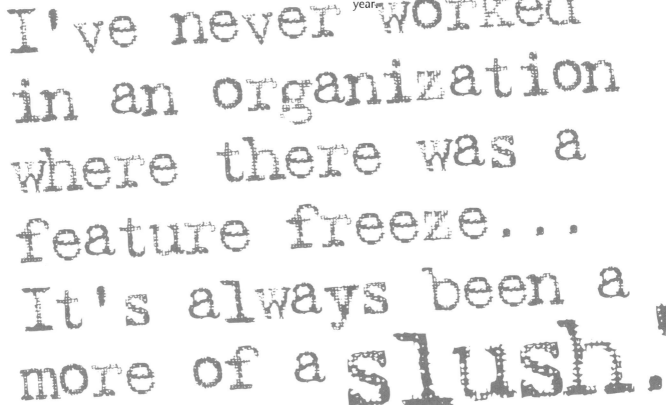

"I've never worked in an organization where there was a feature freeze... It's always been a more of a slush."

Tester

What They Do

A **tester** works under the direction of a test manager and puts a product through many series of tests to make sure it obtains the highest level of quality assurance under the given project constraints. It can be a thankless job because the primary focus is to find and isolate problems in the product. It also means running seemingly endless tests on the same parts of the product. But for people who are bothered by poorly constructed products and who take great pride in having a hand in producing quality ones, this position can be a rewarding one and one that is ultimately critical to the success of a product.

Testers fit primarily in the **production** phase and in the **testing** phase. One or two may participate earlier in development in assisting the test manager in developing the test plan. During production, they are used primarily as a form of check and balance to the development team. They will verify the progress of development by how well the product matches the milestones laid out in the production schedule. People have a tendency to overestimate the amount of completion in any task they are working on. Testers can be invaluable to a producer in auditing the work of media production and programming staffs in order to determine what is realistic. Once formal testing begins, marked by the development of alpha and beta versions of the product, testers will follow a regimented process, implementing test plans and reporting bugs and monitoring their status up until the time of shipping and beyond.

Process

The process a tester uses closely follows the software testing process. A **test plan** should be created before production begins. This plan lists the resources needed for testing (people, hardware, and software), the procedures, the schedule, and a set of test scripts and list of configurations. This information will outline all the procedures and tests to run.

There are several types of testing that occur. One type of testing is **unit testing**, which is the verification of discrete programming modules. Programmers usually perform these tests as they develop each section but a tester may help design the tests and verify their completion. Another type of testing is **functional testing**. Testing of this nature makes sure that the product performs as described in the functional specification which is usually created at the end of the design phase. If navigation or tools do not work as they are supposed to, for example, a tester will create a bug report listing the problem. The programming team will then try to correct it. When a new build occurs, the tester records whether the problem was fixed or not.

A third form of testing is **configuration** or **compatibility testing**. This type checks the product on a variety of different configurations of hardware and software. The sheer number and variations in platforms and components, especially with Windows and PC machines, make this area one of the most difficult ones to cover with complete confidence. Many businesses cut corners here, much to their peril, simply because the cost and logistics of testing all the possible avenues may seem prohibitive. The hardware components to test can include processors, memory size, sound cards, video cards, monitors, mice, joysticks, CD-ROM drives, modems, fax cards, and printers. The software components include audio and video playback systems, web browsers, fonts, other applications (especially those that the product imports or exports to), and even software utilities and extensions.

A variation of configuration testing is **environment testing**, which is where particular issues relevant to the location a product will be used in are addressed. This testing is important for **kiosks** ▶ 47, **presentations** ▶ 48, **performances** ▶ 39, and any other projects that put a great deal of emphasis on the environment it is played or viewed in. All products, though, should have some amount of testing in the type of space they

Other titles for tester are quality engineer and design verification engineer.

Lots of **game designers** ▸ 178 start out as testers and, in the process, learn what makes games enjoyable.

have been designed for. This extends to include home and business products.

A final form of testing is **content testing**. **Content experts** ▸ 195 or **researchers** will typically perform this task but possibly under the direction of the testing staff. Testers might verify this testing has occurred and possibly audit the permissions to make sure the publisher or developer has the rights to use any content or programming included in the product.

Tools and Techniques

The biggest tools a tester needs, besides a test plan, test scripts, bug reports, and test automation tools, are a wide variety of machines that enable comprehensive analysis of consistency, quality, and compatibility. The ideal testing situation involves a host of computers containing different processors and running at different clock speeds, all with an array of operating systems and extensions. Numerous manufacturers should be represented in terms of general hardware as well as cards and peripherals. However, since few can afford establishing complete **test suites** ▸ 117, many developers take advantage of access to labs at larger companies such as Apple Computer or they hire independent contract testing firms. Another option is to rent space and hardware in testing labs. These are found in areas with a high concentration of software or multimedia development.

Qualifications

Testers need to be diligent, attentive, and assertive. The combination of technology and interactivity means that there are a huge number of configurations and pathways through a product. The magnitude of testing means that the tester needs to be diligent in isolating and testing as many different permutations as defined in the test plan. They need to record their progress and their findings in order not to miss sections of the product or repeat unnecessary work.

The ever-changing nature of the underlying software during the development process means that a tester needs to be attentive to problems that may appear in previously tested sections. They also need to be able to help isolate problems. Noticing a bug in a program is one thing. Helping to find the cause and thereby the solu-

tion is another. Good testers will isolate the problem to repeatable steps and write a clear description of the steps needed to reproduce it.

Strength is needed in order to stand up to pressures to cover up problems and ship products on schedule regardless of the level of quality. Many multimedia companies do not allow adequate time and budget for testing products and, even if they do, they often end up eating into the testing schedule because of development overruns. A tester needs to stand up to these pressures and be an advocate for the user. While people are likely to initially resent someone who delays shipping a product because of problems, that treatment in no way compares to the wrath that will result should a product go out that has catastrophic problems with it. The recent cases of Intel, Intuit, and Disney should make this point clear.

How to Hire

People do not have to have prior experience to be good testers. The easy way to find people besides word of mouth is to post job descriptions about the positions and the tasks and then look through the resulting resumes for people with experiences that point toward having good analytical skills and being detail-oriented. It is sometimes difficult to find these things out about a person until after you have hired them. Nevertheless, someone who is organized, attentive, and well-presented and can follow instructions has the potential to be an excellent tester.

How to Be Hired

The test manager or producer in a production studio, publisher, or online service is the most likely person to hire testers. A full-time **test manager** especially will continually be on the lookout for people that will make good testers. Enthusiastic and qualified people who approach them stand a good chance of being hired. It goes without saying that any resumes, cover letters, or other materials should be error free. Also, you should call when you say you will and be on time or early for interviews. Test managers and producers will look at your behavior and how you present yourself to see if your habits match what is needed for the job of a tester.

Pamela 'Bondy' Bondurant
QA Lead Engineer, vivid studios

Bondy Bondurant stumbled into quality assurance and found it a far better fit for her personality than she had ever expected. "It's easy to become passionate about testing—it's simply a matter of being committed to helping the team turn out the best product possible."

After spending several years ensconced in a top secret lab, writing test plans and training test engineers, Bondy was ready to make the jump to testing something less Orwellian. Her natural choice was multimedia, though whether her new field actually is less riddled with newspeak than matters of national security is anyone's guess. She enjoys testing multimedia projects because there is such a tremendous variety within them, and her skills as a multimedia specialist are highly valued. Her work at vivid studios has been mission critical and very much appreciated.

Her years at the University of Northern Colorado had prepared her for a career in education, and multimedia let her reconnect with those interests. "I've had the opportunity to work on some educational products, which I think were of a very useful nature, and I was glad to get to work on them...Also, I got to perform testing on the Amnesty International CD-ROM. Not only is it an outstanding CD-ROM, but I got to put my skills toward something that I feel is important, something that works toward social change."

Bondy notes that one of the critical lessons that QA has taught her is the value of diplomacy and straightforward communication skills. She casts the tester as the "bearer of bad news" all the way through to the end of the project, "when you get to give a product your blessing and the whole team forgets what a showstopper you were during the development of the product. You almost always approach a product to criticize it and break it, but you're on the same side as the developers and must always value the 3,000 things that were done correctly as opposed to the five that were done incorrectly."

Her goal in testing is similar to her theory of motorcycle riding—in essence, there is no safe way to do it. Riding the bike or building the project requires the acceptance of a certain amount of risk. Once the decision has been made that the risk is worth it, you simply wear a helmet and pay close attention to the road, to try to find Zen and the art of product design.

As Bondy puts it, "Testing is a way to minimize risks, the greatest ones first, working down to the lesser risks. Finishing with a really polished product—right down to spelling errors, screen redraws, consistent interfaces, etc.—is much more rewarding than passing something off with a 'good enough' mindset." Where testing becomes quality assurance, and outstanding quality becomes the requirement, the detail-oriented individual can find a very satisfying career. Bondy notes that testing can be a career in itself or a foot in the door to design, as long as you're committed to turning out superior products and standing up for quality in the face of ever impending deadlines.

Compensation

The compensation for a tester in multimedia at the moment tends to pay less than it does in software. Rates for contractors can range between $10/hr and $30/hr and for full-time positions $25,000–$40,000. The way to increase in compensation is to either accept greater testing responsibilty, manage other testers, or move into programming or interaction design.

Sales Roles

What They Do

A **sales manager** coordinates the efforts of salespeople by helping them identify and approach potential clients in a consistent and focused manner. Sales managers also implement systems for tracking and analyzing the cost of sales. Without these systems, a sales organization can spend more resources getting business than the business is worth. Another big part of a sales manager's job is to hire and train salespeople. **Salespeople** meet with potential customers either in person, over the phone, through email, or via some other form of communication to try and sell products or services.

Sales organizations are a part of almost every company. They are especially prominent with publishers, distributors, online services, and digital periodicals. In many production studios, especially the smaller ones, the executive producer will often act as the sales manager. They may have one or more full-time salespeople or sales representatives, or use producers as the sales staff with a marketing coordinator to assist them.

With most products and with services that are well understood, sales managers and salespeople have the authority to close. This means that they can negotiate the terms and sign an agreement. With custom-built products or complex services, the sales group will often develop a relationship with potential clients but hand these contacts to a producer to prepare proposals and handle negotiations.

Sales is an ongoing process of every business so sales organizations are a continuous part of the management structure. Sales activities often take place both before a project starts and after it is finished. The sales efforts prior to the beginning of a project are usually directed toward obtaining funds to develop it. In the case of a CD-ROM title, an executive producer or producer might pitch the idea to a publisher. In the case of a kiosk, a salesperson might pitch the idea to a museum, mall, or large retailer. Sometimes the sales organization is used to test whether there is interest in products at the retail level prior to giving them the green light. The sales efforts afterward involve selling the completed product or access to it. Sales organizations for publishers, online services, or digital magazines direct their efforts toward selling products to retailers, memberships to customers, or advertising space to media buyers.

Process

The **sales process** has five steps: identify, qualify, approach, propose, and close. Some sales groups only work on the first three, leaving the proposing and closing to people more knowledgeable about the costs and deliverables involved in a project. In other cases, sales managers and salespeople handle all the steps, though often within a given framework established by the management team. This framework can include the range for negotiating items such as the delivery schedule, discount rate, and payment terms.

Each of these steps can take place within a matter of minutes or stretch out over the course of weeks or months. A good sales manager guides and motivates salespeople to meet with qualified contacts and move towards a sale. Not adequately qualifying prospects is a fundamental mistake that most inexperienced salespeople make. They end up spending a lot of time educating prospects, only to find out later they either do not have the money or were just looking for information. A good salesperson makes the effort to find out who makes the buying decision, whether they have the budget to make a purchase, and what their time frame is.

Tools and Techniques

A sales manager uses several tools to help them and the people they manage identify and keep track of potential customers and competitors. These tools include contact databases, marketing lists and directories, and possibly geographic information systems (GIS). The latter tool consists of mapping software that allows salespeople to see the areas containing current or potential

Marketing ▶ 148 involves establishing and communicating a company's strategy to a wide audience. Sales involves the application of sales tactics to develop a one-on-one relationship and complete a transaction.

customers and make decisions based on that information. Also important are tools that help them contact people. Sophisticated call-routing systems for telephones are becoming increasingly popular, especially with businesses that sell directly to customers. Online services and companies selling business-to-business products usually have large telephone sales staffs. Increasingly, a sales manager's responsibilities are being extended to include setting up and managing online transaction systems.

Qualifications

Most sales managers have a **background in sales**. Although some managers may be able to get away with not having one, it comes in handy not only for helping salespeople close deals, but also for knowing how to manage and motivate salespeople. Sales managers need to know the steps in a sales process so they can train and manage others in the process. They also need to know who to hire and when to replace someone not doing their job. It can be hard to tell how a salesperson will perform until they are performing. Once there, however, experienced sales managers can quickly tell which ones hold promise and which ones do not. This intuition will help them decide how many resources to devote to each salesperson and when to let someone go.

How to Hire

The way to hire a sales manager or salesperson for interactive media is really no different than the way to hire people for similar positions in other industries. Posting job openings and using recruiters are common and appropriate ways to find people, as is looking for people in similar positions in traditional industries. A sales manager at a print magazine, for example, is a very good candidate for the same position at an online magazine. Although the pricing and form of advertising are different, the principles and the goals of the position are the same. You want to look for someone that has run a successful sales operation before. Barring this qualification you may want to look for a sales person with experience selling the same products or services along with great management skills. Many salespeople do not have the skills for the manager position, but some do.

How to Be Hired

Getting hired as a sales manager or salesperson at a company working in multimedia means first understanding the type of sales that is taking place and then **positioning** ▶ 80 yourself appropriately. A business that creates interactive marketing presentations will be looking for someone not only knowledgeable about selling presentations but also presentable to their business clientele. Understanding the products, services, and technology can be an asset but not as much as understanding the sales process and knowing the marketplace.

Compensation

Most sales managers are salaried, while most salespeople receive some form of a commission based on the business that they bring in. The wages, commissions, benefits, and "perks" will be similar to those found in any other industry. There are few rules and so a lot of the compensation package is negotiable.

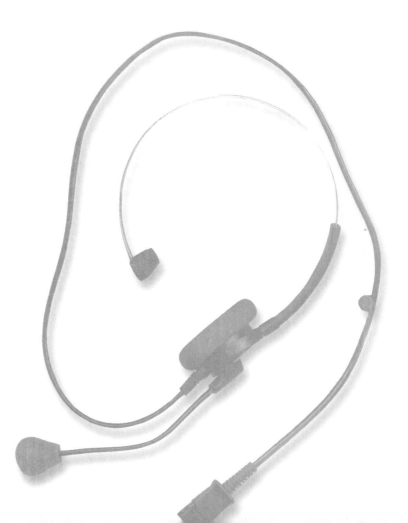

Customer Support

Some companies will use phone menus or artificial intelligence software to route strategic users to special handlers.

What They Do

Customer support is one of the fastest growing areas in multimedia and in the computer industry in general. As computer products increasingly move into the consumer marketplace, there is a growing need to respond to customers with questions and problems. It is a huge area for computer hardware manufacturers and software publishers and is becoming an increasingly larger issue for multimedia publishers and online services. Businesses that do not take support into account are making a fatal mistake. Support costs, along with marketing costs, are two of the major reasons why small publishers and online services are having a difficult time competing with larger companies.

Most positions in customer support are treated as entry level positions, but this is one of the few areas that offers the chance to move into either marketing or development. Over the course of their job, a support person will develop in-depth knowledge of the product as well as have the opportunity to talk directly with customers. Few people in the company get the chance to do both. This experience can pave the way for you to move into testing and then into development (provided you have the skills and aptitudes for those roles). Or, you can make a lateral move into marketing.

Customer support for a multimedia product can occur for as long as the product is on the market and that cost can approximate or even exceed a product's development cost. These facts alone make multimedia publishing strikingly different from book, music, or film publishing. Unless something goes wrong and a printer drops the final pages, a book publisher almost never receives calls asking for help, whereas multimedia companies sometimes hear from customers having trouble turning their computers on.

Process

There are two issues involved in customer support. The first is a top level concern and has to do with accounting for and implementing a **customer support system**. Accounting for these costs needs to take place before a product or service is even created. Somewhere in every production agreement should be a section which spells out who is responsible for supporting a project. Most publishers assume this cost, but no one should take on this responsibility without adequately estimating and recovering the costs of doing so. More sales typically implies more support calls and so support costs are usually allocated as a percentage of revenue as opposed to a fixed cost.

Setting up the support systems and procedures also needs to happen early, before a product ships. Customers who buy a product right after it ships will not be happy being told to call back in a week when things are in better order. This is especially important for products that are widely released or intended as Christmas or other holiday gifts. Customers will not be happy opening presents, running into problems, and not being able to get in touch with someone to help resolve the problem, either because the line is busy or everbody is on vacation.

The second issue is within the realm of a **single customer inquiry**. The typical process is to get the caller to ask the question as clearly and calmly as possible and have the support person answer the question and end the call. Many times, though, the solution is either not readily apparent or the customer does not adequately explain the problem. In this case, the customer support person needs to walk the user through a series of steps to either reproduce the problem or to locate the area where it is occurring.

In the course of answering inquiries, customer support people should **compile statistics** on the number and length of calls and the types of questions asked. They should also **record the correspondence** that takes place and each question and eventual solution. This information can be invaluable for both managing current operations and responding to future inquiries.

Tools and Techniques

The primary tool in customer support is the telephone, but many large companies also use relational databases and sophisticated call-routing systems to help handle calls efficiently and economically. A **relational database** helps in cataloging known problems with a product or platform as well as previously asked questions. A good database can help someone in customer support identify and resolve a problem without having prior knowledge of the problem. Call-routing systems perform two functions: the first is to route the call to the appropriate person or department, and the second is to satsify the customer. Having a customer receive a busy signal is not an appropriate response, nor is leaving them on the line indefinitely. More than a few companies have systems that pick up the call, present a list of options, and then place the call in a queue for the next available representative. The best companies have systems that periodically give estimates of the wait time or allow people to leave voicemail messages for later responses.

Many companies are also taking advantage of **online services** ▶ 16, 61 and **bulletin board systems** to reduce the number of calls that need to be handled in person. These companies either create their own bulletin board systems for customers to directly dial into or they create places in online systems for people to either look up questions in reference facilities or ask questions in discussion areas. Often, customer support people will monitor these discussion groups and supply answers and offer guidance.

Qualifications

Customer support people need to be **knowledgeable about computers**, especially Windows and PCs, considering these typically have the most problems over all other computer platforms. Most people who call customer support centers have general problems with their computers as opposed to a particular product. For example, people may not have read the requirements on the packaging for a CD-ROM and don't have a computer capable of playing the title. Or, they have non-standard sound or video cards in their computers that are not supported by the authoring tool used to create the product. As a result, people in customer support need to be familiar with the typical components and set-ups of a variety of platforms and be able to spot these types of problems quickly.

Customer support people also need good **instructional skills**. They need to be able to walk a person through a series of steps and explain various points along the way. They should be able to give clear instructions and make complex issues appear understand-

Never make any assumptions about a person's computer knowledge. Customers will ask the strangest questions or perform the most amusing steps in response to basic instructions.

Stephanie Davis
Customer Service Representative, O'Reilly & Associates

Stephanie Davis is full of answers. As a customer service representative for the Global Network Navigator, one of the first publications on the World Wide Web, she's fielded all types of questions from the basic ("How do I subscribe?") to the complex ("How do I choose a service provider?" "How do I configure my server?"). She's even had calls from people who don't have computers, but have heard about the Internet and want to learn more.

It's hard to believe she wasn't born wearing a telephone headset and toting a keyboard. Yet, as Stephanie was growing up in California wine country, she never had any interest in computers. "I thought I'd be a beautician or horse trainer," she laughs. "I had horrid grades, and didn't want to go to college. I can't tell you how many times my teachers said, 'You are so bright, you really should do something about your grades.'" She decided to "do something" when she graduated, so she enrolled in the local business school. And dropped out after

four months. Through a series of temp jobs she eventually landed at O'Reilly & Associates, where she's been working happily since 1989. "Everything I know about computers and customer service, I learned here, mostly through doing," she explains, adding "I'm sure I'll die here."

Her advice for aspiring service reps: "Know what you are talking about. If you don't know, don't be afraid to let the customer know, and tell them you'll find the answer. And then follow through—get back to people, even if you don't have the answer yet." Steph has also devised many shortcuts to make her job easier, from writing macros to preparing "canned" files for common questions. Because she is the first (and often only) point of human contact for sometimes frustrated users, she has others listen in on her calls to make sure she sounds confident, helpful, and friendly. "Be pleasant, but not too chatty on the phone," she advises. "Don't waste words."

able. Someone who leaves the caller more confused than when they started is not a good candidate.

Finally, people in customer support need **tact and patience**. There will be many cases when they will have to deal with someone who is very angry. A person who is unable to handle these situations either because they take issues too personally or they respond in a disrespectful manner will not be effective in this role.

How to Hire
Posting a print or online job opening for customer support people will generate a lot of response, but finding people who can do the job without the need for a lot of training can be difficult. Look for candidates with prior experience handling people, such as teachers, counselors, or guides. They should have a positive attitude and clear, confident communication skills. Customer support people are often the first and only representatives of a company that people come in contact with. Therefore, you need people that will not reflect poorly on the company.

You also want customer support people to have a certain level of knowledge about computers, especially about components and configurations. Best of all are people who can think quickly and logically and walk through steps to help isolate problems. You can test all these skills in an interview by seeing how candidates handle themselves and respond to your questions. Some people like to pose hypothetical questions, but recognize that some people may need a few days to become knowledgeable on a particular platform or product. Using this method may dis-

In December 1994, Packard Bell, the leading seller of PCs through retail stores, added 200 people to its existing customer support staff of 800. Dell computer had 500 people fielding 4,000-16,000 calls a day, every day, and Microsoft averaged 25,000 calls per day.

—Forbes, March 13, 1995

qualify a person who could eventually grow into the position.

How to Be Hired
Prior customer support experience can help but most companies are willing to consider people without direct experience. Instead, these companies want to see an ability to quickly and calmly solve people's problems. You should highlight any experience that you have in public speaking, counseling, or teaching. Also, the interview is critical because you will be directly applying all the skills you will use in the position. If you handle the interview well, you'll have a great advantage.

Compensation
Customer support people, especially those answering the phones, responding to email messages, and monitoring bulletin boards, are not usually highly paid. The position itself is often viewed as entry level, and many of the people in it are paid by the hour. Also, support centers, especially for large companies, tend to be in less expensive areas, making it less attractive to relocate.

Customer support managers, however, have more leverage, especially if they understand ways to integrate technology into the process and reduce the cost and headaches often associated with customer support. There are ample opportunities for people with these capabilities to approach firms and offer to improve their operations. There are also opportunities to consult with companies in setting up support systems as well as setting up independent companies to contract support services.

Jeff Braun
President, Maxis

As I recently told the L.A. Times, Windows isn't a consumer operating system, it's a pain in the ass. We have so many problems developing for that environment, worrying about setting up RAM configurations, monitor configurations, sound board configurations, etc. You have to be a hacker to work the basic functions. How's grandma in St. Louis going to deal with it when the first "Interrupt DMARIQ" pops onto her screen? All you have to do is go into the

technical support department of any software company that supports both the Mac and Windows and ask them how many calls they get for each system. If you took this survey across the entire industry, and you stacked up the numbers, I guarantee you that Windows users have ten times the problems that Mac users have. And that translates to customer dissatisfaction.

—From an interview with The Red Herring, December 1994

Books

This collection of books is a small but qualified sampling of the many resources available on interactive media and related topics. The list contains some books that focus on ideas, others that focus on processes, and still others that focus on tools.

BUSINESS AND MARKETING

Bionomics
Michael Rothschild
Henry Holt and Company, 1990
New York, NY
ISBN: 8050-1979-0
A great book with wonderful new thoughts about how to view business. Excellent insight on innovation and technology.

Graphic Artists Guild Handbook of Pricing and Ethical Guidelines
Graphic Artists Guild, 1991
New York, NY
ISBN: 0-932102-07-7
An essential business tool for professionals from all disciplines. Includes information on how artwork is priced and commissioned, legislative developments, writing contracts and proposals, and much more.

Making Money with Multimedia
David Rosen and Caryn Mladen
Addison-Wesley, 1995
Reading, MA
ISBN: 0-201-82283-0
Multimedia developers who need business training quickly can benefit from the advice and insight in this new book sponsored by the Apple Multimedia Program.

Relationship Marketing
Regis McKenna
Addison-Wesley, 1991
Reading, MA
ISBN: 0-201-56769-5
Powerful text on understanding the why and how of real marketing. Great for beginners, and inspirational for more experienced marketing and sales people.

CD-ROM

Apple CD-ROM Handbook
Joel Nagy
Addison-Wesley, 1992
Reading, MA
ISBN: 0-201-63230-6
Well written book covering all phases of CD-ROM production.

CD-ROM Handbook
Chris Serman
McGraw-Hill
New York, NY
ISBN: 0-07-056693-3
A large reference source on hardware and software tools and the CD-ROM production process (data preparation, mastering, and manufacturing). Written by more than 20 leading experts in the field. Contains appendices detailing CD-ROM standards.

COMPUTERS

Danny Goodman's Macintosh Handbook
Danny Goodman
Bantam Books, 1992
New York, NY
ISBN: 0-679-79094-2
A comprehensive book on using a Macintosh computer based on an information design layout.

How Computers Work
Ron White
Ziff-Davis Press, 1994
Emeryville, CA
ISBN: 1-56276-250-8
A full-color graphical approach to what happens inside your computer. Explains how information is sent from the keyboard, mouse, and other connections, and how memory works.

How Windows Works
Kaare Christian
Ziff-Davis Press, 1994
Emeryville, CA
ISBN: 1-56276-193-5
Tells how DOS and Windows cooperate and how menus, toolbars, dialog boxes, and fonts work.

New Inside Macintosh (15 volumes)
Apple Computer
Addison-Wesley, 1992-1993
Reading, MA
ISBN: 0-201-63242-X
Documents tools and resources in the Macintosh system software.

Understanding Computers
Nathan Shedroff, J. Sterling Hutto & Ken Fromm
Sybex, 1993
Alameda, CA
ISBN: 0-7821-1284-X
A four-color, highly graphical book on computers that has sections on uses, components, technology, and buying and selling.

DESIGN, GENERAL

Art & Physics
Leonard Shlain
WIlliam Morrow and Company, 1991
New York, NY
ISBN: 0-688-12305-8
A provocative book that tracks the breakthroughs in art and physics as they occur side by side throughout history. A case is made for how artists have foreshadowed the insights of physicists on many occasions.

A Primer of Visual Literacy
Donis A. Dondis
MIT Press, 1973
Cambridge, MA
ISBN: 0-262-54029-0
Ideas and elements of graphic design such as form, layout, movement, type, and grids makes this recommended reading for illustrators, animators, and graphic and interface designers.

Living Colors, A Designer's Guide to 80 Essential Palettes from Ancient to Modern Times
Margaret Walch and Augustine Hope
Chronicle Books, 1995
San Francisco, CA
ISBN: 0-8118-0558-1
A wonderful guide to color use throughout history, in mediums ranging from architecture and apparel to paintings and pottery. Illustrated in a gatefold format with four-color images and color chips for matching against projects at hand.

The Map Catalog
Joel Makower
Vintage Books, 1990
New York, NY
ISBN: 6797-4257-3
A catalog of the many types and styles of maps in existence.

Notes on Graphic Design and Visual Communication
Gregg Berryman
William Kaufmann, 1984
Los Altos, CA
ISBN: 1-560-52044-2
A wonderfully simple resource giving thumbnail rules for graphic art design. Highly recommended for graphic designers and illustrators.

Symbol Sourcebook
Henry Dreyfus
McGraw-Hill, 1972
New York, NY
ISBN: 0-442-221806-0
An excellent source of information about the power and meaning of symbols. Includes information on the history and development of symbols and what distinguishes good symbols from bad ones.

DESIGN, INFORMATION

Information Anxiety
Richard Saul Wurman
Doubleday, 1989
New York, NY
ISBN: 0-553-34856-6
If you are interested in the design of information, this book will help you sort out the meaningful from the meaningless. It offers valuable insight into organization of information, although the book can, at times, produce a little anxiety itself.

Mapping Hypertext
Robert E. Horn
Lexington Institute, 1989
Lexington, MA
ISBN: 0-962-55650-5
A book on hypertext with some busic ideas on information mapping technique. Goes hand in hand with Wurman's work on information design and Tufte's aesthetic analysis of thematic mapping.

Mapping the Next Millennium
Stephen S. Hall
Vintage Books, 1992
New York, NY
ISBN: 0-679-74175-5
A nicely written and conceptually enthralling look at modern day maps and spatial models that are used by astronomers, neuroscientists, geneticists, and mathematicians to chart new and strange terrain in space, on Earth, in living beings, and in subatomic particles.

The Visual Display of Quantitative Information
Edward R. Tufte
Graphics Press, 1983
Cheshire, CT
ISBN: 0-961-39210-X
A superb book explaining and illustrating basic principles of graphic illustration, thematic mapping, and good information design. By the author of Envisioning Information, 1990.

DESIGN, INTERACTION

The Great Good Place
Ray Oldenburg
Paragon House, 1989
New York, NY
ISBN: 1-569-24907-5
Makes a convincing case for the basic human need to have "a sense of place." Though a bit winded and academic in tone, it is an underground hit with many online developers who are finding that its arguments transfer quite readily from the real world into the virtual world.

A Pattern Language
Towns•Buildings•Construction
Christopher Alexander and others
Oxford University Press, 1977
New York, NY
ISBN: 0-195-01919-9
A book full of fascinating insights into what makes healthy and useful environments. It lists numerous patterns for the construction of towns and buildings for achieving a higher aesthetic. It holds insights for designers of all kinds.

The Virtual Community, Homesteading on the Electronic Frontier
Howard Rheingold
HarperPerennial, 1993
New York, NY
ISBN: 0-06-097641-1
An interesting look at life on the Net with particular attention paid to the many communities of shared interests found there. It's the first book to reveal the human side of online interactions.

DESIGN, INTERFACE

Computers as Theater
Brenda Laurel
Addison-Wesley, 1993
Reading, MA
ISBN: 0-201-55060-1
An advanced aesthetic philosophy and observation on the design of virtual reality and modern interfaces is developed. This book literally transcribes the principles of Aristotle's On Poetics as a basis for interactive design.

The Art of Human-Computer Interface Design
Brenda Laurel, Editor
Addison-Wesley, 1991
Reading, MA
ISBN: 0-201-51797-3
Articles by many writers covering most elements of the interface discipline.

The Design of Everyday Things
Donald A. Norman
Doubleday, 1988
New York, NY
ISBN: 3-852-6774-6
An introduction to some basic principles of user-centered design based on a study of the obvious and the ordinary.

Macintosh Human Interface Guidelines
Apple Computer
Addison-Wesley, 1992
Reading, MA
ISBN: 0-201-62216-5
This book consists of guidelines for Macintosh computers plus color capabilities, open architecture, and enhanced system software.

Making It Macintosh
Apple Computer, 1993
Cupertino, CA
ISBN: 0-201-62626-8
This CD-ROM interactively demonstrates the interface design practices discussed in the book Macintosh Human Interface Guidelines.

Tog on Interface
Bruce Tognazzini
Addison-Wesley, 1992
Reading, MA
ISBN: 0-201-60842-1
Good running commentary and general lessons in computer interface design.

Understanding Comics
Scott McCloud
Kitchen Sink Press, 1993
Northampton, MA
ISBN: 0-060-97625-X
A must-read for anyone interested in interface design. Explains many of the visual communication elements found in comic books—and done within a comic book format.

FILM, VIDEO, AND ANIMATION

The Book of Video Photography
David Cheshire
Alfred Knopf, 1990
New York, NY
ISBN: 0-394-58744-8
A highly visual book on every aspect of video movie-making including equipment, lighting, capturing a subject, editing, sound, and special techniques.

Disney Animation—The Illusion of Life
Frank Thomas & Ollie Johnson
Abbeville Press, 1981
New York, NY
A coffee table book of grand illustrations with a great section covering many of the principles of 2D animation.

The Film Sense by Sergei Eisenstein
Jay Leyda, Editor
Harcourt Brace, & World, Inc., 1942
New York, NY
ISBN: 0-156-30935-1
Motion picture analysis and lessons. Good for videographers, and film producers, and editors.

MacWeek Guide to Desktop Video
Erik Holsinger
Ziff-Davis Press, 1994
Emeryville, CA
ISBN: 1-56276-127-7
Details costs and capabilities of desktop video. Explains how to integrate traditional video equipment with video tools for the computer. Covers some style and formatting.

Premiere With a Passion, The Essential Guide to Adobe Premiere Movie Making and Video Editing
Michael Feerer
Peachpit Press, 1994
Berkeley, CA
ISBN: 1-56609-165-9
Advanced tips and techniques for using Premiere.

Shoot Video Like a Pro (CD-ROM)
Red Hill Studios
Zelos Digital Learning, 1994
San Francisco, CA
ISBN: 1-883387-09-4
Well presented interactive CD that is intended for the camcorder enthusiast. Shows you how to create and compose professional looking video.

Video Lighting & Special Effects
J. Caruso & M. Arthur
Prentice Hall, 1990
Englewood Cliffs, New Jersey
ISBN: 0-138-24756-0
Knowledgeable production book on the subject.

GAME DESIGN

Behind the Scenes at Sega, The Making of a Video Game
Nicholas Lavroff
Prima Publishing, 1995
Rocklin, CA
ISBN: 1-55958-525-0
Discusses the history of arcade games and explains how to merge roles to create a successful video game. A highly graphical book that is a must for game designers, illustrators, and animators.

Rebel Assault, The Official Insider's Guide
Joe Hutsko
Prima Publishing, 1994
Rocklin, CA
ISBN: 1-55958-789-X
An inside look at Lucas Arts' making of Rebel Assault. Includes original artwork, concept sketches, and behind-the-scenes decisions. (Also contains tips for playing.)

INTERACTIVE TELEVISION

Interactive Television, A Comprehensive Guide for Multimedia Technologists
Winston William Hodge
McGraw Hill, 1994
New York, NY
ISBN: 0-07-029151-9
Covers the concepts design and approaches to ITV. Gives technical requirements for video on demand, pay per view, interactive TV, and advanced multimedia.

INTERNET

The Whole Internet User's Guide and Catalog
Ed Krol
O'Reilly & Associates, 1992
Sebastopol, CA
ISBN: 1-56592-025-2
Covers everything from electronic mail and newsgroups to the newest developments. Shows you the way to find the resources you want.

LAW

Intellectual Property: Patents, Trademarks, and Copyrights
Richard Stim
Lawyer's Cooperative, 1993
ISBN: 0-8273-5487-8
Written by an attorney who has experience managing licensing for Microsoft, Adobe Systems, Lucas Arts, and Colossal Pictures.

Multimedia Law Handbook
Dianne Brinson and Mark Radcliffe
Ladera Press, 1994
Menlo Park, CA
Designed for the non-lawyer, this book is a practical guide for developers and publishers. Includes a PC diskette with forms and ready-to-use contracts.

The Software Publishers' Association Legal Guide to Multimedia
Thomas J. Smedinghoff
Addison-Wesley, 1994
Reading, MA
ISBN: 0-201-40931-3
Contains a disk with templates and agreements. Covers copyrights, licenses, and using preexisting content. Also, how to develop, protect, and distribute your material.

MULTIMEDIA

CyberArts: Exploring Art and Technology
Linda Jacobson, Editor
Miller Freeman, 1992
San Francisco, CA
ISBN: 0-87930-253-4
A well-edited series of articles from the individual speakers at the CyberArts forums. A great modern resource covering subjects like binaural sound, new computer art, and music.

The Cyberspace Lexicon
Bob Cotton and Richard Oliver
Phaidon Press, 1994
London, England
ISBN: 0-7148-3267-7
A colorful, oversized reference book that covers everything from arcade games to artificial intelligence, data superhighways to DTP, and video graphics to virtual reality. This book explains all the essential concepts and technical terms.

How Multimedia Works
Erik Holsinger
Ziff-Davis Press, 1994
Emeryville, CA
ISBN: 1-56276-208-7
Part of the How It Works series, it shows not just how the hardware and software work but also how multimedia can enrich our lives.

The Medium is the Massage: An Inventory of Effects
Marshall McLuhan and Quentin Fiore
Bantam Books, 1967
New York, NY
ISBN: 0-671-68997-5
Interesting book that shows how media transforms society. Introduces many stimulating ideas about experience, sense ratios, and media as extensions of the mind and body.

Multimedia Resources Catalog
Future Systems, Inc.
Falls Church, VA
[+1 800] 323 3472
A collection of top-notch books, reports, market studies, and directories for multimedia developers.

Multimedia Demystified, A Guide to the World of Multimedia
vivid studios/Apple Computer
Random House, 1994
New York, NY
ISBN: 0-679-75603-5
A comprehensive book on the process of developing multimedia projects. Written and produced by the same people who created this book.

Understanding Media
Marshall McLuhan
Signet Paperback, 1964
New York, NY
ISBN: 0-262-63159-8
Probing look at the effects of many media types and technologies in modern and past societies.

MUSIC AND SOUND

The Art of Music Licensing
Al and Bob Kohn, Editors
Prentice Hall Law & Business
Englewood Cliffs, NJ
ISBN: 0-130-68792-8
A 1,000-page guide on granting licenses and obtaining permissions to use music.

The Musician's Home Recording Handbook
Ted Greenwald
Miller Freeman/GPI Books, 1992
San Francisco, CA
ISBN: 0-879-30237-2
Many common issues of acoustics and recording are covered.

PHOTOGRAPHY, ILLUSTRATION, AND IMAGE MANIPULATION

Adobe Illustrator 5.0, The Official Handbook for Designers
Tony Bové & Cheryl Rhodes
Random House, 1993
New York, NY
ISBN: 0-679-791639
Tips and techniques for working with Adobe Illustrator's interactive modeless dialog boxes, type tools, plug-ins, typefitting, and much more. Written by the co-founders of Publish magazine.

where was that great quote

Photoshop 3.0: Knock Their Socks Off!
Peter Fink
Ziff-Davis Press, 1994
Emeryville, CA
ISBN: 1-56276-273-7
Written for commercial artists who want to get better, faster results from Photoshop. Lots of tips for producing commercial effects.

The Photographer's Handbook, Third Edition
John Hedgecoe
Alfred A. Knopf, 1992
New York, NY
ISBN: 0-679-74204-2
A complete reference manual of photographic techniques, procedures, equipment, and style. Full of illustrations, examples, and comparison photos.

The Photoshop Wow! Book
Linnea Dayton & Jack Davis
Peachpit Press, 1993
Berkeley, CA
ISBN: 1-56609-004-0
Contains step by step instructions on using the multitude of features found in Photoshop.

PERSONAL GROWTH/JOB HUNTING

What Color is Your Parachute?
Richard Nelson Bolles
Ten Speed Press, 1995
Berkeley, CA
ISBN: 0-89815-568-1
A practical job manual for people looking for jobs or changing careers. This book offers general advice that is highly informative and inspirational.

First Things First
Stephen Covey
Simon and Schuster, 1994
New York, NY
ISBN: 0-671-86441-6
Written by the author of Seven Habits of Highly Effective People, Covey transcends traditional time management of faster, harder, and smarter, and offers readers a compass instead of a clock to navigate to where you're heading.

PROGRAMMING

HTML Specifications
Yahoo website
Stanford University
http://akebono.stanford.edu/yahoo/
Computers/World_Wide_Web/HTML/
Contains a comprehensive list of webpages that discuss the specification and implementation of HTML code.

Learning Perl
Randal Schwartz
O'Reilly and Associates, 1993
Sebastopol, CA
ISBN: 1-56592-042-2
The official guide for both formal and informal learning of Perl. Accessible to the novice programmer.

Mythical Man-month, Essays on Software Engineering
Frederick P. Brooks Jr.
Addison-Wesley, 1975
Reading, MA
ISBN: 0-201-00650-2
"Everybody quotes it, few people read it, and nobody obeys it." A classic book on software development.

SCRIPTWRITING

Adventures in the Screen Trade
WIlliam Goldman
Warner Books, 1983
New York, NY
ISBN: 0-446-39117-4
An highly enjoyable book on scriptwriting and the film industry.

Screenplay, The Foundations of Screenwriting
Syd Field
Dell Publishing, 1982
New York, NY
ISBN: 0-440-57647-4
Provides a detailed look at the structure and format of a screenplay. Useful for thinking about how this structure may or may not apply to interactive media.

TESTING

The Art of Software Testing
Glenford J. Myers
John Wiley And Sons, 1979
New York, NY
ISBN: 0-471-04328-1
Like Boris Beizer's book, another testing classic. Gives practical rather than theoretical methods for effective test cases.

Software Testing Techniques
Boris Beizer
Van Nostrand Reinhold, 1990
New York, NY
ISBN: 0-442-20672-0
A popular quality assurance guide. Informative for quality assurance personnel and others.

about graphic designers?

Testing Computer Software
Cem Kaner, Jack Falk, Hung Quoc Nguyen
Van Nostrand Reinhold, 1993
New York, NY
ISBN: 0-442-01361-2
For testers, test managers, project managers, programmers, and students. Discusses the importance of finding crucial bugs first, describing software errors, designing test plans, tracking, timing of testing, compatibility, and even some legal issues.

VIRTUAL REALITY

Garage Virtual Reality
Linda Jacobson
Sams Publishing/Prentice Hall
Indianapolis, IN
ISBN: 0-672-30270-5
A resource-rich book for those who want to make affordable virtual reality.

Magazines

In combination with reading books and attending conference exhibits, subscribing to a few trusted magazines can be the most cost-effective way to stay informed on developments within a discipline and within an industry.

Advertising Age
Crain Communications
Detroit, MI
[+1 800] 678 9595
Weekly
51 issues/$99.00
Circulation: 75,000
One of the more influential magazines covering the advertising industry, it contains a very good interactive media and marketing section.

AV Video
Montage Publishing
White Plains, NY
[+1 914] 328 9157
Monthly
12 issues/$53.00
Circulation: 70,000
The latest news on production and presentation technology.

BMUG
BMUG Inc.
Berkeley, CA
[+1 510] 549 BMUG
Semi-yearly
Membership/$45.00
Circulation: 13,000 members/15,000 distributed
Five hundred pages of commentary on a variety of Macintosh issues from a grassroots organization known for its integrity.

Byte
MacGraw-Hill, Inc.
Peterborough, NH
[+1 800] 257 9402
Monthly
12 issues/$29.95
Circulation: 520,000
Technical information on advanced computer technology from a cross-platform perspective.

CD-ROM Professional
Pemberton Press Inc.
Wilton, CT
[+1 800] 248 8466
Monthly
12 issues/$98.00 corporate; $55.00 individual
Circulation: 19,000
Practical how-to advice for CD-ROM end-users and developers.

Communications of the ACM
Association for Computing Machinery
New York, NY
[+1 800] 342 6626
Monthly
12 issues/$82.00 with membership
12 issues/$124.00 without membership
Circulation: 100,000
Slightly academic but still thoughtful articles on computer technology, security, and ethics.

Computer Pictures
Montage Publishing
White Plains, NY
ISSN: 0883-5683
[+1 914] 328 9157
Bimonthly
6 issues/$40.00
Circulation: 55,000
Current tools and tips in digital imaging production, 3D rendering, animation, and still images.

Desktop Video World
IDG Communications Publishing
Peterborough, NH
[+1 603] 924 0100
Monthly
12 issues/$24.97
Circulation: 40,000
Caters to those working in the digital video and multimedia information markets.

Edupage
Educom
Washington, D.C.
comments@educom.edu
150 issues/free
Circulation: 35,000 addresses (300,000-500,000 estimated readers)
An online summary of news items on information technology provided three times each week by Educom—a consortium of leading colleges and

universities. It is free and may be obtained by sending mail to listproc@educom.edu and in the body of the message saying, "subscribe edupage <your name>".

Electronic Entertainment
Infotainment World
San Mateo, CA
[+1 415] 349 4300
Monthly
12 issues/$12.00
Circulation: 100,000
A popular magazine on multimedia, games, and edutainment products.

Electronic Media
Crain Communications
Chicago, IL
[+1 800] 678 9595
Weekly
52 issues/$93.00
Circulation: 25,700
Information on the television and cable industries with emphasis on business and government issues.

Electronic Musician
Act III Publishing
Emeryville, CA
[+1 800] 843 4086
Monthly
12 issues/$19.95
Circulation: 62,000
Includes buyers guides, reviews, and tips and techniques for digital musicians.

Entertainment Weekly
Entertainment Weekly, Inc.
New York, NY
[+1 800] 828 6882
Weekly
52 issues/$51.48
Circulation: 1,125,000
Quick read covering personalities, trends, and news in film, television, music, books, games, and multimedia.

Forbes ASAP
Forbes Inc
New York, NY
[+1 800] 888 9896
Bimonthly
6 issues/$57.00 (also includes 27 issues of Forbes Magazine)
Circulation: 135,000
A technology supplement to Forbes magazine covering how the digital revolution is affecting business.

HotWired
Wired USA
San Francisco, CA
http://www.hotwired.com
A unique publication showcasing online activities and news/gossip related to the online industry from the creators of Wired magazine.

How
F&W Publications, Inc
Cincinnati, OH
[+1 513] 531 2222
Bimonthly
6 issues/$49.00
Circulation: 38,000
A lively graphic design magazine geared toward describing the process of design. Contains lots of examples.

ID Magazine
Magazine Publications, L.P.
New York, NY
ISSN: 0894-5373
[+1 800] 284 3728
Bimonthly
7 issues/$60.00
Circulation: 10,000
A visually appealing magazine that addresses the art, culture, and business of creating objects and images. ID explores design's role in society as a link between ideas, form, aesthetics, and commerce.

Imaging
Telecom Library
New York, NY
[+1 800] 999 0345
Monthly
12 issues/$17.95
Circulation: 85,000
Practical advice and straightforward information on the tools and process of working with images and text on a computer.

Innovation
NewsScan, Inc.
Atlanta, GA
comments@newsscan.com
Weekly
52 issues/ $15.00
A weekly online summary of trends, strategies, and innovations in business & technology. Produced by the same people who produce Edupage. A free trial subscription to Innovation can be obtained by sending mail to: Innovation-request@NewsScan.com, and in the body of the message saying simply: "subscribe".

Inter@ctive Week
Ziff-Davis Publishing
Garden City, NY
[+1 516] 229 3700
http://www.interactive-week.com
Biweekly
29 issues/$60.00
A relatively new magazine combining lots of late-breaking news on interactive media.

Internet World
Meckler Media Publishing
Westport, CT
[+1 203] 226 696/
neubarth@mecklermedia.com
Monthly
12 issues/$49.00
Circulation: 160,000
Emphasis on multimedia, sports, government, and business with Internet news coverage, cultural issues, profiles, and resources.

MacUser
Ziff-Davis Publishing
Foster City, CA
[+1 800] 627 2247
Monthly
12 issues/$27.00
Circulation: 470,000
A magazine for Macintosh users featuring multimedia and software reviews, product comparisons, and how-to articles.

MacWEEK
Ziff-Davis Publishing
New York, NY
[+1 609] 786 8230
Weekly
52 issues/$125.00
Circulation: 110,000
A timely resource for developments and trends in the Macintosh industry.

Macworld
Macworld Communications
San Francisco, CA
[+1 800] 288 6848
Monthly
12 issues/$30.00
Circulation: 575,000
Hardware and software product information for the Macintosh.

Mondo 2000
MONDO 2000
Berkeley, CA
[+1 510] 845 9018
Quarterly
5 issues/$24.00
Circulation: 100,000
A wild mix of technology, art, and cyberpunk lifestyle.

Morph's Outpost
Morph's Outpost, Inc.
Orinda, CA
[+1 800] 55 MORPH
Monthly
12 issues/$39.95
Circulation: 36,000
Articles about the development of multimedia, communications, software, hardware, and authoring systems, written by developers for developers.

MultiMedia Merchandising
Eastman Media L.P.
Santa Monica, CA
[+1 310] 458 3102
Monthly
12 issues/$50.00
Circulation: 35,000
A great new magazine for information on marketing, packaging, distributing, and retailing game and multimedia titles.

Multimedia Producer
Montage Publishing
White Plains, NY
[+1 914] 328 9157
Monthly
12 issues/$40.00
Circulation: 40,000
Geared for creators and developers of multimedia.

Multimedia World
PC World Communications, Inc.
San Francisco, CA
[+1 415] 281 8650
Monthly
12 issues/$29.90
Circulation: 900,000
A resource for in-depth feature articles, how-tos, and reviews of the latest multimedia titles.

NewMedia
Hypermedia Communications, Inc.
San Mateo, CA
[+1 415] 573 5170
Monthly
13 issues/$38.00
Circulation: 250,000
A prominent magazine about multimedia technology for desktop computer users. It contains information on processes, resources, and products, as well as insightful articles, interviews, and editorials.

OnLine Design
OnLine Design Publication Inc.
San Francisco, CA
[+1 415] 334 3800
Monthly
12 issues/$15.00
Circulation: 50,000
A large-format magazine serving electronic designers and graphic artists in California.

PC Magazine
Ziff-Davis Publishing
New York, NY
[+1 800] 289-0429
Semi-monthly
22 issues/$49.97
Circulation: 1,051,000
Information on PC technology, software, multimedia titles, as well as advice and how-to tips to maximize enjoyment and productivity with PCs.

PC WEEK
Ziff-Davis Publishing
Riverton, NJ
[+1 609] 786 8230
Weekly
51 issues/$195.00
Circulation: 260,000
A timely trade resource for products, developments, trends, and news items in the personal computer industry.

PHOTO Electronic Imaging
PPA Publications & Events
Atlanta, GA
[+1 404] 522 8600
Monthly
12 issues/$18.00
Circulation: 40,000
Information on integrating photography, electronic imaging, and computer graphics.

Publish
Integrated Media, Inc.
San Francisco, CA
[+1 800] 685 3435
Monthly
12 issues/$23.95
Circulation: 90,000
Reviews, new product listings, editorials, goings-on, and calendar of information for high end electronic publishing professionals.

Publishers Weekly
Cahners Publishing Co.
New York, NY
[+1 800] 278 2991
Weekly
51 issues/$139.00
The primary source of information on the publishing industry.

The Red Herring
Flipside Communications, Inc.
Redwood City, CA
[+1 415] 865 2277
Monthly
12 issues/$180.00
Refreshing look at entertainment, communications, and technology companies from an investor's viewpoint.

Santa Cruz Comic News
Santa Cruz, CA
[+1 408] 426 0113
Semi-monthly
24 issues/$22.00
A summary of some of the best political and humor cartoons appearing in newspapers across the country. (Can't work all the time, now can you?)

Telemedia Week
Cahners Publishing Co.
Washington, D.C.
[+1 800] 554 5729
Weekly
Covers infrastructure elements of the information superhighway from the point of view of the television industry. Includes information on legislative and regulatory issues.

Upside
Upside Publishing Company
Foster City, CA
[+1 619] 745 2809
Monthly
12 issues/$48.00
Circulation: 60,000
Information on people, companies, trends, and future developments in technology written for business executives and managers.

Variety
Variety
Los Angeles, CA
[+1 800] 323 4345
Daily/$157.00
Weekly/$167.00
Circulation: 58,000
Authoritative source on all aspects of film, television and cable, home video, legitimate theater/live performance and music, as well as areas such as new media and technology and finance.

Videography
P.S.N. Publications
New York, NY
[+1 212] 779 1919
Monthly
12 issues/$32.00
Circulation: 39,000
Magazine of professional video production technology and applications.

Wired
Wired USA
San Francisco, CA
[+1 800] SO WIRED
subscriptions@wired.com
Monthly
12 issues/$39.95
Circulation: 160,000
Coverage on the digital revolution for people who are making it happen. Focuses on individuals, companies, and ideas.

Newsletters

Newsletters, though expensive, can be valuable because of the experienced point of view of the editor and because of their timeliness and independence from advertising.

California Technology Stock Letter
Michael Murphy, editor and publisher
[+1 415] 726 8495
Semi-monthly
24 issues/$265.00
Covers technology investing with clear explanations of the technology and information on current research topics.

ComputerLetter
Richard Shaffer, editor
[+1 212] 696 9330
Weekly
40 issues/$595.00
Covers the business side of the computer industry. Highly recommended by many.

Content
Gene DeRose, editor and publisher
[+1 212] 941 9252
Monthly
12 issues/$495.00
Covers the online services industry with emphasis on providing entry strategies for mainstream media.

Digital Media
Mitch Ratcliffe, editor-in-chief
[+1 800] 325 3830
customer-service@seyboldpub.ziff.com
Monthly
12 issues/$395.00
Provides an overview of the battles going on in the consumer electronics, computer, entertainment, telephone, cable and broadcast media fields.

Electronic Education Report
SIMBA Information Inc.
[+1 203] 834 0033
Semi-monthly
24 issues/$319.00
Provides information regarding the market for educational technologies. Has news and analysis of K–12, higher education, and consumer education markets.

Electronic Information Report
Lorraine Sileo, editorial director
Semi-weekly
46 issues/$399.00
Coverage of market trends and news. Includes strategies, new companies, mergers and acquisitions, and legislative issues.

Interactive Publishing Alert
Rosalind Resnick, editor and publisher
[+1 305] 926 7655 fax
71333.1473@compuserve.com
Monthly
12 issues/paper $174.00, email $149.00
Tracks developments in interactive publishing and electronic media.

Internet Letter
Jayne Levin, editor
[+1 800] NET WEEK
info@netweek.com
http://www.infosphere.com
Monthly
12 issues/$299.00
Includes a list of new Internet databases and services and covers commerce and policy of the Internet.

Microprocessor Report
Michael Slater, editor and publisher
[+1 707] 824 4001
17 issues/$495.00
Circulation: 2,000
Covers technical information on microprocessor developments.

Multimedia Monitor
Rockley Miller, editor and publisher
Future Systems
[+1 800] 323 3472
Monthly
12 issues/$395.00 ($150.00/educational)
Contains information about interactive multimedia technologies, applications, and markets.

Multimedia Week
Phillips Business Information
[+1 800] 777 5015
Weekly
50 issues/$597
Circulation: 5,200
Short information newsletter full of late-breaking events in the industry.

P.C. Letter
David Coursey, editor
Stewart Alsop, publisher
[+1 415] 312 0691
Semi-monthly
22 issues/$495.00
Information on PC products, companies, personalities, and technologies.

Release 1.0
Gerald Michalski, editor
Esther Dyson, publisher
[+1 212] 924 8800
Monthly
12 issues/$395.00
Covers industry trends and software technology with increasing coverage of the online industry.

Soft•letter
Jeffrey Tarter, editor and publisher
[+1 617] 924 3944
Semi-monthly
24 issues/$345.00
Circulation: 1,500
Summaries of trends and strategies in software publishing with a focus on company management issues, operations and finance research, and new technology and marketing concepts.

Professional Groups

American Society of Composers, Authors, and Publishers (ASCAP)
New York, NY
[+1 212] 621 6000
A content-licensing source for sound and music.

Apple Multimedia Program (AMP)
20525 Mariani Avenue, MS 303-2D
Cupertino, CA 95014
[+1 408] 974 4897
A program at Apple Computer designed to assist multimedia developers.

Apple Programmers and Developers Association (APDA)
P.O. Box 319
Buffalo, NY 14207-0319
U.S. [+1 800] 282 2732
Canada [+1 800] 637 0029
International AppleLink APDA
[+1 716] 871 6555
A source for Apple developer information and tools.

Association of Computing Machinery
SigCHI (Computer-Human Interaction)
SigGRAPH (Computer Graphics)
1515 Broadway, 17th Floor
New York, NY 10036
[+1 212] 869 7440
http://www.acm.org
Ongoing meetings of professional and academic individuals to advance the knowledge of interface and multimedia uses of computers.

Audio Engineering Society
60 East 42nd Street
New York, NY 10165
[+1 212] 661 8528
Technical association for audio professionals and music engineers. They also cover issues like licensing and royalties.

Boston Computer Society (BCS)
Boston, MA
[+1 617] 290 5700
An association containing over 23,000 members whose mission is to help people improve their ability to use personal computers.

BMUG
Berkeley, CA
[+1 510] 549 2684
The largest membership-based consumer advocacy Macintosh users' group in the world (12,000+ members) with a goal of providing information and critical direction to users and developers, beginners and experts alike.

Broadcast Music, Inc. (BMI)
New York, NY [+1 212] 586 2000
Los Angeles, CA [+1 310] 659 9109
A content-licensing source for sound and music.

Computer Professionals for Social Responsibility (CPSR)
Palo Alto, CA
[+1 415] 322 3778
cpsr@csli.stanford.edu

Electronic Frontier Foundation (EFF)
1001 G ST NW, Ste 950E
Washington, DC 20001
[+1 202] 347 5400
Association leading the dialogue on social, legal, and political issues of multimedia computing.

Human Factors and Ergonomics Society (HFES)
P.O. Box 1369
Santa Monica CA 90406
[+1 310] 394 1811
A group concerned with studying human characteristics and capabilities and applying that knowledge to the design of the products, systems, and environments that people use.

IMA Intellectual Property Task Force
1 Fifth Street
Cambridge, MA 02141
[+1 617] 864 6606
In charge of figuring out appropriate legal and business models for the multimedia industry.

Meeting people of similar mind and interest can be reassuring in a time of tremendous change.

Interactive Multimedia Association
3 Church Circle, Suite 800
Annapolis, MD 21401-1933
[+1 410] 626 1380
An organization whose mission is to promote the development of interactive multimedia applications and reduce barriers to the widespread use of multimedia technology.

International Interactive Communications Society (IICS)
14657 SW Teal Blvd. Suite 119
Beavertown, OR 97007
[+1 503] 579 4427
mltmedia@aol.com
Organization of individuals concerned with issues of interface and multimedia design. Local chapters exist in many cities around the world.

International MIDI Association
23634 Emelita Street
Woodland Hills, CA 91367
[+1 818] 598 0088
Distributes MIDI specifications.

Multimedia Development Group (MDG)
2601 Mariposa Street
San Francisco, CA 94110
[+1 415] 553 2300
A non-profit trade association providing information to the multimedia community on business, technology, tools, and professional services.

Multimedia PC (MPC) Marketing Council
1730 M Street NW, Suite 700
Washington, D.C. 20036
[+1 202] 452 1600
Issues and promotes the Microsoft MPC standard.

National Multimedia Association of America (NMAA)
9750 52nd Ave.
College Park, MD 20740
[+1 800] 214 9531
membership@nmaa.org

Screen Actors Guild (SAG)
5757 Wilshire Boulevard
Los Angeles, CA 90036-3600
[+1 213] 549 6847

Society for Technical Communication (STC)
901 North Stuart Street, Suite 304
Arlington, VA 22203
[+1 703] 522 4114
A group that keeps its 18,000 communicators aware of the latest trends and technology in technical communication.

Without the right skills, few can hope to reach the opportunities they dream of. Training can provide a foundation. The rest is up to you.

Software Publishers Association (SPA)
1730 M Street NW, Suite 700
Washington, D.C. 20036
[+1 202] 452 1600
Organization of computer vendors who occasionally develop multimedia policies.

United States Office of Copywriting
[+1 202] 707 3000

Usability Professionals Association (UPA)
10875 Plano Road, Suite 115
Dallas, TX 75238
[+1 214] 349 8841

The Writers Connection
P.O. Box 24770
San Jose, CA 95154-4770
[+1 408] 445-3600
A West Coast-based organization that provides writing, interactive writing, publishing, and film industry information, resources, and services to members, writers, and other publishing and entertainment industry professionals.

United Digital Artists
New York, NY
[+1 212] 777-7200
UDIGART@applelink.apple.com
A new media agency representing more than 400 artists (photographers, designers, videographers, and multimedia developers), programmers, and consultants engaged in developing interactive products and online services.

Training & Schools

American Film Institute
Los Angeles, CA
[+1 213] 856 7664
This affordable and well-respected school offers a multitude of classes with tracks in screenwriting, directing, producing, editing/cameras, systems, animation, digital imaging, digital film and video, and multimedia. Reinventing Hollywood is part of their charter.

Apple Developer University
DEVUNIV@applelink.apple.com
Provides expert instruction for all levels of Macintosh programmers.

Center for Creative Imaging
Camden, ME
[+1 800] 428 7400
An innovative art and learning facility.

Center for Electronic Art
San Francisco, CA
[+1 415] 956 6500
info@cea.edu
http://1www.cea.edu
*Intensive training in developing CD-ROM
prototypes, World Wide Web sites, and interactive
digital art.*

Multimedia Training Library
DEVSUPPORT@applelink.apple.com
*Contains a worldwide database of multimedia
training providers.*

New Media Centers Program
[+1 415] 329 1316
*Nationwide program based on a new model that
fosters the widespread integration of interactive
media in teaching, learning, and communicating.
Founders include Adobe Systems, Apple
Computer, FWB, Macromedia, Prentice Hall, Sony
Electronics, and SuperMac Technology.*

San Francisco Digital Media Center
San Francisco, CA
[+1 415] 824 9394
sfdmc@well.com
*Unique training and production environment for
new media technologies with access to state-of-
the-art desktop media facilities for the general
public.*

**San Francisco State University Multimedia
Extension**
San Francisco, CA
[+1 415] 904 7700
sfsummsp@aol.com
*One of the largest multimedia instruction
programs in the world, SFSU provides classes on
every part of the production process including
interaction design, production management,
scriptwriting, programming, and animation. Also
includes classes on marketing, finance, and law.*

United Digital Artists
New York, NY
[+1 212] 777-7200
UDIGART@applelink.apple.com
*An agency representing new media artists that
also provides extensive training in a variety of
interactive design disciplines.*

Conferences

*There are many con-
ferences on multime-
dia; the largest and
most important ones
are listed here. A
complete listing can
be found in the
MediaSense calendar
produced by
MediaSense and pub-
lished by the Interac-
tive Media Festival
[+1 415] 357 0100.
Conferences are useful
for meeting people
and learning about
titles and tools.*

JANUARY

Consumer Electronics Show (CES)
Electronics Industries Association
Las Vegas, NV
[+1 202] 457 4900

MacWorld Expo
Mitch Hall Associates
San Francisco, CA
[+1 617] 361 2001

MILIA
Midem Organization
Cannes, France
[+1 212] 689 4220

NATPE
National Association of Television Program
Executives
Las Vegas, NV
[+1 310] 453 4440

FEBRUARY

Consumer Online Services
Jupiter Communications
New York, NY
[+1 212] 941 9252

Demo
InfoWorld Editorial Events
Indian Wells, CA
[+1 415] 312 0545

Digital Hollywood
American Expositions
Beverly Hills, CA
[+1 212] 226 4141

Intermedia
Reed Exhibitions
San Francisco, CA
[+1 203] 840 4800

Interactive Television
Multichannel CommPerspectives/ITA
Philadelphia, PA
[+1 303] 393 7449

MacWorld Expo
World Expo Corporation
Tokyo, Japan
[+1 508] 879 6700

MARCH

Electronic Books International
Mecklermedia
London, UK
US [+1 203] 226 6967
Europe [+44 071] 976 0405

National Association of Broadcasters (NAB)
Las Vegas, NV
[+1 202] 429 5346

New Media Expo
The Interface Group
Los Angeles, CA
[+1 617] 449 6600

Seybold Seminars Exposition
Seybold Seminars
Boston, MA
[+1 310] 457 8500

Software Publishers Association (SPA)
San Diego, CA
[+1 202] 452 1600

APRIL

Computer Game Developers Conference
Computer Game Developers Association
San Jose, CA
[+1 415] 948 CGDC

COMDEX Spring
The Interface Group
Atlanta, GA
[+1 617] 449 6600

MAY

Apple Worldwide Developer Conference
Apple Computer, Inc.
San Jose, CA
[+1 408] 974 4897

Electronic Entertainment Expo (E3)
Los Angeles, CA
[+1 800] 800 5474

Interactive Marketing East
Interactive Marketing, Inc.
New Orleans, LA
[+1 310] 798 0433

MacWorld Expo
Washington D.C.
[+1 508] 872 8237

SGI Developer's Conference
Silicon Graphics, Inc.
San Jose, CA

JUNE

American Booksellers Association (ABA)
Chicago, IL
[+1 203] 840 4820

Art Teco
Morph's Outpost, Inc.
San Francisco, CA
[+1 800] GO MORPH

Digital World
Seybold Seminars
Los Angeles, CA
[+1 415] 578 6900

IICS Annual Conference
International Interactive Communications
Society
Anaheim, CA
[+1 503] 579 4427

Interactive Media Festival
Cunningham Communications & Seybold
Seminars
Anaheim, CA
[+1 800] 573 1212

NECC
National Education Computing Conference
Boston, MA
[+1 503] 346 4414

VISCOMM
United Digital Artists
San Francisco, CA
[+1 212] 777 7200

JULY

MacWorld Expo
Singapore
[+1 508] 872 8237

AUGUST

Interactive Multimedia 95
Society for Applied Learning Technology
Washington, DC
[+1 800] 457 6812

MacWorld Expo
Mitch Hall Associates
Boston, MA
[+1 617] 361 2001

SIGGRAPH
Special Interest Group-Graphics
Association for Computing Machinery
[+1 312] 644 6610

SEPTEMBER

Agenda
InfoWorld Editorial Events
Scottsdale, AZ
[+1 415] 312 0545

Multimedia Expo West
American Expositions
San Francisco, CA
[+1 212] 226 4141

Online Developers Conference
Jupiter Communications
San Francisco, CA
[+1 212] 941 9252

Seybold San Francisco Expo
Seybold Seminars
San Francisco, CA
[+1 310] 457 8500

OCTOBER

ACM Multimedia
Association for Computing Machinery
San Francisco, CA
[+1 212] 944 1318 (fax)
ACMHELP@acm.org

CD-ROM Expo
Online
San Francisco, CA
[+1 203] 761 1466

COMDEX Asia
Singapore
[+1 617] 449 6600

Interactive Marketing West
Interactive Marketing, Inc.
Scottsdale, AZ
[+1 310] 798 0433

Macromedia Developers Conference
Reed Exhibition Companies
San Francisco, CA
[+1 203] 352 8296

MacWorld Expo
Frankfurt, Germany
[+49 61] 51 26121

National Storytelling Festival
National Association for the Preservation &
Perpetuation of Storytelling
Jonesborough, TN
[+1 800] 525 4514

NOVEMBER

San Francisco Bay Area Book Festival
San Francisco Bay Area Book Council
San Francisco, CA
[+1 415] 861 2665

COMDEX Fall
The Interface Group
Las Vegas, NV
[+1 617] 449 6600

MacWorld
Hong Kong
[+1 508] 872 8237

NICOGRAPH
Nippon Computer Graphics Association
Tokyo, Japan
[+81 3] 3233 3475

Virtual Reality
Mecklermedia
New York, NY
[+1 800] 632 5537

VISCOMM
United Digital Artists
New York, NY
[+1 212] 777 7200

Western Cable Show
California Cable Television Association
Anaheim, CA
[+1 510] 428 2225

you need a vacation

you will take a vacation

Glossary/Index

Symbols

This is a combined glossary and alphabetical index. Where appropriate, definitions of terms are provided.

2D animation ▶ 129, 210-213

3D animation ▶ 101, 116, 210, 214-221

4-bit color
Representing colors using 4-bits. 16 colors can be displayed.

8-bit color
Representing colors using 8-bits. 256 colors can be displayed.

24-bit color
Representing colors using 24-bits. Over 16 million colors can be displayed.

A

accelerator card
A card or board that can be placed into a computer to improve the performance of the CPU.

access time
The time it takes to search, retrieve, and return data from computer media. Video tape takes minutes, CD-ROM a couple hundred milliseconds, hard disk 10-20 milliseconds, and random access memory (RAM) microseconds.

acquisition
The process of transferring data from analog to digital form; specifically video material. Also referred to as capturing.

actor ▶ 246, 247

adaptive feature ▶ 171
A feature that allows a product to adapt to the actions or profile of the user.

advertising ▶ 32, 33, 53, 91

affiliated label
A distribution option where a publisher provides marketing and distribution for a product developed by a production studio. Less popular now than a few years ago.

agent ▶ 32, 54, 58, 87, 96, 148, 189, 190, 195, 198, 246
A person that represents and acts on another person's behalf, usually in terms of finding work or licensing or selling publishable materials. Also, a software component that acts on behalf of a user to find information or perform transactions.

alpha test ▶ 259, 265
The first formal testing period for a software or multimedia product. Followed by beta testing.

analog
Any physical system indexed, controlled, or represented by continuously variable physical quantities, often electrically based. A digital system by contrast uses discrete representations.

animation ▶ 32, 203, 210-222
A sequence of illustrations that give the illusion of motion. The two basic branches of animation are 2D and 3D animation.

anti-aliasing
A process of blurring a jagged line with intermediary colors to give the appearance of a smooth line. Also refers to the process of sampling a signal at more than twice its natural frequency.

Appleton, Bill ▶ 123, 124

application
A software program that performs a specific task such as page layout, word processing, or illustration.

art director ▶ 83, 158, 164-170, 211, 222

ASCII ▶ 33
(American Standard Code for Information Interchange) A widely used convention for encoding characters using 8-bit pieces of data.

aspect ratio
The ratio of width to height of an image or screen generally expressed as a fraction. Consumer television has a 4:3 aspect ratio. Images will become distorted if forced into a different aspect ratio during enlargement or reduction.

asymmetric compression ▶ 240
A compression scheme that takes longer to compress than to decompress. These tend to be lossy schemes but have extremely high compression ratios.

Atchley, Dana ▶ 88, 191, 247

audio
The medium of sound. It includes voice, music, sound effects, and background sound.

Audio Video Interleaved ▶ 217, 240, 245
(AVI) A file format for digital video under Microsoft Windows.

auteur ▶ 170
A person who has a strong personal influence on a work. In filmmaking, directors are often referred to as the auteurs. In interactive media, there is a debate about who the auteur is, or if there even is one.

authoring tool ▶ 14, 124, 174, 253, 259, 275
A tool that is used for creating multimedia projects.

avatar ▶ 31

B

bandwidth ▶ 35, 63
The capacity of an analog or digital signal transmission or network.

Barry, Claire ▶ 169

baud rate/bps rate
(bps - bits per second) Rates at which packets of data are sent and received through the net-

work. Baud rates vary from 2,400 bps (quite slow) to 56,000 bps (56K leased line—faster) to 1,500,000 bps (T1—pretty darn zippy). The networks that form the backbone of the Internet often use T3 lines, which are capable of transmitting 45,000,000 bps. The higher the baud rate, the faster the connection.

Betacam ▸ 115, 240, 243

beta test ▸ 259, 265
A second and final testing period which often includes tests by actual users in real-world situations.

Bickford, Peter ▸ 175

binary
A system with only two possible states such as on or off, 1 or 0, high or low.

binaural sound
Sound specially recorded and played that gives a listener a three-dimensional audio perception.

bit depth
The number of bits used to represent black and white, grayscale, or color values. Common bit depths are 1, 4, 8, and 24.

bitmap
Images or fonts that are described as pixels. Commonly used to describe black-and-white images as opposed to grayscale or color ones.

Bliss, Lucille ▸ 230, 231

blue screen ▸ 238, 240, 246

Blum, Eric ▸ 249

Bondurant, Pamela ▸ 271

bookkeeper ▸ 145

book publisher ▸ 54, 71, 91, 275

Boorstin, Daniel J. ▸ 11

Boosman, Frank ▸ 11, 50, 250

brainstorming ▸ 159, 165, 174, 197
A technique for generating ideas in a group situation that ignores many of the project constraints and is supportive of all ideas. Ideas developed here can then be refined to fit the scope of the project.

Braun, Jeff ▸ 24, 276

Brenner, Don ▸ 259

Brown, Lisa ▸ 79

Bruno, Angelina ▸ 199

budget ▸ 19, 22, 38, 59, 120, 126, 249, 252, 264

bug ▸ 266
A problem or incompatibility in software or hardware.

build ▸ 253, 259
An intermediary version of software in which code resources are resolved and integrated prior to its creation.

bulletin board system ▸ 15, 62, 86, 274
(BBS) An online area where people can view messages and post responses.

bump map
A kind of texture map in 3D animation that simulates physical surfaces by imparting imperfections or random patterns.

Burch, Karen ▸ 77, 131

business model ▸ 121
The strategy in a business for generating revenue. Typically based on the model from an existing company or industry.

byte
A measure of data equal to eight bits.

C

camcorder
A small consumer video camera typically recording an NTSC signal and using either VHS or 8mm tape.

Canavan, AnnD ▸ 265

cartridge ▸ 13, 14, 114, 213, 228, 235, 265
A form of removable computer storage. Game cartridges are used in many of the early game machines. Syquest cartridges are popular with desktop computer users for transporting portfolios, audio and video segments, and other large files. (They can hold either 44MB or 88MB.)

CD-i ▸ 13, 75
(Compact Disc-interactive) A compact disc storage format created by Philips and Sony that is similar to CD-ROM and intended for the consumer electronics market. The CD-i specification includes an operating system standard and proprietary hardware compression methods.

CD-R
(Compact Disc-Recordable) A special type of CD that can be written to with the use of a special drive. The costs of the discs and the drives are dropping rapidly making them excellent systems for creating archives, delivering materials, and testing builds. CD-Rs are also referred to as "one-offs." The specification is known as the Orange Book.

CD-ROM ▸ 13, 14, 32, 58, 83, 102, 114, 156, 189, 228, 234, 242, 255
(Compact Disc-Read-Only Memory) A format for storing computer data or compressed audio or video data on a compact disc in a digital form. (The specification for CD-ROM is known as the Yellow Book.) Used generically to refer to a compact disc that contains computer data in a read-only format. They have space for approximately 650MB of data and track information.

CD-ROM/XA
(Compact Disc-Read-Only Memory/Extended Architecture) An extension of the original CD-ROM standard which adds the capability for interleaving data to enhance real-time playback of time-based data. Closely related to CD-i but intended for use with computer systems.

CD-WO
(Compact Disc-Write Once) Another term for CD-R.

Chait, Jonathan ▶ 85

character ▶ 20, 25, 26, 188, 222, 224

chart of accounts ▶ 146

chat ▶ 15, 30, 36, 61
A forum for real-time text-based public discussions of issues among multiple participants.

children ▶ 20, 21, 40, 184

clip art
Preexisting and widely available illustrations and artwork that can be incorporated into projects.

Coates, George ▶ 39

Coburn, Brian ▶ 234

codec ▶ 239
(Derived from compressor/decompressor) A hardware chip or software algorithm that compresses or decompresses data.

Cole, Brooks ▶ 165

Coleman, Dennis ▶ 81

Collins, Jim ▶ 94

communication ▶ 15, 16, 28, 30, 41, 134, 149

community ▶ 18, 27, 30, 31

compositing
The process of accumulating separately rendered video, graphics, animations, backgrounds, and sounds into a single final track using transparency and additive and subtractive algorithms.

compression ▶ 14, 224, 239, 245
Encoding a file, image, sound, or movie with a special algorithm to reduce space requirements for storage or transmission. Compression may be done with either software or hardware.

compression ratio ▶ 245
A measure of the efficiency of compression expressed as the ratio of the original size of the data to its compressed size.

computer-based training (CBT) ▶ 45

concept
The general idea for a product that embodies set goals and messages. Also, a stage in the development process.

conference ▶ 15, 37, 61, 85, 107, 140, 150, 187, 255, 261
A non-real-time online discussion area. Also, a series of seminars held at a specific location.

content
The information, media, or story used in a multimedia product to educate, entertain, communicate, or in any way affect an audience.

content expert ▶ 195-199, 203, 270

content licenser ▶ 195

content manager ▶ 167, 191

content provider ▶ 27, 57, 61
A generic term used to describe an individual or company that provides material for interactive projects.

contract ▶ 95, 135, 137, 141
A legal document that establishes a binding agreement between two or more parties.

contractor
See independent contractor.

controller ▶ 16, 180

conversation ▶ 12, 174

copyright ▶ 32, 90, 102, 110, 119, 137, 142, 199, 207
The right of ownership to an original work of art. Automatically granted to the creator except under certain provisions in the work-for-hire doctrine. They can be transferred or licensed to another party.

cost accountant ▶ 144

CPU
(Central Processing Unit) The processor in a computer that performs the primary computations.

creative director ▶ 158-163, 170, 177

creative feature ▶ 171
A feature in an interactive product that lets users have a role in performing a job or developing a piece of work.

credit ▶ 105, 219

credit list ▶ 84, 190, 198, 236

critique
A review of art material with the primary intent of improving future work.

crop
A process used in editing images and video that removes or obscures portions of the frame.

cross-platform ▶ 256
A strategy or method to develop media or software to run on more than one computer system.

cursor
A symbol on a computer screen that acts as a pointer or an indicator for some action currently taking place.

customer support ▶ 56, 79, 264, 272, 274-276

custom project
A project created for a client that has limited distribution. Technical requirements and support issues are often different for this type of project than for one created for general consumers.

custom tool
A software component created outside of an authoring tool that provides expanded capabilities.

cut
Editing term that refers to a piece of sound, video, or film media that is abruptly followed by another piece of media.

cyberspace ▶ 28, **30**
A term for the world of online connectivity that highlights its social aspects and its weblike nature.

D

DAC
(Digital to Analog Converter) A device that reads digital sound data and converts it to sound waves that can be played out of a speaker.

Daniels, Maya ▸ 233

database ▸ 146, 149, 152, 266, 275
An organized set of data within a file or set of files in a prescribed format that can be accessed with structured routines for storage and retrieval.

Davis, Stephanie ▸ 275

decompression
Restoring a file or image from its compressed form to its original format.

delivery media ▸ 244
The storage media containing the product that is delivered to the customer or client.

delivery platform ▸ 41, 113, 158, 165
The platform or platforms typical users will play or view a product on. Often different from the platform used to develop the project.

demonstration rights ▸ 105, 137
Rights to publicly display a copyrighted work. Many contractors and companies will preserve these rights in order to show their work to prospective clients.

demo reel ▸ 83, 218, 241
A videotape with video samples on it.

demo tape ▸ 83, 230, 231, 236
An audio cassette tape with audio samples on it.

derivative product
A work that recasts, transforms, or adapts material from preexistent works. These works are protected under copyright law.

developer
A person or company that creates a product. Often used in reference to game developers.

development platform ▸ 113, 165
The platform used to develop a project.

digital
The representation of a signal by a set of discrete numerical values. Commonly represented on a computer in binary form.

digital audio tape ▸ 223, 226, 230, 235, 237
(DAT) A delivery medium used for high definition sound recording and computer file backup. DAT has far greater storage capacity and better time synchronizing quality than analog tape.

digital camera ▸ 114, 202
A filmless camera that uses charge coupled devices (CCDs) and computer memory to take and store photographs. Low resolution digital cameras are widely available and reasonably priced.

digital periodical ▸ 184

digital sound processor
(DSP) A computer chip specifically designed for playing and performing various operations on digital sound data.

digitizer
Any multimedia device that records media to a computer disc in digital form. There are sound, video, and image digitizers.

disc
A plate of optical or magnetic material used to store data in digital form.

diskette
A transportable, light weight diskette that has a flexible disk encased in either a flexible or a rigid plastic case. Commonly called a floppy disk.

dissolve
Media editing term that refers to overlapping two pieces of media to make a transition from one to the other. A dissolve is usually the fading out of one overlay and the fading in of the other.

distribution ▸ 37, 127, 155

distributor ▸ 55, 57
A company that carries and supplies a product to retailers and end-users.

dithering
A way of assigning colors to pixels in order to simulate a color unavailable in a particular output device.

Dolby, Thomas ▸ 38, 170, 223, 226-228, 241

Don, Abbe ▸ 26, 27, 176

Doyle, Larry ▸ 251

dpi
(Dots Per Inch) A measure of resolution or detail used for monitors, printers, and other pixel-based devices.

drive
A computer or CD-ROM disc device that accepts, reads, and in most cases, writes data to a disc or diskette. Can refer to a hard drive, floppy drive, CD-ROM drive, cartridge drive, or other.

E

early adopters ▸ 262
People who buy and use early technology in new markets.

edit decision list ▸ 239
(EDL) A list of timing and other editing information for sound and video segments that is used in assembly.

editor ▸ 173, 192-194

edutainment ▸ 21
An often overused term that refers to media products that serve both education and entertainment purposes.

F

file
A set of data created with a software application or multimedia product and stored on a computer by name.

The name and standard specification for the storage of a particular kind of data. TIFF, EPS, and Microsoft Word are file formats.

file server
A remote and common disk storage device connected to computers by a network that manages the sharing of common data and applications.

file type
A code that identifies a particular file format.

filter
A software algorithm or device that modifies audio or visual signals to create special effects.

A contract bid that lists a set price. Fixed-price bids can be beneficial for clients because they allow them to better estimate costs.

A chart that shows the nodes of a story or set of content for a CD-ROM, website, or other interactive project. The structure of nodes can be hierarchical, web-like, or any other form.

Modeling and animating physical structures in real-time 3D in order to give the illusion of flying through the space.

A term used in the film industry for referring to a sound effects specialist.

font
A complete set of characters. Sometimes it refers it a particular size and style and other times it refers to an entire typeface family.

Frames per second.

frame
The basic unit of video information. Essentially a single screen.

frame dropping
The process of dropping video to stay synchronized with an accompanying soundtrack.

frame grabber
A device that converts a screen's worth of analog video signal into a digital form.

The number of frames displayed per second. Used with animation and video. TV and film support frame rates of 24-30 frames per second. Digital video often has frame rates that are far less due to performance limitations.

frequency
The number of times a sound wave oscillates as measured in hertz or cycles per second.

fulfillment
A service provided by a printer, duplicator, or disc manufacturer that can entail warehousing inventory, processing orders, and shipping to customers.

Used to describe video that moves at 24 to 30 frames per second, a rate fast enough to give the eye the perception of continuous motion. Frame rates of 12-18 fps provide relatively smooth movement.

A document that is produced prior to production that describes how the product should work and what the interface should look like.

G

A map of a gaming region that is used in the design and development of a game. Designers, programmers, animators, and others use the game map in order to understand what interactions occur and where the media elements go.

game play ▶ 22, 178, 223
A measure for that which makes a game captivating and fun.

Gates, Bill ▶ 11, 16

gigabyte
(GB) A unit of computer memory equal to 1024 megabytes (1,073,741,824 bytes).

Gilbert, Paul ▶ 240

Gilburne, Miles ▶ 42, 60

golden master ▶ 125, 259, 266
The designated copy of a software or multimedia project that is suitable for replication or release.

gopher ▶ 46, 87, 197
A tool used to search for information on the Internet.

Gourard shading ▶ 215
A rendering algorithm that averages the color and illumination of each corner of a polygonal shape. It renders faster than Phong shading and is more realistic than flat shading.

graphic design ▶ 200
The discipline of communicating messages visually.

grayscale
An image using levels of gray as opposed to just black and white.

The Great Good Place ▶ 28

Green Book
Refers to the specification documents for the CD-i format.

Grosso, Vincent ▶ 9, 16, 53, 191

groupware ▶ 42
Software that allows several people working on the same tasks to better interact and work together.

guide
A software resource that shares information but does so only upon being triggered by the user. Guides are often represented as animated characters.

H

Habitat ▶ 25, 31
A pioneering 2D graphical online system developed several years ago.

Hampton, Sheryl ▶ 238, 242

Hanlon, Pat ▶ 41, 196

hard drive
A disk drive containing one or more disc platters for storing data. Characterized by moderate to high volume and extremely fast access times. Also commonly referred to as a hard disk.

Harrington, Cody ▶ 219

hidden-line animation ▶ 215
A simple 3D animation rendering technique that removes lines in a wireframe model that are blocked by surfaces at the perspective rendered.

Hi-8 ▶ 115, 240, 244
A video format originated by Sony that uses standard 8mm videotapes.

high concept ▶ 185
A term used in film production for a synopsis of a project.

higher-level language ▶ 263
A software language more closely aligned with human forms of expression as opposed to ones more readily understood by computers. Object-oriented and scripting languages fit into this category.

Holland, Gray ▶ 216

Hollywood ▶ 51, 54, 57, 70, 134, 149, 185, 189, 214, 229

HotWired ▶ 33, 67, 160, 193

Hourvitz, Leo ▶ 252

HTML ▶ 15, 76, 160, 258
(Hypertext Markup Language) The programming language used to develop webpages. Browsers decipher documents encoded with HTML and display them as a mixture of text and graphics.

http ▶ 15
(hypertext transfer protocol) The protocol used by a web browser to retrieve HTML documents.

Hutto, J. Sterling ▶ 86

hypermedia
An organizational structure for presenting information where text, graphics, and other media are associated in a dynamic and navigable form.

hypertext
Text that lets users jump from one area to an associated area. One of the primary features of the World Wide Web is its use of hypertext links to form connections between webpages on local and remote websites.

I

icon ▶ 201
A graphic or pictographic symbol used to represent an abstract or concrete object or process.

illustration ▶ 202
Any picture drawn to depict a subject.

image manipulation ▶ 203
The art of using software tools to create and modify pixellated images.

in-betweening ▶ 215
An animation technique where frames are rendered by interpolating between two key frames.

indemnification ▶ 103, 141, 198
A guarantee to compensate or reimburse another party for losses or expenses they might have incurred. Often used to protect a person or company from a contractual party's infringement of someone else's intellectual property rights.

independent contractor ▶ 97, 110

Someone who works for, and receives payment from, an employer but whose working conditions or methods are not controlled by the employer.

information ▶ 14, 16, 18, 27, 34, 43, 46

information design ▶ 9, 170, 172

A form of design directed at making information clear and understandable as opposed to merely visually attractive. An approach to arranging data into a meaningful organization.

information superhighway ▶ 15, 26

A metaphor for the world of online connectivity that highlights its mercantile and transactional nature.

initial public offering ▶ 57

(IPO) The first offering of a company's stock to the public.

in-point

The beginning point of a piece of media that is selected for editing.

instructional design ▶ 44

Designing products for educational purposes. A part of the field of interface design.

integration

Merging code resources and media elements to create a build. The integration process can go smoothly or can be problematic depending on the software tools used and the development procedures in place.

intellectual property ▶ 57, 110

Property that results from intellectual endeavors. Often separated into trademarks, trade secrets, copyrights, and patents.

interaction design ▶ 170, 172

A discipline under the field of interface design that is concerned with the type of experience created as users navigate and interact with a product.

interactive ▶ 9, 20, 31, 58, 171, 187, 225, 250, 264

Products and services that respond quickly to the choices and commands users make.

interactive TV ▶ 9, 12, 16, 53, 63, 64, 78, 189, 191

interface design ▶ 163, 170-177, 256

Designing the organization, interaction, and visual display of media elements in order to create a cohesive experience.

interface designer ▶ 158, 170-177, 179

interleaving ▶ 243

The practice of sector-by-sector alternation between data types within files on a CD-ROM disc. Interleaving permits different types of data to be routed to different hardware or software components. Also used in the broadcast of television signals.

Internet ▶ 15, 30, 43, 46, 69

A collection of interconnected networks that share a worldwide backbone. There are millions of computers connected to the Internet and more are added each day.

internship ▶ 91, 176, 242

interpreted language

A computer language that is decoded into machine readable format and processed at the same time. They offer more flexibility but tend to perform slower than compiled languages.

ISO

(International Standards Organization) An active worldwide body which develops, promotes, and establishes standards and protocols for data communications and storage. They have established international CD-ROM, compression, and character encoding standards.

ISO 9660 ▶ 14

An international standard for a CD-ROM file structure that is supported by most major computer platforms.

J

Jacobson, Linda ▶ 220

jewel box

A clear, hinged polystyrene case commonly used for compact disc storage.

job description ▶ 90, 95, 151, 198

A detailed outline of the responsibilities, reporting structure, and compensation for a free-lance job or employment position.

joint venture

A relationship between two or more business partners to collectively research, develop, or market a technology, product, or service.

JPEG

(Joint Photographers Experts Group) An international set of standard ISO protocols for compressing and decompressing still digital images. It can be implemented in either software or hardware.

K

Kapor, Mitch ▶ 15, 28, 29

Kay, Larry ▶ 21

key frame ▶ 210, 214

An animation frame that is used to guide subsequent action or interpolation when paired with another key frame.

kilobyte

(K) A unit of computer memory equal to 1,024 bytes (2 to the 10th power).

kiosk ▶ 17, 47, 269

An installation for public use, often providing directions or information pertinent to the space the installation is in.

Kreth, Will ▸ 193

Kuhr, Barbara ▸ 160

L

Lanier, Jaron ▸ 27

Lau, Clifford ▸ 23, 58, 199, 215

Laurel, Brenda ▸ 27

lawyer ▸ 91, 134-143, 176, 242

leasing ▸ 112

light source
An algorithmic or programmatic device that gives the appearance of light from a particular angle and intensity in a 3D model, showing reflections, color shadings, and shadows.

linear ▸ 26

linear editing system
A film editing system in which video segments can only be accessed sequentially. Digital non-linear editing systems are rapidly replacing linear systems.

link
A connection between one area and another. A primary feature of interactive products is the ability for users to explore linked materials.

list server ▸ 29, 192
A software module that maintains email lists. Considered a necessity for people who maintain large dynamic email lists.

local area network
(LAN) A collection of interconnected computers and other devices within a small geographical space, typically a single building.

localization ▸ 232
The act of tailoring a product to the specific requirements of a particular culture. Localization extends beyond language translation to include modifying visual, audio, and video elements that might confuse or offend people of another culture.

location-based entertainment ▸ 17, 25, 70, 75
(LBE) An interactive gaming setup often featuring special-purpose hardware and containing some form of virtual reality aspect to it.

Lopuck, Lisa ▸ 201

Lord, Sean ▸ 78, 88, 107, 153

lossless
Refers to compression and decompression algorithms that result in reconstructed images that have no degradation in picture quality. Commonly takes longer and provides a smaller compression ratio than lossy algorithms.

lossy
Refers to compression and decompression algorithms that produce reconstructed images containing less information than the original source. They are typically faster and offer better compression ratios than lossless algorithms, but cannot be used when data integrity is essential as in the case of text data.

Lovell, Pamela ▸ 86

M

Maddux, Scott ▸ 174, 180, 256

magnetic-optical
(MO) Small optical disks that can be rewritten.

marketing ▸ 80, 149, 154

master
A CD-ROM mold, diskette, audio or video tape, or other image used to make copies. Mastering is the process of producing this image.

McBride, Stewart ▸ 59, 65

megabyte
(MB) A unit of computer memory equal to about a million bytes (1,048,576 bytes).

microphone ▸ 223, 230, 237, 240, 244

MIDI ▸ 38, 115, 226, 237
(Musical Instrument Digital Interface) A communications standard for representing time-based data for the generation of digital music. MIDI is event-based and can be interpreted by both software and hardware MIDI devices.

Miller, Larry ▸ 36

Milligan, Patrick ▸ 9, 262

mixed mode ▸ 38
A CD-ROM disc which contains data and Red Book audio tracks.

mixer
An audio or video board that is used to mix multiple signals into one.

modeling ▸ 214, 215
Creating 3D wireframe forms, applying shades and textures to them.

model release ▸ 134
A legal release to use a person's image within a product. The image itself will likely need a separate release from the photographer, illustrator, or current copyright holder.

modem
A device that allows a computer to transmit and receive data over phone lines.

moderator ▸ 192-194

Molnár, Dezsö ▸ 222, 225, 231

monochrome
A display that uses only two color values, most commonly black and white.

Moriarty, Brian ▸ 179

morphing
A common video transition that blends one scene or object into another by interpolating between them.

Mountford, S. Joy ▸ 49, 162, 234

MPEG ▶ 245
(Motion Picture Experts Group) An international set of standard ISO protocols for compressing and decompressing digital video and sound.

MUD and MOO ▶ 30
(Multi-User Dungeons and MUD Object-Oriented) Online environments that create a rich scenario for role-playing activities. Most are currently text-based—users type in commands to navigate, perform actions, and communicate with others—but a few support the use of images and, in some cases, sound.

multimedia ▶ 9, 50, 185
Combining text, graphics, sound, animation, video, or other media, most commonly in digital format.

multisession disc
A CD-ROM disc containing more than one recording session. (It needs a multi-session drive.)

Myst ▶ 8, 23, 25, 170, 178, 179, 238

N

narrative ▶ 21, 22, 26, 27, 39, 124, 180

navigable movie ▶ 169
An interactive movie that allows users to move in various directions.

navigation ▶ 15, 63, 159
The act of moving through an interactive product.

negotiation ▶ 51, 97, 133, 136, 139, 272

Nelson, J.A. ▶ 257

netiquette
A code of behavior for interacting with others in cyberspace.

netizen
A net citizen.

network ▶ 15, 41
A collection of connected computers that share resources and data.

new media
A term for interactive multimedia.

newsgroup ▶ 29
Conferences found in the USENET portion of the Internet.

Nguyen, Minh-Hang ▶ 147

Nilsen, Spencer ▶ 13, 223, 224, 235

non-compete clause ▶ 104
A clause that prevents one party from performing work that might compete with its current or past work.

non-disclosure agreement ▶ 90, 130
(NDA) A legal agreement that warrants that a person keep subsequently disclosed information in confidence (unless it becomes public knowledge). NDAs should ideally be mutual.

non-linear ▶ 21, 26, 223

non-linear editing system
A video editing system, usually digital, that allows video editors greater flexibility in manipulating video. Editors can cut, paste, and otherwise rearrange video segments almost instantly.

NTSC
A television transmission standard that supports 30 frames per second that was established by the National Television Standards Committee and is used in the United States, Canada, and Japan.

O

object-oriented programming ▶ 258, 263
A programming approach that encapsulates data and operations on the data into discrete modular components.

Okada, Corrine ▶ 210

Oldenberg, Ray ▶ 30

one-off
A writable compact disc used for testing CD-ROM production.

One-offs contain an actual CD-ROM image and can play in CD-ROM drives.

online ▶ 15, 32, 46, 61, 84, 185, 192-194
Connected to others in cyberspace.

online service ▶ 18, 30, 61, 84, 87, 154, 274
A service that offers electronic mail, conferences, chat, information resources, and other content and communication services. Users connect to online services through the use of computers, modems, and phone lines.

operating system ▶ 15, 215, 253
Software running in a computer that contains general instructions to manage processes, memory, communications, and other system-level responsibilities.

optimization
Techniques used near the end of prototype or production stages to improve the performance of a product.

Orange Book
Standards for the recordable compact disc. There are two parts, one for write once (WO) and one for magnetic optical (MO) rewritable discs.

Oren, Tim ▶ 10, 14, 15, 25, 30, 188, **194**

Ores, David J. ▶ 51

out-point
The ending point of a piece of time-based media that is selected for editing. The in-point and out-point specify an editing cut of a fixed duration.

P

Pacheco, Candice ▶ 39

page-layout application
A class of computer software that allows the user to arrange text and graphic images more creatively than word processing

software.

paint software
Computer applications that let the user create images by manipulating individual pixels on the screen.

PAL
(Phase Alternation Line) A color video broadcast standard that supports 25 frames per second; used in China and many European nations. It offers slightly better resolution and color than the NTSC standard.

palette
A collection of colors or shades available to a software program, authoring tool, or graphics system.

patent ▶ 142
A non-obvious, novel invention that is recognized as such by a governing body, which in the U.S. is the U.S. Patent and Trademark Office. Patent protection lasts for 17 years.

payment ▶ 100, 109

performance ▶ 17, 39, 269

performer ▶ 246, 247

peripheral
A piece of hardware connected to a computer that gives a computer certain external capabilities.

Perkins, Anthony ▶ 8, 56

Perrault, Bill ▶ 154

personal computer

personal digital assistant ▶ 17
(PDA) A handheld computer primarily used for organizing names, addresses, and other personal information, but increasingly offering communication capabilities such as fax and email.

perspective ▶ 26, 187

Phong shading ▶ 215
A high-quality shading technique that calculates a color for each pixel in a 3D model. It cannot, however, render more advanced lighting effects such as transparency or reflection.

Photo CD
An image file format and color standard conforming to Kodak's specifications for CD photo finishing. It stores about 100 pictures and is recorded on CD-ROM/XA discs.

photorealism
Exactingly real presentation or imaging of a scene by a computer. The rendering of the scene pays attention to light, reflection, texture, shadow, and other visual details.

PICT
A standard data format in which many Macintosh illustrations are encoded. PICT data can be created, displayed on a screen, and printed by routines incorporated in the Macintosh system.

Pinney, Nancy ▶ 206

pitch meeting ▶ 126, 181, 185, 198
A term from Hollywood that refers to a meeting with an agent, a producer, or a director where an idea is introduced.

pixel
(Picture Element) The smallest unit within an image or computer screen that can be assigned a color value.

place ▶ 25, 228, 80, 170, 222
Any distinctive area in cyberspace that provides an entertaining and enlightening experience.

placeholder
The technique of putting working media in place until finished media can be produced.

platform ▶ 10, 12, 50, 80, 113, 137, 244
A set of hardware components, operating system, and delivery media that provides specific functions and capabilities for the production or playback of digital programming.

platform release ▶ 52
A product launch strategy used

in the film industry that tries to create strong word of mouth by initially limiting the availability of the film.

player ▶ 13, 23, 26, 234
A small computer or device that plays back multimedia. Also, a person that interacts with a product.

Plunkett, John ▶ 160

point of view ▶ 27, 32, 54, 176, 192, 187

Poole, Henri ▶ 121

portfolio ▶ 82, 108, 161, 167, 206, 207

positioning ▶ 80, 107, 273

post mortem ▶ 108
A meeting held after the completion of a project to go over the development process with the specific intent of improving future productions.

post-production
Processing of video or sound data after it has been captured.

Power, Todd ▶ 20, 128

premastering
A CD-ROM or videodisc production step in which all the individual files are combined into a single large file for a mastering machine.

premise ▶ 185
A term from TV production for the general structure of a programming concept.

presentation ▶ 12, 17, 39, 48, 269

presentation software ▶ 17, 40, 48
Computer software that helps users create presentations. The presentations are usually given by a speaker, but they can be made to be self-running.

producer ▶ 51, 119, 126-133, 134, 142, 170, 197, 222, 255

production
The work phase in a multimedia project that comes after the design phase and before the for-

mal testing phase.

production studio ▶ 57, 59, 63, 119, 133, 155

production tool
A tool used in the creation of a project. Often refers to tools that help in preparing media elements such as word processors, image manipulation software, and illustration programs.

productivity tools ▶ 42

programmer ▶ 73, 78, 151, 153, 250-263

project plan
A document that provides budgets, schedules, task charts, resource needs, and other information needed to produce a project.

proof-of-concept
A simple form of prototype intended to either prove the viability of a project or spark the interest of investors.

property ▶ 51, 57, 148
A tangible work that has value. Or, a person or group whose future work is valuable.

proposal ▶ 120, 126, 131, 158
A written document stating an intent and providing a bid to produce a product or perform a service.

protocol ▶ 12, 61
A set of rules that governs the way information is exchanged between processes or machines.

prototype ▶ 120, 148, 172
The inventive phase in a multimedia project that comes after concept and planning and explores many possible designs. Also, a working demonstration that can be used to get financing and distribution and/or test out design ideas.

publisher ▶ 40, 57
A company that manages the funding and distribution of a product.

Q

quality assurance ▶ 128, 264, 265
A discipline that improves quality by addressing all activities and processes within a business.

QuickTime ▶ 217, 232, 240, 242, 245
A system extension developed by Apple Computer that displays video and animation on Macintosh computers and under Windows without additional video hardware. It gives developers a common set of routines for manipulating, compressing, and synchronizing moving images and sound in real time.

R

RAM ▶ 114-117
(Random Access Memory) Principal memory used by a computer in which data and instructions are momentarily used. Most RAM memory chips do not preserve the data when the power is turned off.

raster display
A raster image is divided into scan lines. Each line consists of a series of dots from a thin section of the final image. The pattern of dots corresponds to a bit pattern in memory.

ray tracing ▶ 215
A sophisticated 3D rendering algorithm that traces rays of light as they bounce off objects. It can add effects such as transparency, true reflection, light refraction, and shadows.

real time ▶ 29, 39, 47
Transmitting, receiving, processing, and displaying results as they happen.

recruiter ▶ 151-153, 157

Red Book ▶ 224
The CD-Audio format developed by Philips and Sony, used to record sound for conventional stereo CD.

The Red Herring ▶ 8, 24, 40, 56, 276

rendering ▶ 214
The final stage of painting the image in the creation of a 3D image. It includes blending of various light sources and surface textures.

repurpose
A term referring to the reuse of content. Commonly used when taking existing print or film products and putting them to digital uses.

request for proposal ▶ 120, 125
(RFP) A formal document issued by a client to a group of contractors requesting work to be done.

resolution
The granularity of a display or image typically indicated by a dots-per-inch measurement. Apparent resolution can be increased by allowing the dot to have a wider color range.

return on investment ▶ 56, 145
(ROI) The profit or loss from an investment. Riskier investments tend to have higher ROIs but not all investments are for ROI purposes. Some investments are for strategic reasons.

review ▶ 101, 107, 158, 211

RGB
(Red, Green, and Blue) A model for defining color within a computer system which assigns values to the percentage of the three primary colors of light which make up a color.

Rheingold, Howard ▶ 28, 30, 192

Rinkus, Allan ▶ 148, 150

RISC
(Reduced Instruction Set Chip) A fast and efficient CPU design that limits the size and number of instructions in the instruction set.

role
A set of logically related responsibilities performed by a member of a project team.

Rollinson, Bill ▸ 163, 232

ROM
(Read Only Memory) A stable, permanent or semipermanent type of memory which stores key data used by a computer. It can only be read and is not erased when the power is turned off.

royalty ▸ 58, 59, 97, 100, 119, 133, 257
Payment made by a publisher to a person or company usually in the form of a percentage of gross or net revenues from the sale of a product.

Rubinstein, Rhonda ▸ 32

S

Saffo, Paul ▸ 32, 37, 42, 43, 47, 54, 122, 157, 192

salesperson ▸ 120, 126, 272-273

sample size ▸ 38
The number of bits in a digital sample. The greater the size, the greater the fidelity.

sampling ▸ 38
A process by which analog audio signals are put into digital form. A sample is a snapshot of sound pressure at one instant in time. Samples are taken quickly enough so that their replay in sequence gives the impression of actual sound.

sampling rate ▸ 38
The frequency in which sampling occurs during digital audio recording. The higher the sampling rate, the greater the rate of pitches accurately recorded.

scalable
Property of being able to take a finished product and transmit to a number of receivers of differing quality. Many digital standards are designed to scale in areas such as bit depth, sampling rate, and cpu performance.

Scales, Frank ▸ 239

scanner ▸ 114
A graphical input device that converts printed matter into digital image data.

Schafer, Tim ▸ 23

schedule ▸ 101, 126, 252

Schoen, Claire ▸ 40

Schwartz, William ▸ 137

script ▸ 51, 124, 148, 178, 186, 214
A text description of scenes and dialogue as well as computer commands written in a scripting language.

scripting language ▸ 258
An interpreted higher level language often found within an authoring tool.

scriptwriter ▸ 51, 129, 178, 184-191, 197

SCSI
(Small Computer System Interface, pronounced "scuzzy") An industry-standard interface between computers and peripheral device controllers.

SECAM
(Sequential Couleur a Memoire) A television standard that supports 25 frames per second; developed by the French, and used in 20 countries, including France.

self-publishing ▸ 55
A person or company that creates and publishes products.

sensorial design ▸ 170
A discipline under interface design that takes into account human perception through areas such as sight, sound, touch, and smell.

sequencer
A digital machine that records, mixes, and plays back MIDI tracks. Other synthesizers connect to a sequencer.

service provider ▸ 62, 84
A business that provides access to a service such as online service providers.

set-top box ▸ 16, 63
A device intended to connect with a TV to allow interactive television capabilities.

Seventh Guest ▸ 8, 22, 68

SGML
(Standard Generalized Markup Language) An international standard (ISO 8879) for defining page layout markup codes. HTML began as a subset of SGML.

Shedroff, Nathan ▸ 169, 172, 173, 174

Shen, Chris ▸ 179, 181

shrink-wrapped
Off-the-shelf products for general consumption as opposed to custom products.

Silicon Valley ▸ 57, 67, 149, 163, 189

SimCity ▸ 24, 178, 181

simulation ▸ 24
Use of computer-generated multimedia to create the illusion of a real process or place.

single session disc
A CD-ROM that only supports a single recording session. Once created, additional material cannot be added to it.

Smith, Ray ▸ 64

software
A set of instructions written in a computer language which performs various operations within a computer.

software industry ▸ 54, 56, 131, 134, 149

sound ▸ 38, 49, 222-237

sound digitizing board
A board that fits into a computer and connects to sound playback equipment. Used for digitizing analog sound signals.

sound engineer ▸ 237, 243

trade show ▸ 68, 88, 149

training ▸ 44

transaction ▸ 15, 16, 43, 46

transfer rate
A measure of the speed at which data can be transferred within computer machinery or networks. CD-ROMs transfer 150-300 kilobits per second.

transition ▸ 210, 224, 245
A movement from one scene to another, often done using cuts, wipes, dissolves, or other video effects.

treatment ▸ 148, 178, 186
A brief description of a product intended to elicit interest from producers, publishers, agents, and others.

true color
A term used to indicate a device or software application which can accommodate 24 bits of color information or over 16 million different color values. Reportedly surpasses the capabilities of the human eye resulting in color that appears natural.

turnaround time
The amount of time it takes for a job to be completed. An example is the time it takes to get a CD pressed.

typeface
A set of characters with design features that make them similar to one another.

typography ▸ 32, 201
The art of designing with type.

U

UNICODE
Worldwide text standard that represents characters as 16-bit sequences. ASCII uses only 8 bits and is not suited for non-Roman languages.

unions ▸ 52, 96, 230, 247

unit testing ▸ 269

A form of testing that concentrates on the workings of individual components. Typically performed by programmers as they are developing.

UNIX ▸
Operating system developed by Bell Labs and owned by Novell that features multitasking and virtual memory. It is popular for machines connected to the Internet because of its built-in communications facilities.

Updike, John ▸ 27

Upside ▸ 64, 81

URL
(Universal or Uniform Resource Locator) The address of a website expressed in the http protocol. Every website has a unique URL ("http://<something>").

USENET ▸ 29, 36, 46, 87, 187, 192
An area on the Internet containing bulletin board-like discussion groups which, unlike chat, are not in real-time.

user group
A group of people interested in a specific type or brand of computer or software who share tips, information, advice, and activities.

user testing ▸ 128
A type of testing that studies the use of a product by typical customers in order to find ways to improve the interface and the interaction.

V

van Duyne, Doug ▸ 133

venture capital ▸ 56, 121, 145
(VC) A form of funding. VC companies obtain funds from large institutional investors and invest them in a number of high risk ventures, typically startups and small companies with the potential for high growth and return on investment.

VHS

A standard consumer video format that uses 1/2 inch tape.

video ▸ 36, 238-249

video digitizing board ▸ 245
A board that fits into a computer and connects to video playback equipment. Used for digitizing analog video signals.

videodisc
A storage medium of video information that uses large thin circular plates primarily composed of translucent plastic.

video editor ▸ 44, 101, 245

videographer ▸ 243

video producer ▸ 44, 238-242

videotext
A standard used by older systems to transmit a limited graphic and character set.

virtual community ▸ 9, 28, 30, 184

virtual corporation
A business structure that uses a collection of independent individuals and businesses to simulate the functionings of a large organization.

virtual memory
A means of using memory on a computer storage disk to simulate a seemingly limitless supply of random access memory.

virtual reality ▸ 25, 75, 220
(VR) Input or output technology and accompanying content and software that provide a highly interactive and immersive environment.

visual designer ▸ 175, 200-209, 211

voice artist ▸ 83, 230-232

W

Wasserman, David ▸ 209

web browser ▸ 15, 62
Software that allows you to visit websites in the World Wide Web.

webpage ▸ 15, 62, 82

A separate screen in a website. A website consists of many webpages, each of which is transmitted individually. (A page is scrollable and therefore could be many "screens" long.)

website ▶ 15, 82
A unique address in the World Wide Web that contains one or more webpages. A website can be created for individuals, companies, educational institutions, and other entities.

Weiner, Dr. Cheryl ▶ 21

The WELL ▶ 15, 62, 84, 193

Wicks, David ▶ 19

wide area networks
(WAN) A network of connected computers which covers a large geographic area.

wide release ▶ 51
Used in the film industry to refer to a film that is released in many theaters.

Willoughby, Scott ▶ 17, 48

Wilmunder, Aric ▶ 256

Wired **magazine** ▶ 11, 16, 67, 160, 193

wireframe ▶ 210, 214
A computer animation technique of modeling a three-dimensional object with line segments.

work agreement ▶ 95, 100, 109, 134, 218
An agreement between an employer and employee or a client and contractor that describes work issues such as the deliverables and payment terms.

work for hire ▶ 102, 136, 207
A doctrine specifying a certain working relationship that has implications for the copyright ownership of authored works.

World Wide Web ▶ 15, 33, 34, 36, 46, 61, 62, 160
A part of the Internet that is made up of an ever-increasing number of websites. The protocol of the Web supports the use of hyperlinks between webpages on local and remote websites, hence the name "Web."

Y

Yawitz, Mitchell ▶ 8

Yellow Book
The specification documents for the original CD-ROM format developed by Philips and Sony.

Z

'zine ▶ 33

Zolt, Nina ▶ 78